Previous Books by Jon Naar

The New Wind Power
New York: Penguin, 1982

Your Space
New York: St. Martin's, 1979

Design for a Limited Planet
(with Norma Skurka), New York: Ballantine, 1976

Living in One Room
(with Molly Siple), New York: Random House, 1976

The Faith of Graffiti
(with Norman Mailer and Mervyn Kurlansky), New York: Praeger, 1974

Christopher Columbus
New York: Picture Progress, 1955

DESIGN FOR A LIVABLE PLANET

HOW YOU CAN HELP CLEAN UP THE ENVIRONMENT

JON NAAR

FOREWORD BY FREDERIC D. KRUPP
EXECUTIVE DIRECTOR, ENVIRONMENTAL DEFENSE FUND

PERENNIAL LIBRARY

HARPER & ROW, PUBLISHERS, NEW YORK

GRAND RAPIDS, PHILADELPHIA, ST. LOUIS, SAN FRANCISCO
LONDON, SINGAPORE, SYDNEY, TOKYO, TORONTO

Dedication

Design for a Livable Planet is dedicated to Henry David Thoreau, John Muir, David Ross Brower, Rachel Carson, Chico Mendes, Jacques Cousteau, Pete Seeger, Ralph Nader, Gary Null, Lois Marie Gibbs, Dave Foreman, Murray Bookchin, James Lovelock, Lynn Margulis, Nancy Jack Todd, John Todd, and to everyone else who has shown us the way to understand the world of which we are indeed a very small part.

Jon Naar and his literary agent Sarah Jane Freymann are donating ten percent of their profits from *Design for a Livable Planet* to the Cousteau Society, Earth First!, Greenpeace, Citizen's Clearinghouse for Hazardous Wastes, and other environmentally active organizations.

All photography © 1990 by Jon Naar except: p. 2, p. 8, p. 36, p. 76 – EPA; Cover and p. 60 – DiskImagery Inc.; p. 96 – The Conservation Group at Washington University Technology Associates courtesy of the Art Commission of New York; p. 152 and p. 188 © Alex Naar, 1990.

FIRST EDITION

Book Design by Joseph L. Santoro

Design for a Livable Planet is printed on recycled paper.

LIBRARY OF CONGRESS CATALOG CARD NUMBER 89-45697

ISBN 0-06-055165-8   ISBN 0-06-096387-5 (pbk.)

91 92 93 94 RRD 10 9 8 7 6 5 4

2/92

CONTENTS

FOREWORD

*by Frederic D. Krupp, Executive Director,
Environmental Defense Fund*

The past few years have seen a great public reawakening to environmental problems. Not since 1970, the time of the last arousal, have so many people in so many different countries and walks of life been moved to ask the all-important question: "What can I do to help?"

Jon Naar's *Design for a Livable Planet* comes at exactly the right moment. When specific steps toward change are not perceptible, when the need to be part of the solution is unanswered by good information, we begin to feel powerless and alienated. This book, with its emphasis on practical things *you and I* can do, is a valuable guide to help us envision and thus undertake change. What's more, because environmental problems will only be solved by action at all levels – government and corporate, as well as individual – Jon Naar has outlined steps for each.

To me the work of an environmentalist is akin to that of an architect. Presented with a need or problem, the good architect devises practical solutions and brings them into being with available resources and within budget. Thus, Jon Naar's choice of title, *Design for a Livable Planet*, is on the mark. He has given us plans that – if faithfully followed – will get us through the next few hundred years with the diversity of terrestrial life thriving and the planetary support systems intact.

As this book goes to press, however, our planet's problems are greater in magnitude than ever before. The most all-encompassing of those problems – climate change – has indeed only recently been fully recognized. We now understand that the thinning of the stratospheric ozone layer, the "hole" over Antarctica, and the warming of the planet are threats so potentially severe and global that they deserve to stand in our consciousness beside the nightmare image of the atomic mushroom cloud, now mercifully receding as Cold War tensions ease.

The new threats pose unparalleled challenges that will test our societies at every level of organization. World leaders will need to rise to these challenges by exercising their political skills in the best sense, readying and rallying the public for change, and by entering into international accords that limit the emissions of waste gases that cause these problems. State and local governments and individuals will need to change their investment patterns and modes of living.

Individuals will play a critical role in the solution by changing their buying and living habits. As more environmentally sound products appear in the marketplace, it will become easier for consumers to find and buy good ones and corporations will either change their production processes and products, to answer society's needs, or they will become antiquated. As people make recycling a part of their lives, they will expect their public officials to propose up-to-date, efficient programs. When government officials make curbside and apartment collection of recyclables the standard, it will become even more convenient for citizens to participate and recycling will be the norm.

Of course, good information will continue to be key to all of this, in order to prevent gimmicks like "biodegradable" plastics from exploiting the public's desire to do good with misguided products.

But all this will not be enough. We need continued strong rules against polluting our environment. These must be supplemented by economic incentives that will speed to market technologies like solar energy, and we need disincentives to harmful behavior. We also need treaties between nations. And we need action in every community. But it *can* start with you and me, for a nation of practicing environmentalists is far more likely to be a nation that demands action from its elected officials.

Fortunately, there is already persuasive evidence that people at all levels – as individuals, corporations, and nations – can respond to overarching environmental problems. In the 1970s, for example, when scientists first discovered the threats to the ozone layer posed by chlorofluorocarbons (CFCs), some corporations acted voluntarily to remove these chemicals from aerosol propellants, one of the major sources. This change was led by the S.C. Johnson Company, which conspicuously labelled its products to let consumers know they contained no

CFCs. People responded enthusiastically, favoring sprays that did not harm the environment. By the time Congress passed legislation banning CFCs in propellants, two-thirds of the containers on the market had already eliminated them.

Of course, the elimination of this use of aerosol CFCs in one country could not by itself stop the depletion of the stratospheric ozone layer, but it provided a model that helped persuade thirty-one nations to agree in Montreal in 1987 to reduce other sources as well. The Montreal Protocol, which has since been signed by eighty-seven nations, is the first case of the governments of the world coming together to address a global atmospheric issue. Unlike many international conventions, this protocol contains an important provision that allows it to be strengthened if new scientific data show that further steps need to be taken to reduce sources of ozone depletion.

Such willingness to reevaluate old regulations on the basis of new information is critical to our capacity to solve global environmental problems. Experience with complex environmental problems shows again and again that when we tamper with global systems we cannot foresee the consequences. In the early 1980s, scientists measuring rates and distribution of ozone depletion programmed their computers to look for a relatively even worldwide thinning of ozone. No experience led them to consider that the depletion might be concentrated by particular climatic conditions. When the data fed to the computers consistently showed heavy depletion over Antarctica and insignificant loss elsewhere, the computers rejected the data, matched it with other corroborating measurements, and were able to conclude that the Antarctic ozone "hole" was a real phenomenon that no one had been able to predict.

Indispensable in science, such flexibility is also crucial to an economic system. Luckily, flexibility is one of the great strengths of free enterprise. It is to this book's credit that, in addition to the detailed, worthy suggestions of dozens of actions each of us can undertake, it calls for economic incentives that can harness the engine of the marketplace to develop the innovative devices that we need.

If the environmentalist is seen as the architect rebuilding our society, the entrepreneur might be seen as the consulting engineer. And what better resource could we summon than the American engineer? Indeed, entrepreneurs all around the globe are beginning to understand that to meet the increasingly urgent demands of consumers and societies for environmentally sound products – and production methods – is an unparalleled opportunity. For the sake of our own country's economy, I hope we Americans rise to the challenge with tremendous energy. To fail to contribute our share of ideas will weaken us economically. To succeed will contribute to our children's prosperity and, at the same time, protect the planet.

As valuable as Jon Naar's compendium is, it would be less interesting if we agreed on everything. Neither I nor the Environmental Defense Fund (and probably most readers) would endorse each and every viewpoint expressed, and he recognizes that the suggestions will not be applicable to everyone. But the 1990s must be a decade in which we commit ourselves to solving the world's problems and rebuilding society to deliver to all people a higher standard of living in a sustainable way. The informed, creative suggestions in this book are a welcome blueprint toward the realization of that goal.

Frederic D. Krupp

"What is the use of a house
if you don't have a decent planet to put it on?"
– Henry David Thoreau

DESIGN FOR A LIVABLE PLANET

INTRODUCTION

It's a Small World, after All

"Viewed from the distance of the moon,
the astonishing thing about the earth, catching the
breath, is that it is alive."
– Dr. Lewis Thomas, Lives of a Cell

Before 1961 no human being had actually seen the whole earth, what Plato had described as "a living creature, one and visible, containing within itself all living creatures." It took more than 2,000 years for modern science to rediscover the ancient wisdom that planet Earth – the Greeks called it *Gaia* or Mother Earth – functions as a single living organism and that we, as part of the planet, are life *within* life.

With the publication of the first photographs of the earth as seen from the moon and the pioneering research of British chemist James Lovelock, who had worked with NASA on the exploration of Mars, the old Gaian concept was recast into a new hypothesis. "The evolution of the species of living organisms," wrote Lovelock, "is so closely coupled with the evolution of their physical and chemical environment that together they constitute a single and indivisible evolutionary process."[1]

The notion that symbiosis (the state of living together) and cooperation between organisms are integral to successful existence and a spur to evolution did not originate with Lovelock. For most of human history there was respect for the natural world because human life depended then on an intimate knowledge of its land, water, air, trees, plants, and animals. The idea of human domination of nature emerged during the "Age of Enlightenment" and was given a full head of steam by the Industrial Revolution some 150 years ago. The earth's bounty, believed to be unlimited, was now at man's disposal to rape, plunder, and exploit.[2]

Ours is the age of fossil fuels, built on the use of coal and developed on the use of oil. If these fuels brought overall material prosperity to the Western world, they also brought misery – urban overcrowding, poverty, and pollution from what the poet William Blake called "dark satanic mills." And, as the world found out in 1973 with the OPEC oil embargo, the supply or at least the accessibility of these industrial-age fuels is severely limited.

As we know from our study of ancient civilizations, pollution is not a new phenomenon. What is new is the scale that it has now reached. As we shall see in the course of this book, there are no corners of the earth untouched by its effects. The land is poisoned with chemical fertilizers and pesticides. The seas are cesspools of trash and toxic waste. There is even the danger that atmospheric pollution, creating global warming, has reached a point of no return, that the impact of existing pollution will radically change our climate *regardless of what preventive measures we take.*[3]

The thrust of this book is that there *still* is time to do something about pollution – to clean it up, and even more importantly to prevent more of it from happening. How much time we have left is debatable, but there's no question about the need to start right now and to do it on the same kind of massive scale that has been employed to produce it in the first place. Ours is the throwaway society with no "away" left.

To cynics who say there's nothing we can do, I say look to those who have helped to change the world – Rachel Carson, Martin Luther King, Jacques Cousteau, Mother Teresa, Pete Seeger, and many others. They show that change is made up of thousands of small acts and decisions. Or consider the elegant simplicity of Paul Connett's "unmaking of trash" described in chapter 1 and many other examples of success in the fight against pollution in the following chapters.

The main purpose of *Design for a Livable Planet* is to show the literally hundreds of ways that we, as individuals and in groups, can make the planet less polluted, more livable. The way to begin is to take charge of one's own "ecology," to clean up one's own pollution, and then to move in concert with others in ever increasing circles of action. In so doing, one begins to see that many other people are moving in the same direction. As we shall see throughout the book, many people and communities are practicing what, with Jacques Cousteau's encouragement, I call Positive Ecology – turning the negative force of pollution into the positive energy of environmental and ecological cleanup. In the process, we will learn to respect ourselves and respect nature, of which we are only a small part. It is, we realize, a small world, after all. However, because it's the only one we have, we will do well to look after it more carefully.

We will do well to heed the words of J.R.R. Tolkien:

The rule of no realm is mine, but all worthy things that are in peril as the world now stands, those are my care. And for my part, I shall not wholly fail my task if anything passes through this night that can still grow fair or bear fruit and flower again in days to come. For I too am a steward. Did you not know?

The Language of Ecology

Throughout this book are references to many aspects of "ecology." Although these terms are described in the contexts where they are used, the following short glossary is a general guide to what is becoming an important new vocabulary for the 1990s and beyond.

Bioregion: A region defined by the givens of nature (e.g., rivers, mountains, forests) rather than by human (political) dictates. Bioregions range from larger (*ecoregions*) to smaller (*morphoregions.*)

Biosphere: The world of living (*biotic*) things and their inanimate environment.

Community: A group of animal and plant populations living and interacting in a given place.

Crash: A precipitate decline in species numbers after **overshoot** (see below).

Dieback or die-off: Extensive deaths resulting when a population exceeds the ability of an environment to support it.

Die-out: The extinction of a species, such as the dodo and the passenger pigeon.

Drawdown: The process by which the dominant species in an ecosystem uses up the surrounding resources faster than they can be replaced and ends up borrowing from other places and times. In little more than 100 years, for example, we have used up perhaps 80 percent of the buried remains of the Carboniferous Period – oil, coal, and gas – that were deposited over a period of 100 million years or more.[4]

Ecology: The study of how living things relate to their natural environment. The interrelated natural world.

Ecosystem: A self-supporting and self-regulating community of organisms interacting with each other and their environment – e.g., oceans, lakes, ponds, tundra, forests, grasslands, deserts, metropolitan districts, transportation corridors, small towns, industries, and agroecosystems.

Energy: The ability to do work, measured as *potential* or *stored* energy, or as *kinetic* energy, the energy of motion.

Environment: The sum of external conditions influencing the life of an organism or *population* (group of the same kind of organisms).

Feedback: A signal sent into a self-regulating system eliciting a response.

Food chain: Transfers of food energy in which one type of organism consumes another.

Food web: A complex, interlocking series of food chains.

Fossil fuel: Remains of dead vegetation and animals – such as coal, oil, and natural gas – that can be burned to release energy.

Fuel: A substance that can be burned, be split in a chain reaction, or undergo nuclear fusion to produce heat (energy).

Gaia: A theory, named after the Greek goddess of the earth, put forward by Dr. James Lovelock claiming that the biosphere acts as a single living system.

Habitat: The place where an organism or community of organisms lives.

Holistic: Relating to the study of complete living systems, rather than of their component parts in isolation.

Human ecology: The study of the relations between a human community and its environment.

Hydrosphere: The water portion of the earth.

Lithosphere: The crust of the earth.

Microorganisms: Bacteria, yeasts, fungi, and any other living things of microscopic size.

Monoculture: The cultivation of a single crop to the exclusion of others.

Nonrenewable resource: One that is limited or depleted to such a degree that its recovery is cost prohibitive.

Open system: One in which energy and matter are exchanged between the system and its environment.

Overshoot: The inevitable and irreversible consequence of continued drawdown, when the use of resources in an ecosystem exceeds its carrying capacity and there is no way to recover or replace the loss.

Pollution: An undesirable change in physical, chemical, or biological characteristics of air, land, or water that can harm the health, activities, or survival of living organisms.

Renewable resource: One that is essentially unlimited, such as energy from the sun.

Resource: Anything needed by an organism, population, or ecosystem.

Symbiosis: Two different species living together beneficially.

Synergy: Interaction in which the combined effect is greater than the sum of the separate effects.

How the Book Works

The first eight chapters of *Design for a Livable Planet* describe the main forms of pollution – solid waste, toxic chemicals, water pollution, air pollution, acid rain, deforestation, global warming, and radiation – and provide many examples of *What You Can Do* – practical steps you can take to clean up the pollution that effects your own life and the environment you live in. Throughout the book these "What You Can Do" sections are indicated by a black bar heading accompanied by the following Thumbs-Up symbol which expresses the power of positive ecology in action:

What You Can Do

Chapters 9 through 12 provide *longer-term* solutions to the pollution crisis – how we can move away from dependency on fossil fuels toward clean, safe, renewable energy and more natural ways of growing our food, how we can use the framework of law to achieve environmental cleanup and regeneration, how we can organize for political action and change at local, state, and national levels, and how we can most effectively use our power as "green" consumers.

For added ease of reference each of the 12 chapters is coded on every page with an identifying symbol as shown by the following examples: chapter 1 – circle of recycling; chapter 2 – toxic waste drum; chapter 3 – water pollution, etc.:

At the end of each chapter is a comprehensive "Resources" section referring you to a network of agencies, organizations, groups, associations, research centers, books, periodicals, and other sources that will help you tackle the job of cleaning up different types of pollution.

Immediately after "Resources" are the Endnotes, which give specific references to the material provided in the chapter and, in some cases, amplification of the text.

Note: For easier access and to avoid excessive cross referencing we have preferred in some cases to give addresses of organizations, titles of books, and other information on page as well as in the "Resources" section. For the same reasons we have duplicated certain material in the "What You Can Do" sections – in chapters 5 and 9, for example, referring to energy-saving measures you can take.

ENDNOTES

1. James Lovelock, *Man and Gaia* – in Edward Goldsmith and Nicholas Hildyard, eds., *Earth Report: Monitoring the Battle for Our Environment* (London: Mitchell Beazley, 1988). This is a brilliant book which is unfortunately not widely available in the U.S..

2. It was the celebrated French mathematician and physiologist Rene Descartes (1596-1690) who provided the philosophical justification of the irrelevance of ethics to the relationship between humans and nature. In his view the nonhuman world, which included animals, consisted of "things" to be dominated and possessed. The objectification of nature was – and for many people still is – a prerequisite in the progress of science and civilization. For further discussion of this concept see Roderick Frazier Nash, *The Rights of Nature* (Madison: University of Wisconsin, 1988) and two books by Michael J. Cohen: *Prejudice against Nature* (Freeport, Me.: Cobblesmith, 1983) and *How Nature Works: Regenerating Kinship with Planet Earth* (Walpole, N.H.: Stillpoint, 1988).

3. This is essentially the viewpoint of Bill McKibben's *The End of Nature* (New York: Random House, 1989).

4. *Crash*, *die-off*, *drawdown*, and *overshoot* are pungent words described at greater length in Kirkpatrick Sale's important book *Dwellers in the Land: The Bioregional Vision* (San Francisco: Sierra Club, 1985).

1

GARBAGE

Waging War On Waste

> "*Most of the luxuries, and many of the so-called comforts, of life are not only dispensable, but hindrances to the elevation of mankind.*"
> – *Henry David Thoreau*

Ours is the age of effluence, the most wasteful in human history. Waste, refuse, trash, garbage, rubbish, junk: whatever word you use, it adds up to one of the most pervasive problems of our time. No corner of the earth is immune from the festering mass of waste that's polluting land, air, water, and environment.

Piled high in cities, in rural dumps, on beaches, and in harbors from New York to Shanghai, waste is a problem that won't go away. Landfills burst at the seams, leaking hazardous chemicals into ground and water.

Incinerator smoke and ash foul the air. Garbage-laden ships sail around the world seeking a place to dump toxic cargoes nobody wants.

Waste is an exclusively human problem. Virtually every pound of natural resources we take from forests, mines, wells, aquifers, and earth ends up sooner or later in an unmanageable pile of trash with no place to go or in other forms of pollution. The dimensions of the waste crisis are described by the United States Environmental Protection Agency (EPA) as staggering.[1] The crisis, most of us know, is as close as our own back doors.

The Statistics of Trash[2]

● From manufacturing, mining, and farming in the U.S. we generate 5 billion tons of solid waste a year – more than 20 tons for each one of us, twice as much as any other country in the world. Twenty tons of trash are enough to fill *ten* large city dumpsters to the brim or cover a football field with a two-foot-high pile.

● In our homes and businesses we produce another 230 million tons of garbage annually – more than 5 pounds for each woman, man, and child every day.

● Every year we trash astronomical numbers of products we could replace with durable alternatives – 16 billion plastic diapers (amounting to 5 million tons), 2 billion disposable razors, 1.6 billion ballpoint pens.

● Each household throws out an average of 13,000 pieces of paper, 1,800 plastic items, 500 aluminum cans, and 500 glass bottles a year.

● We discard enough office and writing paper annually to build a 12-foot high wall from Los Angeles to New York, enough glass bottles and jars to fill the 1,350-foot high twin towers of the New York World Trade Center every two weeks, and enough plastic soda bottles and milk jugs to fill a line of dump trucks stretching from New York to Cleveland.

● 216 million pounds of plastic soda bottles and milk jugs are thrown out annually.

● Costs of waste disposal have skyrocketed to $50 and more a ton. If it doesn't sound like a lot, multiply $50 by 160 million tons and you have a bill of $7.5 billion for household and office garbage disposal alone! That's enough to build 1,000 schools and 500 hospitals with more left over for staff salaries and maintenance.

The question is not, Do we have a solid waste crisis? but, How can we avoid being buried in our own refuse?

The obvious answer is to create less in the first place – what the EPA calls waste minimization. But that's easier said than done. Modern industrial society is based on producing goods that are "convenient," disposable, unessential, obsolescent, or all of the above. Making less waste means radically changing what we buy and use. It means persuading manufacturers, suppliers, distributors, advertising agencies, supermarkets, department stores, and other retailers to make and sell products that we really need, will last, and are packaged economically.

Giving up our throwaway lifestyle is no simple matter. Yet with the crisis at our doorsteps, we must respond. The options: send the garbage "away," put it in landfills, burn it, or recycle it. As we shall see, there is really no "away" to be found, either here in the United States or anywhere else.

No Place to Go

Moving trash by truck, barge, or other means costs more than landfilling. And it creates other problems. Even when communities are willing to pay a premium to have their garbage carted away, they discover other people don't want to take it in. Remember the barge *Mobro* in 1987 trying to dump 3,186 tons of solid waste picked up from Islip, Long Island? It was refused unloading permission in North Carolina, Louisiana, Florida, the Bahamas, Mexico, and Honduras. After 164 days and 6,000 miles of frustrated journeying, the vessel came back home to New York where, barred from docking, it languished for another three months in the harbor. The by-then overripe cargo was eventually incinerated in Brooklyn, leaving 400 tons of ash residue to be shipped back to Islip for burial in the local landfill.[3]

A Glossary of Garbage

Bottom ash: A residue that collects in the bottom of the burning chamber of an incinerator.

Compost: Decayed organic material used as a soil fertilizer and conditioner.

Dioxin: The common name for 2,3,7,8-tetrachlorodibenzo(p)dioxin, an organic compound found in incinerator ash that is known to cause cancer in animals and possibly in humans.

Electrostatic precipitator: An air-pollution control device that removes fine dust by charging the particles with an electric field, then attracting them to highly charged collector plates.

Emission: Smoke and other substances discharged into the air.

Fly ash: Fine particles of ash in flue gases produced by trash burning.

HTRR: High-technology resource recovery – a state-of-the-art incinerator.

Incinerator: A furnace, boiler, or other container for burning waste.

Leachate: Liquid that leaks out of a landfill.

Mass burn facility: An incinerator which burns unsorted trash.

MRF: Material recovery facility.

Municipal solid waste (MSW): Waste from households, street litter, commercial refuse, ash, and abandoned automobiles.

Noncombustible waste: Metal, tin cans, dirt, bricks, glass, ceramics, asbestos, ash, and bulk waste such as refrigerators that cannot be burned.

Particulates: Fine solid particles of smoke or soot to which pollutants adhere.

PET (polyethylene terephthalates): Clear plastics from which many soda bottles are made.

Resource recovery: A misleading term for mass burn incinerators, which recover no resources other than small amounts of heat.

Scrubber: A device for removing acid gases and aerosols from the incinerator airstream.

Source separation: Sorting trash (usually at the point of generation) and putting specific materials – newspapers, glass, metal cans – into separate containers for collection.

Tipping fee: The charge to unload waste materials at an incinerator or landfill.

Waste stream: All the garbage produced by a community.

Another ship, the *Khian Sea*, carrying 14,000 tons of Philadelphia incinerator ash (16 pounds for each resident!) that contained heavy metals and cancer-causing dioxin, traveled for more than two years trying to unload its cargo at 11 ports across the world from Delaware Bay to Singapore. Under the pretense of delivering fertilizer, it left 3,000 tons of its cargo in Haiti before the government could be warned of its contents; the ship then changed its name and ownership twice to evade detection and finally dumped the rest of the ash in the ocean.[4]

Landfilling

About 80 percent of U.S. trash currently is dumped in landfills – open sites usually not far from where we live. Landfilling presents serious problems: we are running out of space, especially near towns; uncontrolled landfills pollute surface and ground waters and occasionally catch on fire; they are breeding grounds for rats, flies, and other carriers of disease; food and other vegetable matter rot, producing smelly methane gas and organic acids that leach heavy metals and other toxins from the waste; landfills also attract noisy traffic.

Landfilling also poses an ethical problem, because it deprives future generations of valuable resources. Much of what we throw into landfills could be used again. It is a political problem as well because, understandably, people don't like living near landfills. Politicians know that putting one in their district is committing political suicide.

Most municipal officials, public health experts, and environmentalists agree that we must reduce our dependence on landfilling, but there are two diametrically opposed approaches on how to do this: destroying the waste materials and recovering them.

Incineration

Incineration runs the gamut from burning leaves in your own backyard (now illegal in most communities) to high-technology resource recovery (HTRR), a capital-intensive, complex process designed to dispose of trash by burning it in large incinerators. Because of the difficulty of finding space for new landfills, many local and state officials have endorsed building massive trash incinerators as the "realistic" solution to the garbage dilemma.

HTRR has been tried in several European countries and in Brazil and Japan. Today there are about 160 municipal waste incinerators operating in the U.S. with about twice that number under consideration. Most are "mass burn" units, which burn trash without first separating its components.

Advantages

● Incineration appeals to many decision makers because it offers a way to get rid of trash without making basic changes to existing waste-disposal procedures.
● It reduces the volume of material that has to be landfilled. Some proponents claim the reduction to be as high as 90 percent.
● It can generate useful steam and/or electricity.
● According to its proponents, many of whom (engineers, designers, builders, lawyers, consultants, financiers, operators) stand to gain materially from its development, incineration provides long-term job opportunities.

Disadvantages

● Incineration is very expensive, especially when you include capital and life-time repayment costs. For example, the estimated capital cost of a proposed incinerator at the Brooklyn Navy Yard in New York is more than $535 million.[5]

The lifetime costs of a unit in Detroit will almost certainly exceed $1 billion.[6] The economics of mass burning were put into focus by Dr. Barry Commoner, director of the Center for the Biology of Natural Systems (CBNS) at Queens College, N.Y.: "The proposed nationwide investment of $30 billion, to be made over the next two decades by state, county, and municipal authorities in garbage incineration represents a monumental commitment to a technology which is fast becoming obsolete. If a similar investment were made in setting up and enforcing recycling programs, we would be much closer to solving the solid waste disposal problem, ecologically and economically."[7]

- Aside from short-term work in building the installation, incinerators don't employ many workers in their operation.
- The 90 percent waste-reduction claim is misleading because it measures the difference between the volume of trash *as it arrives at the plant* and the residue (ash) that leaves it after burning. It excludes nonprocessible objects, like refrigerators, that are too big to go into the hoppers.

> *"The proposed nationwide investment of $30 billion . . . in garbage incineration represents a monumental commitment to a technology which is fast becoming obsolete."*

A more realistic figure is probably closer to 60-70 percent.[8]

- Trash is rough on incinerators. A plant in Rome, N.Y. that opened in January 1985 had to have its grates repaired and its furnace linings and all four stacks replaced during the first year of operation.[9]
- Unable to handle unsorted trash, incinerators require a steady flow of garbage to fuel them, which must be guaranteed by the municipality. In effect, this puts a premium on maintaining (not reducing) the amount of trash we produce.
- Most first-generation incinerators in the U.S. had to be closed when they failed to meet air-pollution standards established after they had been built. Many newer-technology plants are not fitted with acid scrubbers (to take out hydrogen chloride), and are believed to be the cause of a pattern of respiratory illness reported in Detroit and neighboring Canada, Oswego, N.Y., Windham, Conn., and Saugus, Mass.[10]
- Mercury, lead, cadmium and other toxic metals cannot be destroyed by incineration, ending up in the unburned bottom ash or released into the air. At sufficiently high exposure levels, mercury causes nervous disorders, cadmium exposure leads to hypertension and kidney failure, while lead is particularly harmful to children's mental development. A proposed trash incinerator in Holyoke, Mass. was turned down by the state Department of Environmental Quality in part because the local population was already overexposed to lead.[11]
- *The ash from incinerators is toxic.* Every three tons of trash burned produces one ton of ash, of which 10 percent is fly ash and 90 percent bottom ash. Fly ash is a fine particulate which gets trapped in the incinerator's control devices. It often contains cancer-causing dioxins.[12] In order to get around EPA toxicity limits, many plant operators dilute fly ash with the less harmful bottom ash. But when the mixture is dumped into landfills, toxic components such as heavy metals leach from the acidic environment of the landfill into the ground water.

In 1985-86 Sweden and Denmark halted building new incinerators because they produced dioxin in mothers' milk.[13] Instead of reducing this carcinogen, incineration actually increases it, a CBNS study showed.[14] "If incinerators had to dispose of their ash as toxic waste, it would make plants ten times more expensive to operate," said Cynthia Pollock of Worldwatch Institute, the highly respected, Washington-based research agency.[15]

Since 1986 at least 50 communities in the United States have reconsidered their projects to build incinerators, including Seattle, where the mayor delayed plans until 1996 in favor of a comprehensive recycling program (see p. 17), Los Angeles, which dropped plans for three proposed plants, and Philadelphia, which shut down two incinerators amid public health concerns.[16] (Examples of how grass-roots organizations have organized to defeat incineration proposals are given in chapter 11, pp. 274-277.)

Recycling and Reuse

Unmaking Trash

"If household trash is made by mixing all our discarded materials together, then clearly the key step to unmaking it is to separate it, or rather to keep it separate, since most of the materials are used separately." – Dr. Paul Connett, cofounder of Work on Waste.[17]

The more trash we reuse, the less there is to get rid of. This saves money and energy as well as conserving natural resources. Recycling is not a new idea. In the 1920s and '30s it was a basic way of life in North America, especially in rural communities, where waste reuse and composting were commonplace. In World War II recycling became a patriotic duty for all citizens, and industry recycled 25 percent of the solid waste stream. Since then, affluence, cheaper consumer products (especially plastics), and the appeal of "convenience" have worked against recycling. However, with an ever-mounting garbage crisis, more and more people are seeing the need to preserve natural resources and conserve energy.

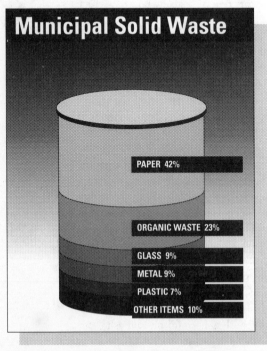

Municipal Solid Waste

PAPER 42%

ORGANIC WASTE 23%

GLASS 9%

METAL 9%

PLASTIC 7%

OTHER ITEMS 10%

Coming Full Circle [18]

The composition of our municipal solid waste shows that many products and materials we usually throw away can be restored to a useful second life.[19]

The largest component (42 percent) is *paper* – corrugated cardboard, newspaper, magazines, books, paperboard, and office paper. Next are *organic wastes* (23 percent), composed of yard waste (16 percent) and food waste (7 percent); *glass containers* (9 percent); *metal* (9 percent); *plastic* (7 percent); and *other items* (10 percent) including wood wastes, rubber, and textiles.

What a Waste!

- The U.S. generates 160 million tons of solid waste a year – enough to fill a line of 10-ton garbage trucks half way to the moon.
- We spend more than $6 billion a year to collect and dispose of our trash. Almost half of it is paper, which can be easily recycled.
- Recycling just one Sunday edition of the *New York Times* would save a forest of 75,000 trees! [20]
- Throwing away one aluminum beer can wastes as much energy as pouring out half a gallon of gasoline.

Estimates of how much solid waste can be recycled range from a low of 20 percent (National Solid Waste Management Association) to a high of 88 percent by weight (CBNS). In fact, many communities in Europe, Asia, and North America are already achieving overall recycling rates as high as 65 percent. Certain products – paper, glass, and aluminum – have high reuse rates. In Denmark an incredible 99.6 percent of bottles and glass containers is recovered.[21] Countries that are more energy-conscious than the U.S. – Japan, West Germany, the Netherlands, and Italy, for instance – recover more than twice what we do.

Classifying Trash

The way we classify the discarded materials in our trash greatly influences what we do with them – or, conversely, what we *want* to do with them will greatly influence how we classify them. This can be illustrated in the following comparison given by Dr. Paul Connett.[22] Imagine three identical cardboard boxes on three conveyor belts, one leading to an incinerator, one to a recycling center, one to a reuse facility. For the incinerator operator the box is combustible and will go into the furnace, the recycler will send the box to a paper mill for pulping, and the reuser might open the box and find a baseball card collection worth hundreds of dollars!

Six Ways to Separate Your Trash

1. *Reusables* – items you no longer need, but which can be used by others (sofas, refrigerators, clothes, books).
- Hold a garage sale, or give them to a friend or a thrift shop run by voluntary organizations such as the Salvation Army.

2. *Recyclables* – items you can no longer use but which contain recyclable materials (newspapers, office paper, aluminum cans, glass, and some plastics).
- Presort them for pickup by your sanitation department or take them to a local recycling center.

3. *Compostables* – material which creates methane and bad smells in landfills, but which can be composted into nutrient-rich soil and fertilizer (food waste, leaves, grass clippings, kitty litter).
- If you have a backyard, compost food waste, leaves and other items into topsoil. Otherwise deliver your compostables to a local composting center.

4. *Avoidables* – "disposables" such as the 1.6 billion pens, 2 billion razors, and 16 billion plastic diapers we throw away every year.
- Buy durable products that can be reused – refillable pens, rechargeable

15

razors, cotton diapers. Get more consumers, manufacturers, and politicians to think about the issue (for more on how to do this, see Tips 24-26, p. 28).

5. *Toxins* – products that contain harmful substances (household and car batteries, paints, solvents, bleaches, cleaners, pesticides).

● For details on how to dispose of them, see chapter 12, pp. 304-305.

6. *The Rest* – what's left over (junk mail, packaging that blends two materials such as plastic and paper – e.g., milk cartons – and plastics that can't be recycled).

● Try to avoid using this material. Support efforts to reduce such use, especially to convince manufactures to use less throwaway packaging and more recyclable materials in their products. (For ways to get rid of junk mail and cut down on excess packaging, see Tips 3 and 4, p. 26.)

An Idea Whose Time Has Come Again

In response to growing public pressure, the EPA in 1988 set a goal of halving the volume of trash going to landfills by 1992 through a combination of burning and recycling. However, many communities are already ahead of this timetable without resorting to incineration. New Jersey, where more than a quarter of the population already sorts its trash, requires all its counties to submit plans to set aside 25 percent of their home and commercial trash for separate pickup and recycling. An even more ambitious plan has been worked out by the city of Seattle, which has one of the country's most successful urban recycling programs. "Our citizens should be given a chance to show how much waste can be recycled" is how Mayor Charles Royer put it.

Reusing Waste

One of the most comprehensive materials recovery facilities is the multipurpose recycling center in Wellesley, Mass., a suburban residential community about 25 minutes from downtown Boston. Affectionately known as "the dump," the center is sited around a defunct incinerator. Its neatly mown grass, picnic tables, and driveways leading to the drop-off areas look more like a park than a garbage dump.

Since Wellesley doesn't have a regular collection service, 85 percent of its residents take their own trash to the dump. Next to the drop-off containers for recyclables is a Goodwill Industries trailer which accepts small appliances and used clothing. In the basement of the old incinerator building is a special section for car batteries, tires, and waste oil. Behind the building is an area where you can drop off grass clippings and leaves and pick up last year's compost. (For more on composting, see "Composting – A Matter of Substance," pp. 24-25.)

The Wellesley center also features a transfer section where you can exchange anything from magazines and books to unwanted furniture and appliances and where commercial haulers can buy metal, cardboard, and other materials. In 1987, more than 16 percent of the 17,677 tons of waste processed at the center was recycled. In 1988, 24 percent of Wellesley's residential trash was recycled with net benefits of $186,000, including sales of recyclables, avoided hauling and landfilling costs, and recycling expenses. [24]

Many other communities have similarly successful reuse centers, including Birmingham and Tuscaloosa, Ala., Mecklenburg County, N.C. (whose over $1 million recycling budget is financed through landfill user fees), San Jose, Calif. (the largest weekly curbside recycling program in the nation), and Wilton, N.H. (with 45 percent recycling). In Portage, Mich., the reuse center incorporates an extensive repair shop that returns appliances to useful service. [25] The Berkeley,

Calif. recycling program includes curbside collection, a drop-off center, a buy-back center, and a large reuse section run by Urban Ore which grosses over $40,000 a month selling bathtubs, windows, doors, and other reusable products.[26]

The System Works in Seattle[*]

In Seattle's North End, brightly-colored crates dot the streets on collection day: yellow for cans and glass, green for paper, and dark green for newsprint. In the South End, one big green 90-gallon wheeled can combines all three items. Both of these curbside recycling programs were begun in February 1988, as part of an ambitious plan calling for rates of recycling higher than anywhere else in the world, with over 60 percent recovery [of the total waste stream] as the goal. In four short months, the curbside program surpassed all others of its kind and currently involves 55 percent of the eligible households in Seattle, far exceeding even the most optimistic predictions for the first year. The city is now recycling 2,500 tons of bottles, cans, and newspapers through its curbside program each month. Add to this Seattle's already successful private recycling efforts, and the city recycles 28 percent of its waste stream.

To promote recycling, Seattle has undertaken a package of programs and incentives such as restructured garbage rates. Residents normally pay $18.55 a month for the city to dispose of two garbage cans of refuse, but if they separate out recyclables and only fill one can, it costs just $13.55. This so-called "variable can" rate reflects the space saved when recyclables are removed from the garbage. Since Seattle saves money when it avoids landfilling the extra amount, it passes some of the savings on to its customers. Super-recyclers will soon be offered the option of an even cheaper minican. The city [has begun to pick up] yard waste (making up 21 percent of residential refuse) to process into compost and paying $30 per ton to private recyclers who make pick-ups from apartment buildings with five or more units.

Seattle's city council chose to try two different methods of recycling by splitting the city into two zones. Rabanco, a local separation plant, took on Seattle's South End, collecting mixed recyclables. Recycle America, run by waste-handling giant Waste Management Inc. (WMI), handles the North End with trucks picking up separated recyclables. While this program is more expensive than the South End's method of combining paper, glass, and cans in one container, it doesn't require as much sorting later. . .

Mining this "urban ore," rather than extracting more of the earth's raw materials, is essential to preserving the environment. Producing a ton of paper from recycled fiber saves some 3,700 pounds of trees and 24,000 gallons of water. Melting down a ton of aluminum cans saves 8,000 pounds of bauxite and 1,000 pounds of petroleum coke. "Our cities are a reliable source of natural resources," says Greenpeace Recycling Project coordinator Bryan Bence. "To ignore minerals and other materials in our cities' waste stream is a crime against the earth."

[*] By Ken Stump and Kathy Doiron from the bimonthly magazine *Greenpeace*, January/February 1989 with permission.

Successful Recycling Programs

Oregon Pioneers[27] – In 1986 Oregon passed a Recycling Opportunity Act to make recycling available to all citizens. It mandates curbside collection of recyclables at least once a month in cities of 4,000 or more; in smaller communities special drop-off sites are provided. Oregon's history of recycling goes back at least to 1981 when the 13,000 inhabitants of West Linn, a small town near Portland, rejected a proposal to put a trash-burning plant just across the river in favor of recycling. Today with some 60 percent of its citizens taking part, West Linn collects $6.70 a container from private haulers to take recycled materials to centers like the cooperative run by the Portland Refuse Recycling Operators Association, where they are prepared for resale to manufacturers. The glass goes to Owens Illinois Inc. (whose Portland plant bought $1.7 million worth of used bottles in 1986), the paper goes to Oregon City paper mills, the tin cans are reclaimed by a company in Tacoma, Wash., and the oil is reused in local furnaces.

Portland Trailblazer

The inspiring force behind the Oregon program is Lorie Parker, state manager of waste reduction. As an environmental activist in the early 1970s, she helped require a city garbage hauler to open a recycling depot as the price of creating a new landfill. In 1983, for a college class project, she wrote an idealized recycling law based on voluntary participation. She got a friendly legislator to introduce it as a state bill and, to her surprise, it became law. Two years later she was invited to administer it. Describing its purpose, Parker said, "Our main priority is to reduce the amount of waste generated, then to reuse the material hopefully for its original purpose. Next we try to recycle what cannot be reused in this way, followed by the recovery of energy from what cannot be reused or recycled, provided that this preserves the quality of air, land, or water resources. Only after all these steps have been taken do we resort to landfilling or other approved methods." [28]

East Hampton Example – One of the United States' most ambitious curbside recycling programs is in East Hampton, N.Y.. Supported by a state research grant and designed by the Center for the Biology of Natural Systems, it aimed to recover at least 70 percent of the town's waste stream. East Hampton provides householders with four plastic containers, for paper and cardboard, metal cans and bottles, food and other organic material, and nonrecyclables (mainly plastic and composites). All recyclables are then taken to the town's processing facilities for conversion into marketable commodities. Paper is sold mixed or separated into different grades; cans and bottles are processed to yield aluminum, tin cans, and crushed glass; the food garbage together with yard waste is converted into compost, a useful soil additive.

In late 1987 East Hampton surveyed 100 households to find out how efficiently residential waste can be recycled when participants are highly motivated. Each participant used the four-container system. The results showed the source-separation rate to be *84 percent* by weight. If yard waste and plastics had been included in the test the rate would have been even higher, claims CBNS.[29]

Cooperation in Canada – In Ontario, Canada, cooperation between the Ministry of the Environment and private industry led to a joint public and private plan for recycling covering 1.2 million households throughout the province. The aluminum and beverage industries have agreed to invest in recycling programs that require weekly curbside collection of newspapers and beverage containers in special receptacles on the same day as regular garbage collection. The province has already committed $40 million to this venture, while 20 corporations have added another $20 million. Ultimately Ontario intends to include all nine million people in the province in an even more comprehensive recycling program.[30]

Hamburg Households – In 1985 the town of Hamburg, N.Y. made recycling obligatory after a voluntary program had produced poor results. In the first year it recycled 650 tons of paper, 150 tons of glass, and 110 tons of metal, saving $24,000 in disposal costs and reducing the amount of trash landfilled by 34 percent. Much of this success is due to an effective enforcement system. For those households that do not separate their waste, refuse collectors leave behind one garbage can to which they attach a bright orange sticker stating the source separation rules. The stickers serve to signal which homes are not cooperating with the program. If, after three weeks, the household does not source-separate, the town sends a letter outlining the rules. Finally, if the household still won't cooperate, the town stops picking up the garbage. This informal but firm approach has led to virtually 100 percent participation.

Islip Initiative – A year after burying the ashes from its infamous garbage barge, Islip, N.Y. became a model for waste disposal. Under a mandatory program initiated in 1987 residents were given green and beige trash cans to separate out paper, glass, and metal for recycling. To date, the program has tripled the yearly volume of recycled materials to 30,000 tons at an annual savings of $2 million and has extended the life of the town landfill.

Mandatory Programs

Recycling is now mandated in ten states and dozens of cities nationwide. Los Angeles, whose more than 6 pounds per capita a day is the highest garbage generation rate in the country,[31] abandoned plans to build an incinerator and is introducing mandatory source separation of waste. Philadelphia, the nation's second largest per-capita trash producer, passed an ordinance requiring the city to recycle at least half of its garbage by 1992. It aims to establish 20 neighborhood service centers, replacing a proposed waste-to-energy project designed to burn 2,000 tons of garbage a day, which was shelved because of widespread opposition from local citizens. Minneapolis now has a comprehensive program in which the city pays private haulers or community groups a "diversion" fee (averaging $15 a ton) for every ton of trash that does not go into a landfill. This is funded by a special landfill surcharge which further discourages wasteful dumping. In 1988 New York City began a major recycling program (see p. 25 for details).

Trash for Cash

Although some recycling has worked well on a nonprofit basis, many programs now incorporate monetary incentives or disincentives. These take many forms – deposits on glass and aluminum containers, the sale of recyclables to manufacturers, surcharges on landfill costs (to discourage dumping), and tax credits for projects that reduce waste and pollution.

Deposits on beverage containers have long been required in other countries. In the U.S. the first bottle law was introduced in Oregon in 1972. Today nine states have such legislation, including New York, where more than 400 million cases of beverages are sold yearly. In the first two years of its operation the New York law saved $50 to $100 million in energy costs, $50 million in cleanup expenditure, and $19 million in solid waste disposal, while increasing net employment by nearly 4,000 jobs.[32]

The Market for Recyclables

The demand for recyclables is growing, especially for newsprint, glass, aluminum, and compost. Corporations such as Owens-Illinois (the largest glass manufacturer in the U.S.), Alcoa, and Reynolds Aluminum that use virgin materials in their manufacturing are finding it profitable to switch to recycled sources. This is also being done increasingly by newsprint and plastics companies. About one-third of United States paper mills now use wastepaper exclusively and another half use 10 to 30 percent wastepaper. According to the American Aluminum Association, over half of today's aluminum cans are made from recovered aluminum.

In some parts of the United States, especially the Northeast and Northwest, material recovery facilities (MRFs) are being set up as the basis for regional recycling. They take in bulk quantities of mixed, dirty bottles, cans, and paper, and turn out marketable products.

Billing by the Bag

In January 1988 the town of High Bridge, N.J. stopped charging households a flat $200 annual fee for garbage collection and began charging for the amount they *actually* discard. Now each household is charged $200 for 52 town stickers, one of which must be placed on each 30-gallon bag or can of trash put out weekly at the curbside. The switch to billing by the bag has already reduced the volume of garbage by 25 percent. "We are stomping all the time, trying to squeeze as much as we can into a bag," explained Cheri Anderson, a local resident. In homes children now set aside empty soda cans for recycling instead of tossing them into the garbage and flatten cereal boxes and milk containers to conserve space in their trash cans. Some people whose cans are less than 100 percent full on the day before collection share their empty space with a neighbor whose can is overflowing. Other communities in New Jersey, Pennsylvania, and as far away as Minnesota and Utah have contacted High Bridge to find out how the system works.[33]

Critics of the program claim that, although it reduces the volume of garbage to be disposed, it doesn't focus on the more important need to reduce the amount of trash generated by our wasteful lifestyles.

A Camden, N.J. facility, which opened in 1982, receives about 75 tons of cans and bottles a day, serving 450,000 people in 40 surrounding cities and towns. New York City and the Community Services Society helped set up the R2/B2* intermediate processing center. This is a for-profit multimaterial buy-back operation, processing newspapers, glass, plastics, tin, aluminum, and other items, which employs 25 people full-time.

According to its contract with the city, R2/B2 must accept a wide range of materials and pay for them by the pound. Nevertheless the center has been very successful in marketing what they take in, including plastic shampoo and antifreeze bottles, used plastic swimming-pool liners, and telephone poles.

* From "Recoverable Resources/Borough of the Bronx

Regional cooperative marketing offers the added advantage of pooled resources that give a variety of benefits, including cost saving, to its members. One such program is run by the New Hampshire Resource Recovery Association, which serves 153 cities and towns and 50 business enterprises. It acts as a broker for smaller recycling programs statewide, negotiating contracts, setting quality specifications, and arranging efficient transportation routes.

In the West, Montana Recycling, a private firm, uses coordinated marketing to overcome high transportation costs in sparsely populated rural areas. With headquarters in Missoula and six branches in Montana and Wyoming, the company sells over 15,000 tons of recycled material annually, including lead-acid batteries and returnable bottles. Another case of recycling enterprise is Rubber Research Elastomerics, Inc. (RRE), in the town of Babbitt in northeastern Minnesota. The RRE plant grinds up used motor vehicle tires and converts them into "Tirecycle," a reclaimed product that substitutes for virgin rubber in a broad range of manufacturing applications.

Recycling Plastics

Although plastics make up only 7 percent of municipal trash by weight, they now account for 30 percent of the space in landfills.[34] At present only 2 percent of plastics (mostly soda bottles) are recycled. The packaging industry, the largest user of plastics, produces 40 percent of plastic waste. Manufacturers and retailers like plastic packaging because it is lightweight, tough, long-lasting, and more resilient than glass. Environmentally, plastics are a nightmare.

Made from petroleum-based chemicals, plastics usually will not degrade, as do the materials they so often replace, such as paper and cardboard. Their manufacture is itself often a toxic process, producing, in the case of styrofoam, ozone-destroying chlorofluorocarbons (CFCs), dioxin, and other harmful gases. One company alone, McDonald's, uses 70 million pounds of polystyrene a year to make its cups and containers, which account for an astronomical 1.6 billion cubic feet of plastic trash – enough to fill 100 million family-sized refrigerators.

Floatable plastics constitute 85 percent of all garbage found on U.S. beaches.[35] Discarded plastic loops from beverage six-packs snare birds, small animals, and fish in such large numbers that eleven states now require they be biodegradable. West Germany has completely outlawed plastic bottles made of polyethylene terephthalates (PET).

Because it is difficult to distinguish one plastic resin from another without some form of coding, most manufacturers refuse to accept plastics for recycling. A concerted campaign by the Washington-based *Coalition for Recyclable Waste* helped persuade the Coca-Cola Company not to introduce a new plastic can which could be easily mistaken for aluminum. When burned, these cans produced dioxin and sudden flares of heat that fouled aluminum smelting.

Widely criticized for their use of plastic packaging that very often ends up as litter, McDonald's and eight large plastics producers announced in late 1989 that they would set up a national program to recycle plastic hamburger containers, cups, and other items. In the program, which will begin in New England and will later be extended to other regions, customers will be asked to separate the polystyrene containers from other trash and deposit them in a separate basket marked "for recyclable plastic only."

Environmental groups reacted cautiously to the announcement because McDonald's and other fast-food chains have not made good on earlier promises to clean up the huge amount of litter they create – according to figures supplied by the plastics industry, each fast-food restaurant produces about 4,000 pounds of plastic waste a year[36] – and because recycling does not address the problems of pollution in the making or the recycling of polystyrene and other plastics.

Smart Plastics?

Imperial Chemicals Industries and other manufacturers are experimenting with "intelligent" plastics designed to degrade either naturally or by application of a chemical reagent. In Nebraska the town of Lincoln is evaluating biodegradable bags for yard waste, which would allow 25,000 tons of grass clippings and leaves to be collected each year between April and November, adding six years to the life of the landfill. To replace the costly process of separating traditional polyethylene bags from the compost pile, the project uses a bright yellow 33-gallon bag whose plastic contains a cornstarch-biodegradable additive and two oxidizing chemicals that supposedly help speed decomposition. In an active compost pile it is claimed that the new bags will degrade within 18 months, compared with 4 to 400 years for traditional plastic.[37]

Another innovation is photodegradable plastics which disintegrate when exposed for a predetermined time to sunlight. Designed for plastic litter (fast-food containers, disposable picnic ware, shopping bags), they are manufactured by Ecoplastics Ltd. of Ontario, Canada, Webster Industries of Peabody, Mass., and other companies. Ecoplastics' product Ecolyte has been approved for use in food contact materials by the Canadian government.[38] Webster's bags are marketed under the trade name Bes-Pak Good Sense.

Discontinuing Styrofoam Peanuts

A leader in the fight for environmental conservation, Nature's Way, a manufacturer of organic herbs and botanicals, stopped its use of styrofoam peanuts in its packaging in favor of a 100 percent recycled tri-paper padding. "If someone sends us a shipment padded with styrofoam peanuts, we send them right back again," said Adam Beutler, the company's shipping manager. "There's no sense in throwing the peanuts away because they are not biodegradable; so if we keep them in the shipping loop, maybe they'll discourage somebody else from buying new peanuts and instead use these old ones." [39] To help those interested in discontinuing the use of styrofoam packaging, the company offers a free information kit. Write to Environment, c/o Nature's Way, P.O. Box 4000, Springville, UT 84663.

'Degradable' plastics, now being marketed by companies such as Mobil which makes Hefty bags, have considerable sales appeal because they seemingly offer an easy way out of the garbage impasse. In actual practice, however, these plastics could be causing more problems than they are solving. In today's overloaded (and therefore oxygen-starved) landfills, the plastics degrade very slowly. Also, the elements into which they do eventually break down are likely to be as dangerous as the plastic itself. The greatest disadvantage perhaps is that these widely promoted products, including 'biodegradable' diapers, divert people from taking part in plastic-recycling programs and, even more importantly, from reducing plastic waste at its source. "These plastics are being sold as a way to reduce waste, and that is a hoax," said Jeanne Wirka of the Environmental Action Foundation.[40]

Developing New Technologies[41]

Legislation to reduce plastic trash such as that enacted in Suffolk County, N.Y., which in 1988 banned the use of polystyrene foam packaging, is stimulating the plastics industry to develop the technology for recycling its products after they have been used by consumers. A division of General Electric, GE Plastics, is researching the possibility of building houses and cars with recycled or recyclable plastics. Wellman Inc., a Shrewsbury, N.J. firm, reprocesses PET beverage bottles into 200 million pounds of polyester and nylon fibers a year. In early 1989 Plastics Again, of Leominster, Mass., opened a plant for recycling polystyrene from food containers and cups into material used for flowerpots and insulation.[42] Plastic Recycling Inc., of Iowa Falls, Iowa, recycles 15,000 pounds of plastics a day into car stops for parking lots and other products.[43] At Rutgers University in New Jersey the Center for Plastics Research has developed an automated system that converts plastic soft-drink bottles and milk jugs into raw materials from which park benches, fence posts, carpet backing, and other products are made.

In 1989 Du Pont and Waste Management Inc., the largest U.S. plastics maker and waste hauler respectively, announced joint plans to build several plastics recycling centers that will separate and clean about 40 million pounds of plastic containers annually and turn them into raw material for new products. Commenting on the venture, John Ruston, an Environmental Defense Fund (EDF) analyst, said, "It will show the rest of the industry that plastic recycling can be done on a large scale." [44]

Despite the efforts of some manufacturers to address the problems posed by plastics, most producers and retailers haven't done enough to detoxify their products and make recycling easier for consumers. Many manufacturers pay lip service to the solid-waste problem by promoting such items as "biodegradable" disposable diapers and plastic bags that have little chance of decomposing in tightly packed landfills. At the same time, they are using less and less recyclable glass in favor of plastic containers that, except for redeemable soda bottles, end up in the landfills or, worse still, in our oceans and lakes. To replace petrochemical-based plastics with glass and other materials less harmful to the environment will require extensive pressure from consumers backed by the power of the government (especially on the part of the EPA) to help move the market forces in the right direction.

Sustaining the Market for Recyclables

The commercial success of recycling depends on suppliers having reliable markets for the recovered materials. In addition to tax incentives to encourage this process, federal, state, and local governments can play an important role as purchasers of recyclables. The Resource Conservation and Recovery Act of 1976 (RCRA) requires federal agencies to purchase products made from recovered materials – paper, tires, insulation, and lubricating oils, for example – whenever they are suitable and available at a reasonable price. The EPA was made responsible for designating the products and issuing purchasing guidelines, but took no action until the summer of 1988 when they were compelled to do so as the result of a lawsuit initiated by the Environmental Defense Fund. "This is a turning point for an important program too long delayed. It is a major gain for recycling," said EPA lawyer Michael Herz, lead attorney for the suit, which was joined by the Environmental Task Force, the Coalition for Recyclable Waste, and the National Recycling Coalition.[45] (For more on RCRA and other environmental laws, see chapter 10.)

Composting – a Matter of Substance

Organic material makes up more than 20 percent of the waste stream. If we throw it away, we lose a great and easily accessible source of energy: composting. This is what happens naturally when leaves fall to the ground, slowly decay, and provide nutrients for soil, plants, worms, and microorganisms. Home composting – mixing vegetation with organic household wastes – speeds up the process when you add air, heat, and moisture. The product, compost, is a sweet-smelling, dark-brown, earthy substance called humus. Rich in nutrients and minerals, it can be used as a natural soil fertilizer or conditioner, as topsoil, and as a landfill cover.

Although farmers have used composting since time immemorial, its full potential, as the basis of organic food growing and as an inexpensive yet highly marketable replacement for synthetic chemical fertilizers, is only now becoming widely appreciated. It also significantly saves the amount of landfill used for trash disposal by diverting wastes to productive uses.

The beauty of composting is that it can be done from virtually any biodegradable waste in almost any quantity, from the small pile of leaves in your backyard to industrial-scale "windrows" (long rows of cut vegetation heaped up as if by the wind) by the simple process of layering the different materials – leaves, sawdust, kitchen wastes, grass clippings, garden debris, animal manure – exposing them to the sun, aerating them, and allowing them to decompose. Through the heat generated by the aerobic process most pathogens and disease vectors are destroyed. Organic waste can also be composted with sewage sludge, although this increases the chance of contamination with toxic chemicals or heavy metals discharged by industry into the sewage system. Under recent pressure from the EPA, industries are slowly beginning to pretreat their wastewater discharges upstream of wastewater treatment plants and some firms are substituting less hazardous process chemicals to avoid large pretreatment costs. However, this still does not make sludge innocuous.

Composting in city landfills has been successfully carried out in Palo Alto, Calif. since 1979. San Diego, San Francisco, and Portland, Ore. also have ongoing composting projects.[46]

Cattle- and dairy-farming states such as Minnesota (which passed a far-reaching Waste Management Act in 1980) and Wisconsin were among the first states to recognize its importance. In Portage County, Wis., just across the Minnesota border, a pilot composting project has been a valuable showcase for those from both states who want to see how it works.

In Japan there is widespread use of composting both in rural and urban areas. In many cases the community runs its own composting plant, while in others they

> *The beauty of composting is that it can be done from virtually any biodegradable waste in almost any quantity . . . its full potential, as the basis of organic food growing and as an inexpensive yet highly marketable replacement for synthetic chemical fertilizers, is only now becoming widely appreciated.*

commission fertilizer manufacturers to produce compost from dewatered sewage sludge provided by the municipality. State-of-the-art technology is now supplying high-quality compost in large quantities directly to local farmers and to outside customers including agricultural cooperatives and fertilizer retailers.

The town of Duisberg in West Germany's Rhineland has been processing household waste from 95,000 residents since 1957. During the three autumn months the composting plant treats leaves from the entire city as well as manure from the slaughterhouse and zoo. The town has developed a permanent market for its compost, which is used extensively in the growing of grapes, in local agriculture, and in landscaping parks and sports fields. Considerable amounts of the end product are also used as soil filters for deodorizing exhaust air from the town's sewage plants, slaughterhouses, and local industries.[47]

Recycling at Apartment and Office Buildings

The higher population density in large buildings offers greater recycling potential than single-household collection. In New York City, which generates the most garbage of any city in the world – more than 22,000 tons a day – the Environmental Action Coalition (EAC) is showing that recycling works in apartment buildings and complexes. Having started with 70 buildings in 1984, the enterprise now covers more than 200,000 apartment units and includes metal and glass as well as newspapers.

After identifying a building for possible participation, EAC explains the program to the building's management and maintenance employees, and in certain cases provides storage and collection equipment. Educational literature is distributed to tenants explaining their part in the process. Then it arranges for a private carting firm or area jobber to collect the materials. Each building's collection schedule is suited to its generation rate.

At the outset EAC emphasizes the advantages of recycling to building personnel – reduced compactor damage due to removal of newspaper and glass from the waste stream, and fewer plastic bags needed to put trash out for city pickup. EAC coordinates an agreement between the building and private haulers who collect the newspaper, glass, and other materials and sell them to brokers and other customers at current market prices. The building and the city both gain by having less garbage to handle.[48]

In addition to this program, the New York City Sanitation Department has started its own newspaper, metal, and glass recycling program in larger buildings, making use of "EZ Pack" dumpsters that are loaded at street level by specially designed trucks.

Office Paper Recycling Service (OPRS) is operated by the Council on the Environment of New York City, targeting private businesses, banks, insurance companies, and other offices that generate large amounts of paper and other recyclables. More than 50 companies take part in the program, which recovers some 1,500 tons of paper a year. When a specific program has been arranged, OPRS assists in implementation, supplying desktop folders, central collection boxes, signs, posters, and brochures. Under a mandatory program set up in 1987 for its 34 municipal agencies, the New York City Sanitation Department collects and sells about 1,000 tons of office paper, which more than pays for itself. Similar office paper recycling programs are now operating successfully in San Francisco, Oakland, and Huntington Beach, Calif., Ocala, Fla., Delaware County, Penn., and many other locations.

The Zen of Recycling –
Yes We CAN (Make a Difference)

In much of the world recycling is seen as a way to save waste, energy, and money *and* to extend the life of products and materials. The regenerative aspect of recycling brings special rewards because it is a process you can share with others – family, neighbors, and friends. As we have seen in the examples above, recycling is taking root in communities across North America. However, by its nature it does not have to be something *they* are doing. It is very much something *we* can do, as is shown in the following section.

28 Ways to Beat the Garbage Crisis

The following suggestions are based on the most successful recycling programs in the U.S. and abroad. Some may not apply to your particular situation. Select those that do. You'll be surprised how much you save – things, materials, and money – and how satisfying it is to take part in the process of reducing waste and helping clean up and prevent environmental pollution.

1. *Recycle at home and at work.* Separate newspapers (in bundles), bottles, and cans for delivery to (or pickup by) your local recycling unit. If you don't have one, see tip 24 below.

2. *Use paper scraps* for notes and memos. Reuse manila envelopes by putting on new labels (this was done widely in World War II).

3. *Reduce junk mail* by writing to the Direct Marketing Association, 6 East 43rd Street, New York, NY 10017, and asking to be taken off mailing lists. This will reduce unsolicited mail by 75 percent but will not affect mail from companies that already have your name and address. To control the latter you can send the mail back to its originator by circling the return address with a felt pen and having your name taken off mailing lists of publications you don't want.

4. *Complain* to companies that have started to package their periodicals and other products in plastic; include the wrapper in your letter. Persuade them to use wrappers made of 100 percent plant-fiber cellulose, which are more transparent than most plastics. For more information on this and on other recycled paper products contact Conservatree Paper Company at (800) 522-9200 or, in California, (415) 433-1000.

5. *Buy products packaged in glass, paper, or metal containers.* Where possible, avoid aluminum (unless it is recycled) because it requires huge amounts of energy to produce. It is also thought by some researchers to be associated with Alzheimer's disease. For food, glass is safest, compared with plastics, which may diffuse to the liquids they hold, or paper products, which may contain trace amounts of dioxin.

6. *Reuse glass containers* for storing flour, rice, oatmeal, nuts, grains, and other staples you can buy in bulk to save unnecessary packaging and money. They are also handy for pencils, pens, paper clips, pushpins, screws, and other household or office items.

7. *Shop where you find produce without plastic wrapping,* preferably organically grown and sold at local farmers' markets.

8. *Take along your own shopping bag,* as do consumers in other parts of the world, and have it packed with groceries and other purchases. String bags are very good for this purpose. Be careful, however, that you don't get accused of shoplifting! Some supermarkets now charge for plastic bags or give discounts to customers who bring in their own bags. Encourage your local managers to adopt a similar policy.

9. *If you must choose between paper and plastic products, the better choice depends on where you live.* If they are likely to get into the ocean or lake, use paper. If you live away from water, some plastics are preferable, *with the major exception of PVCs (polyvinyl chlorides), styrofoam, and PET plastics, which are highly toxic in their manufacture and when incinerated.* Polyethylene, the very thin plastic used for bags, baggies, and translucent products such as cups and "glasses," is less polluting than paper on a per pound basis.[49]

10. *Invest in durables.* A leather bag may cost more than a plastic one, but will outlive it by five or six times. The same principle applies to appliances, machinery, automobiles, and toys. Remember those great products from the 1950s and before – Waring blenders (mine goes back to 1947 and still works), Parker fountain pens, and Singer sewing machines. Many are still manufactured, while others you can find secondhand or discarded at recycling centers.

11. *Be an informed buyer.* Check carefully with *Consumer Reports* and other independent consumer guides before making major purchases so that you buy durable products. (See also chapter 12 for more on environment-friendly shopping.)

12. *Use cloth diapers*, if you have a baby, instead of plastic ones that dump an estimated 2.8 million tons of feces and urine into our overcrowded landfills and spread harmful bacteria. If you don't want to wash diapers, find a rental service or persuade one to serve your area. They are at least 20 percent cheaper than buying plastic diapers. For further information contact the *National Association of Diaper Services*, 2017 Walnut Street, Philadelphia, PA 19103, who will help you find a local cloth diaper service.

13. *Take a china coffee mug or teacup and metal spoon to work* so that you don't have to use tacky plastic cups and stirrers. This usually gets you more coffee or tea, is more enjoyable to use, and cuts down on waste.

14. *Avoid styrofoam.* For picnics and cookouts, wash and reuse heavy paper plates and plastic spoons and forks instead of lightweight styrofoam. If you do a lot of outdoor entertaining, consider metal camping pots and utensils, available at camping supply stores.

15. *Compost your food and other organic wastes* (leaves, grass clippings) for your garden, if you have a backyard, If you live in an apartment, propose to your neighbors to have the entire building's organic garbage sent to a local composting center.

16. *Use scrap paper and cardboard packaging as fire starters*, if you have a wood-burning stove.

17. *Reuse materials to make things you need*: old sheets, curtains, or clothes can be cut into small pieces for rags or made into hooked rugs or quilts (a few years ago I made camera lens protectors out of a 10-year-old wool shirt that had seen better days). Old lumber can be used in small home-carpentry projects or, if it is not painted or pressure-treated, as firewood (I salvage lumber and other building materials from construction sites, dumpsters, and – with permission – from our local landfill); old bricks and broken concrete make good retaining walls, garden walkways, or patios. Large (2-liter) plastic soda bottles make wonderful mini-greenhouses for growing seeds and plants: all you need is a utility knife or a pair of scissors to separate the bottle into two parts; punch holes in the bottom and use for germinating seeds; the top half works well as a solar dome to put over the plants when they have grown to about two inches. This method will save you money and give you a jump of 3 to 4 weeks on the growing season.[50]

18. *Rent or borrow items you use infrequently* – specialized power tools, ladders, or audiovisual equipment, for example.

19. *Maintain and repair* appliances, tools, and other equipment to lengthen their lives.

20. *Share, barter, trade, or donate* what you no longer need, but which has value to others – magazines, books, toys, clothes, and other items. Thrift shops are excellent places to find what you want and to give what you don't need. You often can get a better tax deduction by donating equipment to a nonprofit group such as Greenpeace or your local Sierra Club chapter rather than by trying to resell it.

21. *Have a garage sale or charity drop-off* instead of trashing household goods.

22. *Get children interested* in making things out of newspaper, toilet paper rolls, ice-cream sticks and other throwaways. You can't be too young to get the recycling "bug."

23. *Support the national campaign to boycott styrofoam and limit the use of plastics.* Vermont and Maine have already banned state use of plastic packages. Suffolk County, N.Y. has banned plastic grocery bags and plastic food containers. Santa Monica, Calif., has banned styrofoam at two McDonald's and is considering a citywide prohibition of styrofoam cups. (For how to organize boycotting and protest campaigns, see chapter 11, pp. 268-281.)

24. *Support recycling projects in your community.* If there isn't one, consider getting a group together. Talk to neighbors and at social gatherings. Speak up at PTA and town meetings. Write to your local newspaper explaining the advantages of recycling. Ask at your local food co-op. If you have a modem, put a notice on your computer bulletin board. If not, leave a note at your local supermarket. With the help of organizations like the Environmental Action Coalition, U.S. PIRG, Greenpeace, EDF, and others listed in "Resources," pp. 30-32, you can find out how to get a recycling center started in your area.

25. *Contact local officials*, your mayor or first selectperson, and your local sanitation department to voice support for far-reaching recycling and waste reduction programs to save landfill space and avoid the need for expensive and hazardous burn plants. If you can't get through by telephone, write letters or postcards, or send telegrams. Most local officials respond to hearing from their constituents; complain they don't hear enough. Ask them where they stand on recycling. Follow up to keep the issue alive. Thank them when they do take action of which you approve. (For more on how to take part in the local government process, see Chapter 11, pp. 264-269.)

26. *Contact state and federal officials.* Write to your state senator and assemblyperson, and to your national senators and congresspeople, to ask them what legislative action is being taken to encourage recycling. Enlist their support for ecologically sound recycling and waste reduction programs as mandated by the law.

27. *Share your recycling experience with others.* If you carry out half of the suggestions listed above, you will already be practicing Positive Ecology!

28. *You are invited to send me one recycling tip from your own experience*, c/o Harper & Row, 10 East 53rd Street, New York, N.Y. 10022.

RESOURCES

The following is provided to help you locate additional resources on the topics covered in this chapter.

1. U.S. Government

Among all the federal agencies the EPA has prime responsibility for protecting the environment. The agency consists of five main administrative divisions: Solid Waste; Pesticides and Toxic Substances; Water; Air and Radiation; and Research and Development (which includes Acid Rain and Global Warming). For convenience of reference we list the main EPA offices and telephone hotlines immediately following. There will, however, be additional EPA references provided in subsequent chapters. When contacting the EPA for information or assistance it is usually advisable to address your inquiries either to the *EPA Public Center* at (202) 382-2080 or to the public information offices in one of the ten *EPA Regional Offices* nearest to you.

(Note: Unless specifically given, the addresses of federal offices and subdepartments are the same as those for the main agency or department listed.)

Environmental Protection Agency

401 M Street SW, Washington, DC 20460; (202) 541-4040:
— Office of Drinking Water and Criteria and Standards
— Office of Emergency and Remedial Response
— Office of Public Awareness
— Office of Radiation Programs
— Office of Solid Waste
— Office of Toxic Substances
— Radon Action Programs
— Small Business Ombudsman's Program

EPA Hotlines and Special Telephone Numbers

— *Asbestos Hotline*, (800) 334-8571, ext. 6741.
— *Chemical Emergency Preparedness Hotline*, (800) 535-0202, in Washington, D.C., 479-2449.
— *The Emergency Planning and Community Right-to-Know Hotline*, (800)535-0202, in Washington, D.C., 479-2449.
— *Inspector General's Whistle Blower Hotline*, (800) 424-4000, in Washington, D.C., 382-4977. Receives reports of EPA-related waste, fraud, abuse, or mismanagement from the public and from EPA and other government employees.
— *National Pesticides Telecommunications Network*, (800) 858- PEST, in Texas, (806) 743-3091. Operates 24 hours a day, every day of the year. Provides information on pesticides to the general public, and the medical, veterinary, and professional communities.
— *National Response Center*, (800) 424-8802, in Washington, D.C., 426-2675. To report releases of oil and hazardous substances.
— *RCRA/Superfund Hotline*, (800) 424-9346, in Washington, D.C., 382-3000.
— *Safe Drinking Water Hotline*, (800) 426-4791, in Washington,D.C., 382-5533.
— *Small Business Hotline*, (800) 368-5888, in Washington, D.C., (703) 557-1938. Helps small businesses in complying with environmental laws and EPA regulations.
— *Solid Waste Hotline*, (800) 424-9346, in Washington, D.C., 382-3000.
— *Toxic Substances Control Act* (TSCA) Assistance Information Service, (202) 554-1404. Provides information under the TSCA program.

EPA Regional Offices
— *Region 1*: New England
JFK Federal Building, Boston, MA 02203; (617) 565-3715.
— *Region 2*: New York, New Jersey, Puerto Rico, Virgin Islands
26 Federal Plaza, New York, NY 10007; (212) 264-2525.
— *Region 3*: Delaware, Maryland, Pennsylvania, Virginia, West Virginia, District of Columbia
Curtis Building, 6th and Walnut, Philadelphia, PA 19106; (215) 597-9800.
— *Region 4*: Alabama, Florida, Georgia, Kentucky, Mississippi, North and South Carolina, Tennessee
345 Courtland Street NE, Atlanta, GA 30365; (404) 347-4727.
— *Region 5*: Illinois, Indiana, Michigan, Minnesota, Ohio, Wisconsin
230 S. Dearborn Street, Chicago, IL 60604; (312) 353-2000.
— *Region 6*: Arkansas, Louisiana, New Mexico, Oklahoma, Texas
Allied Bank Tower, 1445 Ross Avenue, Dallas, TX 75202; (214) 655-6444.
— *Region 7*: Iowa, Kansas, Missouri, Nebraska
726 Minnesota Avenue, Kansas City, KS, 66101; (913) 236-2800.
— *Region 8*: Colorado, Montana, North and South Dakota, Utah, Wyoming
1 Denver Place, 999 18th Street, Denver, CO 80202; (303) 293-1603.
— *Region 9*: Arizona, California, Guam, Hawaii, Nevada, American Samoa
215 Fremont Street, San Francisco, CA 94105; (415) 974-8071.
— *Region 10*: Idaho, Oregon, Washington, Alaska
1200 6th Avenue, Seattle, WA 98101; (206) 442-5810.

2. *States*

State Recycling Agency Hotlines

Alabama .... (800) 392-1924
California (L.A.) .... (800) RECYCAL
Colorado (except Denver) .... (800) 438-8800
Delaware .... (800) CASHCAN
Maryland .... (800) 345-BIRP
Minnesota .... (800) 592-9528
New Jersey .... (800) 492-4242
Ohio .... (800) 282-6040
Rhode Island .... (800) RICLEAN
Tennessee .... (800) 342-4038
Texas .... (800) CLEANTX
Virginia .... (800) KEEPITT
Washington .... (800) RECYCLE

You can get a complete listing of state recycling offices from the EPA Office of Solid Waste (see above) or in their booklet *Recycling Works!* (EPA/530-SW-89-014) which is available on request at (800) 424-9346 or, in Washington, D.C., 382-3000.
Note: you can also get statewide recycling help via the tollfree line of the Environmental Defense Fund at (800) CALLEDF.

3. *Organizations*

— *Center for the Biology of Natural Systems*, Queens College, Flushing, NY 11367; (718) 670-4180. Research studies on municipal solid waste disposal, renewable energy, and other environmental subjects.
— *Center for Plastics Recycling Research*, Busch Campus/Rutgers University, Piscataway, NJ 08855; (201) 932-2303.
— *Citizen's Clearinghouse for Hazardous Wastes*, P.O. Box 926, Arlington, VA 22216; (703) 276-7070. An important national grass-roots organization (for more details see chapter 2, "Resources," p. 56).
— *Coalition for Recyclable Waste*, P.O. Box 1091, Absecon, NJ 08201; (609) 641-2197. A citi-

zens' group that fought the plastic Coke can and other issues.

— *Environmental Action Coalition*, 625 Broadway, New York, NY 10012; (212) 677-1601. An independent group that works with the New York City Department of Sanitation to organize recycling of newspapers, glass, tin cans, and plastic containers.

— *Environmental Action Inc.*, 1346 Connecticut Avenue NW, Washington, DC 20036; (202) 833-1845. Education and lobbying on air quality, bottle-deposit legislation, nuclear energy, solid waste, toxic substances.

— *Environmental Defense Fund*, 257 Park Avenue South, New York, NY 10010; (212) 505-2100, recycling hotline (800) CALLEDF. A nonprofit membership organization that combines scientific research with legal action on a wide range of subjects including recycling, radon, toxic waste, and global warming. Through its environmental information exchange EDF helps state-level groups find technical, scientific, and legal information. Publishes the bimonthly *EDF Letter* and numerous excellent reports.

— *Environmental Research Foundation*, P.O. Box 3541, Princeton, NJ 08543; (609) 683-0707. Provides assistance to grass-roots environmental groups in fighting landfills and incinerators. Publishes the excellent weekly bulletin, *Rachel's Hazardous Waste News*, giving news and resources on toxins.

— *INFORM*, 381 Park Avenue South, New York, NY 10016; (212) 689-4040. Research on garbage, toxic waste, water pollution, and other environmental topics. Publisher of *Garbage Burning*, 1986.

— *Institute for Local Self-Reliance*, 2425 18th Street NW, Washington, DC 20009; (202) 232-4108. Provides community consultations for solid waste management and economic development.

— *National Association of Diaper Services*, 2017 Walnut Street, Philadelphia, PA 19103; (215) 569-3650. Will help locate local cloth diaper services.

— *National Coalition Against Mass Burn Incineration*, 1329-A Hopkins, Berkeley, CA 94702. Publishes *Network Against Incineration* newsletter focusing on efforts to stop siting and construction of solid-waste burn facilities.

— *Natural Resources Defense Council*, 40 West 20th Street, New York, NY 10011; (212) 727-2700. A national organization dedicated to protecting the natural and human environment. It combines research, education, advocacy, and litigation on toxic substances, air and water pollution, nuclear safety, and other subjects. Publishes a bimonthly newsletter and the outstanding quarterly *Amicus Journal*.

— *New York Public Interest Research Group* (NYPIRG), 9 Murray Street, New York, NY 10007; (212) 349-6460. A grass-roots environmental action organization involved in many aspects of solid-waste management. Published *The Burning Question*, 1986 and other important materials. (Note: There are PIRGs in 21 states. Check in your local telephone directory.)

— *U.S. Public Research Interest Group*, 215 Pennsylvania Avenue SE, Washington, DC 20003; (202) 546-9707. The parent organization of the 21 PIRGs.

— *Work on Waste* (WOW-USA), 82 Judson Street, Canton, NY 13617; (315) 379-9200. Founded by Dr. Paul Connett, a research and educational group focusing on resource management programs for municipal solid waste and promoting reuse, recycling, composting, and waste reduction. Publishes the weekly newsletter *Waste Not* for rational resource management.

4. Recycling Industry Associations

— *Aluminum Recycling Association*, 900 17th Street NW, Washington, DC 20006; (202) 785-5100.

— *American Iron and Steel Institute*, 1000 16th Street NW, Washington, DC 20006; (202) 452-7100.

— *Automotive Dismantlers and Recyclers Association*, 1133 15th Street NW, Washington, DC 20005; (202) 293-2372.

— *Institute of Scrap Recycling Industries*, 1647 K Street NW, Washington, DC 20006; (202) 466-4050.

— *National Recycling Coalition*, 45 Rockefeller Plaza, Room 2350, New York, NY 10111; (212) 765-1800. A coalition of recycling industries and groups.

— *National Solid Waste Management Association*, 1730 Rhode Island Avenue NW, Washington, DC 20036; (202) 659-4613.

— *Society of the Plastics Industry*, 335 Lexington Avenue, New York, NY 10017; (212) 503-0600; 1275 K Street NW, Washington, DC 20005.

— *World Association for Solid Waste*, 130 Freight Street, Waterbury, CT 06702; (203) 755-2283.

5. Further Reading
Books and Articles

— *Aluminum Recycling Case Book*. Washington, D.C.: Aluminum Association, 1985.

— *The Art of Composting*, Portland, Ore.: Metro Service District, undated; can be ordered from Earth Care Paper, P.O. Box 3335, Madison, WI 53704.

— *The Burning Question: Garbage Incineration Versus Total Recycling in New York City*. New York: NYPIRG, 1986.

— *Case Studies of California Curbside Recycling Programs*, Sacramento: California Waste Management Board, 1982.

— *The Characterization of Municipal Solid Wastes in the United States, 1960-2000*, Washington, D.C.: U.S. Environmental Protection Agency, 1986.

— *Coming Full Circle*. New York: Environmental Defense Fund, 1988.

— "The Cost of Burning Garbage," David Morris, *Alternative Sources of Energy*, April 1986.

— *Developing Markets for Recycled Materials* (working paper), New York: Environmental Defense Fund, 1988.

— *An Environmental Review of Incineration Technologies*, Neil N. Seldman. Washington, D.C.: Institute for Local Self-Reliance, 1986.

— *Garbage Burning: Lessons from Europe*, Allen Hershkowitz. New York: INFORM, 1986.

— *Garbage — Practices, Problems, and Remedies*, Joanna D. Underwood, Allen Hershkowitz, and Maarten de Kadt. New York: INFORM, 1988.

— "How States Implement Recycling Programs," Dawn Schauer, *BioCycle*, March 1986.

— *Here Today Here Tomorrow*, Trenton, N.J.: New Jersey Department of Environmental Protection, 1989. A well-designed teachers guide on solid-waste management for grades 4 through 8, but valid at all levels.

— *How to Start a Recycling Center*, Sacramento: California Waste Management Board, undated.

— *An Intensive Trash Separation and Recycling System for the Town of East Hampton, NY*, Barry Commoner et al. New York: Center for the Biology of Natural Systems, 1986.

— *Materials Recycling: The Virtue of Necessity*, William U. Chandler. Washington, D.C.: Worldwatch Institute Paper 56, 1983.

— *Mining Urban Wastes: The Potential for Recycling*, Cynthia Pollock, Washington, D.C.: Worldwatch Institute Paper 76, 1987.

— *Oregon's Pioneering Recycling Act* (mimeograph), Portland, Ore.: Oregon State Department of Environmental Quality, 1986.

— *Recycling Plan of Action*, Newark, N.J.: Office of Recycling, 1985.

— *Recycling Works!: State and Local Solutions to Solid Waste Management Problems*, Washington, D.C.: EPA Office of Solid Waste, 1989.

— *Solid Waste Action Project Guidebook*, Lois Gibbs and Will Collette, Arlington, Va.: Citizen's Clearinghouse for Hazardous Waste, 1987.

— *Rush To Burn: Solving America's Garbage Crisis?* Newsday, Washington, D.C.: Island Press, 1989.

— *The Solid Waste Handbook: A Practical Guide*, New York: John Wiley, 1986.

— *To Burn or Not to Burn: The Economic Advantages of Recycling Over Garbage Incineration for New York City*, New York: EDF, 1985.

— *Waste – Choices for Communities*, Washington, D.C.: CONCERN Inc., 1988.

— *Waste Management: As If the Future Mattered*, Dr. Paul Connett. Lecture given at St. Lawrence University, May 1988, issued as a videotape under the same title, Video-Active Productions, Canton, NY, 1989.

— *Waste Minimization – Environmental Quality with Economic Benefits*, Washington, D.C.: EPA, Office of Solid Waste and Emergency Response, 1987.

Periodicals

— *BioCycle: Journal of Waste Recycling*, JG Press, 18 South Seventh Street, Emmaus, PA 18049. Treats all aspects of recycling, waste reduction, and composting; 10 issues a year.

— *Compost Patch*, 306 Coleridge Avenue, Altoona, PA 16602. A newsletter devoted to promoting ideas to encourage positive social change.

— *Garbage*, P.O. Box 56520, Boulder,CO 80321. A bimonthly magazine designed for homeowners.

— *Materials Recovery Report*, 1089 Curtis Street, Albany, CA, 94706. A monthly newsletter on recycling with some attention to landfilling and incineration.

— *Resource Recovery Report*, 5313 18th Street NW, Washington DC 20015.

— *Solid Waste Report, Business Publishers Inc.*, 951 Pershing Drive, Silver Spring, MD 20912-4464. A biweekly newsletter covering all aspects of solid waste management.

— *Waste Age* (monthly) and *Waste Alternatives* (quarterly), National Solid Waste Management Association, 1730 New Hampshire Avenue NW, Washington, DC 20036. Industry-oriented publications covering all aspects of solid waste management.

ENDNOTES

1. Philip Shabecoff, "EPA Sets Strategy to End 'Staggering' Garbage Crisis," *New York Times*, September 23, 1988.

2. Information from *The Solid Waste Dilemma – An Agenda for Action*, Final Report of the Municipal Solid Waste Task Force, Office of Solid Waste (Washington D.C.: U.S. EPA, February 1989).

3. Barbara Hogan, "All Baled Up and No Place to Go," *Conservationist*, vol.42, January-February 1988.

4. "Ship Dumps Philadelphia Ash, but Where?," *New York Times*, November 10, 1988; "After 2 Years, Ship Dumps Toxic Ash," *New York Times*, November 28, 1988.

5. Letter from Environmental Defense Fund, *New York Times*, December 9, 1988.

6. The capital costs of an incinerator in Detroit, as reported in the *Detroit Times*, April 27, 1986, were $460 million. If the municipal bonds are repaid over a 20-year period, the lifetime costs (excluding major repair) will exceed $1 billion. Cited in Dr. Paul Connett, "Waste Management: As If the Future Mattered," a 48-page booklet published by Work on Waste, Canton, NY, 1988 (referred to henceforth as Connett), p.9.

7. Dr. Barry Commoner, Testimony before Hazardous Waste and Toxic Substances Subcommittee, Committee on Environment and Public Works, U.S. Senate, August 6, 1987.

8. Connett, p. 10.

9. Ibid.

10. Ibid, p. 12.

11. *Morning Union*, Springfield, Mass., November 21, 1986, cited in Connett, p. 13.

12. Dioxin refers to a set of 75 closely related chemicals, one of which, 2,3,7,8-TCDD — notorious for contaminating Times Beach, Mo. – is the most potent synthetic carcinogen ever found. Recent tests show low levels of TCDD in such widely-used products as paper plates, paper towels, office bond paper, and coffee filters. *EDF Letter*, vol. 14, no. 5 [December 1988].

13. Cynthia Pollock,"Realizing Recycling's Potential," chapter 6 of *State of the World*, 1987 (Washington, D.C.: Worldwatch Institute, 1988), pp. 107-108.

14. Commoner, Testimony, August 6, 1987.

15. Quoted in Carolyn Mann, "Garbage In, Garbage Out," *Sierra*, September/October, 1987.

16. *Waste Not* (monthly newsletter of Work on Waste) quoted in *Hudson Valley Green Times*, Holidays 1988.

17. Connett, p. 24.

18. *Coming Full Circle* is the title of a comprehensive book on recycling published by Environmental Defense Fund (New York: 1988).

19. Data are from EPA and Dr. Paul Connett, *Waste Management: As if the Future Mattered*, videotape, Canton, N.Y.: Video-Active Productions, 1989.

20. Cynthia Pollock, "Mining Urban Wastes" (Washington, DC: Worldwatch Paper 76, 1987), p. 23.

21. *Coming Full Circle*, p.10.

22. Connett, p. 25.

23. Quoted in Connett, p. 29.

24. *Recycling Works!*, EPA/530-SW-89-014, (Washington, D.C.: EPA Office of Solid Waste, 1989), pp. 44-46. For further information on the Wellesley program contact Maurice "Pat" Berdan, director, Wellesley Department of Public Works, 455 Worcester Street, Wellesley, MA 02181; (617) 235-7600.

25. For more details contact the repair shop operator, Jay Eaton, 1122 Romence Road, Portage, MI 49002; (616) 323-2550.

26. Connett, p. 31. For information on Urban Ore, contact Dan Knapp, 1089 Curtis Street, Albany, CA 94706; (415) 526-7080.

27. Based on information from *Coming Full Circle*, pp. 65-66.

28. Lorie Parker, *Oregon's Pioneering Recycling Act*, Portland, Ore.: Department of Environmental Quality, 1986.

29. Commoner et al, *Intensive Recycling: Preliminary Results from East Hampton and Buffalo*, New York: CBNS, 1988, p. 9.

30. *Coming Full Circle*, p. 14.

31. National Solid Waste Association quoted in *New York Times*, October 23, 1988.

32. Pollock, "Realizing Recycling's Potential," p. 114.

33. *New York Times*, November 24, 1988.

34. Myra Klockenbrink, "Plastics Industry, Under Pressure, Begins to Invest in Recycling," *New York Times*, August 30, 1988; Michael deCourcy Hinds, "In Sorting Trash, Householders Get Little Help From Industry," *New York Times*, July 29, 1989.

35. William Reilly, EPA administrator, *Wall Street Journal*, April 26, 1989; see also Kathryn J. O'Hara et al., "A Citizen's Guide to Plastics in the Ocean," Washington, D.C.: Center for Environmental Education, 1988, pp. 5-12.

36. John Holusha, "McDonald's Plastic Recycling Plan," *New York Times*, October 27, 1989.

37. *BioCycle*, September 1988, pp. 34-39.

38. Personal communication from A. E. Redpath, president, Ecoplastics Ltd., Willowdale, Ontario, Canada.

39. News release, *Nature's Way*, September 1989.

40. John Holusha, "Doubts Are Voiced on 'Degradable' Plastic Waste," *New York Times*, October 25, 1989.

41. Much of the information in this section is based on chapter 7 of *Coming Full Circle*, pp. 89-123.

42. "Plastic Recycling Gains Steam," *Wall Street Journal*, January 12, 1989.

43. Klockenbrink, "Plastics Industry," *New York Times*, August 30, 1988.

44. Bill Richards and Amal Kumar Naj, "Du Pont and Waste Management Plan to Build Largest U.S. Recycling Plant," *Wall Street Journal*, April 26, 1989.

45. *EDF Letter*, vol. 19, no. 4, September 1988.

46. *BioCycle*, October 1987 and July 1988. Both issues are devoted to composting.

47. *BioCycle*, July 1988, pp. 34-42.

48. David J. Hurd, "Apartment House Recycling," mimeograph, *New York: Environmental Action Coalition*, September 1988, pp.1-4.

49. Dr. Jan Beyea, "Paper vs. Plastics," *Audubon Activist*, March/April, 1989 p. 5.

50. For further instructions consult Sydney Eddison, "A Recycler's Guide to Seed Growing," *New York Times*, December 11, 1988.

2
BAD CHEMISTRY

Defusing the Toxic Time Bomb

> *"It is ironic to think that man might determine his future by something so seemingly trivial as the choice of an insect spray."*
> – Rachel Carson

In the United States there are some 75,000 chemicals in everyday use, many of which endanger the lives of millions of people who live near where they are produced, handled, transported, or dumped. Contained in pesticides, herbicides, food additives, drinking water, building materials, household goods, and many other carriers, toxic chemicals threaten every woman, man, child, and animal. We are literally poisoning ourselves to death.

The dimensions of controlling toxics are so vast that even the Environmental Protection Agency finds them "almost impossible to comprehend." A ticking time bomb primed to go off is how the agency described the toxic waste problem in 1980. The surgeon general declared it an environmental emergency. Some action has been taken since then and there is certainly more governmental and public awareness, but the EPA crash program initiated at that time (Superfund) has failed to clean up the toxic chemical mess and the danger continues to rise.

Preventing toxics from ever reaching the environment may be an easier task than disposing of them once they have gotten there. Today, more than ten years after Love Canal was declared a Federal Disaster Area, toxic waste is still a problem that can't be buried.

15,000 Superdomes

700,000 tons of toxic waste are produced in the U.S. every day. That's 250 million tons a year – enough to fill the New Orleans Superdome 15,000 times.[1] To this add 12 million tons of pesticides sprayed annually on food crops, forests, lakes, parks, lawns, playing fields, and playgrounds, as well as untold amounts of

Dangerous at 200 Feet[2]

Widely used chemicals that are very toxic in small quantities to a person 200 feet from a leak in "worst case" weather conditions.

Chemical and uses	Amount dangerous	U.S. annual production in pounds
Benzyl chloride Drugs, dyes, perfumes	1.4 pounds	160 million
Chlorine Bleach, water purifier	2.5 pounds	30 billion
Demeton Insecticide	13 ounces	Not available
Hydrogen cyanide Electroplating, photo processing	1.5 pounds	1.3 billion
Formaldehyde Insulation, fertilizers, dyes, preservatives, resin	3.5 pounds	9 million
Lead, tetraethyl Gasoline additives	1.5 pounds	510 million
Methyl isocyanate Pesticide	1.3 pounds	12 million
Phosgene Dyes, pesticides	6.5 ounces	2 billion
Sulfuric acid Batteries, dyes, glues, metals, explosives	2.5 pounds	110 billion

chemicals contained in the products we use at home and work, from shampoo to shelf paper.

Knowledge of the harmful effects of chemicals has lagged far behind their introduction into the marketplace. For example, there is no information on toxicity for 80 percent of the more than 48,500 chemicals listed by the EPA; less than a fifth have been tested for acute effects and less than a tenth for longer-term (e.g. cancer-causing or genetic) impact.[3]

Only in December 1985 did the federal government release detailed information on 403 chemicals they termed "highly toxic" with an explanation of how dangerous they could be, especially in the event of an accident.

Many of the 403 were at least as dangerous as methyl isocyanate, the substance that leaked in the Bhopal, India, disaster in 1984, killing more than 2,000 people and injuring 200,000 others. The chemicals posing severe health problems in amounts less than five pounds include widely produced

> *"The chemical industry is way, way behind."*
> Risk Expert Alvin M. Weinberg[4]

sulfuric acid, chlorine, and formaldehyde, as well as less familiar but highly toxic phosgene, a dye and pesticide component used as a poison gas weapon in World War I, and carbon disulfide, a solvent so flammable that "vapors may be ignited by contact with an ordinary light bulb."[5]

Chemical Accidents

"This country has been very lucky it has not had a major chemical accident killing a lot of people. There have been many warnings. Those who try to minimize the hazards are totally wrong. And if there aren't many changes in the next couple of years, there probably will be a major accident here." Such was the assessment by Roger J. Batstone, a chemical engineer and hazardous chemicals consultant for the U.K. government and the World Bank, in a major *New York Times* report on chemical accidents, one year after Bhopal and three months after a similar leak at another Union Carbide plant (in Institute, W. Va) had injured 135 people.[6]

Between 1980 and 1985 in the United States there were an estimated 20,000 toxic-chemical accidents, killing perhaps 400 people and injuring 4,500.[7] Nearly three-quarters of these took place during production or storage of chemicals, the rest during transportation. Causes of the accidents included storage-tank failures, valve problems, overpressurized tanks, broken gauges left unrepaired, and other human errors. They included a pesticide leak injuring 161 people in New Jersey, a nitric acid explosion killing 3 and injuring 61 in Mississippi, a solvent leak injuring 40 in New York City, and a chlorine cloud from a plant in Niagara Falls, N.Y., which came down on a high school football game causing 76 injuries and one death. Ammonia, which is widely used for cooling, killed 4 people in San Antonio, Texas, and injured more than 270 people in bakeries, ice-cream factories, and other enterprises nationwide.

Preventive Measures

Efforts to reduce the likelihood of a major accident or indeed to monitor safety at chemical plants are hampered by the sheer size of the industry: 12,000 chemical manufacturing plants; 400,000 major chemical storage facilities; and several million users or storers of potentially dangerous amounts of toxic chemicals, including dry cleaners, hospitals, food warehouses, paint dealers, and other small

Case History: "Just Don't Touch the Food..."*

JACKSONVILLE, ARK. - It is a quiet Sunday afternoon in this city of 30,000 residents 12 miles northeast of Little Rock. Patty Frase turns her station wagon off the freeway and onto Route 67 leading into town, then says, "Just don't touch the food, drink the water, or even wash your hands in Jacksonville."

Some local citizens don't call their hometown Jacksonville. They refer to it as "Dioxinville." And with good reason: in its heart the Vertac chemical plant that the Environmental Protection Agency (EPA) called "one of the most serious uncontrolled hazardous waste sites in the U.S." is now abandoned and secluded behind locked iron gates. Inside the plant, some 30,000 barrels of poison, including many containing dioxin-laden waste from cancer causing herbicides, await disposal. Many continue to leak into the ground water.

The city sewer system, a creek adjacent to the plant, the flood plain, parts of the nearby Little Rock Air Force Base, and two city dumpsites have already been severely contaminated. TCDD dioxin, the deadliest manmade chemical known, has been detected here at the highest levels ever found in U.S. soil. Many residents who live near the chemical plant or the dumpsites suffer severe health problems.

"Everyone Here Is Dying of Cancer"

"In 1974 my father had just retired from the military at 51 and was in good shape," Frase says, "then he woke up one morning, went into a coma and was dead by noon. There was a major fire at the Vertac plant right before this. It destroyed everything around the area. All the oaks and hardwood practically disintegrated overnight. There were dead dogs, dead squirrels. All the fish died in the discharge area into Rocky Branch Creek. For years we'd lived a few blocks away and I have no doubt my father died of chemical poisoning. My mother started checking around and said, 'Everyone here is dying of cancer.' Right after that she went into the hospital with liver cancer. She had just turned 50, and nobody had ever had cancer on either side of my family. The day before she died she told me, 'Go get 'em, Patty, and watch out for your health.'" So she did. Despite her own mounting health problems, Frase organized the Arkansas Chemical Clean-Up Alliance and eventually was named to the Governor's Task Force on Hazardous Waste. Moving with her husband 30 miles on the other side of Little Rock, she had six miscarriages before conceiving a daughter who is deaf in one ear from peripheral nerve damage, and suffers periodic bouts of severe chloracne (skin lesions resulting from contact with dioxin) as well as a hormonal imbalance that finds her gaining and then losing large amounts of weight, was one of 65 Jacksonville residents who settled out of court with Vertac in a personal injury and wrongful death class-action lawsuit the day before Vertac shut down its operations.

A survey taken in 1985 by the *Arkansas Democrat* of children living near the dumpsites found 10 of 18 with serious health problems, including some

---

* This case history is based with permission on "Dioxinville," a three-part series by Dick Russell which appeared in *In These Times*, March 9, 16, and 23, 1988.

with fluid on the brain and seizures, an infant with a hole between the chambers of the heart, and a baby born with part of her brain outside her skull. Some of Jacksonville's children never survived at all. "This is one of the most serious public health disasters in the United States," says Adrienne Anderson, western director of the National Toxics Campaign. "The number of mysterious SIDSs [Sudden Infant Death Syndromes] is horrifying."

Today a chemical odor lingers in the air for blocks around the Vertac site. Despite public complaints going back to the 1950s, it was only in 1987 that EPA sent in a team of workers to begin the cleanup. They found more than 100,000 cubic yards of contaminated material, enough to cover 20 football fields 3 feet deep, including "Vertac mountain," where 20,000 cubic yards of dioxin-contaminated sludge had been piled 20 feet high. In 1988 EPA added the two city dumpsites to the Superfund cleanup list.

Passing the Buck, Burning the Evidence

In January 1987 Vertac had declared itself unable to fulfill its financial responsibilities for maintaining the corroding waste drums and left Arkansas, transferring its assets to a new Tennessee-based corporation. In federal court, the EPA, the Department of Justice, and the state of Arkansas are now attempting to force Vertac to follow through on its cleanup obligations. The EPA and the state don't want to get saddled with a cleanup tab that the agency has estimated could reach nearly $400 million. They propose having the hazardous wastes incinerated on-site by a private company with a dubious reputation, overturning a Jacksonville City Council ordinance and a people's referendum against incineration.

The townspeople, along with many experts, are concerned that the relatively untested incineration process will send more dioxin into the environment, even as it destroys most of the wastes. Yet the EPA and the state are ignoring alternate solutions, adamant that incineration is the only answer.[8]

In July 1989, the state signed a $10.7 million contract with a Louisiana company, MRK Incineration, to commence the burning of about 30,000 barrels of hazardous waste – including Agent Orange – in the near future. But MRK's chief executive officer, Chip Efferson, admits that this will be the first time for his company to incinerate hazardous wastes. An inexperienced firm handling such lethal materials is expected to lead to widespread citizen protests.

Meanwhile, both Jacksonville and national environmental groups are up in arms over the EPA's decision to award some $150,000 in Technical Assistance Grants to an industry-backed local coalition. Under the federal Superfund Law, such grants are supposed to go to legitimate citizen groups to enable them to monitor clean-up efforts with their own experts. But the Jacksonville People with Pride Organization, established in 1986 to downplay the rising tide of indignation about the city's pollution problems, was heavily funded by Hercules, Inc., which manufactured dioxin-containing Agent Orange at the Jacksonville chemical site during the Vietnam era. The latest uproar from Jacksonville has prompted EPA headquarters to cancel the award, but Greenpeace and other groups are demanding a Congressional investigation into the EPA Region 6 office's motives in granting the allotment in the first place. ▶

The conclusion of Dick Russell's investigation into the dioxin contamination of Jacksonville reveals "a situation more dire than Love Canal," in which a tangled web of government bureaucracy, legal delays, and multinational corporate maneuvering poses troubling questions that go far beyond Arkansas.

businesses, many of which are in densely populated regions. A study by the Congressional Research Service found more than 6,300 chemical and allied manufacturing plants in the 25 largest metropolitan areas of the country in which 75 percent of Americans live. 800 of these plants are located in northern New Jersey.[9]

According to Lee M. Thomas, EPA administrator in the Reagan administration, the key to success lies in "far greater awareness on the part of plant management about process-system safety."[10] He was in agreement with other experts interviewed in the *New York Times* series that risks of accidents could be reduced if companies were more willing to tell the public what hazards their plants present, rather than claiming that every substance they make is a trade secret; chemical plants and the communities around them should be better equipped to cope with toxic accidents and chemical

> *"The question now is whether America's manufacturers will . . . reduce their toxic emissions voluntarily – or wait for their workers, their communities, or their government to prod them into action."*

emergencies; safety precautions should not depend on considerations of financial profitability; and better preparedness would result from the wider use of computerized training simulators, common among airlines and other industries.

Although the chemical industry says the chance of a major accident is very small, few companies do detailed risk assessments that would determine which procedures are most likely to fail. Ultimately, prevention of accidents depends on how well a plant is managed and how it responds to the Emergency Planning and Community Right-to-Know Act of 1986 and other federal toxic-chemicals cleanup regulations (for more on this legislation see chapter 10, p. 236).

Coming Clean

Two companies that have responded constructively to new federal and state reporting requirements on toxic chemical emissions are Monsanto, the multinational giant, and Yale Materials Handling Corporation, a small manufacturer of forklifts in Flemington, N.J.

After Monsanto had taken inventory as required by the new regulations, it found that in 1987 its 35 plants across the country released a total of more than 374 million pounds of toxic substances into the environment. More than 20 million pounds were emitted into the air of the communities surrounding Monsanto's facilities, with the remainder going into streams, rivers, underground injection wells, landfills, and waste-treatment plants. Many of the chemicals were linked to cancer, neurological and reproductive disorders, and other chronic health problems.

"When Montsanto's data on the release of chemicals were collected in one place for the first time, company executives, especially those not directly involved in manufacturing or regulatory compliance, said they were taken aback by the amount of toxic substances they were discharging into the environment," reported Charles L. Elkins, director of the EPA's Office of Toxic Substances, in an article specially prepared for the *New York Times*.[11]

In the summer of 1988 Monsanto's chairman, Richard J. Mahoney, pledged the company to a 90-percent reduction in air emissions of hazardous chemicals worldwide by the end of 1992. "For a number of years, we have had a campaign to reduce plant releases," said Mahoney. "Good progress has been made, but it is clear that the process should be accelerated – and we intend to do so." [12]

The experience of Yale Materials was similar to Montsanto's but on a smaller scale. At Yale's plant in Lenoir, N.C., their senior engineer, Garland Ross, found that they were routinely emitting 2,000 pounds a year of the volatile toxic chemical 1,1,1-trichloroethane, a solvent used in large quantities to clean and degrease metal cylinders. Yale had been looking for a workable substitute for this chemical and in early 1988 they began using a safer, water-based rinse for cleaning and degreasing. The switch cut Yale's plant-cylinder-cleaning costs by almost half, while eliminating the growing cost of hazardous-waste disposal.

According to the EPA, Monsanto and Yale are among many companies that are only now discovering the extent to which they are discharging potentially harmful substances – not just as a result of plant accidents, but also during routine daily operations. As this information is gathered and reported to the EPA, to the states, and to the public, pressure will mount on manufacturing facilities to lower their toxic emissions, Elkins said, adding that "in many cases, companies will find that doing so is good business as well as good community relations. The savings from controlling waste and improving process efficiencies often outweigh the costs."

Guidance on process changes, recycling or reuse of toxic wastes, better containment of volatile chemicals and chemical dust, and many other techniques for controlling toxic chemicals at the source is now available from the EPA's nationwide clearinghouse. "The question now," said Elkins, "is whether America's manufacturers will seize the initiative to reduce their toxic emissions voluntarily – or wait for their workers, their communities, or their government to prod them into action. Here's hoping many other companies follow the good example set by Monsanto and Yale." [13]

Toxic-Waste Disposal

The main disposal methods are as follows:

● *Dumping in pits, ponds, and lagoons* is all too common. It is the cheapest of all disposal methods and the least regulated. Because many such sites are illegal, it is hard to tell how many there are and what they contain. Virtually everyone agrees that they represent the worst possible way to deal with the problem.

● *"Secure" landfills* are similar to older, unregulated landfills, but are fitted with liners, first of clay, then of plastic; these landfills present the same problems of limited available space and potential leaching of toxic substances into ground and water. In practice, all liners leak to some extent. Ideally, they have underground drainage to collect leachate for pretreatment or discharge to the sewer.

● *Aboveground storage* involves containing liquid or solid waste in tanks or sheds. They require continuous surveillance and present the danger of fire or explosion.

● *Incineration* is the process in which combustion is used to destroy toxic materials. In addition to producing carbon, oxygen, and water, incineration produces air pollution and residual ash containing dioxin and other toxic substances.

- *Underground injection* sinks the waste into deep wells located below drinking water sources. Defended by some industries as safe, injection is opposed by many environmental groups and public health experts concerned over the growing need to dig deeper for our drinking water supplies and the impact of earthquakes on the course of underground rivers and streams.
- *Fixation* involves treating liquid waste, sludge, or contaminated soil with chemicals which bind them up into a solid material *(solidification)* or coat the waste with an impermeable substance *(encapsulation)*. The agents used in this process include fly ash and kiln dust (which may contain heavy metals) or lime (which may contain radioactive contaminants).
- *Neutralization* – treating toxic substances with chemicals or microorganisms to render them harmless – has yet to be demonstrated as effective or safe over long periods of time.

Health Effects of Toxic Chemicals

Much of what we know about the toxic effects of exposure to hazardous chemicals has come from accidents and industrial exposures. Symptoms experienced by the public at large, however, are usually more subtle and less easy to recognize.

While an industrial worker may face the rupture of a sulfur-dioxide cylinder, which causes fatal swelling of tissues in the upper respiratory tract – nose, throat, windpipe, and bronchial tubes – low levels of SO_2 in the outdoor air may affect the general population almost imperceptibly. Only severe episodes of poor air quality result in respiratory distress among asthmatics and other susceptible individuals. Over the long term, however, there may be a larger, unidentified part of the population whose health is in some way compromised by this and other environmental insults.

With this in mind, it is useful to have a general overview of the different kinds of chemicals associated with pollution, and realize the difference between acute (immediate) and chronic (delayed, long-term) effects, which are a function of the amount (dose) received and the duration of exposure.

Let's start with the headlines. Many times, reported incidents of contaminated drinking water are based on the discovery of parts-per-billion (ppb) or parts-per-million (ppm) of *chlorinated solvents* in ground water. Trichloroethylene, chloroform, vinyl chloride, carbon tetrachloride, chlorobenzene, and methylene chloride are among the chemicals commonly named in toxic leaks and accidents. The *chlor* or *chloro* in the name indicates the presence of chlorine. These are non-flammable liquids used for degreasing, cleaning, and other purposes. Furniture strippers, for example, typically contain chlorinated solvents "to be used in well-ventilated areas" – check your cabinets!

The two most common industrial (or household) effects of chlorinated solvents are depression of the central nervous system and irritation of tissue. The greater the extent of chlorination, generally, the greater the anesthetic effect. Carbon tetrachloride (with 4 chlorines per molecule) is a more potent anesthetic than chloroform (with 3), which is more potent than methylene chloride (with 2).

All chlorinated solvents are irritants because they are defatting agents – capable of stripping the naturally protective oils from the skin, lung tissue, or eyes, and damaging human cells.

However, the public concern over chlorinated solvents in drinking water is related to chronic effects on the liver, kidneys, and heart. Also, except for chlorobenzene, all of the chemicals named above are suspected of causing cancer. So, the EPA has set limits, generally around the 5 ppb level (2 ppb for vinyl chloride) for these substances in drinking water.

Metals are another broad class of chemicals. They differ widely in toxic effects and activity. Many metals which are nutritionally essential elements in trace quantities – like copper, iron, and chromium – are toxic in larger doses.

Generally, metals exert "systemic" effects – they are distributed via the bloodstream to the body's systems and organs such as the nervous, gastrointestinal, and respiratory systems, or the kidneys and liver. There they may bind to enzymes to inhibit their action, or they may attach to cell constituents and alter cell function, substitute for essential metals, or cause essential metal imbalance.

Exposure to *lead* is of great concern because of its devastating effects, including learning disabilities in children who, in their own homes, find and eat leaded paint chips or drink water containing lead from solder or pipes in the water supply system. Any additional exposure in the air or from lead-contaminated soil can put children (and other people) over the edge in terms of risk.

> *"Exposure to lead is of great concern because of its devastating effects, including learning disabilities in children. . ."*

Polychlorinated biphenyls (PCBs) are also found as contaminants in soil, where there may have been spills from electrical transformers, for example. Generally, PCBs are not highly volatile, and so exposure may come directly from soil contact, hand-to-mouth transfer, or food. PCBs are extremely persistent and have been identified in almost every person tested for them. One-third of the U.S. population is estimated to have PCB levels of 1 ppm or more in fatty tissue, including the liver, kidneys, brain, and blood plasma.

PCBs induce liver enzymes. Some evidence indicates that they may cause cancer and that they may be associated with hypertension and heart disease. The well-documented "Yusho" incident in Japan, in which fish was accidently contaminated with oil containing PCBs during processing, resulted in stomach and liver cancer, elevated estrogen and progesterone levels in women, skin pigmentation, diarrhea, nausea, and vomiting. One theory holds that trace impurities of dioxin and polychlorinated dibenzofurans, not PCBs, were responsible. The jury is still out on what may be the subtle effect of PCBs and other similar substances.

The Creation of Superfund

In response to public outrage, the United States Congress in 1980 created Superfund, a $1.6 billion, five-year crash program run by the EPA and intended to clean up thousands of leaking dumps such as Love Canal that contaminated underground water supplies and seriously threatened public health. The program was funded with taxes on crude oil and on 42 different commercial chemicals. State governments paid 10 percent of the cost of work at privately owned toxic-waste sites and 50 percent of the cost at those that were publicly owned.

In the early years the Superfund program achieved very little. As more and more communities discovered they were living near dumps contaminated with dioxin, vinyl chloride, PCBs, lead, mercury, arsenic, and other deadly poisons, it became clear that the hazardous waste problem was larger and more complex than originally thought.[14]

In late 1986, under mounting public pressure, Congress renewed the program under the Superfund Amendments and Reauthorization Act (SARA). Providing funding of $8.5 billion from 1986 to 1991 – more than five times the original budget – SARA stiffened EPA's enforcement powers and increased criminal penalties for failure to report releases of hazardous waste. It was, EPA said, "certain to strengthen Superfund in the years ahead." [15]

The EPA Record

In Superfund's first six years EPA investigated some 6,500 of 25,000 potentially dangerous toxic-waste sites nationwide, placing 952 of them on a National Priorities List (NPL) – sites that present the most serious threats to health and environment and are targeted for long-term remedial action under the Superfund program. Aside from evaluating the problem, EPA did little else.

In September 1988 the agency presented the "Superfund Scorecard" in which 26,959 sites were considered potentially hazardous. Of these, only 9,107 had been actually inspected, and 1,175 were on the NPL and were thus eligible for Superfund monies. Remedial Designs were in progress at 103 sites and Remedial Actions at another 124. The number of cleanups claimed by the EPA was 43, not even 1 percent of the potentially hazardous sites and only 5 percent of the Priority sites.[16] In September 1989 the Rand Corporation, a prestigious California nonprofit research organization, reported that only 34 of the 1,175 worst toxic waste dumps in the U.S. were cleaned up in the first eight years of the Superfund program and that polluters paid less than a tenth of the cost.[17]

In its own defense the EPA highlighted:
- completion of a five-year, $14 million study of the Love Canal area that would "lead to habitability decisions and land-use recommendations" by New York State;[18]
- a plan for the Lipari site in Pitman, N.J., first (i.e., worst) on the NPL, committing $21 million for cleaning up the chemically contaminated Lake Alcyon;
- a $5.3 million settlement for the Stringfellow acid pits in Glen Avon, Calif., no. 32 on the NPL, in which the 183 defendants agreed to the remedies, including a ground-water pump system, and site and surface water diversion channels;
- signing a consent decree involving 200 responsible parties and an estimated $20 million remedy of the Conservation Chemical Company NPL site in Kansas City, Mo.;
- agreement by over 200 firms to reimburse the EPA nearly $5 million for cleaning up the Kin-Buc landfill Superfund site in Edison, N.J.;
- an agreement by the EPA and the Department of Justice made with Goodyear Tire and Rubber Company for remedial action at the Phoenix Goodyear-Litchfield Airport Superfund site; and
- Department of Justice suits on behalf of the EPA to recover more than $4 million already incurred in cleaning up the Harvey and Knous Superfund site in New Castle County, Del., and the McAdoo site, Kline Township, Pa.

Right Train, Wrong Track

In mid-1988 six leading national environmental groups – the Environmental Defense Fund (EDF), the National Audubon Society, the National Wildlife Federation, the Natural Resources Defense Council (NRDC), the Sierra Club, and the U.S. Public Interest Research Group (USPIRG) – joined with the nation's largest association of hazardous waste treatment firms, the Hazardous Waste Treatment Council, to issue a first-of-its-kind, comprehensive analysis of Superfund cleanup performance encompassing all 75 records of decision (RODs) that EPA made during 1987.

Titled *Right Train, Wrong Track*, the 102-page report found that, despite the clear and explicit directive of the Superfund law "to use permanent treatment remedies to the maximum extent practical," only 8 percent of the EPA remedies actually complied. Sixty-eight percent of the remedies selected "failed to use any treatment whatsoever on the sources of contamination at Superfund sites." Another 24 percent used only partial or ineffective options in the remedy selection process.[19]

Worst U.S.Toxic Waste Sites

Source: U.S. Environmental Protection Agency

9 **NUMBER OF SITES IN EACH STATE**

THE TOXIC TOP 20 – states with the most sites on the EPA's national priority list

THE LEAST-THREATENED 30 – states with the fewest priority-list sites.

The report criticized EPA for ignoring the national cleanup standards established by Congress in 1986 under SARA, exempting Super-fund cleanups from "the very environmental regulations it imposes on other waste-management facilities, and ignoring the impact of Superfund sites on natural resources in the vast majority of its cleanup decisions." These problems, it said, "combine to create a program which falls far short of that necessary to protect human health and the environment from the dangers of Superfund sites."[20]

The EPA's failure to set standards, the report continued, occurs even in cases in which the toxic chemicals pose a well-documented health threat. At the Renora Inc. site in Edison Township, N.J., for example, it set no standard for lead in the soil, despite high concentrations at the site with levels almost six times the federal drinking water standard. "This omission has particularly disturbing consequences because much of the contamination. . . will be treated on site using biomediation, a technology completely ineffective in eliminating metals."[21] Similarly, at Endicott Village Well Field, N.Y., a well contaminated with numerous toxics including several suspected carcinogens continues to serve as a public drinking water source.

According to the report, the EPA in most cases seeks "to merely *minimize short-term exposure, rather than to treat the waste to permanently eliminate the haz-*

ards, as directed by Congress." At some sites bogus "treatment" technologies, such as the stabilization of highly organic wastes, are selected even when the EPA's own data show them to be ineffective. In other instances, the agency "defers selection of a cleanup technology to an unspecified future time and thereby eliminates review of this important decision by the public and other interested parties." [22] At the Diamond Shamrock site in Newark, N.J., the record of decision "leaves unresolved whether incineration of waste will take place on or off site, thus making it difficult for residents near the site to comment fully on a key issue of tremendous potential interest to them." Similar instances of public exclusion are documented at the Liquid Disposal site in Michigan and at the highly contaminated Soydeco site, Charlotte, N.C.[23]

Despite a generally bleak picture, the report identifies three cases in which EPA followed its Congressional mandate:

● At the Geiger site in Rantoules, S.C. the agency rejected land disposal and other short-term remedies in favor of an on-site, cost-effective solution of thermal treatment and chemical fixation of metal wastes, providing greater protection to human health and the environment.

● At the Rose Township dump in Michigan, the EPA selected a remedy that provided permanent treatment, reducing the volume and toxicity of the contaminated soil, despite its higher short-term cost.

● At the Resolve, Mass., site the EPA selected a promising innovative technology called KPEG to destroy PCB waste based on a pilot study that demonstrated its effectiveness.

These cases, the report states, "serve as a model and as reminders that compliance with SARA's permanent remedy directive is readily achievable." [24]

The prime cause of Superfund's "utter failure" to respond to the public demand for timely action is lack of leadership, the report concludes. The EPA, it urges, must move swiftly to comply with SARA on remedy selection and cleanup standards, to issue simple and workable regulations enabling threatened communities to get technical assistance grants, and to provide guidance on the cost and availability of treatment alternatives.

New Broom Sweeps Cleaner?

In his presidential campaign George Bush promised to attack the toxic waste menace "with every ounce of energy I have, and with every enforcement tool at my disposal." [25] With his appointment of William K. Reilly as head of the EPA, the president appeared to be turning his back on the dismal record of the previous administration.

Reilly, former president of the World Wildlife Fund, has a tough job on his hands. He says he wants the EPA to become more aggressive – to make polluting firms pay for waste removal, for example. To do this he proposes, among other measures, to convert $75 million earmarked for consultants into 500 new enforcement positions within the agency. Such a step raises concern among environmentalists. "When businesses are allowed to do cleanups, history has shown that it leads to less productive cleanups," commented Blakeman Early, a spokesperson for the Sierra Club.[26]

Soaring Costs

Reilly's decision to strengthen enforcement was based on an EPA study warning that the Superfund program was unable to meet its goals and is faced with soaring cleanup costs. The agency needs to review 31,000 dump sites, a number that is growing at the rate of 2,000 a year, the study says. The $8.5 billion yearly

EPA budget would not even cover one-third of the estimated $30 billion necessary to clean sites that have already been reviewed. As the report concludes, any such effort "will take many more decades." [27]

What You Can Do about Toxic Chemicals

1. *Clean up your own mess first!* It's easy to blame Exxon and other corporate polluters, but remember there's more of us than of "them." It may not seem important if you pour a can of old bleach or turpentine down the sink or toilet, but multiply this by 83 million other households in the U.S., each one of which contains an estimated 3 to 8 gallons of hazardous waste. It certainly adds up.

As we see throughout this book, there are dozens of hazardous substances found in products we buy in supermarkets and leave in our homes like so many toxic time bombs. (For information on how to dispose *safely* of these products and find safe alternatives, see chapter 12, pp. 304-305.)

2. *Become informed.* Any action you take as an individual or together with others must be based on accurate, up-to-date facts.

3. *Know your rights.* Under the Superfund law, federal, state, and local governments and industry are required to develop plans to deal with chemical emergencies and community "right-to-know" reporting on hazardous chemicals. (For more on how this works, see chapter 10, pp. 235-236.)

> *There are dozens of hazardous substances found in products we buy in supermarkets and leave in our homes like so many toxic time bombs.*

4. *Contact the EPA.* In addition to its headquarters in Washington, D.C., the agency has ten regional offices (see "Resources", at the end of chapter 1), and a Superfund hotline (800-424-9346). Some calls go unanswered, others reach a machine referring you to other numbers. Be persistent. When you do get through to a live person, explain your problem and she or he will put you in touch with the appropriate department in the agency and/or send you useful background material.

5. *If you are facing a toxic-waste dump threat:*

a. Find out from the EPA which government agency is responsible for the permitting in your area. The EPA is giving more and more states authority to handle their toxic waste disposal. The permitting process allows citizens to ask questions relating to all aspects of toxic-chemical production, transportation, use, and disposal. However, you will discover, as you proceed, that the EPA does not encourage active citizen participation in the process.

b. Work with friends, neighbors, and local groups to compile a dossier on the local toxic waste facility. The information you need should describe what kind of a facility it is, who owns it, what their track record is of compliance with federal and state laws, what particular kinds of waste are or will be handled, what the transportation plans are, and what provisions there are for safeguarding the waste and monitoring the facility's performance.

c. Bring a citizen suit. Superfund authorizes a citizen to sue any person, the United States, or an individual state for violation of standards and requirements of the law. Before taking legal action, see "Citizens' Suits", chapter 10, p. 247.

d. Possible joint legal action can be explored in conjunction with citizens', environmental, and other groups.

6. *Join a national group.* Virtually all national environmental groups such as the Sierra Club, the EDF, and the Natural Resources Defense Council publish important information on toxic chemical issues. These groups influence federal legislation and form part of a growing national environmental movement. (See "Resources" at the end of this chapter for more specifics. See also chapter 11, "Eco-Action," which describes how environmental, citizens', and other types of groups work).

7. *Work with an issue-oriented action group.* One leading organization on toxic waste cleanup is the Citizen's Clearinghouse for Hazardous Wastes (CCHW), with its national headquarters in Arlington, Va. CCHW was founded by Lois Gibbs, who first organized her neighbors to protest conditions at Love Canal in Buffalo, N.Y. It maintains a network of field offices, especially in the South and Appalachia. Contact the CCHW national Office to find the one nearest you. Working with 6,300 local groups, CCHW is in the forefront of environmental action and education. It organizes conferences and workshops, as well as publishing the newsletter *Everyone's Backyard*, the quarterly *Action Bulletin*, and very useful handbooks such as *Fight to Win on Hazardous Waste: A Leader's Manual.*

Another important group is the National Toxics Campaign, 37 Temple Place, Boston, MA 02111; (617) 482-1477. With representatives in most parts of the U.S., this is a grass-roots network that works with Greenpeace and other environmental groups in a concerted effort to induce the federal and state governments to embrace reduction of toxics instead of incineration. The campaign has included organizing a successful national call-in day and a national day of action in the fall of 1989. Its program is outlined in a well-documented report, *From Poison to Prevention: A White Paper on Replacing Hazardous Waste Facility Siting with Toxics Reduction.*

8. *Check "Resources"* at end of this chapter for further leads and information.

The Pesticide Problem

Who's Minding the Store?

Two federal agencies have responsibility for controlling pesticides in food – the EPA, which regulates pesticide sale and use and determines "acceptable" levels (tolerances), and the Food and Drug Administration (FDA), responsible for monitoring food to ensure that pesticide residues do not exceed EPA tolerances.

Unfortunately, the basic law governing pesticides, the Federal Insecticide, Fungicide and Rodenticide Act of 1972, neither sets levels below which pesticides must be reduced nor mandates requirements for reducing the levels. Instead, it authorizes the EPA to evaluate the risks presented by specific chemicals and to decide if the risks would have "unreasonable adverse effects" on health or the environment. The net effect is to leave many harmful pesticides on the market until they have been proven guilty.[28]

Many consumer and citizen groups agree with Jay Feldman, coordinator of the National Coalition Against the Misuse of Pesticides, that the EPA is engaged in a "nightmarish regulatory process in which subjective judgments of benefits ride roughshod over considerations of public health and the environment." [29]

In a rare use of its muscle, the EPA decided to suspend Dinoseb, a pesticide used on peas and beans and other plants, because it caused birth defects in babies of exposed farm workers. The growers took the agency to court, contending there were no suitable alternatives to the product and that its banning would cause them severe economic hardship. As a result, a federal court ordered EPA to modify its decision and allow limited uses to continue.

In the case of the nation's most widely used herbicide, Alachlor, the EPA decided to allow its continued use despite its finding that it posed a cancer risk of one in a million over a lifetime, that it was contaminating water supplies, and that less harmful alternatives were available. The agency defended its decision on the grounds that the risks were "not unreasonable" and because "we have not been sued by any environmental groups." [30]

According to EPA estimates, pesticides have contaminated ground water in 38 states, fouling the drinking water of half of all Americans.

Alar, a toxic chemical used for almost 20 years to enhance the growth and appearance of apples, has also enjoyed remarkable immunity from governmental regulation. (For details on its tortuous chronology, see chapter 11, pp. 259-261.)

Captan, a chemical widely sprayed on fruits and vegetables, is another common residue in food. Although the levels found are usually below EPA's tolerances, they may not be safe because (1) the EPA has called Captan a probable human carcinogen and therefore any level of exposure may cause cancer; (2) the majority of Captan tolerances were set before the EPA knew the chemical caused cancer; (3) the tolerances do not cover one of the compound's breakdown products that may also be a carcinogen; and (4) the EPA's determinations of what levels of Captan in food should be acceptable do not consider exposure to Captan through nonfood sources such as paints, mattresses, shower curtains, and shampoos. Although the EPA began a special review of this chemical in 1980 because of concerns about its hazards, by 1989 the agency had taken no steps to restrict the use of the chemical or protect the public. [31]

Pesticide Alert*

The full extent of environmental contamination by pesticides is not known. Yet what we are finding out is alarming:

● Between 1982 and 1985 the FDA detected pesticide residues in 48 percent of the fresh vegetables and fruits we eat most frequently. Almost certainly this is an underestimate because half the pesticides in food cannot be detected by FDA's routine laboratory methods, and it samples less than 1 percent of what we eat. [32]

● According to EPA estimates, pesticides have contaminated ground water in 38 states, fouling the drinking water of half of all Americans. [33]

● The EPA says pesticide residues on food are more menacing than hazardous-waste dumps or air pollutants. It estimates that some 6,000 cases of cancer a year are caused by just the one-third of the approved pesticides in use today that have been tested. Most of the 50,000 pesticides on the market have *never* been

---

*This is the title of an important book by Lawrie Mott and Karen Snyder, senior scientist and research associate with the Natural Resources Defense Council.

tested for long-term effects. Chemicals known to cause cancer, genetic mutations, birth defects, and testicular atrophy are legally and widely applied to vegetables and fruits.[34]

● There is mounting evidence that farmers, farmworkers, and their families
who are exposed to pesticides and herbicides have a far greater risk than the general population of developing leukemia and other cancers, birth defects, and diseases of the central nervous system.[35]

A California County's Trouble*

BAKERSFIELD, CALIF. – Janice Gary thought she had found her dream
house the first time she saw the ranch-style house in the semirural North
Olive Estates development here. She was especially attracted by the fresh
country air and the beautiful almond orchard across the street.

Then one night in late 1986, shortly after she had moved into the new
housing development, the dream turned into a nightmare. The almond
grower flipped a switch on his tractor-drawn tanks and started spraying
clouds of pesticide into his 500 acres of trees and into North Olive Estates.

"I got the shakes. My lungs hurt so badly, I can't tell you," says the 51-
year-old housewife, clutching her chest as she instinctively recalls the pain.
"It was frightening." Since then, as the sprayings have continued, Mrs. Gary
has spent weeks at a time in bed with burning lips and swollen eyes. Once,
unable to breathe, she was rushed through the chemical fog outside to an
emergency room.

A group of neighbors sought to stop the spraying — to no avail. They
think they know why. In California, as in most states, pesticide regulation
falls to the state department of agriculture, whose main task is to protect and
help farmers, not police them. Critics see a conflict of interest.

"It's the fox guarding the chicken coop," says Richard Wiles, a pesticide
expert at the National Academy of Sciences, a Washington, D.C., research
group.

In the case of Mrs. Gary's neighborhood, the pesticides used were
changed, says Theodore Davis, assistant agricultural commissioner for Kern
County. The orchard owner declines to comment. But the residents
became sickened - and disheartened. One of them says she left a meeting
with the county agricultural commissioner in despair. "I could see there
would be no action," she says. "I felt he was only for the farmers." Mrs.
Gary now evacuates her home seven times a year, when the almond grower
sprays. "I don't know what to do or where to turn." she says.

---

* Condensed with permission from "Health Hazard: Pesticide Regulation, Mainly the
States' Job, Is Spotty and Weak," by Sonia L. Nazario, *Wall Street Journal*, January 18,
1989, © Dow Jones & Company, Inc., 1989.

DDT – Gone, but Not Completely

In 1962 Rachel Carson alerted the world to the devastating effects of DDT on
birds, fish, and other animals. Although banned in the United States, DDT is
still manufactured here and in Western Europe and exported to many countries
such as Mexico and Columbia from whom we import large quantities of food

and coffee. DDT and other pesticides are very persistent and mobile in the environment, having been found in animals in the Antarctic and other areas never sprayed. A 1986 report done for EPA condemned the agency for failing to investigate pesticide poisonings of the bald eagle, brown pelican, Californian condor and other endangered species. The EPA now estimates that more than half of the 450 species on the endangered list are potentially jeopardized by pesticide use in 47 states.[36]

Another consequence of the widespread and long-term use of pesticides, herbicides, and fungicides is that pests, weeds, and fungi are becoming resistant to the chemicals. This calls for even greater amounts being used in a never-ending cycle of poison. Since the 1940s pesticide use has increased tenfold, but crop losses to insects have doubled.[37]

Pesticides in Your Food: Identifying the Risks

In the light of headlines about pesticide-contaminated watermelons, cake mixes, grapes, and many other products, it is important to understand the risks associated with pesticide residues in food.

It is crucial to identify pesticide residues because with many health hazards, especially cancer, any amount may be dangerous. Since most fruits and vegetables often contain several pesticides, there is also the possibility of synergism, which takes place when simultaneous exposure to more than one chemical produces a greater toxic effect than the sum of the chemicals' individual toxicities.

As Pesticide Alert points out, most produce contains pesticides, but some more than others. These include commodities where cosmetic appearance is especially important – apples, strawberries, and peaches, for example. Foods whose edible parts are essentially roots, such as carrots and beets, or tubers such as potatoes, absorb chemicals from the soil. Other vegetables and fruits have thick skins (bananas), husks (corn), or outer leaves (cauliflower) that offer some protection against pesticides.

As already noted, imported foods generally contain much higher pesticide levels than domestic varieties, as well as often containing DDT and other chemicals banned in the United States.

Breaking the Pesticide Chain

The ultimate way to limit exposure to pesticides is to break agriculture's dependence on synthetic chemicals. One effective approach is integrated pest management (IPM) – growing crops as part of an organic ecosystem where many natural forces are allowed to interact. It draws on traditional practices such as crop rotation, interplanting (growing nitrogen-fixing legumes between rows of wheat to keep weeds under control), and mulching, long discarded by factory farming with its intensive use of chemical fertilizers and pesticides.

IPM employs biological controls like planting flowers among vegetables to attract ladybug beetles, praying mantises, and other natural predators of pests. Avoiding the single-crop farming favored by agribusiness, IPM raises a wide variety of crops to create a diversified habitat for useful predators and parasites. It does not eliminate chemicals completely, but makes use of nicotine, pyrethrin, garlic, and mild soap sprays that were used for generations before modern pesticides were developed. If IPM requires farmers to adopt a more thoughtful approach to raising crops, its benefits are impressive. It reduces the need for expensive chemicals and the anxiety about pesticides getting into food and ground water. The system has worked well in China, where import costs have prohibited widespread use of chemical pesticides and fertilizers. When applied to the soybean crop in Brazil, IPM achieved an 85 percent drop in insecticide use.[39]

As might be expected, IPM is not embraced by chemical manufacturers, many of whom have tightened their grip on farming by buying seed companies and reducing the variety of seeds available, a step that works against natural pest control.

The U.S. Department of Agriculture has experimented successfully with IPM and other organic farming techniques pioneered by the Rodale organization in Emmaus, Pa., and the Land Institute in Salina, Kans. Yet the USDA Extension Service funding for IPM has remained at under $8 million a year since 1981, a pitiful 2 percent of its total budget.[40]

An alternative, nontoxic pest killer, undergoing tests in California, is the Bugvac, "a gigantic vacuum cleaner that literally sucks harmful insects out of the strawberry patch, leaving most of the beneficial bugs behind."[41] The experimental device reportedly cleared 15 acres of strawberries of the harmful lygus bug. According to its inventor, entomologist Edgar Show, the vacuum, which is mounted on a tractor, is designed to suck up only the top third of the insects that inhabit strawberry plants. The good bugs apparently live further down under the protection of leaves. "Good bugs tend to be more agile," Shaw said, "It's spooky. They detect the machine coming and escape."[42]

12 Ways to Get Pesticides Out of Your Food

1. *Read the book.* NRDC's *Pesticide Alert* is a comprehensive, product-by-product guide to pesticides and explains how you can demand and get safer food.

2. *Support:*

● *National Coalition Against the Misuse of Pesticides*, 530 Seventh Street SE, Washington, DC 20003; (202) 543-5450. The primary coalition of all grass-roots groups working on pesticide issues. It publishes the important newsletter *Pesticides and You.*

● *Northwest Coalition for Alternatives to Pesticides*, P.O. Box 1393, Eugene, OR 97440; (503) 344-5044.

● *NRDC, EDF, Greenpeace, USPIRG, Public Citizen, Rodale Institute* and other groups working against use of harmful pesticides and for organic farming. See "Resources" immediately below for more information.

3. *Grow your own food organically.* Join the 35 million people in the United States who grow all or part of their own food, especially those who do it organically – i.e., without using chemicals. Organic gardening is based on the principles of using compost[43] instead of chemicals to create a fertile soil and of encouraging natural life – not just birds and bees, but insects and other organisms – to create a healthy growing environment. If you don't have room for a garden plot, raise tomatoes, herbs, and other simple foods on your roof, terrace, or window box. If really pressed for space, try sprouting alfalfa or mung beans in glass jars. When you grow your own food, you don't have to guess what's inside. To find out more, read *Organic Gardening* magazine, published by Rodale Press, Emmaus, Pa., and any one of several excellent books on the subject listed in the "Resources" section.

4. *Buy organic food.* These products are now widely available, not just in health food stores and farmers' markets but increasingly in supermarkets and grocery stores nationwide. For more on organic food, see chapter 12, pp. 290-292.

5. *Wash all produce.* To get rid of some but not all surface pesticide residues, thoroughly wash all vegetables, fruits, grains, and legumes in clean water or a weak solution of hydrogen peroxide.[44]

6. *Peel, scrape, or remove skins.* This will take off surface residues in potatoes, carrots, turnips, zucchini, and other produce. There will inevitably be some loss of nutritional value in this process.

7. *Buy local, buy in season.* The closer to home the produce you get is grown, the fresher it will be and the more likely you can check if it was grown with pesticides. Also, food in season is less liable to be artificially preserved with irradiation or chemicals.

8. *Beware the perfect apple.* Harmful pesticides such as daminozide (marketed as Alar by Uniroyal) are used on apples, peanuts, cherries, peaches, grapes, tomatoes, and pears to enhance their cosmetic appearance because of alleged consumer insistence on perfect-looking produce. However, a campaign by *Public Citizen*, NRDC, and other groups that have sued the EPA to ban daminozide has caused several food store chains to stop selling Alar-treated apples. (For details on the Alar story, see chapter 11, pp. 259-261.)

9. *Meet the manager.* Most stores, especially supermarkets, respond to their customers' requests for new products (e.g., bottled water and organic foods) as well as to their concerns about the hazards of food additives, irradiation, and pesticides. As the case histories in this book show, it often doesn't take many requests or complaints to get harmful practices changed. Ask your manager to post information on the origin of the food and what pesticides have been used on them. Point to the commercial successes of companies that are marketing pesticide-free food and beverages.

10. *Support the pesticide reduction program* of the Consumer Pesticide Reduction Program of the National Toxics Campaign endorsed by ABCO, American Brothers Produce, Bread & Circus, Provigo, Raleys, and other food retailers.

11. *Know your rights.* To find out exactly what the laws and your rights are, contact the EPA office in your region or get in touch with the FDA in Washington D.C., (see also chapters 10 and 11). Also contact influential citizens' groups, including Americans for Safe Food, the National Coalition Against the Misuse of Pesticides, the Natural Resources Defense Council, the Northwest Coalition for Alternatives to Pesticides, Pesticides Action Network, and Public Citizen. For further information on these and other groups, see "Resources," immediately below.

12. *Contact your congressional representatives:* write and speak to them about your pesticide concerns. Urge support for Senator Fowler's Farm Conservation and Water Protection Act. Ask them to press the EPA, FDA, the U.S. Department of Agriculture, and other federal agencies to do a better job of protecting consumers from pesticides and other toxic substances in food and water. Work also with your elected officials at state and local levels, including particularly those on the boards of health.

RESOURCES

The following is provided to help you locate additional resources on the topics covered in this chapter.

1. U.S. Government

— *EPA*:

RCRA Hotline answering questions about the Resource Conservation and Recovery Act, the basic law regulating hazardous waste (800) 424-9346

SARA Hotline. (800) 535-0202.

(For more on EPA, see chapter 1, "Resources.")

— *Food and Drug Administration*, Department of Health and Welfare, 5600 Fishers Lane, Rockville, MD 20857.

— *Occupational Safety and Health Administration*, Department of Labor, 200 Constitution Avenue NW, Washington, DC 202210 .

2. Organizations

— *ACORN* (Association of Community Associations for Reform Now), 413 8th Street SE, Washington, DC 20003; (202) 547-9292. Deals with community improvement, health care, toxics.

— *Americans for Safe Food*, 1501 16th Street NW, Washington, DC 20036; (202) 332-9110. A coalition of over 40 consumer, environmental, and rural groups working for contaminant-free food.

— *California Certified Organic Farmers*, P.O. Box 8136, Santa Cruz, CA; (408) 423-2263. Representing some 500 organic farms, it monitors and inspects the state's organic farms.

— *Center for Science in the Public Interest*, 1755 S Street NW, Washington, DC 20009; (202) 332-9110.

— *Citizen's Clearinghouse for Hazardous Wastes*, P.O. Box 926, Arlington, VA 22216; (703) 276-7070; field offices nationwide, especially in the South and Appalachia. Does research and action-oriented work on toxic waste, water pollution, solid waste incineration, asbestos in schools.

— *CONCERN Inc.*, 794 Columbia Road NW, Washington, DC 20009; (202) 328-8160. Provides information and education to individuals and groups, encouraging them to act in their communities.

— *Environmental Law Institute*, 1525 18th Street NW, Washington DC 20036; (202) 452-9600. Research, lobbying, litigation on toxics victim compensation.

— *Environmental Research Foundation*, P.O. Box 3541, Princeton, NJ 08543; 609) 683-0707. Sponsors computer databases and publishes the weekly *Rachel's Hazardous Waste News*, both filled with useful information for citizens working on toxics problems.

— *Greenpeace*, 1436 U Street NW, Washington, DC 20009; (202) 462-1177. An international organization with offices in Anchorage, Alaska, Cambridge, Mass., Chicago, San Francisco, Seattle, Wilton Manors, Fla., Toronto, Montreal, and Vancouver, Canada. Lobbying and direct action on all forms of pollution and toxics, especially water-related and nuclear.

— *Greenpeace U.S.A.* Toxics Campaign, 1017 W. Jackson Boulevard, Chicago, IL 60607. Greenpeace Action, Waste Trade Project, 1436 U Street NW, Washington, DC 20009. Documents waste trafficking worldwide.

— *National Association of Farm Worker Organizations*, 1316 Tenth Street NW, Washington, DC 20001; (202) 328-9777. Research and education on pesticides and other farm hazards.

— *National Toxics Campaign*, 37 Temple Place, Boston, MA 02111; (617) 482-1477. Formerly called the National Campaign Against Toxic Hazards, this is a coalition of citizens, community leaders, scientists, consumer organizations, environmentalists, health activists, and dumpsite groups formed to develop and implement solutions to the toxics crisis.

— *National Center for Policy Alternatives*, 2000 Florida Avenue NW, Washington, DC 20003; (202) 387-6030.
— *National Coalition Against Misuse of Pesticides*, 530 Seventh Street SE, Washington, DC 20003; (202) 543-5450. The primary coalition of all grass-roots groups working on pesticide issues, it publishes the important newsletter *Pesticides and You*.
— *Northwest Coalition for Alternatives to Pesticides*, P.O. Box 1393, Eugene, OR 97440; (503) 344-5044.
— *Organic Crop Improvement Organization*, P.O. Box 729A, New Holland, PA 17557. Farmer-owned group that provides information on how to reduce or eliminate pesticides; certifies farmers that meet its organic farming standards. Send self-addressed, stamped envelope to get list of OCIO-approved organic food in your area.
— *Organic Food Production Association of North America*, P.O. Box 31, Belchertown, MA 01007. Trade association of organic farmers, processors, and distributors. Marketing network that should be contacted by supermarkets seeking supplies of high-quality, authentic organic food.
— *Pesticides Action Network*, P.O. Box 610, San Francisco, CA 94101; (415) 771-7327. International coalition of organizations and individuals opposed to global misuse of pesticides.
— *U.S. Public Interest Research Group* (USPIRG), 215 Pennsylvania Avenue SE, Washington, DC 20003; (202) 546-9707.
— *Working Group on Community Right-to-Know*, 215 Pennsylvania Avenue SE, Washington, DC 20003; (202) 546-9707. A coalition of national environmental groups that supplies information on right-to-know to toxics activists.

3. Further Reading

— *Approaches to Source Reduction of Hazardous Waste: Practical Guidance From Existing Policies and Programs*, New York: Environmental Defense Fund, 1986.
— *A Citizen's Toxic Waste Audit Manual: Zero Discharge*, Ben Gordon and Peter Montague. Washington, D.C.: Greenpeace and Environmental Research Foundation, 1989.
— *Community Relations in Superfund: A Handbook*. Washington, D.C.: EPA, Office of Emergency and Remedial Response, June 1988.
— *Detox*, Phyllis Saifer, MD, and Merla Zellerbach. Los Angeles: Jeremy P. Tarcher, 1984.
— *Dumpsite Cleanups: A Citizen's Guide to the Superfund Program*. Washington, D.C.: Environmental Defense Fund, n.d..
— *The Hazardous Waste System*. Washington, D.C.: EPA, Office of Solid Waste and Emergency Response, June 1987.
— *Health Effects of Environmental Pollutants*, George L. Waldbott, M.D. Saint Louis: C.V. Mosby, 1973.
— *How to Survive in Your Toxic Environment*, Edward J. Bergin with Ronald E. Grandon. New York: Avon, 1984.
— *Intolerable Risk: Pesticides in our Children's Food*. New York: NRDC, 1989.
— *Laying Waste: The Poisoning of America by Toxic Chemicals*, Michael Brown. New York: Pantheon, 1980.
— *Leaking Underground Storage Tanks - Secondary Containment: A Second Line of Defense*. New York: Environmental Defense Fund, 1988.
— *Love Canal: A Chronology of Events that Shaped a Movement*. Arlington, Va.: Citizen's Clearinghouse for Hazardous Waste, n.d.
— *Making a Difference*. Arlington, Va. : Citizen's Clearinghouse for Hazardous Wastes, n.d..
— *No Time to Waste*, a report by the Toxics Project of the New York Public Interest Research Group, Walter L. T. Hang and Steven A. Romalewski. New York: NYPIRG, 1989.
— *Pesticide Alert: A Guide to Pesticides in Fruits and Vegetables*, Lawrie Mott and Karen Snyder. San Francisco: NRDC/Sierra Club, 1987.
— *Proven Profits from Pollution Prevention*, Donald Huisingh, Larry Martin, Helene Hilger, and Neil Seldman. Washington, D.C.: Institute for Local Self-Reliance, 1986.
— *Right Train, Wrong Track: Failed Leadership in the Superfund Cleanup Program*, EDF, Hazardous Waste Council, National Audubon Society, National Wildlife Federation,

NRDC, Sierra Club, and USPIRG. Mimeograph. June 1988.

— *Serious Reduction of Hazardous Waste*. Washington, D.C.: U.S. Congress Office of Technology Assessment, U.S. Government Printing Office, 1986.

— *Shadow on the Land: A Special Report on America's Hazardous Harvest*, John T. O'Connor and Sanford Lewis. Boston: National Toxics Campaign, 1988.

— *Superfund 1987: Public Health Remains at Risk*, Henry S. Cole and Bill Walsh. Washington, D.C.: USPIRG, 1987.

— *Work Is Dangerous to Your Health*, Jeanne M. Stellman, Ph.D and Susan M. Daum, M.D. New York: Vintage, 1973.

— *Zero Discharge: A Citizen's Toxic Waste Manual*, Ben Gordon and Peter Montague. Washington, D.C.: Greenpeace, 1989.

ENDNOTES

1. "Superfund: Looking Back, Looking Ahead," *EPA Journal*, January/February 1987.

2. EPA, SRI Directory of Chemical Products, and individual chemical companies cited in *New York Times*, December 17, 1985.

3. "Controlling Toxic Chemicals," Sandra Postel in *State of the World, 1988*, Washington, D.C.: Worldwatch Institute, 1988, p. 120.

4. Alvin M. Weinberg, former director of Oak Ridge National Laboratory, quoted in "Chemical Accidents: The Hidden Danger," *New York Times*, November 25, 1985.

5. Stuart Diamond, "E.P.A. Lists Dangers of More Than 400 Chemicals," *New York Times*, December 17, 1985.

6. Stuart Diamond, "Problems at Chemical Plants Raise Broad Safety Concerns," *New York Times*, November 25, 1985.

7. Industrial Economics Inc., Cambridge, Mass., lead consultant of an EPA-commissioned study, reported in "U.S. Toxic Mishaps in Chemicals Put At 6,928 In 5 Years," *New York Times*, October 5, 1985.

8. According to a study by the Center for the Biology of Natural Systems, incineration of waste can increase the amount of dioxin contained in it. See chapter 1, pp. 13-14 for further information.

9. Diamond, "Problems at Chemical Plants," *New York Times*, November 25, 1985.

10. Ibid.

11. "Toxic Chemicals, the Right Response," *New York Times*, November 13, 1988.

12. Ibid.

13. Ibid.

14. *The New Superfund: What It Is, How It Works*, booklet (Washington, D.C.: August 1987).

15. "Superfund: Looking Back, Looking Ahead," p. 9.

16. *EPA Superfund Advisory* (Office of Solid Waste and Emergency Response, U.S. EPA OS-110, Washington, D.C.) Summer/Fall 1988.

17. AP report, "Toxic Site Cleanup Reported Lagging," *New York Times*, September 10, 1989.

18. Ibid.

19. *Right Train, Wrong Track* (New York: Environmental Defense Fund et al., June 20, 1988), p. 2.

20. Ibid., p. 2.

21. Ibid. pp. 44-45.

22. Ibid., pp. 18-19.

23. Ibid. pp. 34-35.

24. Ibid. p. 35.

25. From a speech delivered in Erie Metropark, Mich., August 31, 1988, reported in *New York Times*, September 24, 1988.

26. Quoted in Bill McAllister, " EPA to Become More Aggressive," *Washington Post*, June 15, 1989.

27. Ibid.

28. For further information on this law, see chapter 10, pp. 237-238.

29. Philip Shabecoff, "Odds Increase for Sharp Increase in Testing of U.S. Pesticides," *New York Times*, September 27, 1988.

30. Ibid.

31. Lawrie Mott and Karen Snyder, *Pesticide Alert* (San Francisco: NRDC/Sierra Club, 1987), pp. 10-11.

32. *Pesticides: Need to Enhance FDA`s Ability to Protect the Public from Illegal Residues* (Washington, D.C.: General Accounting Office, October 1986).

33. Sonia L. Nazario, "Pesticide Regulation," *Wall Street Journal*, January 18, 1989.

34. Ibid.

35. Mary Strange, Liz Krupicka and Dan Looker, "The Hidden Health Effect of Pesticides," in *It's Not All Sunshine and Fresh Air* (Walthill, Neb.: Center for Rural Affairs, 1984), pp. 55-61.

36. Mott and Snyder, *Pesticide Alert*, p. 58.

37. Ibid., p. 7.

38. Ibid. p. 21.

39. Postel, "Controlling Toxic Chemicals," p. 126.

40. Ibid., p. 133.

41. Sandra Blakeslee, "The Good, the Bad and the Berries," *New York Times*, November 8, 1988.

42. Ibid.

43. For further information on how composting works, see chapter 1, pp. 24-25.

44. For more on water purification, see chapter 12, pp. 295-298.

3

TROUBLED WATERS

Protecting the Sources

"All is born of water, all is sustained by water"
– Goethe

Ours is a water planet. Water covers three quarters of its surface, makes up two-thirds of our bodies. It is so vital to life we can't live more than four days without it. If all the earth's water – an estimated 325 trillion gallons – were squeezed into a gallon jug and you poured off what was not drinkable (too salty, frozen or polluted) you'd be left with one drop. And even that might not pass U.S. water quality standards.

Because water pollution is an insidious and all-pervasive environmental problem, cleaning it up is a matter of greatest urgency. It involves a complexity of scientific, technological, economic, and political factors that cut across state, national, and international borders.

From Sea to Stinking Sea

In the summer of 1988 the unsightly appearance of hypodermic needles, vials of blood, and medical waste on the shores of the eastern United States dramatized what had existed for decades – the filthy condition of our oceans and coastal waters.

Although the sea can handle its own natural waste – gray whales, even anchovies, contribute more excrement to the oceans than the Los Angeles sewer system,[1] but they spread it over a far wider area – the ocean can't absorb the infinitely greater concentrations of poisons we relentlessly dump into it from our sewage, industrial waste, oil spills, fertilizer and pesticide runoff, and many other sources.

Recipe for Pollution Soup

To contaminating agricultural and industrial runoff discharged by rivers and streams into estuaries, add the following lethal ingredients:

- sulfuric and nitric acids from acid rain
- toxic chemicals from wind-borne pesticides
- oil spills from tankers and offshore drilling rigs
- uncounted tons of garbage (mainly nonbiodegradable plastics) dumped from oceangoing ships, fishermen, and recreational boaters
- raw human and animal sewage
- radioactive wastes
- dioxin-laced ash from ocean incinerators and illegal dump ships
- medical and surgical debris

MIX THOROUGHLY AND RUN LIKE THE PLAGUE (NOT RECOMMENDED FOR EATING WASHING, SWIMMING, OR DRINKING).

For the United States the problem is intensified by rampant building development along all our coasts. Today well over half of the population lives within 50 miles of the Pacific, Atlantic, or Gulf of Mexico, discharging 30 billion gallons of industrial and municipal waste into the sea every year.

According to members of the Cousteau ship *Calypso*, there is no place, even in the remotest corners of the globe, free of styrofoam and other plastic trash bobbing on the surface of the water. Bays and estuaries from Chesapeake to Rio de Janeiro and the Sea of Japan are choked with garbage, plagued with red and brown tides of algae, suffocating fish and other marine life. Dead whales washed up on Cape Cod in 1988 had most likely ingested poisons passed up the food chain from shellfish to the polluted mackerel the whales had eaten.

The more we learn about our troubled oceans, the grimmer the picture.

Oil and Water Don't Mix

"It is not just that once-pure water is now marbled with globs of oil. . . that beaches have been so dirtied one would rather not look at them . . . that I saw even bald eagles, the very symbols of the United States, sullied with grease, or that these great birds will feed on oil-soaked animals and may die. It is that in Prince William Sound the spill has created ecological anarchy." – Jean-Michel Cousteau, June 1989

When the oil tanker Exxon *Valdez* ran aground in March 1989, dumping 11 million gallons of crude oil into Alaska's Prince William Sound in the largest spill in U.S. history, it was an ecological disaster of epic proportions. In addition to killing untold thousands of birds, fish, and sea otters, the spill threatens the survival of zooplankton, microorganisms that form the basis of the food chain for all marine creatures.

As it was later revealed,[3] the *Valdez* spill was only one of thousands of oil spills a year – another Exxon tanker had spilled crude oil 15 miles from Waikiki Beach, Hawaii, just three weeks before the Prince William Sound disaster, in January 1989 an Argentine navy supply ship leaked thousands of gallons of diesel oil in Arthur Harbor in the Antarctic, and in late June there were three substantial oil spills within hours of each other (in Narragansett Bay, R.I., the Delaware River, and the Houston Ship Channel). In April of the same year a supertanker ran aground in the Red Sea, leaking nearly a million gallons of oil and imperiling coral reefs and turtle breeding grounds. It merited a 17-line report buried deep inside the voluminous pages of the *New York Times*. In January, 1990 the Iranian supertanker *Kharg-5* exploded, spilling 20 million gallons of crude oil along the Moroccan coast.

In 1988 alone there were 5,000 to 6,000 spills involving oil and other toxic substances along the coasts and other navigable waters of the U.S., according to the chief of the U.S. Coast Guard's investigation division. Of these, 12 were classified as major because they involved more than 100,000 gallons. Between 1980 and 1986 91 million gallons of oil and 36 million gallons of other toxic substances were recorded as being spilled into U.S. waters.[4]

"Neither Government nor industry has the will or technology to respond successfully to oil spills – even relatively small ones," was how a *New York Times* lead editorial commented on the aftermath of the Exxon *Valdez* spill.[5] Stronger regulation by the government was recommended by the *Los Angeles Times*, which

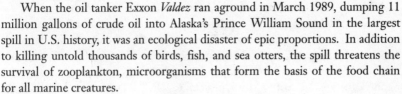

World's Worst Oil Spills

1. February 1983 – *Nowruz* oil field, Persian Gulf, offshore well collapses: estimated spill of 220 million gallons

2. June 1979 – *Ixtoc* 1 oil well explodes in Bay of Campeche near the Yucatán Peninsula, Mexico: 200 million gallons

3. July 1979 – Collision of *Atlantic Empress* and *Aegean Captain*, off Trinidad: 110 million gallons

4. August 1983 – Fire aboard *Castillo de Beliver* off Cape Town, South Africa: 75 million gallons

5. March 1978 – *Amoco Cadiz* runs aground off Brittany, France: 70 million gallons

6. March 1967 – *Torrey Canyon* runs aground off Land's End, England: 36 million gallons

7. February 1980 – *Irenes Serenade* catches fire and sinks off Pylos, Greece: 35 million gallons

8. January 1990 – *Kharg-5* explodes off the Moroccan coast: 20 million gallons

9. March 1989 – Exxon *Valdez* runs aground in Prince William Sound, Alaska: 11 million gallons

said the "spill has demonstrated that Americans cannot rely on the good will of corporations to clean up their own messes adequately." The Alaskan tragedy, it stated, "makes the case for strong federal regulations and controls closely monitored and strongly enforced. There must be stiff penalties for failure to comply. And whenever a company assumes a less-than-urgent approach to such a cleanup, the government must not hesitate to take direct command of the situation." Since 1980, the editorial concluded, the national administration has complained about the cost of government regulation of business and has worked to reduce the reduce the number of rules. "Now, the nation knows the cost of insufficient regulation." [6]

> *"Americans cannot rely on the good will of corporations to clean up their own messes adequately."*

Whose Water Is It Anyway?

The oceans belong to our common heritage. Their state of health or disease is a matter of common concern. This concept has been acknowledged by international law since at least 1609 when a young Dutch jurist named Hugo Grotius published a treatise called *Mare Liberum* (The Free Sea).

Based on the belief that oceans were boundless and their resources inexhaustible, the Grotius principle lasted as long as it served the needs of the international community – for more than 300 years. However, when President Truman in 1945 claimed the resources of the continental shelf for the United States (to exploit oil deposits), it triggered a chain reaction of territorial claims by other nations.[7]

For the next 25 years freedom of the sea was interpreted to mean a free-for-all grab of its resources – fishing, oil, and minerals – with little regard for its ecological integrity. In the process the oceans became the garbage can of the world, particularly of the alphabetic nuclear powers – U.S., U.K., and U.S.S.R – who found it convenient to dump their radioactive wastes there.

Thanks mainly to the efforts of the United Nations, the ocean dumping of high-level radioactive and other very toxic wastes was banned by the London Dumping Convention, signed in 1972 by 90 countries including the U.S. However, ten years later, when 132 nations adopted the U.N.'s Law of the Sea Treaty to control ocean pollution and exploitation, President Reagan refused to sign.

By this time the dumping of plastics in the ocean had become a major world problem, entangling and drowning marine animals, starving and killing others which eat plastic junk mistaking it for food, and disrupting valuable fishery resources. In late 1987 the United States ratified Annex V of an international marine pollution (MARPOL) treaty. The annex specifically prohibits dumping all plastics into the ocean and requires ships to carry their plastic trash back into port for proper disposal.[8]

For the United States compliance with MARPOL is vested in the Clean Water Act, which regulates discharge of industrial wastes into the nation's fresh and salt water and which set up a national estuaries program to involve the federal government in state and local cleanup efforts. Other important federal clean-water legislation includes the Marine Protection, Research and Sanctuaries Act and the Nuclear Waste Policy Act, both of which prohibit the dumping of waste into the ocean. (For more on these and other environmental laws, see chapter 10.)

Coast and River Cleanups

The federal government's success (or failure) in complying with MARPOL depends on the cooperation of individual states, few of which have comprehensive cleanup programs, and on individual people – professionals, government employees, businessmen and women, and concerned citizens. Here are four cases in which some progress has been achieved.

The Delaware Decision – Fifty years ago pollution in the Delaware River Estuary was so bad that shad and most other fish could not survive there. Gases from the river, detectable at 5,000 feet by pilots landing at Philadelphia's airport, corroded ship's engines and fittings and tarnished products being manufactured in nearby factories. In warm weather the estuary resembled the contents of a septic tank.

The pollution was caused by vast amounts of oxygen-demanding wastes entering the river from cities and industries. During a century of neglect, municipal officials, industrial managers, and even the general public took it for granted that the price of the industrial revolution was grossly polluted water.

The first cleanup effort, begun in the late 1930s, was interrupted by World War II. A second program was started by the Delaware River Basin states and the federal government. This was a massive effort based on the

> *"When they see a black scum or a little slick, they let us know about it."*
> *Thomas Hubbard,*
> *Seattle water-quality planner*

enforcement of stricter state and federal pollution water-control legislation, including the 1972 federal Clean Water Act.

Completion of the program in 1987 resulted in a 75-percent decrease in oxygen-demanding wastes, improving water quality to levels better than at any time in fifty years. Studies in 1985-1987 found 36 species of fish, including the migratory shad whose spawning grounds now extend over a hundred miles of the estuary and river.

Before the program ended, a third-generation effort by state, federal, and Delaware River Basin Commission scientists was launched to make the entire estuary "completely fishable and swimmable," as required by the national estuary program of the 1987 Clean Water Act. This is a long-term project addressing the impact of toxic chemicals, agricultural runoff, and other pollutants on the ecology of the Delaware River, estuary, and bay.[9]

Puget Program – In 1985 in Washington State the Puget Sound Water Quality Authority initiated a program for cleaning up the heavily polluted 3,200-square-mile body of water. It is in part funded by an 8 cents-a-pack surtax on cigarettes, which brings in about $8 million a year. The discharge of waste from all sources is closely monitored by the authority and other state agencies working with private industry to reduce the flow of effluent into the Sound.

The project also includes limiting runoff from farmland, stringent construction zoning in the critical watershed area, and an areawide educational program that, in the words of *Time* magazine, teaches everything from the history of the sound to what not to put down the kitchen sink.[10]

The control of pollution is promoted as everybody's task. High school students take water samples and local citizens are trained to spot oil spills and other types of water pollution. According to Thomas Hubbard, a water-quality planner for Seattle, bridge tenders are great at calling in violations: "They are up high, and when they see a black scum or a little slick, they let us know about it." [11] It's a concerted community effort and it works.

Texas Beach Campaign[12] – In September 1986 the Center for Environmental Education's Gulf Coast States regional office sponsored the first Texas statewide beach cleanup. Orchestrated by the office's director, Linda Maraniss, it was a tremendous success – some 3,000 volunteers came out for a day and spent three hours picking up trash. However, for one "beach buddy" who participated, the cleanup would become more than just a one-day event.

Maraniss had persuaded Texas State Land Commissioner Garry Mauro to help in the cleanup. Mauro says he expected to go out to the beach, pick up a few cans and bottles, and go home. But the volume of trash collected that day opened his eyes to the extent of the debris problem in Texas. Since that day Commissioner Mauro and his staff have gone on to organize an Adopt-a-Beach program in Texas, in which groups or individuals adopt a particular section of beach for one year and sponsor at least three cleanup efforts at the site.

Commissioner Mauro has become a leader in the campaign to fight marine debris. To date, all of the 172 miles of accessible coastline in Texas has been adopted and is being cared for by concerned citizens.

> *"Someday, though maybe not this year, my Hudson and my country will run clear."*
> Pete Seeger, folksinger and activist.

Saving the Hudson with a Song – Those of us who knew the Hudson River in the 1960s recall the sight and stench of sewage and industrial waste that fouled its waters from north of Albany down to the Atlantic Ocean. Much of the credit for the cleanup goes to Pete Seeger and the sloop *Clearwater*, the building of which he inspired in the mid '60s.

Clearwater is a full-scale replica of the sailing vessels that plied the Hudson in the nineteenth century. For over twenty years the sloop has served as a floating classroom to hundreds of thousands of schoolchildren, community leaders, and other concerned citizens including 10,000 members of *Clearwater* itself, each of whom is a part owner of the tall, proud ship.

Since its founding *Clearwater* has joined in some of the most significant initiatives to make the Hudson a clean river once again. Among its achievements are:

● helping lead the fight to clean the riverbed of tons of cancer-causing PCBs which are poisoning fish and plants and threatening human life.

● exposing the scandal that two-thirds of industries with permits to discharge chemicals dumped illegal amounts of lead, mercury, and other poisons into the river.

● helping beat back the wasteful, environmentally disastrous Westway proposed in federal court.

● saving a National Historic Landmark threatened with destruction in Poughkeepsie, N.Y., and successfully promoting the 107th Street pier in East Harlem.

● persuading New York state to set numerical water-quality standards instead of vague "guidelines" and fighting to save 95 new water standards in the face of intensive industry challenge.

For further information contact *Hudson River Sloop Clearwater*, 112 Market Street, Poughkeepsie, NY 12601; (914) 454-7673.

A Mini Handbook: What You Can Do about Ocean or River Pollution

1. *Small counts:* The extent and diversity of contamination should not discourage your desire to clean it up. Obviously, no one person working alone can address the whole scope of the problem, but you can effectively zero in on whatever aspect is appropriate for you. Even the smallest contribution you make is important, because it adds to work being done by other people, just as a single piece of a jigsaw puzzle fits into a bigger picture.

2. *Combined efforts* of many individuals add up to success. In some cases your action, small as it may seem at the time, can trigger a chain reaction of influence that moves mountainous corporations, legislatures, governors, even U.S. presidents.

3. *Define your goals:* A first principle of any action is to define what concerns you most and concentrate on that objective. Make it specific.

4. *Ask questions:* If you live near an estuary or river, question the condition of the water. Does it meet federal standards? How polluted is the water? Is the shellfish safe to eat? What are the main sources of contamination? What action is being taken by local agencies? by the press? Are any environmental groups working on the problem? Are the state or federal governments involved? Once you get the ball rolling, you'll soon discover you are not alone.

5. *Vote and communicate:* Even if you don't have at hand the resources available to a corporation or other large polluter, remember you possess one extremely valuable weapon – the vote. It is doubly meaningful. It can select and elect a representative sympathetic to the cause you are interested in, *and* can add muscle to your communications as you keep the representative constantly aware of where you stand on a particular issue. For example, the hundreds of individual letters of support sent to Californian congressional representatives and to the U.S. Department of Commerce in 1981 helped get Point Reyes and the Farallon Islands designated as a national marine sanctuary.

6. *Become part of the process:* City councils, local planning commissions, county boards of supervisors, state legislatures, and other government agencies will respond to your input – remember, they want to get reelected. By attending their meetings, most of which are by law open to the public, you can learn how they develop programs for wetland conservation, coastal management, ocean protection, and related issues. As you discover how the legislative system works, you become part of the process itself by raising questions and getting heard. (For more on this process, see chapter 11.)

7. *Join a group* like *Clearwater* in your own area; if there isn't one, be inspired by Pete Seeger and help create your own. Thus you can add your voice and contribution to a growing grass-roots movement that is becoming a major political force in the 1990s.

8. *For further information* on government agencies and environmental and other groups concerned with cleaning up ocean and coastal environments, see "Resources" at the end of this chapter.

Drinking Water - Toxins from Your Tap

About half the U.S. population drinks surface water – supplied from streams, rivers, lakes, and reservoirs – that may be polluted with acid rain, pesticides, radioactivity from nuclear plants, or wastes from industry and farms. The other half relies on ground water – from wells, springs, and aquifers (vast underground reservoirs) – that may be contaminated with human and animal wastes, chemicals from toxic waste dumps, or leaking oil-storage tanks. One gallon of gasoline, for example, can poison the drinking water for a community of 50,000 people. And there are more than two million underground gasoline storage tanks in the United States, one quarter of which are thought to be leaking. Once contaminated, ground water may stay that way for decades or longer, although the ground does, to some extent, act as a filter.

> *"You can use the latest toothpaste, then rinse your mouth with industrial waste."*
>
> *"Pollution," a song by Tom Lehrer*

In addition to gasoline and oil leakage, at least 42 million people in the United States, including 10 million children, are exposed to dangerous amounts of lead in their drinking water, according to the EPA. As we have seen (on p. 45), exposure to lead is extremely dangerous, especially in children. In general there has a decrease in lead exposure in the U.S. as a result of the ban on lead-based paints and the phasing out of leaded gasoline. However, the presence of lead in drinking water may be on the increase because acid rain "mobilizes" the lead that was used in water pipes for many years. (For more on this, see chapter 5, p. 100.)

If you live in the country, your water most probably comes from the ground; in a town, you are most likely to get surface water. As we shall see below, both sources are equally vulnerable.

Main Sources of Water Contamination:

Natural minerals and salts; decay products of uranium, radon, and uranium; human and animal organic waste; defective oil-storage tanks; leaking hazardous-waste landfills, ponds, and pits; intrusion of salt water into depleted aquifers near the seashore; agricultural runoff (fertilizers, pesticides, herbicides, fungicides); surface runoff (overflowing storm sewers, rainwater from oil-slicked or salt-treated highways, parking lots, etc.); underground injection of industrial waste; acid rain and snow.

Cancer-causing trihalomethanes (THMs) created by chlorination of water *(Treatment with chlorine is one of the most serious sources of drinking- water contamination!)*; copper sulfate, lime, and alum added to purify water.

Corrosion of piping materials, including lead and asbestos; bacteria and dirt from leaking pipes; cross connections (incorrect pressure gradients that can suck polluted water into pipes instead of pushing it out); contamination by chlorination and lead, which can also occur after treatment.

Five Main Contaminants in Water Supplies

Substance	Source	Effects
Chlorinated solvents	Industrial pollution – degreasing, chemical manufacture	Cancer
Trihalomethanes	Created by chemical reactions in water purified with chlorine	Liver/kidney damage; cancer
Lead	Old pipes and solder in public water-supply systems and older homes	Brain damage, high blood pressure, nerve disorders
PCBs	Waste from manufacturing, electric transformers	Liver damage, cancer
Bacteria and viruses	Overflow from sewers or septic tanks	Gastrointestinal diseases, meningitis

We All Live Downstream

Drinking-water pollution is at least as old as the Roman Empire, when aqueducts were poisoned by lead leaching from the pipes. In 1849 an English physician showed conclusively that contaminated water from the River Thames caused cholera epidemics in London. Yet in the United States it was not until the 20th century that adequate steps were taken to stem the spread of waterborne diseases with sand filters, sedimentation, chlorination, and other sanitary measures.

Bacterial infection is still a problem where shallow wells are infiltrated by seepage from antiquated septic systems. There is also widespread pollution by toxic chemicals from industry, farming, and other sources, including perhaps your own home.

Because it is such a widespread threat to public health, water pollution is a problem that must not be shelved. It can be cleaned up significantly, provided we are willing to make the effort. Many ways that we can address the problem are given in the following pages.

Long-Term Strategies

When President Ford signed the Safe Drinking Water Act in 1974, he promised safe drinking water for every single American.

Unfortunately, this promise has yet to be kept. It can only be done if the EPA, the responsible agency, carries out its congressional mandate. This means getting tough with states, public water systems, private industry, and others who are openly breaking the law. In 1988, for example, it devoted a pitiful 1.3 percent of its effort to enforcement – at a time when there were 98,000 violations from the previous year against which no action had apparently been taken.[13]

Contamination of drinking water stems from many causes, one of which is the use of antiquated treatment systems that could be easily changed. In Canada and Europe two technologies – granular activated carbon filtration (GAC) and a process known as packed tower aeration – have been proven much more effective in removing organic pollutants than chlorination, still widely used in the United States and itself a source of dangerous contamination. Yet less than 100 of 79,000 publicly regulated water systems in this country have switched over. In Cincinnati, the first major utility to install GAC, the projected increase in cost was only 21 cents per thousand gallons – $27 per household a year – hardly an extortionate price to pay for clean, safe water.[14]

Toxic Dumping

A pervasive cause of drinking water pollution, toxic dumping is the direct result of policies and programs sanctioned by the government that allow astronomical amounts of toxic chemicals to be simply poured into rivers, lakes, streams, and other parts of the environment. In the words of an important 1988 study, *Troubled Waters on Tap*, published by the Center for Study of Responsive Law: "In effect, hundreds of thousands of sanctioned waste dumps, millions of permitted wastewater discharges and a spectrum of unregulated indirect releases of toxic contamination into air, land and water have created the drinking water crisis." [15]

Solar Aquatics: The Ecological Solution

" *Every time the restrictions on one type of pollutant get stronger, the chemicals to remove it get stronger. That can't be the right way to go. It must be possible to use sunshine and ecology to purify water the way nature does.* " – John Todd, president, Ocean Arks International[16]

To show that ecological purification of water wastes – solar aquatics – is feasible, Todd founded Ocean Arks International, a nonprofit research center, and the for-profit Ecological Engineering Associates (EEA) in Woods Hole, Mass.

> *The system had the natural purifying cycles of a lake or stream, except that the processes we established were much faster than those occurring in nature.*

The first project was a small prototype facility at the Sugarbush Ski Resort in Vermont with the capacity of treating the wastes of about ten households. It represented a new direction in wastewater treatment, depending on sunlight and photosynthesis for its primary energy source and entirely avoiding the use of hazardous chemicals. The system, said Todd, "broke ranks with the wastewater industry by purposely not separating the solids from the liquid portion of the waste. We did not add chemicals, like aluminum salts, to produce two separate waste streams, sludges, and supernatents. Instead, the whole waste stream was kept into suspension and integrated into a wide range of ecological food chains, the end points of which were fish, flowers, trees, and clean water. The system had the natural purifying cycles of a lake or stream, except that the processes we established were much faster than those occurring in nature." [17]

In the summer of 1988 Ocean Arks undertook an experiment at Harwich on Cape Cod, Mass., to treat septage, the highly concentrated wastes from septic tanks, which is hard to purify and almost impossible to treat cost effectively. It is thirty to one hundred times more concentrated than sewage and contains toxic substances, greases, and fats which gum up the works in conventional treatment plants.

The Harwich research project was unique in that half the construction cost was supported by a vote of local taxpayers at their annual meeting. The state paid for the rest through its Centers of Excellence program and three private foundations provided design, logistical, and staff support. The design is unique in the annals of waste treatment. Twenty one interconnected tanks were placed in a row on a gentle slope. The septage entered at the uphill end and reemerged, purified, some ten days later. At the halfway point, the flow was diverted into a 120-foot-long, engineered marsh, then pumped back into the remaining tanks for the rest of the treatment journey. The facility produced clean water and, in so doing, changed the rules for the treatment of concentrated liquid wastes. The total capacity of the solar aquatic facility was 12,000 gallons. It treated one-tenth of Harwich's waste or up to 1,200 gallons a day.

> *"It must be possible to use sunshine and ecology to purify water the way nature does."*
> John Todd, president,
> Ocean Arks International

As Todd reports, the results of the project were extraordinary: "During the [four-and-a-half-month] trials we pumped wastes which were loaded with fats and greases from restaurants, oils and solvents from households and small businesses, as well as cleaning agents and assorted wastes from an open pit lagoon. Metals, including lead and mercury, were present." [18] The influent before treatment contained 14 of 15 top EPA priority organic pollutants, most of them carcinogenic, and fecal coliform bacteria in the millions per one hundred milliliter (ml) sample. The septage lagoons were, in effect, toxic waste sites. Heavy metals and 13 of the 14 priority pollutants were removed from the water by hundreds of species of organisms. The remainder, toluene, was 99.9 percent removed by the treatment process. When fish in the downstream end of the system were analyzed for PCBs, dioxin, and related toxic compounds, their livers and flesh were found free of the contaminants. Fecal coliform bacteria were largely eliminated, with coliform levels as low as 2 per 100 ml, compared with 200 per 100 ml allowed for swimming water. Nitrate levels were reduced significantly below well drinkingwater standards.

In May 1989 the town of Harwich voted to pay EEA to treat 4,800 gallons of septage a day in a new prototype commercial facility. Shortly after that Ocean Arks and EEA were invited to set up and operate a major solar aquatics research unit at the Narragansett Bay Commission's Field Point center, the main wastewater treatment center for the city of Providence, R.I.

The success of Ocean Arks-EEA projects has attracted attention from Scandinavia, Spain, Yugoslavia, and other countries, as well as from the federal and state governments in the U.S. from which, it is to be hoped, funding might come for additional research in innovative solar aquatics work at Harwich, Providence and other locations.

What You Can Do about Water Pollution

As we have seen from the above examples, technological solutions to clearing up our water are available. The reason they are not being applied more vigorously is political. When sufficiently large numbers of people (us) become aware of the threat of polluted water and when we demand action by our elected representatives at all levels from the local board of health to the president of the United States, the problem will be solved. The keys are in your hands.

1. *The Safe Drinking Water Act* (SDWA) gives you the right to know from your local water supplier where your water comes from, how it is purified, which contaminants it has been tested for, what, if any, are past or current pollutant levels that violate federal standards, and how the public was informed of the violation. (For more information on safe drinking water laws, see chapter 10, pp. 233-235.)

2. SDWA gives you the right to bring civil suit against your local water system, your state, or the federal government if they fail to do their job. It requires your public-water system to treat contaminated water chemically or to install cleanup equipment to reduce the contaminants to safe levels. Current amendments to SDWA require the EPA to set standards for 83 chemicals, including the most common drinking-water contaminants. They also require public notification of contaminant-level violations within 14 days of their detection and, so long as the violations continue, every 3 months thereafter. Other provisions of the act include an immediate ban on lead pipe and solder, protection of sole-source aquifers, and special monitoring of industrial and municipal underground injection wells.

3. *Join the efforts* already underway by numerous environmental and consumer groups to enforce the law. That these efforts are so widespread is testimony to the generally dismal track record of federal and state enforcement agencies. *But do not be discouraged.* These offices are staffed by people very much like yourself. Most of them are conscientious and hardworking. They are also concerned about their own and the public's health and will usually try to do their best to help you. As in any situation where you are seeking information or advice, it helps to know the right agency and the right person to approach.

4. Although you can, for example, contact the EPA through their Safe Drinking Water Hotline – (800) 426-4791 or, in Washington, D.C. 382-5533 – it might be more productive first to *contact your local or state environmental department or public health office.*

5. *Multiply the effect* of your effort by enlisting the help and resources of one or more of the independent groups already engaged in the campaign for cleaning up our troubled waters. These include the Clean Water Action Project, the Center for Study of Responsive Law, Citizen's Clearinghouse for Hazardous Waste, Water Quality Association, NRDC, Ocean Arks International, Sierra Club, Friends of the Earth, INFORM, and the Environmental Task Force. (For details on how to contact these organizations, see "Resources," immediately below.) From these groups and from your local press and yellow pages you will discover a vast network of citizens' committees, study groups, and task forces that are focusing on specific water-quality issues, some of which may be identical or similar to your own problem or concern. You will also be able to enlist their help in approaching local, state, and federal bodies.

6. For details on how to organize your efforts at community, state and national levels see chapter 11.

7. For specifics on *drinking water safety* see chapter 12, pp. 292-298.

RESOURCES

In addition to the sources listed below, the material in this chapter is based primarily on information provided by the EPA, the National Oceanic and Atmospheric Administration, the U.S. Coast Guard, the University of Maryland Sea Grant College, the University of Massachusetts Water Resources Research Center, the Cousteau Society, Concern Inc., INFORM, the Center for the Study of Responsive Law, as well as chapter 20, "Water Pollution," in the indispensable textbook *Living in the Environment* by G. Tyler Miller, Jr., (Belmont, Calif.: Wadsworth, 1987).

The following is provided to help you locate additional resources on the topics covered in this chapter.

1. International Organizations

— *International Association of Hydrological Sciences*, 2000 Florida Avenue NW, Washington, DC 20009; (202) 462-6903.
— *International Bottled Water Association*, 113 North Henry Street, Alexandria, VA 22314.
— *International Maritime Organization*, 4 Albert Embankment, London SE1 7SR, England.
— *Law of the Sea Treaty*, Secretariat, United Nations, Room 1827A, New York, NY 10017.
— *Regional Seas Activity Center*, United Nations Environmental Program, Palais des Nations, 1121 Geneva 10, Switzerland.

2. U.S. Government

— *Department of Commerce*, 14th Street and Constitution Avenue NW, Washington, DC 20230:
  National Oceanic and Atmospheric Administration.
  National Marine Fisheries Service, 1825 Connecticut Avenue NW, Washington, DC 20235.
— *National Ocean Service*, Marine Pollution Programs Office, Ocean and Coastal Resource Management, 11400 Rockville Pike, Rockville, MD 20852.
— *Department of Energy*, Sub Seabed Disposal Program, Geologic Repositories Office, 1000 Independence Avenue SW, Washington, DC 20585.
— *Department of State*, Oceans and International Environmental and Scientific Affairs Bureau, 2201 C Street SW, Washington, DC 20520.
— *EPA*: Office of Drinking Water and Criteria and Standards Division, Safe Drinking Water Hotline (800) 426-4791.
Office of Groundwater; (202) 382-7077.
— *Marine Mammal Commission*, 1625 Eye Street NW, Washington, DC 20460.
— *National Advisory Committee on Oceans and Atmosphere*, 3300 Whitehaven Street NW, Washington, DC 20235
— *National Ocean Policy Study*, U.S. Senate Commerce Committee, 527 Hart Senate Office Building, Washington, DC 20510.
— *National Oceanic and Atmospheric Administration*, Rockville, MD 20852.

3. Environmental Organizations

— *Antarctica Project*, 1845 Calvert Street NW, Washington, DC 20009.
— *Center for Environmental Education*, 1725 DeSales Street, NW, Washington, DC 20036. Publishes many important reference works on the oceans.
— *Citizens for Ocean Law*, 1601 Connecticut Avenue NW, Washington, DC 20009.
— *Clean Water Action Project*, 317 Pennsylvania Avenue SE, Washington, DC, 20003.
— *Cousteau Society*, 930 West 21st Street, Norfolk, VA 23517.
— *Earth Island Institute*, 300 Broadway, San Francisco, CA 94133.

— *Greenpeace*, 1436 U Street, Washington, DC 20009; (202) 462-1177.

— *Hudson River Sloop Clearwater*, 112 Market Street, Poughkeepsie, NY 12601; (914) 454-7673.

— *National Demonstration Water Project*, 602 South King Street, Arlington, VA 22209; (703) 478-8652. Works through affiliates to address water-quality issues.

— *Oceanic Society*, 1536 16th Street NW, Washington, DC 20036.

— *Sea Shepherd*, P.O. Box 7000-S, Redondo Beach, CA 90277.

4. Trade, Industry, and Research Organizations

— *National Ocean Industries Association*, 1050 17th Street NW, Washington, DC 20036.

— *Ocean Arks International and Solar Aquatics*, One Locust Street, Falmouth, MA 02540; (508) 540-6801.

— *Society of the Plastics Industry*, 1275 K Street NW, Washington, DC 20005.

— *Water Quality Association*, 4151 Napierville Road, Lisle, IL 60532; (312) 369-1600.

5. Water-Testing Laboratories and Consultants

— *Clean Water Fund of North Carolina*, Asheville, NC; (704) 251-0518.

— *Hach Chemical Company*, P.O. Box 389, Loveland, CO 80537.

— *National Sanitation Foundation*, 3475 Plymouth Road, P.O. Box 1468, Ann Arbor, MI 48106. This is an independent not-for-profit organization that tests home water filters for the Water Quality Association and other manufacturers.

— *Pure Water Place*, P.O. Box 6715, Longmont, CO 80501 (303) 776-0056.

— *Rocky Mountain Student Environmental Health Program*, Colorado; (303) 491-5128.

— *Virginia Student Environmental Health Program*, Arlington, VA; (703) 961-6683.

— *Water Information Network*, P.O. Box 909, Ashland, OR 97520; (503) 488-5029. Provides information on water contamination problems, purification options, and product evaluations.

— *WaterTest Corporation*, Box 186, New London, NH 03257; (800) H20-TEST.

(Note: There are many more testing labs than those given here. This list is for general guidance only, and inclusion does not imply endorsement of their work.)

6. Further Reading

— *Citizens Guide to Plastics in the Ocean.* Washington, D.C.: Center for Environmental Education, 1988.

— *Coastal Waters in Jeopardy: Reversing the Decline and Protecting America's Coastal Resources.* Oversight report of the Committee on Merchant Marine and Fisheries, December 1988, Serial No. 100-E. Washington, D.C.: U.S. Government Printing Office, 1989.

— *The Cousteau Almanac*, Jacques-Yves Cousteau. New York: Doubleday, 1981.

— *The Delaware Estuary*, Tracey L. Bryant and Jonathan R. Pennock. Newark, Del.: University of Delaware Sea Grant College, 1988.

— *The Edge of the Sea*, Rachel Carson. Boston: Houghton Mifflin, 1979.

— *The Frail Ocean*, Wesley Marx. New York: Ballantine Books, 1970.

— *Plastics in the Ocean*, K.J. O'Hara, N. Atkins, and S. Iudicello. Washington, D.C.: Center for Environmental Education, 1987.

— *The Poisoned Well: New Strategies for Groundwater Protection*, ed. Eric P. Jorgensen. Sierra Club Legal Defense Fund. Washington, D.C.: Island Press, 1989.

— *The Sea Around Us*, Rachel Carson. New York: Oxford University Press, 1950.

— *Tracing a River's Toxic Pollution: A Case Study of the Hudson*, Steven O. Rohmann. New York: INFORM, Phase 1, 1985, Phase II, 1987.

Note: For a list of publications on drinking water see "Resources" at the end of chapter 12.

4

AIR POLLUTION

Clearing the Air

"At least 150 million Americans live in places where air quality, if that's the word, is below federal standards." – Senator Max Baucus[1]

Take a deep breath. Hold it in for a moment. The odds are that what you have just inhaled is polluted. In Chicago, Denver, Los Angeles, Washington, D.C., New York, Boston, or virtually any urban area you live in, the air you take in every five seconds almost certainly does not meet federal standards. . . . Now you can let it out!

Air pollution is one of the oldest human plagues, as we know from smoke-charred walls and ceilings in prehistoric cave dwellings. In 13th-century England the king banned coal burning while Parliament was in session because smog hampered the work of government.

Fossil-Fuel Pollution

Now, as then, the prime culprits are fossil fuels – basically coal and oil. From electric power plants, factories, smelters, cars, buses, trucks, airplanes, and even lawn mowers these fuels produce toxic air pollutants that endanger public health, wildlife, vegetation, buildings, railroads, statues, gravestones – all they touch. Causing the damage are the substances these fuels produce when burned: sulfur dioxide, carbon monoxide, nitrogen dioxide, particulate matter, hydrocarbons, ozone, and lead and other metals.

"Far Exceeds Our Worst Fears"

A first national survey of industrial air pollution, issued by the EPA in 1989, reported that an estimated 2.4 billion pounds of chemicals believed to cause cancer, neurological disease, or birth defects were emitted into the air in 1987. Over one third came from the chemical industry; other major sources are factories that produce metals, paper, plastics, rubber, electric equipment, petroleum and oil products, and furniture.

The actual totals are far higher, the EPA says, because the study did not include pollution from automobiles, toxic-waste dumps, and the many companies emitting under 75,000 pounds of toxic substances a year. The distribution of these toxic industrial pollutants on a state-by-state basis is shown in the map below.

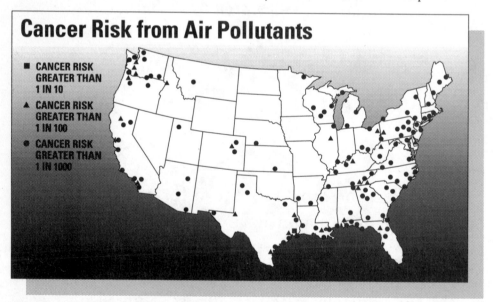

Cancer Risk from Air Pollutants

- ■ CANCER RISK GREATER THAN 1 IN 10
- ▲ CANCER RISK GREATER THAN 1 IN 100
- ● CANCER RISK GREATER THAN 1 IN 1000

"The magnitude of this problem far exceeds our worst fears" said Representative Henry A. Waxman, a California Democrat, chairperson of the House Energy and Commerce Committee's Subcommittee on Health and the Environment that made the EPA survey public.[2]

Polluted Air: What's in It for You?

Air pollution takes many forms, all harmful to human health and the environment – smoke, soot, grit, smog, fog, and acid precipitation (rain, snow, mist, dry acid deposition). Those regulated by the EPA since the 1970s include the following:

- *Sulfur dioxide (SO₂)*, an acrid, colorless gas created by fossil-fuel combustion; when mixed with water vapor in the atmosphere, it produces sulfuric acid in the form of a highly irritating mist that is corrosive to just about anything it contacts, including marble, iron, and steel. At moderately high concentrations, sulfur oxides can affect breathing and irritate the upper respiratory tract.
- *Carbon monoxide (CO)*, another product of burning fossil fuels; it forms in the air when fuel is incompletely burned (does not get enough oxygen). Some two-thirds of this pollutant comes from internal-combustion engines. CO reacts with hemoglobin in the blood, and can deprive the body of oxygen, resulting in symptoms such as impaired judgment, headache, and fatigue. Levels of CO inside vehicles may approach 100 parts per million (ppm) in traffic jams and 50 ppm on freeways during rush hours, contributing to Los Angeles-style smogs.

When the burning fuel gets enough oxygen, as in an automobile catalytic converter, the carbon monoxide is oxidized into carbon dioxide (CO_2), which is nontoxic but an important contributor to the greenhouse effect (see chapter 7, pp. 137-144).
- *Nitrogen dioxide (NO₂)*, a suffocating, reddish-brown gas formed from the reaction of oxygen with nitric oxide, which is produced when fuel is burned at high temperatures; it comes mainly from motor-vehicle exhausts, power stations, and industrial boilers, but is also emitted directly in the manufacture of fertilizers and other chemicals. Under the influence of sunlight, nitrogen dioxide reacts with gaseous hydrocarbons to form photochemical oxidants (like ozone) which, along with particulates, form photochemical smog. It irritates the lungs, causes bronchitis and pneumonia, and lowers resistance to influenza and other respiratory infections.

Nitrogen oxides are also a major component of acid rain (see chapter 5) as well as adding excess nitrate ions to aquatic ecosystems. This oversupply of nitrates can stimulate extremely rapid growth of algae and other aquatic plants, which depletes the water of vital oxygen and causes massive fish kills (in Chesapeake Bay, for example).
- *Particulates*, known also as TSPs (total suspended particulates); these are minute dusts or liquid droplets given off by fossil-fuel combustion and other sources. Borne up by air currents, they are prevalent in industrialized urban areas.

Small particles (which average 10 microns or 1/1000 of a millimeter in size), known as "respirable" particles, have recently been added to the list of regulated pollutants because of their ability to penetrate deep into the lungs and into the bloodstream. Larger TSPs, thrown into the air by stone-crushing operations, soil erosion, forest fires, and volcanic eruptions, are found mainly in rural regions.
- *Hydrocarbons* – benzene, methane, and butane – come from incomplete combustion of fossil fuels in automobiles and furnaces, and from evaporation of industrial solvents and oil spills, forest fires, and plant decay. Hydrocarbon pollutants are converted into photochemical smog by the action of sunlight.
- *Ozone*, a pale blue, highly reactive gas, is created by electrical discharges from lightning and high-voltage equipment or from the interaction of nitrogen oxides and hydrocarbons from motor vehicles and industry, under the influence of sunlight. Ozone is irritating to mucous membranes and inflames eyes and the upper respiratory tract.

Ironically, the ozone in the upper atmosphere is life-protecting and shields the earth from the sun's harmful ultraviolet radiation. (The role of the ozone layer is discussed at greater length in chapter 7, pp. 139-140.)

● *Lead*, once commonly added to gasoline to raise the octane rating, is emitted from automobile tailpipes, industrial smelting, and battery manufacture. Its use in gasoline has been systematically reduced by the EPA over the past ten years. In the U.S. most of the industrial use of lead is located in the Midwest, particularly in urban centers and in areas where metal smelting is carried out. Concentrating in blood, bone, and soft tissue, lead is not readily excreted from the body, affecting the nervous system and the kidneys and other organs. Lead from auto exhausts accumulates in city streets and presents a serious health threat to children who play there.

Effects of Air Pollution on the Human Body

Dizziness

Headache/migraine

Irritation of eyes

Stuffy nose, sneezing, nasal discharge

Nausea, vomiting

Coughing, sore throat, colds laryngitis

Constricted airway, asthma, bronchitis, shortness of breath, emphysema, chest pains, pneumonia, lung cancer

Heart disease

Stomach poisoning, stomach cancer

Diseases of blood vessels

Kidney damage

Allergies

Because of the decrease in lead content in unleaded gas and because more cars are using unleaded fuel, there has been a substantial reduction in atmospheric lead from this source – from 34,800 tons of lead in 1984 to an estimated 1,100 tons in 1988. However, the *overall* use of lead – in indoor paints and tin cans, for example – has increased to the point that many experts consider it to be our number 1 toxics problem.

How Air Pollution Affects Your Health

Air pollution is particularly harmful to the young, the old, the poor in industrialized, urban areas, and cigarette smokers and people afflicted with lung and heart diseases. These groups account for well over half the total population of the United States and other industrialized countries. Injurious to animal and plant life, it has also become a serious public-health and environmental problem in the developing world.

Some effects of air pollution on the human body – from dizziness to allergies can be visualized in the adjacent diagram.

Damage to the Environment

The effects of air pollution on plant life include leaf spotting and decay, decreased rate of photosynthesis, decreased crop yields – vegetables and fruit grown near large cities are particularly vulnerable – and severe damage to trees. (For details on forest destruction by acid rain, see the next chapter.) In Ontario, Canada, pollution from an iron-sintering factory virtually destroyed an entire forest ecosystem 5 miles downwind and caused plant and tree damage 20 miles away. Photo-chemical smog produced in Los Angeles has severely damaged trees in most of the San Bernardino National Forest 78 miles to the east.[3] Yearly damage from air pollution to plants, crops, and trees in North America is estimated by the EPA to amount to considerably more than $1 billion in lost value.

The Risk Is Growing

In response to a series of air pollution disasters in the 1950s and '60s, the federal government acted to offset the worst effects of industrial and urban smog. Since the passage of the Clean Air Act in 1970 some pollutants have been reduced, but others – carbon monoxide and ozone, especially – remain at danger levels in most big cities nationwide.

At least 150 million people in the United States live in places where air quality is below public-health standards.

In 1988 urban air pollution reached record levels, posing a serious and growing health threat, especially to children.[4]

Smog from Vehicles

In the cities the campaign to control smog from cars, trucks, and buses has lost ground because of the enormous increase in the volume of vehicles on the road. Technical measures such as improved catalytic converters, more efficient engines, and cleaner fuels simply have not kept pace with the sheer weight of numbers.

According to the National Highway Traffic Safety Administration, there were 183 million vehicles on the roads in 1988, compared with 147 million in 1977, a 25-percent increase. The number of trucks, mostly with heavily polluting diesel engines, went up by 40 percent to a total of 41 million.[5]

Drop in the Bucket

In response to a federal mandate, sales of gasoline containing lead have dropped sharply, but oil refiners have been allowed to add more light hydrocarbons to their fuel. This saves them money but has made the gasoline more volatile, especially in warm weather. To protect the health of gas-station attendants and customers, and to reduce vapor escaping into the atmosphere, gas stations in California, New Jersey, and New York are now required to dispense fuel from pressurized pumps with hose tips that make a tight seal with the car's filling pipe and return vapor to underground tanks – a drop in the bucket, but every little bit helps.

Experiments are being carried out with alternative, nonpetroleum fuels, the two most promising of which are ethanol (a corn-based product) and compressed natural gas. These significantly cleaner but somewhat more costly fuels are being tested in a small number of vehicles in New York, Los Angeles, and other cities. But, as long as gasoline prices are kept low, there is little financial incentive for the automobile industry to mass-produce such engines. Many experts agree with William Chameides, a geophysicist at Georgia Institute of Technology studying smog formation, who believes the problem can't be solved as long as internal-combustion engines dominate the roads: "In the long run I believe we must get away from all forms of combustion and perhaps go to electric vehicles. Every other approach is just a stopgap remedy."[6]

Gray Air

In terms of amount emitted in the United States, *carbon monoxide* is the number-one air pollutant and the automobile by far the major source. However, in terms of human health, *sulfur dioxide* and *particulates* rank as the top two offenders. The major source of these hazards is burning coal and oil at electricity power plants and in a wide range of industrial operations, particularly pulp and paper mills, iron and steel mills, smelters, chemical plants, and petroleum refineries.

Industrial air pollution, sometimes called gray air, is prevalent in regions with cold, wet, winter climates – Chicago, Pittsburgh, Detroit, Cleveland, Philadelphia, Boston, and New York, cities that depend heavily on burning coal and oil for heating, manufacturing, and electric power and on the automobile as a prime means of transportation. Sulfur dioxide and particulates are also major components of acid rain. (The role they play and how they can be controlled are examined in the next chapter.)

Dust Bowl Revisited

For many people, soil erosion and dust bowls are thought of as something that happened in the Depression years of the 1930s. However, the highly mechanized "factory farming" methods practiced by agribusiness during the last 30 years have eroded vast areas of the North American breadbasket from Texas to Saskatchewan. Nationwide, 5 billion tons of topsoil are displaced annually along with thousands of farmers who can no longer pay their mortgages. For every ton of grain produced they lose six tons of topsoil.[7] Much of it is added to the already polluted air, along with pesticides and additional dusts churned up by cattle feedlots. The remainder goes into our rivers, lakes, and streams.

A possible consequence of the greenhouse effect, drought is an additional source of soil erosion. This was dramatically recorded in a *New York Times* report of March 19, 1989: "Then on Tuesday [March 14] one of the worst fears of Kansas farmers in a drought year was realized. High winds, with gusts up to 72 miles an hour at one point, raised great clouds of dust with tops up to 10,000 feet high. By midafternoon much of Kansas's wind-driven topsoil was blasting Kansas City, Mo., to the east, and the next day it was sifting down on lawns in Arkansas."[8]

Los Angeles Cleanup Scenario

"You can either preserve the California dream, or preside over the California nightmare." – Jan Heidt, mayor, Santa Clarita, Calif.

Los Angeles is an environmental disaster zone, on a par with the world's most polluted cities – Mexico City, Beijing, São Paulo, and New Delhi. The L.A. basin with its 12 million inhabitants and 8 million cars suffers choking air pollution, the worst of any North American city. In 1988 the 13,000 square-mile region violated federal health standards for ozone on 176 days. Its carbon monoxide pollution is greater than New York's.

In addition to highway driving, the leading contaminators of L.A.'s air include major automobile-connected companies – Chevron, Arco, Mobil, and a large GM assembly plant – Universal Studios, and Disneyland.

Triple Play: As well as inflicting widespread respiratory and health damage on many of its inhabitants, L.A.'s chemically contaminated air could cause cancers in an estimated 44,000 people when the state population hits 40 million in the next decade.[9]

On March 17, 1989, Los Angeles, or more precisely the South Coast Association of Governments (SCAG) and the South Coast Air Quality Management District (SCAQMD), overwhelmingly approved a far-reaching plan to make the air in their region clean enough to meet federal standards by the early 2000s.

The Southern California officials voted to impose drastic measures that will impact on every aspect of life in the region. The three-stage plan requires all cars to be converted to electric power or other clean fuels by 2007. Other measures, some starting in 1989, include stepped-up ride sharing, building housing closer to job centers, and new controls on electric utilities, oil refineries, industries, and even on businesses such as commercial bakeries, breweries, and paint manufacturers.

Lifestyle Changes. The plan also calls for significant changes in lifestyle that will be brought about by virtually eliminating free parking, outlawing gasoline-powered lawn mowers, and a ban on using starter fluid for barbecues.

"With today's action, we cast off the attitude that this region is doomed to smog." said Pat Nemeth, deputy executive officer of SCAQMD.[10]

Resistance from Business and Labor. Although there is heated protest from some business interests and labor-union officials that stringent controls will result in the loss of thousands of jobs, and despite deep concern from the automobile industry that the restrictions will force "premature and technologically unfeasible" changes on cars, the four-county region is under the gun of a federal court order to comply with national standards for ozone, carbon monoxide, nitrogen oxides, and particulates by 2010. SCAQMD estimates that compliance will cost $2.8 billion a year for the first five years but will also result in 80,000 new jobs by that time.

"Everyone Is Being Enlisted." Stage 1 of the plan places sharp control on any materials – deodorant sprays, paints, solvents – that emit hydrocarbons or ozone-producing gases. It also calls for new controls on boilers, trashburners, and industrial heaters. Stage 2, from 1993 to 1998, will require conversion of 40 percent of cars and 70 percent of trucks and buses to clean fuels. The third stage, which assumes breakthroughs in technology, would ban all gasoline vehicles by 2007. Between now and that date the plan calls for the adoption of 120 separate air-pollution controls.

As the *Los Angeles Times* pointed out in its endorsement of the plan, the struggle for clean air over Southern California has taken a turn for the better. Pollution control, they wrote, is no longer a matter of low-intensity conflict with a few big, obvious targets – automobile tailpipes, power-plant smokestacks, oil refineries and the like. "Now, everybody in Southern California is being invited to join in spreading the clean-air campaign to cover dozens of polluting activities rather than just a few big ones. More precisely, everyone is being enlisted."[11] The L.A. plan is strongly supported by the American Lung Association, Clean Air Coalition, and other environmental groups. It promises to be the forerunner of similar air-quality campaigns throughout the United States.

Indoor Air Pollution

Assuming that you are reading this book indoors, take another deep breath and prepare for a surprise. You have almost certainly inhaled more air pollutants than if you were outside!

The evidence is not as visibly dramatic as a chemically orange New Jersey sunset or a hazy brown L.A. smog. But, according to the EPA, the level of air pollutants in your own home or workplace or your children's school is often five times or more higher than outside levels.[13] Aside from specific sources of pollution that we will examine below, one reason for increased indoor air pollution is the tighter construction of new buildings.

Indoor air pollutants are mostly colorless and odorless and, because you don't suspect them, they often remain undetected. This can pose a serious health threat when you consider that most of us spend 12 hours a day indoors – young children, the elderly, and the ill even longer. The National Academy of Sciences estimates the annual national health-care cost of indoor air pollution to be between $15 billion and $100 billion.[14]

Now for the good news: You can improve indoor air pollution more easily than outdoor. To discover how, let's look first at the underlying causes.

Indoor Air Pollution – Causes and Effects

Some pollutants are instantly detectable: smoke from a fire or vapor from ammonia, causing breathing difficulty, burning eyes, choking, even asphyxiation. Others are more insidious because they act over long periods of time, sometimes many years: asbestos, formaldehyde, and radon. Their symptoms (ranging from dizziness, headaches, and fatigue to damage to the central nervous system, lungs, heart, kidneys, and liver, and eventually to cancer) are harder to link directly with the source. While many of these may seem to be minor irritants, they become a real and present danger when added together and concentrated within four walls over the long periods of time we spend indoors.

● *Detectable contaminants:* The more common sources of indoor air pollution are wood, coal, or kerosene fires, unvented gas stoves and ovens, gas or oil furnaces and water heaters, aerosol cleaners and disinfectants, cleaners that include chlorine or ammonia, self-cleaning floor waxes, air fresheners, insect sprays, and perhaps the most deadly of all – cigarette smoke.

● *Undetectable contaminants:* Many building materials, finishes, and furnishings contain substances that are injurious, but whose effects are not always immediately apparent. Most threatening are asbestos, formaldehyde, lead, and radon.[15]

Asbestos, used widely by the construction industry until quite recently, is a material made of natural minerals that separate into strong, very fine fibers. Once prized for its heat resistance and durability, it was used extensively for insulating heating pipes and boilers and in asbestos-cement boards placed behind wood stoves. It is now linked to severe lung diseases – asbestosis, mesothelioma, and lung cancer. When released indoors asbestos's tiny fibers remain suspended in the air for long periods of time, staying in the lungs when inhaled.

Because each exposure can increase the buildup of asbestos in the body, government control programs are aimed primarily at protecting schoolchildren and persons whose work involves exposure to the substance. The EPA has prohibited most asbestos use and is currently planning a total ban.[16]

What You Can Do about Indoor Air Pollution

1. Ventilators and Air Cleaners

Ventilators. You can significantly lower the concentrations of air pollution in your own home by increasing the circulation between outdoors and indoors. Opening windows and doors, when weather permits, increases the natural ventilation rate. Turning on kitchen, bathroom, or workshop exhaust fans is a simple way to remove contaminants from those areas.

It is especially important to take these steps whenever you get involved in activities that create high levels of pollution – painting, paint stripping, floor waxing, photographic processing, model making, and many other hobbies.

Another way to increase indoor air flow is to install *heat-recovery ventilators* (also known as air-to-air heat exchangers) in your home. These devices increase ventilation by drawing outside air indoors and conserve energy by recovering heat from air that is exhausted outdoors. They can be installed either as window units in existing homes or in central air systems in new homes (or when remodeling).

Before buying a mechanical ventilation device, however, write to *Renewable Energy Information*, P.O. Box 8900, Silver Spring, MD 20907, for the U.S. Department of Energy fact sheet, *Air-to-Air Heat Exchangers*. Then consult a mechanical engineer either through your local yellow pages (under "Engineers") or the nearest branch of the American Society of Heating, Refrigerating, and Air Conditioning Engineers (ASHRAE); for address see "Resources," p.94.

Air Cleaners: There are many types and sizes on the market, from cheap tabletop models to sophisticated (and expensive) whole-house systems. Some are effective at removing airborne particles; others, including most smaller units, don't do a very good job. Air cleaners are generally not designed to remove gases or vapors and are not substitutes for adequate ventilation.

How well an air cleaner works depends on how well it collects aerosols and particles from indoor air (usually measured as a percentage efficiency rate) and how much air it draws through the cleaning or filtering agent (measured in cubic feet per minute). Another important factor is the *strength* of the polluting source, which might overpower most tabletop units.

People sensitive to particular pollutants often find that air cleaners are helpful only when used in conjunction with efforts to remove the polluting source. *Note: The EPA advises NOT using air cleaners for radon contamination because they do not diminish the amount of radon entering the home.*[17]

2. Asbestos

Asbestos is an extremely dangerous substance found in many buildings constructed before the mid-1970s. If you suspect the presence of asbestos in your home or one you are thinking of buying, have it checked by a specialist.

You can also get advice from the *EPA Consumer Product Safety Commission* hotline (800-638-2772 or, in Maryland, 800-492-8363). There is an asbestos coordinator at each of the EPA's regional offices (see list on p. 30).

Many states have asbestos-control programs and can be contacted for a list of approved laboratories which will analyze materials for asbestos content at a fee of about $50.

If the presence of asbestos is confirmed – and especially if the material in question is crumbling or powdery – you have three options, all of which should be carried out by a professional:

Removal is the most radical solution. If the cost of repairing the damage is 60 percent or more of removal, it is preferable to have the offending material completely taken out. This is usually a time-consuming and expensive process, costing $100 or more an hour, and must be done according to EPA guidelines that require sealing off the affected area and maintaining it under "negative air pressure."

In most cases, it's a good idea to vacate the premises while asbestos removal is under way. However, an independent inspector such as an industrial hygienist can often provide an invaluable service on major removal projects by making sure work is carried out properly. The industrial hygienist inspects the work and takes air samples to measure the potential presence of airborne asbestos outside the enclosure and upon completion of the work.

Enclosure means permanently covering up asbestos-containing areas (crawlspaces, for example) and caulking all joints so that they are airtight. If the asbestos is not badly damaged or disturbed, enclosure is preferable to removal (and considerably cheaper).

Encapsulation is used to seal in objects that are not easily enclosed (such as a boiler); it is usually done with paint, epoxy, or fiberglass cloth. Both enclosure and encapsulation must be done by an EPA- or state-certified asbestos contractor. If the asbestos is intact and there is little potential for it to become airborne, your safest bet may be just to leave it alone.

For further information, refer to the EPA's *Guidance for Controlling Asbestos-Containing Materials in Buildings* or their *Asbestos Waste Management Guidance* booklet (see "Resources," p. 94).

For information on how to deal with asbestos in schools contact the *Asbestos School Hazard Abatement Act (ASHAA) hotline* at (800) 835-6700 (554-1404 in Washington D.C.).

3. Formaldehyde

Formaldehyde is a strong irritant that causes burning eyes and throat, nausea, and difficulty in breathing; it is the tenth leading cause of dermatitis. It causes cancer in animals and possibly humans. It is used widely in the manufacture of building materials and many household products. A component of many glues, paints, and surface coatings, it also serves as a permanent-press agent in draperies and clothing. Indoors the most common sources of formaldehyde are particle board (used in shelves, cabinets, furniture, and subflooring), wood paneling, fiberboard (used for furniture tops, and drawer and cabinet fronts), carpets, and upholstery.

In the 1970s as many as half a million homes were built with urea-formaldehyde foam insulation (UFFI) in their wall cavities as an energy conservation measure. It was also used extensively in mobile homes, where high indoor levels of formaldehyde are also found. According to the EPA these emissions decline with time, although more slowly if the insulation is damp or if there are cracks in interior walls that expose the foam. In hot and humid climates formaldehyde outgasses at a greater rate.

What You Should Do about Formaldehyde

The best way to avoid the effects of formaldehyde is *not* to buy or use products that contain it. If you suspect you have dangerous levels in your home, have a test done by a qualified lab. Many state and local health agencies do this at no cost or for a small charge. The federal Occupational Safety and Health Administration (OSHA) recommends a test known as the chromotropic acid method which is used by many commercial laboratories (check with OSHA or your local yellow pages for further leads).

If it is in your home, school, or workplace, you should consider getting rid of its source – taking out pressed-wood products, particle-board subflooring, or UFFI – although this can be an expensive undertaking. Other steps to reduce exposure to formaldehyde recommended by the EPA include:

● Increase ventilation, particularly after bringing new sources of formaldehyde into the room.

● Use air conditioning and dehumidifiers to maintain moderate temperature and reduce humidity, even though this will raise your electric bill.

"Yes. I Do!"

Tobacco smoke is best eliminated by not smoking and not allowing others to do so. Because of increased public awareness of the severe health hazard that smoking presents, most people will now ask if you mind their lighting up, and will refrain if you politely but firmly reply, "Yes. I do." (Five years ago I put a No Smoking sign on my front door and no one has smoked in my apartment since.)

The smoking problem is now widely and in general successfully addressed throughout North America (less so in other parts of the world) by local regulation and ordinance in offices, factories, restaurants, public places, planes. trains, and buses.

Once tobacco smoke gets into a space, removing it by fans, opening windows, and other ventilation systems takes considerably longer than the few minutes it takes five or six smokers to generate dangerous particulate levels, according to the National Research Council.

4. Taking the Lead Out

Indoor air pollution from *lead* is caused by automobile exhaust fumes which are obviously more prevalent the closer you live or work to the street. The effect can be minimized by improving ventilation and surrounding the building with trees and plants. (For information on how plants can help clean up indoor air, see p. 89.)

5. Other Sources of Indoor Air Pollution

Bathrooms and kitchens or any room where there is standing water or excessive damp can be breeding grounds for bacteria, molds, and mildew. Bathrooms and kitchens also house many aerosol products containing such air pollutants as methylene chloride (found in many hair sprays), creosol (found in disinfectants), lye and ammonia (in drain and toilet-bowl cleaners), and chlorine (cleansers and laundry bleach).

These chemicals irritate mucous membranes and affect the central nervous system, liver, kidneys, and other organs. *Be careful not to mix a chlorine-based cleanser with a product containing ammonia, as I did once. You'll be producing a toxic gas – ammonium chloride.*

Other common indoor air pollutants include paints, paint removers and thinners, polyurethane, varnish, shellac, and glues used in do-it-yourself projects, as well as solvents, spray adhesives, rubber cement, and other chemicals used in offices. Such products contain various organic chemicals and other compounds which give off harmful gases and vapors.

Caution: Cigarette smoking IS dangerous to your health – Tobacco causes more death and suffering in adults and children than any other form of environmental pollution.

That cigarette smoking is directly responsible for at least 325,000 deaths from lung cancer and another 50,000 deaths from other lung diseases every year in the United States is a widely known fact. But it is now feared that passive smoking – involuntary exposure to other people's smoke – causes more cancer deaths than any other pollutant.[18]

Before you take another deep breath or drag on a cigarette, remember this warning you won't find on a cigarette pack: *cigarette burnoff smoke puts into the air 50 times more carcinogens than those inhaled by the smoker.*

It contains carbon monoxide, nitrogen dioxide, nicotine, hydrocarbons, and hundreds of other pollutants including 50 chemicals, such as benzene, that are known to cause cancer. And, as the U.S. surgeon general warned in 1986, passive smoking takes an especially harsh toll on children and fetuses.

Children with parents who smoke have much higher rates of colds, bronchitis, influenza, and pneumonia; they are also more likely to have learning disabilities and reduced intellectual development.[19]

You should also note that cigarette smoke is often the carrier of radon into lungs of young and old alike.

6. Air Conditioners, Humidifiers, and Heaters

Air conditioners and humidifiers often harbor harmful bacteria, molds, fungi, and viruses that are spread into the air, causing infection and allergic reactions. In schools, office buildings, and other workplaces "humidifier lung" – chills, headaches, and difficulty in breathing – is often traceable to central humidifiers that add moisture to heated incoming air.

Air conditioners must be kept scrupulously clean, especially filters and coils, which should be professionally changed or cleaned at least once a year, depending on how much use they get.

Humidifiers should be cleaned every day with a strong solution of white vinegar and very hot water. According to Consumers Union, ultrasonic units spread fewer microbes than cool-mist types. If you use the latter: (1) be sure to empty any leftover water before use; (2) start up with fresh water. However, when ultrasonic humidifiers are used with hard water (or water with high levels of minerals), minerals are vaporized and made airborne, producing irritating fine dust and eventually leading to dust deposits on plants, floors, and other surfaces.

Heaters: Care and Maintenance of Gas, Oil, and Wood-burning Systems

● *All* heating appliances should be regularly maintained and, if defective, replaced with energy-efficient models.

● Vent all furnaces to outdoors; keep doors to the rest of the house open when using unvented space heaters.

● Have a trained professional inspect, clean, and tune up central heating system (furnace, flues, and chimneys) annually. It will pay for itself in terms of fuel savings as well as reducing air pollution..

- *Repair any leaks immediately.*
- Change filters on central heating and cooling systems according to manufacturer's directions.
- Choose wood stoves that meet or exceed current EPA emission standards, i.e., are fitted with low-pollution high-efficiency catalytic burners. These will usually pay for themselves with fuel saving in less than three years. If necessary, replace the entire stove with a state-of-the-art model, which should pay for itself over a 5- to 6- year period.
- Make sure doors on all wood stoves fit tightly; burn only aged or dried wood (not pressure-treated wood, which contains chemicals). Do not burn leaves: (1) it's highly polluting and against the law; (2) they are extremely valuable for garden mulch and composting.

Note: Unvented kerosene heaters are virtually impossible to prevent from polluting and should be replaced with electric or vented gas units.

The Common Houseplant Does Its Bit for Cleaner Indoor Air

That houseplants have a natural ability to rid the air of harmful pollutants has been common knowledge since time immemorial. But we now have scientific validation: in June 1988 NASA's Stennis Space Center at Bay St. Louis, Miss., reported that of eight plants tested with benzene, the chrysanthemum and the Gerbera daisy rated "superior" in removing the pollutant from an experimental chamber in a 24-hour exposure.[20]

Other greenery found to be effective air cleaners are spider plants (superior at removing carbon monoxide) and philodendron, especially the elephant-ear species which has the added ability to absorb large quantities of formaldehyde.

To clean the air in a typical 1,500-square foot house 15 to 20 plants would probably be adequate. If feasible, the ventilation system in a house or office might be modified so that a fan pulls the air across the filtering leaves of the green plants. Another suggestion is to pot the plants with a mixture of soil and granular charcoal (used in water filters), which absorb and degrade organic pollutants from the air.

So take a tip from NASA or Mother Nature: If you want to stay clean, grow green!

Household Chemicals

Many products we use in our homes are to be avoided because they contain hazardous chemicals, some of which give off noxious fumes and vapors. Because these items have other dangerous side effects, they are reviewed, together with other household products and tips on finding or making environmentally friendly alternatives, in chapter 12, pp. 298-309.

Auto Pollution

Mostly we think of automobile pollution as that created by the exhaust on the outside. Yet some of it comes inside, both from your own engine and from the exhaust of other vehicles on the road.

Also, the automobile's sealed interior can release many organic chemicals, including polyvinyl chloride (PVC) used in upholstery. PVC is responsible for the "new car" smell prevalent for the first months of its use.

What you can do: Minimize indoor car pollution by leaving the windows open, especially if they have been closed for long periods of time. However, a small percentage of cars are chronically contaminated with organic chemicals. So, if the pollution persists, classify your car as a lemon and return it to the manufacturer.

Indoor Air Pollution in Public Spaces

The quality of air in schools, offices, and other workspaces is a matter of growing concern, especially in modern buildings where it is usually not possible to open windows and let in fresh air. For reasons of economy these buildings are engineered with air distribution systems that centralize heating, cooling, and humidity control.

In many cases polluted indoor air (containing stale tobacco smoke, chemicals from copying machines and cleaning materials, and formaldehyde outgases from new furniture, carpets, and draperies) is recirculated throughout the working day, giving rise to chronic discomfort and respiratory ailments.

When Working Is Good for Your Health

"Filled with daylight, clean air and trees, the new national headquarters of the Environmental Defense Fund brings the outdoors inside. . . it is the result of a yearlong collaboration among architects and environmentalists who wanted, literally and symbolically, to provide a breath of fresh air in a midtown office building." [22]

The Environmental Defense Fund, a leading environmental research and advocacy group based in New York, faced an extraordinary challenge in planning its new national headquarters in 1986.

As a nonprofit agency, it did not have the funds for an expensive building – the budget was $400,000. Yet it was morally committed to setting an example of environmental quality and to being as free as possible of indoor air pollution. "Our prime goal was the quality of life in the workplace," said Frederic D. Krupp, the fund's executive director. [23]

Like a City within a City

Designed by William McDonough, a New York architect with an impressive track record in environmentally conscious building design, the EDF headquarters are divided into work areas or "districts" – one for EDF's scientists, another for its lawyers, and a third for the administrators. The relatively small (10,000- square foot) space in a 20-story, 75-year-old building is defined by "boulevards" (corridors) that lead to a central plaza paved in polished granite. The 30-person EDF staff works under graceful street lamps, separated not by conventional cubicles but by leafy ficus trees in wood and wrought-iron planters. The space, which has 14-foot-high ceilings and windows that open, also comfortably accommodates a reception area, a conference room, and a library. At the outset of the project Krupp and McDonough, with the help of outside consultants, defined the need to minimize the use of harmful products and maximize natural ventilation.

Many of the materials they considered potentially least toxic – solid wood, stone, wool – were expensive. But McDonough refused to use cheaper fiberboard (it contains formaldehyde). To meet the budget solid wood was out of the question except for chairs, said McDonough, "so we chose a high-density plywood with a low percentage of glue. We couldn't afford wool floor covering, but put a jute pad under the carpet so no glue was necessary." A wood floor was prepared with nontoxic sealers and a beeswax finish.[24] Desk tops are granite or plywood sealed with laminates.

Quality of Light

Special attention was paid to the quality of light inside the offices. A new type of fluorescent (called a triphosphor lamp) is used as the main source of interior lighting. These lamps have a very high color rendition index, which makes objects look more natural than conventional lamps; they use less energy and are more cost-effective than incandescents. Housed in inexpensive industrial fixtures, they aim up at the reflective ceiling giving a soft, glare-free light, which combines with deeply penetrating daylight from high windows to give an active, balanced field of illumination.

Natural Ventilation

A large part of the budget went into air conditioning, which, combined with the open windows, provides the excellent indoor air quality that client and architect insisted upon. Because they were reusing an existing air-conditioning plant, special care was taken to clean thoroughly and refurbish the equipment and to check the quantity of fresh air being delivered to the space. During and for two months after construction, ventilation was put at maximum levels to let the space air out fully. The facility was thoroughly cleaned, carpets vacuumed often, ducts washed, and new air filters installed. "We prepared the space for long-term use," said McDonough, "and took care to make the occupants aware of the importance of a regular cleaning and maintenance schedule using nontoxic products."[25]

The ultimate payoff is in terms of user satisfaction – the space is exhilarating to visit and to work in – and in the fact that the project was brought in under budget. Both Krupp and McDonough agree that a multidisciplinary effort is needed to tackle the pressing issue of indoor atmosphere and to make our buildings pleasant and healthful. The example of the EDF headquarters sends an impressive message on how this goal can be achieved and applied in other situations.

Ozone Hazard

Poorly ventilated spaces may accumulate dangerous levels of ozone produced by electrostatic copying machines, mercury-enhanced light bulbs, and by some electrostatic cleaners. You can recognize it by its acrid, pungent odor. Its effects – headaches, dryness in the nose and throat, chest pains – are increased by low humidity, tobacco smoke and other pollutants.

Research has shown that negative ions in the air are generally good for your health while high levels of positive ions can make you feel tired, irritable, and depressed. Depletion of negative ions from the air is a harmful byproduct of inadequate ventilation combined with high density of people. Because an estimated three-quarters of the population, especially women, may be ion-sensitive, this can present a serious health hazard.[21]

How to Improve Air Quality in Public Buildings

As in other examples discussed throughout this guide, it is better to attack the problem at the source rather than to deal with its symptoms. In the case of large modern buildings it is difficult but not impossible to influence decisions on how they will be built. In schools, offices, and other workplaces your voice will carry far more weight if you join with an organized group such as a PTA, trade union, or consumer association, preferably at the planning stage of the building. Increasing numbers of architects, designers, and even developers now solicit input from the people who will eventually use the space. You can also help create a healthier indoor environment when a space is being remodeled. A successful example of how a healthy and pleasant indoor environment can be created on a relatively low budget is (appropriately) the national headquarters of the Environmental Defense Fund in New York featured on pp. 90-91.

To Keep in Mind When You Are Building a New Home[26]

Building a new home provides the opportunity for preventing indoor air problems. However, it can also expose you to higher levels of indoor air contaminants if careful attention is not paid to potential pollution sources.

Express your concerns about indoor air quality to your architect or builder and enlist his or her cooperation in taking measures to provide good indoor air quality. Talk about proper selection of building materials and providing an adequate amount of ventilation.

ASHRAE recommends a ventilation rate of one complete air change every three hours for new homes, and some energy-efficient homes built to tighter specifications require even more ventilation. Particular care should be given in such homes to preventing the buildup of indoor air pollution to high levels.

Here are six important actions that can make a difference:

● *Use radon-resistant construction techniques.* Get a copy of the EPA booklet *Radon Reduction in New Construction* from your state radon or health agency, homebuilder's association, EPA regional office, or the EPA Public Information Center.

● *Choose building materials and furnishings that will keep indoor air pollution to a minimum.* Wherever possible, use natural wood products for furniture, wall covering, and floors, but avoid exotic hardwoods such as teak and mahogany that come from endangered rainforests.

● *Do not permanently adhere carpets directly to cement floors,* because they tend to be cold, and moisture condenses on the carpet, providing a place for mold and dust mites to grow. Also, carpets laid this way do not dry thoroughly if they get wet.

● *Provide proper drainage and seal foundations in new construction.* Air that enters the home through the foundation can contain more moisture than is generated from all occupant activities.

● *Become familiar with how heat recovery ventilators* (air-to-air heat exchangers) work and consider installing one. A whole-house system permits occupants to enjoy the air-quality benefits of drawing more outdoor air into the home while reducing the costs of heating or cooling the air.

● *Install exterior-vented ducts into wood-stove fireboxes and near fireplaces.* The supplementary air supply from these ducts will provide adequate oxygen for complete combustion, minimize infiltration of cold outside air into the rest of the house, and prevent backdrafts from bringing combustion down the chimney. Do not close the duct until all embers are extinguished.

Clearing the Air

As we have seen, much remains to be done before air pollution is brought down to reasonably healthy levels. In the case of outdoor pollution a truly concerted effort must be made at the national and state levels to implement and strengthen laws that are on the books and to create new ones to deal with such overriding problems as urban smog and acid rain, which is the subject of our next chapter. Because of the magnitude of these problems, it may seem that one's own efforts are pitifully inadequate.

We must, therefore, constantly keep in mind that our "small" individual contributions (of conserving energy, using fuels that pollute less than coal or oil, avoiding toxic products in our home, and developing more ecologically conscious lifestyles) add up to a considerable total when multiplied by thousands, perhaps hundreds of thousands of other people taking similar action. In addition to the real impact these efforts will have on improving air quality indoors and out, they will also serve to press our political and industrial leaders into making sounder decisions that will positively affect the environment we are seeking to clean up.

RESOURCES

The following is provided to help you locate additional resources on the topics covered in this chapter.

1. U.S. Government

— *Consumer Product Safety Commission* (CPSC), 5401 Westbard Avenue, Bethesda, MD 20207; hotline (800) 638-CPSC.

— *Department of Health and Human Services,* 200 Independence Avenue SW, Washington, DC 20201:

    Hazard Evaluations and Technical Assistance Branch (R-9), Division of Surveillance, Hazard Evaluation and Field Studies, 4676 Columbia Parkway, Cincinnati, OH 45226.

    Office on Smoking and Health, Rockville, MD 20857.

— *Department of Labor,* Occupational Safety and Health Administration:

    National Institute for Occupational Safety and Health, Division of Respiratory Disease Studies, 944 Chestnut Ridge Road, Morgantown, WV 26505.

— *Environmental Protection Agency,* 401 M Street SW, Washington, DC 20460:

    Office of Air and Radiation, (202) 382-7400.

    Public Information Center, (202) 382-2080.

    Toxic Substances Control Act (TSCA) information service for help on asbestos, (202) 554-1404.

    (For further information on the EPA see also chapter 1, "Resources," pp. 29-30).

2. State Agencies

Many of your concerns about indoor and outdoor air problems can be answered by state or local government agencies, which are usually listed in your local telephone directories.

3. Associations

— *Air Pollution Control Association*, P.O. Box 2861, Pittsburgh, PA 15230.

— *American Gas Association*, 1515 Wilson Boulevard, Arlington, VA 22209.

— *American Institute of Architects*, 1350 New York Avenue NW, Washington, DC 20006.

— *American Lung Association*, 1740 Broadway, New York, NY 10019 (also has local chapters).

— *American Society of Heating, Refrigerating, and Air Conditioning Engineers* (ASHRAE), 1791 Tullie Circle NE, Atlanta, GA 30329.

— *Asthma and Allergy Foundation of America*, 1302 Eighteenth Street NW, Washington, DC 20036.

— *Building Owners and Managers Association*, 1250 Eye Street NW, Washington, DC 20005.

— *National Association of Home Builders*, Technology and Codes Department, 15th and M Streets NW, Washington, DC 20005.

4. Environmental and Citizens Groups

— *National Clean Air Coalition*, 530 Seventh Street SE, Washington, DC 20003; (202) 543-8200. The coalition includes 35 national organizations and a network of thousands of state and local groups concerned with the problems of air pollution. Among the leading members of the coalition are the American Lung Association, EDF, National Audubon Society, NRDC, the Sierra Club, and the Wilderness Society.

5. Further Reading

— *Asbestos Fact Book*, EPA A-107 86-002. Washington, D.C.: EPA, 1986.

— *Asbestos Waste Management Guidance*, EPA/530-SW-85-007, Washington, D.C.: EPA, 1985.

— *Air Pollution in Your Home*. New York: American Lung Association, 1987.

— "Blueprint for the Nontoxic Home," interview with Paul Bierman Lytle, *East West Journal*, March 1987.

— "EPA Will Consider Regulation of Formaldehyde," Philip Shabecoff, *New York Times*, May 19, 1984.

— *Formaldehyde: Everything You Wanted to Know But Were Afraid to Ask*. Washington, D.C.: Consumer Federation of America, 1987.

— "Heat-Recovery Ventilators," *Consumer Reports*, October 1985.

— "High Efficiency Wood Stoves," *Consumer Reports*, October 1985.

— *The Home Book*. Washington, D.C.: Center for Study of Responsive Law, 1989.

— *House Dangerous*, Ellen J. Greenfield. New York: Vintage, 1987.

— *Indoor Air Pollutants*. Washington, D.C.: National Research Council, National Academy Press, 1981.

— "How To Clean Up Your Cleanser Act," Debra Lynn Dadd, *East West Journal*, March 1987.

— *Indoor Air Facts No. 3: Ventilation and Air Quality in Offices*. Washington, D.C.: EPA Office of Air and Radiation, February 1988.

— *Indoor Air Quality Handbook — For Designers, Builders and Users of Energy-Efficient Residences*. Albuquerque, N M : Sandia National Laboratories, U.S. Department of Energy, 1982.

— "Indoor Pollution Alert," Lynne Lohmeier, *East West Journal*, March 1987.

— *The Natural Choice*, Livos Plantchemistry catalog (nontoxic home products), Santa Fe, N M : Livos, 1988.

— "New Tactics Emerge in Struggle Against Smog," Malcolm W. Browne, *New York Times*, February 21, 1989.

— "Nontoxic Floor Finishes," Rudolf Reitz, *Livos Natural Choice newsletter*, Spring 1987.

— *The Nontoxic Home*, Debra Lynn Dadd, Los Angeles: J.P. Tarcher, 1986.

— *The Toxic Cloud. The Poisoning of America's Air*, Michael H. Brown. New York: Harper & Row, 1988.
— *The Healthy Home: Guide to Toxin Free Living*, Linda Mason Hunter. Emmaus, Pa.: Rodale, 1989.

ENDNOTES

1. *The Washington Spectator*, September 1, 1989.
2. Quoted in Philip Shabecoff, "U.S. Calls Poisoning of Air Far Worse Than Expected and Threat to Public," *New York Times*, March 23, 1989.
3. G. Tyler Miller, Jr., *Living in the Environment* (Belmont, Calif.: Wadsworth, 1987), p. 397.
4. Philip Shabecoff, "Health Risk from Smog Is Growing, Official Says," *New York Times*, March 1, 1989.
5. Malcolm W. Browne, "New Tactics Emerge in Struggle Against Smog," *New York Times*, February 21, 1989.
6. Ibid.
7. *State of the World 1988*, Washington, D.C.: Worldwatch Institute, 1988, p. 173.
8. William Robbins, "Crop Dried in Kansas, Focus Now Is the Land," *New York Times*, March 19, 1989.
9. Dick Russell, "L.A. Air," *Amicus Journal*, Summer 1988, p. 13.
10. Robert Rheinhold, "Drastic Steps Are Voted to Reduce Southern California Air Pollution," *New York Times*, March 18, 1989.
11. "First Step to Clean Air," lead editorial, *Los Angeles Times*, March 18, 1989.
12. *New York Times*, January 29, 1987.
13. *Newsweek*, January 7, 1985.
14. Ellen Greenfield, *House Dangerous* (New York: Vintage Books, 1987), p.4.
15. For a comprehensive discussion of the radon problem and how to deal with it, see chapter 8, pp. 171-173.
16. Asbestos Waste Management Guidance, EPA/530-SW-85-007 (Washington, D.C.: EPA, 1985).
17. *The Inside Story: A Guide to Indoor Air Quality* (Washington, D.C.: EPA Office of Air and Radiation, September 1988).
18. William U. Chandler, "Banishing Tobacco," in *State of the World 1986* (Washington, D.C.: Worldwatch Institute, 1986), p. 139.
19. Ibid., pp. 149-50.
20. John Noble Wilford, "The Common Houseplant Does Its Bit for Cleaner Air," *New York Times*, July 26, 1988.
21. Dr. Jacqueline C. Vischer, *Environmental Quality in Offices*, (New York: Van Nostrand Rheinhold, 1989), pp. 206-216.
22. Linda Martin, "New Office Tries for a Pollution-free Environment, *New York Times*, January 27, 1987.
23. Jon Naar, "When Working Is Good For Your Health," *Interiors*, December 1989.
24. An extensive line of nontoxic, organic paints, sealers, stains, finishes, and other products can be ordered from Livos Plantchemistry, 614 Agua Fria Street, Santa Fe, NM 87501.
25. "When Working Is Good for Your Health."
26. Excerpt from *The Inside Story: A Guide to Indoor Air Quality* (Washington, D.C.: EPA, 1988).

5

ACID RAIN

Stopping the Damage

> *"Acid rain spares nothing. What has taken*
> *humankind decades to build and nature millennia to*
> *evolve is being impoverished and destroyed in a matter*
> *of a few years – a mere blink in geologic time."*
> *– Don Hinrichsen*[1]

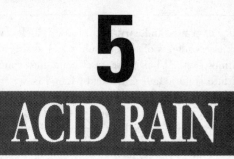

In her landmark book *Silent Spring* the biologist and author Rachel Carson warned of the dangers of pesticides and herbicides on all life. A generation later spring is again losing its voice. Forests are dying, fish are not surviving in lakes and streams, birds are unable to lay eggs, deer are sustaining liver damage, and drinking water is being poisoned. Once more the culprit is chemical – acidification. It is an ecological problem that transcends national and political boundaries.

Acidification is produced from the burning of fossil

fuels by power plants, industry, and motor vehicles, whose smokestacks and tailpipes release millions of tons of sulfur and nitrogen oxides (SO_2 and NO_X) into the atmosphere. When these gases come into contact with water, they are converted into sulfuric and nitric acids, found in water droplets in clouds and particles in the air mass. The acid compounds are often carried thousands of miles in the atmosphere before dropping to the ground as deadly acid rain.

Few environmental issues have generated so much controversy as acid rain (more properly termed acid deposition). It is the cause of friction between the U.S. and both Canada and Mexico, between the northeastern U.S. and the

How Acid Rain Affects Your Health and Welfare[7]

● Acidic drinking water can corrode distribution pipes, causing metal levels higher than the maximum allowed by the EPA.
● In a national survey of rural drinking water supplies, drinking water standards for lead were exceeded in the Northeast by 9.6 percent of households for lead, 16 percent for iron, and 22 percent for mercury.
● Increased sulfate from acid deposition may cause an increase in the conversion of mercury into its most toxic form.
● Increased atmospheric sulfate and nitrate pollution correlates with increasing hospitalization for heart and lung ailments.
● Regional haze from sulfate particles in the air causes a decline in visibility in rural areas. (New England shows a 50–percent decline since the 1950s.)

Midwest, and among many European countries. The acid-rain phenomenon is now an international problem affecting life and resources located downwind of major industrial regions of the world from Canton, Ohio to Canton, China. It increasingly endangers your health, costs you money, and will undoubtedly affect your children's future.

Every year some 160 million tons of SO_2 and slightly less NO_X are spewed into the world's atmosphere as the result of human activities. The leading contributors to this pollution are the U.S., the U.S.S.R., Poland, East and West Germany, the U.K., Canada, and China. Seventy percent of SO_2 emissions come from coal-burning electric–power plants, while the largest share of NO_X pollution (about 40 percent) comes from the ever-growing numbers of automobiles, although utilities and industry contribute significantly. Controlling nitrous oxides is particularly difficult because their sources are so varied and dispersed.

When SO_2 is emitted from tall industrial smokestacks (so as not to pollute the immediate backyard!), the dirty gases rise to high altitudes before being swept along by the wind. Depending on emission rates and weather patterns, this chemical brew is carried hundreds, even thousands of miles from its point of origin. In addition to their direct health and ecological impact as air pollutants, SO_2 and NO_X contribute heavily to acidic deposition.

Incalculable Damage

The billions of dollars of damage that acid rain causes to water, soil, food crops, buildings, and human health knows no geographical or political boundaries. In the United States alone the damage is costing at least $10 billion a year.[3]

Lakes, ponds, and streams are the first victims, especially where bedrock and soils are low in carbonates and similar chemicals that can neutralize acids. Thousands of lakes in the northeastern United States, Canada, and Scandinavia are so acidic that fish cannot live in them. A 1988 report by the University of Massachusetts Water Resources Center revealed more acid-rain damage in that state already than the EPA forecasts for the entire Northeast in 50 years.[4] In Sweden and Norway a majority of the streams and lakes are technically "dead" or on the critical list.[5]

Sulfur and nitrogen oxides have long been known to injure vegetation by yellowing leaves and inducing plant diseases. Acid rain-related damage to trees and crops is extensive in California, the Midwest, the northeastern U.S., and most of Western Europe. It has been identified as a prime cause of *waldsterben* (tree death) affecting more than half of the forests in West Germany and those in southern Sweden, Switzerland, and the U.K.

Acid rain presents a triple threat to forests: it prevents nutrients from reaching trees through their leaves; it leaches nutrients out of the root zone; and it concentrates aluminum in the soil, which can block the roots' uptake of vital magnesium and calcium. These attacks can work alone or in combination. When a tree loses nutrients in its foliage, it tries to compensate by taking up more from the soil. And, if these are not available, the tree becomes more susceptible to damage from frost and insects. Studies in West Germany show that

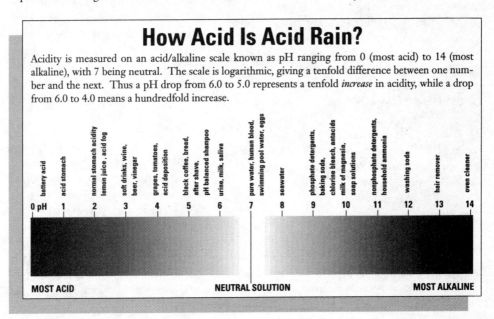

How Acid Is Acid Rain?

Acidity is measured on an acid/alkaline scale known as pH ranging from 0 (most acid) to 14 (most alkaline), with 7 being neutral. The scale is logarithmic, giving a tenfold difference between one number and the next. Thus a pH drop from 6.0 to 5.0 represents a tenfold *increase* in acidity, while a drop from 6.0 to 4.0 means a hundredfold increase.

even minute amounts of aluminum from acid precipitation released into the water and soil during springtime snowmelts can severely damage tree root systems.[6] In Poland's Upper Silesia industrial region acid deposition is eroding metal railroad tracks so rapidly that trains are reportedly limited to 25 mph! Acid-rain pollution is also eating into masonry, metals, and marble in buildings from Massachusetts to the Taj Mahal. In combination with other air pollutants, it has ravaged the Canadian Parliament building in Ottawa with a creeping blight that is turning the facade black. Now even parts of Latin America and Africa are showing signs of acid-rain damage.

Health Impact of Acid Rain

Breathing the gaseous air pollutants connected with acid rain is harmful to your health. Recent findings from Japan and Canada show a close relationship between lung diseases (particularly asthma in children) and concentrations of sulfate in the air. Nitrogen compounds and ozone, combined with sulfur dioxide and/or sulfate, may act in concert to increase the risk of respiratory ailments.

Countdown to Oblivion

In the northeastern United States the average pH of rainfall is 4.6 – in Massachusetts it is 4.2 – but it frequently drops to 4.0, one thousand times more acidic than pure water. Although rain in the western states tends to be less acidic, incidents of smog with a pH of less than 3.0 have been documented in Southern California.

To understand the severity of a rise in acidity (or a drop in pH), here are some examples of how acidity can affect life in a typical pond where a healthy pH is about 7:

6. At pH 6.0 most trout, clam, and crustacean populations begin to decline.

5. At pH 5.5 rainbow and brown trout begin to die and brook trout fail to reproduce. Clams and crustaceans are probably eliminated.

4. At pH 5.0 most fish species experience reproductive difficulty.

3. At pH 4.2 the common toad dies off.

2. At pH 3.5 virtually all fish, clams, snails, and frogs cannot survive.

1. At pH 2.5 only a few species of midges, fungi, and bacteria can survive.

0. No life exists.

Watch the Water

Acid rain's indirect impact on health is caused by its increasing the corrosiveness of surface and ground water. When this water gets into your water supply, it can leach out toxic metals and asbestos from watersheds, sediments, and plumbing into the water you drink. This is particularly dangerous when the pipes are themselves made, even in small part, of toxic metals. A recent survey of 158 Massachusetts municipal drinking waters found that 73 percent were extremely "aggressive" – i.e. able to corrode metals from piping systems.[7] The acidity of the water supply in Boston, where 85 percent of the service pipes from the road to the house are lead, necessitated expensive treatment to protect against lead going into the drinking water.

Acid-rain corrosion of water pipes in Sweden is reported to have caused diarrhea in young children and produced thin-shelled chicken eggs. And, allegedly, several persons who had washed in water with high amounts of copper corroded from household pipes found their blond hair had turned green. Studies of roof catchment/cistern drinking water systems in Ohio and western Pennsylvania found unusual amounts of lead, copper, and cadmium due to acid deposition. (Ironically, the owners had turned to cisterns as a last resort because the ground and surface water was polluted by coal mining.)

Don't Eat the Fish

Dangerously high levels of mercury in fish from acidic waters have been measured in Norway, Sweden, the Adirondack region of upstate New York, in the largest reservoir in Massachusetts (Quabbin), and in Ontario. In Ontario warnings were issued to local inhabitants and anglers throughout the province not to eat fish caught in certain heavily contaminated areas.

Controlling Acid Rain

Acid rain is hard to control because so much of it comes from "somewhere else." Acid-forming emissions are spread unevenly over the United States, with ten states mainly in the central and upper Midwest producing more than half the total.

Because of prevailing winds most of this acid rain falls in New England or eastern Canada, a region which produces a very small percentage of the emissions.

Acid precipitation also threatens many high-altitude lakes in the American West, a phenomenon first noted in 1984. According to research done by the EPA and the Environmental Defense Fund, as many as 2,000 lakes in the Rocky Mountains could be ruined by "as little as one-tenth as much acid as was needed to acidify some less sensitive lakes in the northeastern United States or Scandinavia."[8] Once a high-altitude lake becomes acidified, it can take hundreds of years for it to recover enough to support aquatic life.

Long-distance Pollution. A direct link between acid deposition and copper smelters 600 miles away in Arizona, Utah, Nevada, New Mexico, and across the border in Mexico was also revealed by EDF research. This long-distance pollution is augmented from other sources including power plants and automobiles in the Rocky Mountain region and California.

The Growing Spread of Acid Rain

OTTAWA, CANADA Airborne acid attacks facade of Parliament building	**NOVA SCOTIA, CANADA** 9 rivers no longer support salmon or trout reproduction	**EAST CANADA** 350,000 lakes in six provinces found extremely acid-sensitive	**U.K.** Highest percentage of acid-damaged forests in Europe (64%)	**SOUTH NORWAY** 80% of lakes dead or dying	**WEST GERMANY** Half the forests affected by Waldsterben (tree death)	**SILESIA, POLAND** Trains limited to 25 mph as acid erodes rails	**ATHENS, GREECE** Air pollution threatens Parthenon and other monuments

CANADA Acid rain causes over $1 billion a year

AGRA, INDIA Airborne acids from local oil refinery attacks Taj Mahal

SOUTH CALIF. Acid fog with pH of under 3.0 reported by EPA in 1986.

TOKYO, JAPAN Industrial airborne acid rain now seen as serious health threat

MIDWEST Most U.S. acid rain emissions originate from industry in Ohio River Valley

BEIJING, CHINA Acid rain damages trees and statues in Forbidden City

| **FLORIDA** Over half the lakes in North Floria Highland acidified. | **PENNSYLVANIA** Has the highest incidence of acid rain in the U.S. | **MASSACHU-SETTS** 64% of surface water vulnerable to acid deposition | **SÃO PAOLO, BRAZIL** Rain has annual average pH of less than 4.5. | **YUCATAN, MEX.** Emissions from oilfields eroding pre-Columbian buildings | **SOUTH AFRICA** Acid precipitation damages buildings and vegetation. | **CENTRAL AFRICA** High levels of acid rain reported in virgin rain forests | **SOUTH CHINA** Rain with under 4.5 pH turns rice fields yellow |

Over the Back Fence. Canada and the United States are proud of their peacefully unguarded frontier. But acid rain is one illegal border crosser that has both neighbors up in arms. From the northern perspective the question is how to get the U.S. to clean up air pollution that's pouring across the border from Ohio, Michigan, New York, and other neighboring states. Acid rain is causing serious economic and ecological problems in eastern Canada, endangering forests, fisheries, agriculture, the maple syrup industry, and tourism. (For a detailed map showing the impact of acid rain in the United States and Canada see page 111.)

When the U.S. criticizes the Inco nickel smelter at Sudbury, Ontario as the largest single source of sulfur dioxide emissions in North America, the Canadians point out that its output is dwarfed by the combined numbers of coal-fueled plants in the U.S. Midwest. Because the U.S. repeatedly rejected proposals for a joint cleanup campaign, Canada in 1985 opted for a go-it-alone program to cut its SO_2 emissions by 65 percent by 1994. Seventy-five percent of these reductions will come from the provinces of Ontario and Quebec.

Canada employs a variety of approaches to reducing emissions. The Sudbury smelter – which has reduced emissions by more than 50 percent – recycles some of its SO_2 as marketable sulfuric acid or liquid SO_2, in addition to cutting back on production. Ontario Hydro, which operates three coal-fired plants in southern Ontario, has been granted leeway only if it can show legitimate cause such as exceptionally high electricity demand.

"The United States has to be part of the solution. It is in their interest to respect treaties with and obligations to a sovereign, neighboring nation."

If the cutback is successful, Canada will have achieved a significant reduction of acid-rain pollutants. But it will not be free of the problem, because half of its acid rain comes from U.S. smokestacks and tailpipes. "The United States has to be part of the solution. It is in their interest to respect treaties with and obligations to a sovereign, neighboring nation. Acid rain is the litmus test of bilateral issues," said an official of Environment Canada, the federal ministry concerned with pollution cleanup.[9]

Causes and Effects

At the heart of the acid-rain controversy is the fact that the *components* of acid rain are created in regions economically dependent on "smokestack" industries that produce the pollution, while the *effects* are experienced in regions that get much of their income from tourism, agriculture, and forest products, all of which depend on a clean environment. This basic divergence of interest is reflected in the U.S. Congress, where Republicans and Democrats from the Midwest oppose acid-rain control while those from the Northeast bipartisanly advocate it.

An indication of change in U.S. policy came in January 1989 when the new head of the EPA said the first item on his agenda was legislation to reduce acid rain (especially that caused by pollution from coal-burning power plants). The Reagan administration had firmly resisted all efforts to control acid rain for eight years even though that position made it awkward for President Reagan to ask another neighboring country, Mexico, to control pollution at its huge new copper smelter at Nacozari, a mere 60 miles south of the Arizona border.

Acid Rain Strikes the Third World

"At times, it seems as if cities such as Beijing, Jakarta, Tehran, Mexico City, and Lagos have been locked inside gigantic Hefty bags of pollution." – Don Hinrichsen[10]

On my first visit to India I attended a symposium in Bombay on renewable energy. At one point I looked out of the window and remarked that the smog looked "just like Los Angeles." To my surprise this observation met with a sharp rejoinder from my hosts: "Don't we have the right to do what you are doing?" Air pollution, it seemed, was a sign of progress, along with traffic jams, Wonder Bread, and Kentucky Fried Chicken.

Brazil's São Paulo, with more than 20 million inhabitants, is home to an estimated 45,000 industries of all types and sizes. Only half have bothered to register with the government for air-pollution controls. Of those, 80 percent are considered polluters.[11] Meanwhile, increasingly high levels of sulfur and nitrogen oxides are found in the larger cities of India, China, and Nigeria due mainly to the burning of coal (and some oil) by power plants and industry, and the enormous growth of automobile use. In Lagos, Nigeria, population 6 million, traffic volumes are almost as heavy as those in New York City or Los Angeles.

In Beijing I asked the chief engineer of the city what was being done about acid rain. With a shrug of the shoulders he replied, "It is a matter of priority. Right now we are more concerned with industrializing our country than with acid rain."[12]

In the summer of 1989 high levels of acid rain and ozone, heretofore associated with industrial regions, were found for the first time over the virgin rain forests of Central Africa. The findings raised new concerns about the future of these forests, which are already under siege from a fast-growing population and intensive commercial lumbering.

With most Third World countries rushing into industrial development, acid rain and other forms of air pollution are taking a heavy toll on public health and the environment. However, as longtime polluters ourselves, First World nations must be mindful of the proverb that people who live in glass houses should not throw stones. *We should try instead to help developing countries learn from our mistakes instead of repeating them.*

What Is Being Done about Acid Rain

Promising Initiatives

Norway and Sweden suffer extensive damage from acid rain, which is acidifying lakes and rivers and causing a serious decline in fish populations. Seventy percent of this comes from the United Kingdom and other parts of Western Europe that until recently have not taken the problem seriously. Like Canada, the two Scandinavian countries decided to clean up their own act, with a cut of some 60 percent in SO_2 emissions by a combination of energy conservation and switching to low-sulfur fuels. West Germany, one of the world's leading exporters of sulfur dioxide, is also committed to a major reduction in SO_2 output, as are nearly all European countries excepting the U.K. and the U.S.S.R..

Liming the Lakes

To offset acidification, Norway and Sweden have "limed" more than 3,000 lakes, a laborious process which involves spreading lime on affected areas to increase the alkalinity of the soil and water. At best it works as a holding action – to protect important fisheries from extinction, for example – until longer-term solutions can be implemented. However, many environmentalists see liming as an undesirable human manipulation of natural ecosystems, on a par with such disastrous efforts of the U.S. Army Corps of Engineers as "straightening out" the Kissimmee River in Florida.

Liming is also being tried in the U.S.. From airplanes, barges, and boats in summer and fertilizer spreaders in winter, fishery experts are applying finely ground limestone to waters in New England, the Adirondacks, and the Great Lakes.

A liming experiment in the Pocono Mountains of western Pennsylvania involved two similar lakes ten miles apart, both declining because of acid rain.

Japanese Cleanup

For Japan with its densely concentrated industries, heavy automobile traffic, and tight island population, acid rain and other forms of air pollution represent a major threat to environmental and human health. Its answer was to clean up sulfur dioxide emissions *before* they could escape into the atmosphere.

This required installation of 1,200 "scrubbers" (devices to desulfurize flue gases) on industrial smokestacks – which has cut SO_2 by more than 70 percent – and the use of efficient catalytic converters in motor vehicles, which reduced their emissions by 90 percent. In fact, Japan now has the world's most stringent limits on air pollution emissions.[14]

One was left untouched, the other treated with 100 tons of limestone spread on the ice in February 1985. The treatment held acidification at bay for two and half years, during which time there were significant increases in organisms sensitive to acid conditions – dragonflies, freshwater mussels, snails, and water lilies. In the untreated lake these species steadily declined.[13]

Other liming projects, in New England and the Midwest, suggest that the process has limitations. Lakes have to be periodically retreated because their water is continuously replaced, flushing out the limestone. The process is prohibitively expensive and thus only a small proportion of lakes (16 percent in Massachusetts, for example) can be treated. As indicated above, liming is not the long-term answer to the ravages of acid rain on the world's water systems. Nor should it be allowed to divert efforts to get to the heart of the matter – namely, reducing the amounts of sulfur and nitrogen oxides discharged into the atmosphere.

Desperately Seeking Solutions

In the United States six states have enacted laws requiring a 25- to 50-percent reduction in SO_2 emissions. However, efforts to control acid rain at the national level have met with stiff resistance from industry and politicians. A major obstacle was the eight years of do-nothing Reaganism. In June 1989 President Bush spoke of a proposed reduction of 10 million tons of SO_2 (almost half the U.S. total) and 2 million tons of NO_X over a ten-year period – amounts greater than expected or wanted by industry and his budgetary advisers. However, when his legislation was presented to Congress, his actual proposal was much less stringent.

He also adopted an acid-rain plan devised by the Environmental Defense Fund that would cut the cost of these reductions and allow affected industries greater flexibility in reaching these targets through the use of economic incentives. Under the plan, 107 major acid-rain producers in 18 states would have the option of switching to lower-sulfur coal, adopting suitable new technologies, installing scrubbers, encouraging consumers to conserve electricity, or using a combination of these measures.

The cost to utilities could be cut by allowing them to sell "pollution rights." For example, if one power plant cut its emissions of pollutants more than required, it could sell the overage to another plant, which could subtract that amount from its required reduction. The total reduction required by the plan would remain the same, but the selling plant could reduce its costs by the money received for the sale and the buyer might save money by having a lower reduction target. The reason for this "bubble concept" (so named because an imaginary bubble is used to delineate a pollution-producing area in which an effort is made to reduce emissions as a whole – i.e., by reducing some emissions more than others) is that a 90-percent reduction at a new plant may be cheaper than a 40-percent reduction at an older plant. As long as the final effect is the same, there is no reason to pay a higher price.

The success of the plan would depend on constant monitoring of smokestack emissions from all 107 of the affected industries included in the president's proposed legislation and on overcoming stiff opposition from states producing high-sulfur coal.

Going to the Law

Frustrated by the federal government's lack of action on acid rain, several states have resorted to lawsuits against the EPA. In one action the New England states, New York, New Jersey, and Ontario sued to force the agency to enforce the transboundary section of the Clean Air Act. Another suit calls for the EPA to regulate air pollution crossing state borders. A third charges the EPA with not limiting the use of tall chimney stacks to evade the Clean Air Act requirements. A fourth would require revision of the act to include national air quality standards dealing with acid deposition. A fifth indicts the EPA with failure to carry out provisions of the Act requiring reduction of pollution that affects visibility in federal parks and wildernesses. Unfortunately, as of this writing none of these suits has had a successful outcome.

Roadblocks to Progress

In addition to power plants and industry, the major cause of acid-rain pollution is transportation, primarily the automobile. However, when it comes to controlling emissions of nitrogen oxide (and carbon monoxide) from motor vehicles, there is powerful opposition from two interests that exert a virtual stranglehold over the federal government and many political leaders – the petroleum companies and the automobile industry.

Efforts by the federal government to increase the low fuel efficiency of new American cars, which increased markedly after the OPEC oil crisis, were blocked when the Reagan administration refused to increase statutory mileage per gallon. General Motors and Ford, in particular, have consistently opposed measures such as installing more effective catalytic converters in their cars on the grounds of cost, even though this has not harmed their competitors in Japan.

Long-Term Can Begin Now

Aside from political and economic barriers, the way to control acid rain and other forms of air pollution is clear. It must come from a combination of energy efficiency (improving efficiency of industrial boilers and motors, generators, turbines, lighting equipment, and consumer appliances) and energy conservation (at least half of what we currently use is needlessly wasted), both of which would significantly reduce fuel burning and the pollution it produces. A cleaner environment would also be a benefit of switching to renewable sources of energy such as wind and water power, photovoltaics, and biomass that are basically nonpolluting. These options are discussed at greater length in chapter 9.

Acid Rain – How Can We Save Our Environment*

- The impacts of acid rain can be reduced by controlling emissions of SO_2 and NO_x.
- Mitigation techniques applied to specific resources can forestall damages but cannot permanently cure them.
- Lakes and ponds can be limed to protect them but in Massachusetts, for example, only 16 percent of the 2900 lakes and ponds can be economically limed.
- Liming has potentially harmful effects on lake and stream ecology, so it must be studied and done with caution.
- Applications of lime to forests, croplands and other terrestrial systems have had limited success to date.
- Temporary protective coatings may be applied to some vulnerable metals such as those used in some statuary, but no effective treatment has been found for stones, mortar, cement, and brick surfaces. Frequent cleaning helps but may itself be destructive.
- Improved atmospheric monitoring can provide better warnings to people whose health is vulnerable to sulfates and nitrates.
- Emission reduction requires interregional and international cooperation.
- Innovative sharing of cleanup costs can reduce financial hardships.
- The United States' refusal to agree to major SO_2 reductions handicaps international efforts which are, nevertheless, expected to have major positive effects outside of North America.

*By Paul J. Godfrey Ph.D., Water Resources Research Center, University of Massachusetts at Amherst,[15] with permission.

What You Can Do about Acid Rain

Keep in mind: the major causes of acid rain – electricity generation, transportation, heating, cooling, and lighting buildings – are *human* activities. We all use electricity, buy food and goods transported over long distances, travel in vehicles powered by internal-combustion engines, live and work in buildings heated and cooled by fossil fuels. These are events that we can influence and change, directly and indirectly. Some of the many steps you can take personally are listed below, while others are cross-referenced to different parts of this book.

Energy conservation is the simplest way to cut down on acid rain – and indeed many other forms of pollution. Thirty-three steps you can take are given here. More details on how to save energy are provided on pp. 216-220.

In the Home and at Work

1. *Get an energy audit.* Many utility companies now do it free or charge a nominal fee; otherwise, check your local yellow pages to find a consultant. Either way you'll end up saving energy and money.

2. *Cut heat loss* from windows and doors. Put storm windows on the outside, weatherstrip and caulk anywhere you can feel cold air coming in. In a new or remodeled building install double- or triple-glazed windows. Curtains and shades placed one inch from the glass can cut heat loss by one-third. Storm doors at about $100 cut loss by a half.

3. *Check walls, floors, and electric outlets* for cracks and openings. Caulk and seal up tight.

4. *Increase your insulation.* Going from R-11 to R-30 will save up to 25 percent on your energy use and heating bill. Don't forget basement, cellar, or crawlspace.

5. *Install ceiling fans* to keep cool in summer and circulate heat in winter. Use an attic fan to ventilate your house in summer. Insulate the attic for protection against heat in summer, cold in winter.

6. *For details on care and maintenance of heating systems,* see chapter 4, pp. 88-89.

7. *Turn down the thermostat.* When you've done steps 1 through 6 above, you won't need to heat up the outside any more. By cutting drafts you'll probably be comfortable in winter at 68 degrees.

8. *Save water and heat* by fixing leaky faucets, taking showers instead of baths, installing an energy-saving showerhead, handwashing dishes in batches without leaving water running.

9. *Turn off lights* when you are not using them.

10. *Install energy-efficient compact light bulbs.* (see pp. 218-219.)

11. *Buy only energy-efficient appliances.* One indispensable help is the DOE Energy Guide tag that now is attached to almost all household appliances. Take a few minutes to compare the estimated annual average operating costs of different models and brands. You can save several hundred dollars a year by selecting the most energy-efficient units. Also buy a copy of *The Most Energy Efficient Appliances*, published annually by the American Council for an Energy-Efficient Economy, Washington, D.C. For less than $5 it may be the best investment you make.

12. *Use nonpetrochemical cleaners, toiletries, cosmetics, and insecticides.* (For details, see "Safe Household Products," chapter 12, p. 303).

13. *Reduce your use of plastic bags, containers, and packaging.* This includes taking bags back to stores for reuse (for details, see chapter 1, pp. 26-27).

14. *Install a simple passive solar system* to provide at least half your hot water. For practical ways to do this, get *Approaching Free Energy* and other energy-related publications from Rodale Press (see "Further Reading," p. 110).

15. *Add a solar greenhouse* as a place to grow food and plants and to help heat your house.

16. *Build a passive solar house* or remodel your existing one to make it more energy efficient.

17. *Consider generating your own electricity with PV panels, a wind turbine, or small-scale hydro,* depending on where you live (see chapter 9, p. 220. See also DOE's booklet *Homemade Electricity* listed in "Further Reading," p.110).

If You Own or Drive an Automobile

18. Make sure the engine is properly tuned.

19. Use only unleaded gas.

20. Economize on gas by driving at less than 65 mph and keeping tires inflated at recommended pressures; keep a light foot on the gas pedal; if your car is standing for more than a minute, switch off the gas; if you are not getting better than 30 mpg, consider trading in for a more fuel-efficient vehicle. (Many newer models get over 40 mpg; Renault and Volvo have working prototypes that get over 80 mpg; see chapter 9, pp.195-196.)

21. Switch to steel-belt radials. They should give you at least 3 more mpg and a safer ride. Check tire pressure weekly.

22. Reduce wind drag by driving with your car windows closed (except when it's very hot) and – according to some experts – by keeping its body highly polished (with a nontoxic wax, of course).

23. Empty the trunk and get rid of any surplus stuff you may be carrying.

24. Don't rev the engine before you switch it off. It thins the oil.

25. Tailgating and beating traffic lights wastes fuel and maybe your life.

26. Concentrate your driving into one longer itinerary, rather than a series of short trips. It will give you better mileage.

27. Wherever possible (e.g., when commuting), carpool, share rides, or use alternative carriers such as trains, which per passenger mile are the least polluting type of transportation.

28. Ride the nonpolluting bicycle – 80 percent of all car trips are under 10 miles. (For more on bicycle power see chapter 9, p. 221.)

29. Walk – it's good exercise and the cheapest way to get around. You might discover that you don't really need a car.

What You Can Do Politically

30. Urge your congressional representatives to: support proposed legislation requiring the U.S. to reduce SO_2 and NO_X emissions significantly; to press the EPA to enforce the Clean Air Act; and to obtain more money for acid-rain research.

31. If you live in Massachusetts, New York, New Jersey, New Hampshire, Michigan, Wisconsin, Minnesota, Ontario, or Quebec, work actively with your state/provincial emission-control programs; monitor their lawsuit actions against the EPA in order to control acid rain.

32. If you live anywhere else, get your representatives to work for similar action in their states. For more on how to work with legislators, see chapter 10.

Working with Environmental and Citizen Groups

33. Almost every environmental group is involved in the fight against air pollution, which includes researching and advocating measures for the control of acid rain. Those that are specifically focussed on acid-rain issues include the Acid Rain Foundation, the Acid Rain Information Clearinghouse, the American Council for an Energy-Efficient Economy, the Energy Conservation Coalition, and the Canadian Coalition on Acid Rain. (For addresses, see "Resources," immediately below) At the state level there is the Acid Rain Precipitation Data Base in Albany, N.Y., and the Acid Rain Monitoring Project at the Water Resources Research Center in Amherst, Mass..

All these groups welcome support (in the form of donations or participation in programs) and the best way to find out how you can take part is to learn more about their activities by reading their prospectuses, annual reports, or newsletters. For details on working with environmental and advocacy groups, see chapter 11, "Eco-Action."

RESOURCES

The following is provided to help you locate additional resources on the topics covered in this chapter.

1. U.S. Government

— *National Acid Precipitation Assessment Program*, jointly chaired by the EPA, the President's Council on Environmental Quality, the National Oceanic and Atmospheric Administration, and the Departments of Agriculture, Energy, and Interior.

— *National Center for Atmospheric Research*, P.O. Box 3000, Boulder, CO 80307. Research on climate change.

Key Political Figures to Contact:

For Acid Rain Controls:
— Representative James Cooper (D-Tenn.)
— Representative Claudine Schneider (R-R.I.)
— Representative Gerry Sikorski (D-Minn.)
— Representative Henry Waxman (D-Calif.)
— Senator John Kerry (D-Mass.)
— Senator Patrick J. Leahy (D-Vt.)
— Senator George J. Mitchell (D-Me.)
— Senator Timothy E. Wirth (D-Colo.)

Against Controls:
— Representative John Dingell (D-Mich.)
— Senator Robert Byrd (D-W. Va.)

2. Environmental and Technical Organizations

— *Acid Rain Foundation*, 1630 Blackhawk Hills, St. Paul, MN 55122.

— *Acid Rain Information Clearinghouse*, Center for Environmental Information, 33 S. Washington Street, Rochester, NY 14608.

— *Acid Rain Precipitation Data Base*, N.Y. State Department of the Environment, 50 Wolf Road, Albany, NY 12233.

— *American Council for an Energy-Efficient Economy*, 1001 Connecticut Avenue NW, Washington, DC 20036.

— *American Forestry Association*, 1319 Eighteenth Street NW, Washington, DC 20036.

— *Canadian Coalition on Acid Rain*, 112 Saint Clair Avenue West, Toronto, Ontario, M4V 2Y3, Canada.

— *Citizens Acid Rain Monitoring Network*, National Audubon Society, 850 Third Avenue, New York, NY 10022. The network, which includes 250 monitors in all 50 states, Washington, D.C., and Mexico, distributes monthly data to the news media and Congress.

— *Energy Conservation Coalition* (A Project of the Environmental Action Foundation), 1525 New Hampshire Avenue NW, Washington, DC 20036.

— *National Clean Air Coalition*, 530 Seventh Street SE, Washington, DC 20003.

— *Pollution Probe*, 43 Queen's Park Crescent, University of Toronto, Toronto, M5S 2C3, Canada.

— *Transportation Alternatives*, 494 Broadway, New York, NY 10012; (212) 941-4600.

— *Water Resources Research Center*, Blaisdell House, University of Massachusetts, Amherst, MA 01003.

3. Further Reading

— *"Acid Indigestion" in Plants?: How Acid Pollutants Affect Forests, Crops, and Other Vegetation*. New York: Environmental Defense Fund, 1987.

— *Acid Rain*, Ross Howard and Michael Perley. New York: McGraw-Hill, 1982.

— "Acid Rain and Forest Decline," Don Hinrichsen in *Earth Report*. London: Mitchell Beazley, 1988.

— *Acid Rain and Electricity Conservation*. Washington, D.C.: Energy Conservation Coalition and American Council for an Energy-Efficient Coalition, 1987.

— *Acid Rain and Related Air Pollutant Damage: A National and International Call for Action*. Boston: Massachusetts Department of Environmental Quality Engineering, 1984.

— *Acid Rain and Transported Air Pollutants*, OTA-O-204. Washington, D.C.: Office of Technology Assessment, U.S. Congress, 1984.

— *Acid Rain Deposition Long-Term Trends*. Washington, D.C.: National Academy of Sciences, 1986.

— *Acid Rain in Massachusetts*, Paul Godfrey. Amherst, Mass.: Water Resources Research Center, University of Massachusetts, 1988.

— *The Acidic Deposition Phenomenon and Its Effects*. Washington, D.C.: EPA Office of Research and Development, 1983.

— *Approaching Free Energy*. Emmaus, Pa.: Rodale, 1980.

— *Energy Smarts: Low-Cost Ways to Shrink Your Energy Bills*, Wesley Cox. New York: Crown, 1984.

— *Homemade Electricity: An Introduction to Small-Scale Wind, Hydro, and Photovoltaic Systems*, DOE/CE/15095-10. Washington, D.C.: U.S. Department of Energy, Appropriate Technology Program, 1984.

— *A Killing Rain*, Thomas Pawlick. San Francisco: Sierra Club, 1984.

— "Like First World, Like Third World," Don Hinrichsen. *Amicus Journal*, Winter 1988.

— *The Most Energy-Efficient Appliances*. Washington, D.C.: American Council for an Energy-Efficient Economy, 1988.

— *The Solar Electric Book: How to Save $$$ Through Clean Solar Power*, Gary Starr. Lower Lake, Calif.: Integral Publishing, 1987.

— *Stop Burning Your Money: The Intelligent Homeowner's Guide to Household Energy Savings*, John Rothchild. New York: Random House, 1981.

— *Thresholds for Acidification: A Framework for Policy and Research*. New York: Environmental Defense Fund, 1988.

ENDNOTES

1. Don Hinrichsen, "Acid Rain and Forest Decline," in *Earth Report* (London: Mitchell Beazley, 1988), p. 65.

2. Paul J. Godfrey Ph.D., *Acid Rain in Massachusetts*. (Amherst, Mass.: Water Resources Research Center, University of Massachusetts, 1988), p. 31.

3. Howard S. Geller et al., "Acid Rain and Electricity Conservation" (Washington, D.C.: American Council for an Energy Efficient Economy and Energy Conservation Coalition, June 1987) p. 1-1.

4. Godfrey, p. 31.

5. Hinrichsen, p. 66.

6. Hinrichsen, pp. 71-73.

7. *National Statistical Assessment of Rural Water Conditions* (Washington, D.C.: EPA Office of Drinking Water, 1984).

8. Thomas Pawlick, *A Killing Rain* (San Francisco: Sierra Club, 1984), p. 112.

9. Mark Mardon, "Canada's View on Acid Rain," *Sierra*, July/August 1987.

10. Don Hinrichsen, "Like First World, Like Third World," *Amicus Journal*, Winter 1988, p.5.

11. Ibid., p. 6.

12. For more on this issue, see James L. Tyson. "What Price Progress, Why China Says Ozone Must Take Back Seat in Drive to Prosperity," *Christian Science Monitor*, March 23, 1989.

13. Wallace K. Stevens, "To Treat the Attack of Acid Rain, Add Limestone to Water and Wait," *New York Times*, January 31, 1989.

14. Anne LaBastille, "The International Acid Test," *Sierra*, May/June 1986.

15. Adapted from Godfrey, *Acid Rain in Massachusetts*, p. 43.

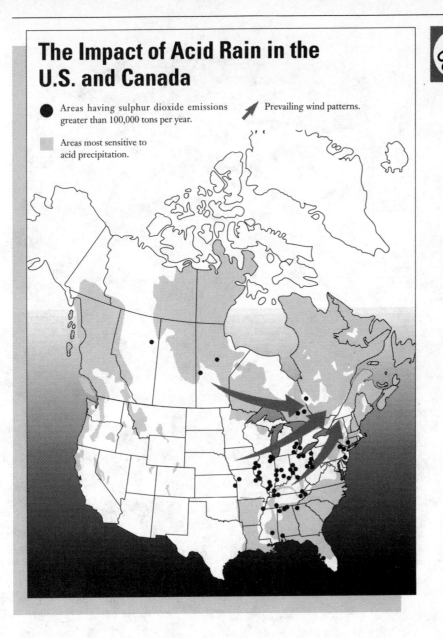

The Impact of Acid Rain in the U.S. and Canada

- Areas having sulphur dioxide emissions greater than 100,000 tons per year.
- Prevailing wind patterns.
- Areas most sensitive to acid precipitation.

6
DEFORESTATION

Saving the Trees

"Trees are the great healers of nature."
– René Dubos

Covering a third of the earth's land surface, forests and woodlands play a vital ecological role. They control climate by influencing wind, rainfall, humidity, and temperature. They recycle water, oxygen, and carbon, which reduces soil erosion, flooding, and air pollution. Providing habitats for half the world's animal and plant species, they are a rich source of food, fuel, and medicines.

Nourished by the energy of the sun, trees are our indispensable link with the biosphere. Perhaps because we take them so much for granted, we have not taken care of nature's great healers. Having already halved the world's original forests by centuries of exploitation, we are now systematically destroying what remains with a combination of greed and neglect. In addition to economic overuse – clearing land for agriculture, cutting down trees for lumber, and gathering fuel wood – there are the devastating effects of acid rain, nuclear radiation, and other pollutants that are accelerating deforestation to a possible point of no return.

Today many parts of the world are treeless, including much of Africa and the Middle East, India, Pakistan, Central Asia, Central America, and the Andean regions of South America. Unfortunately the countries with the largest remaining forests – the U.S.S.R., Brazil, Canada, and the U.S. – are not overly concerned with preserving what remains.

Destroying the Rain Forests

Every year at least 27 million acres of tropical forests – an area as large as Pennsylvania – are destroyed. At this rate, the world's tropical forests will be effectively eliminated by the end of this century, along with the 25 percent of all the world's life that inhabits them.

The damage done may already be irreversible. You do not have to demolish an ecosystem 100 percent to kill it off. The point of no return is often reached when more than half has been destroyed.

The Hamburger Connection – Tropical forests that took hundreds of years to grow are being sacrificed overnight for short-term commercial profit regardless of dire ecological consequences. They are cut down wholesale by chain saw and fire to provide cheap sources of beef for fast-food restaurants in North America and Europe, to harvest teak, mahogany, and other hardwoods for world markets, and to build giant projects – highways, hydroelectric dams, and mining operations.

Although some forests are cleared as a result of government planning, most of the devastation is done piecemeal, without regard to the consequences. The destruction is accelerated by intensive land use on the generally poor soils in tropical regions. Field cropping and cattle grazing deplete soil fertility and cause erosion. As crop yields fall, land is abandoned and more forest has to be cleared. What remains supplies meager subsistence for poverty-stricken local populations.

> *"If you turned the forest-products industry loose on that land, it would all be gone in perhaps 20 years."*
> Dr. Jerry Franklin[1]

The Fuel Wood Factor – In the Third World, where most rain forests are located, two billion people rely on firewood as their prime fuel for cooking and heating. This necessitates their cutting wood many times faster than it grows. It also further decreases soil fertility, because when the firewood runs out, families resort to burning cow dung instead of leaving it in the soil as manure or using it as a feedstock for methane biogas digesters.[2]

Long-term Consequences – Tropical deforestation is collapsing vital ecosystems that will take centuries to revive, if they ever do. It is irrevocably disrupting the lives of 200 million inhabitants who know how to use the rain forests without destroying them. These people and their way of life are fast disappearing with the trees.

The Price of Deforestation – Trees draw up the water from their roots through their branches and release it through their leaves as moisture, which then forms clouds. When they are cut down, rain and wind wash away the topsoil, making it impossible for water from melting mountain snowcaps or monsoons to be absorbed into the earth, eroding the soil.

The loss of trees and soil is taking its toll on the remarkable diversity of species in the rainforests (one out of every four pharmaceuticals used by Western chemists comes from tropical plants, 1,400 of which are under review as possible cancer cures). Because more than half the total biological diversity in the world exists where vegetation is threatened, more than 1.2 million species – a quarter of total biological diversity – are expected to vanish within the next 25 years. *No extinction of this magnitude has occurred during the past 65 million years.*[3]

Annihilation of Indigenous Peoples

In the Carajás region of the Amazon jungle in 1982, an area of rain forest the size of Florida, Georgia, and South Carolina combined, was cleared in 1982 to make way for a $1-billion iron-ore mining project.

The removal of essential sources of food and shelter forced the Guajas, the last nomadic tribe in South America, to the brink of extinction. Two other tribes, the Parakana and the Xikrin, now exist only in photographs and the slums of Rio de Janeiro.[4]

Global WarNing

Trees play a key role in the global cycling of carbon. The earth's vegetation and soils hold 2 trillion tons of carbon, roughly triple the amount stored in the atmosphere. When trees are cut, the carbon they contain is oxidized and released into the air, adding to the atmospheric store of carbon dioxide (CO_2). When trees are burned, the release takes place more rapidly. CO_2, water vapor, and trace amounts of other "greenhouse" gases such as ozone, methane, nitrous oxide, and chlorofluorocarbons play a key role in trapping heat in the earth's lower atmosphere. This warming action, commonly known as the greenhouse effect, is a matter of growing concern throughout the world because it is expected to bring about dramatic changes in global climate and food-growing. (The likely impact of these changes is discussed in the next chapter – "Global Warming.")

Deforestation in the West

The wholesale destruction of trees is not confined to the tropical regions. Sixty percent of the world's closed forests, including 90 percent of the conifers, are in the temperate zone. A large proportion of these forests, especially in North America and Europe, are being cleared by commercial timber and pulpwood production or to make way for agricultural use.

Utilization, not Protection

The ravaging of the virgin forests in the United States began with the first European settlers and reached such proportions by the late 19th century that Congress created a system of national forests and the U.S. Forest Service (USFS) to manage and protect them.

Today USFS "regulates" most of the country's remaining old-growth timber, most of it in the Pacific Northwest and Alaska, including the rain forests of the

Olympic Peninsula in Washington State and Alaska's Tongass National Forest where some of the trees are 500 years old and more. Unfortunately, regulation does not mean protection from cutting. The service is charged with *utilization* of forests. This includes timber production (which means heavy logging of trees) as well as recreation and protection of wildlife habitat and ecosystems.

Although funded exclusively by taxpayers, USFS permits private timber companies to cut federally owned trees, as they deplete their own forests. In the American rain forests, which run from northern California through southeast Alaska, more of the oldest and tallest trees in the world are being cut from public land than ever before.

Nationwide, the amount of timber stripped from 156 national forests reached an all-time high of 12.7 billion board feet in 1987, a record that would have been surpassed in 1988 but for extensive forest fires. *At the present rate of cutting, most of the nation's remaining old forests will vanish within the next 15 to 20 years, along with many of the ecosystems and wildlife species the service is supposed to protect.*

Hidden Subsidies

Much of the nationally owned timberland is being stripped at heavy cost to U.S. taxpayers. In Colorado's San Juan National Forest, timber sales lose 79 cents for every taxpayer dollar invested. In Cherokee National Forest, which surrounds the Great Smoky Mountains National Park, current harvests return only 62 cents for every dollar spent growing and selling trees. All seven national forests surrounding Yellowstone National Park lose money, with four of them returning less than 40 cents for every taxpayer dollar invested.[5]

Between 1982 and 1987 the Forest Service's timber-cutting losses totalled $2.4 billion. This was not a case of government inefficiency, but of incorrect priorities. The loss resulted from the service's lifelong relationship with timber-dependent communities.

When it was first established, USFS invited lumber mills to set up shop near the national forests and many towns grew up totally dependent on the work the industry provided. Although the service's mandate is to serve the nation at large, it is in fact obligated to local interests whose goals are often harmful to the environment.[6]

Conflicting Interests

The multiple use of U.S. national forests – which, along with state and local governments, make up 30 percent of total forestland in the nation – works poorly because those who use them have conflicting interests. Campers and hikers want to enjoy scenery and wildlife and not to be shot by hunters, of whom there are more than 40 million. The latter also have a stake in the continued existence of forests and perform a useful function in keeping deer populations in check. Farmers object to campers who cause forest fires and pollute the water; they don't like timbering because they depend on the trees to prevent soil erosion and flooding. The timber companies dislike anyone who gets in the way of cutting down trees that can be made into newspapers or houses, or, even more profitably, exported to Japan. This includes all of the above and developers with whom they compete in the race to cut down trees.

Responsible for reconciling these divergent interests are the U.S. Departments of Agriculture and Interior, the Bureaus of Land Management and of Wildlife and Fisheries, and the U.S. Forestry Service, which are often in disagreement with each other on how the forests should be managed.

New-style Logging

Most environmentalists agree with the Wilderness Society that no government agency is doing enough to protect old-growth trees (300 or more years old) whose huge size and tight grain make them especially valuable commercially. In the words of Chris Maser, senior author of the encyclopedic *Natural History of Oregon Coast Mammals*, "This is *our* habitat they are destroying. This is the habitat of the human race!"[7]

In many areas of the Pacific Northwest unique old-growth conifer forests composed of many varieties of trees are being cut down and inadequately "replaced" with a single species. Douglas fir saplings planted today will hardly take the place of cedar, spruce, and hemlock planted in the 17th century.

For loggers to get to the trees, thousands of miles of roads are being built, mainly by USFS which is the largest road builder in the world.

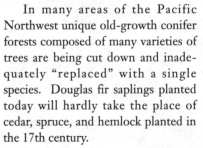

"A precious legacy, our national forest system is being destroyed by commercial logging – and taxpayers are subsidizing this disaster to the tune of almost half a billion dollars every year."

Wilderness Society report [8]

More than 343,000 miles of logging roads – eight times the mileage of the entire United States Interstate Highway System – now crisscross our national forests. These roads necessitate cutting down even more trees, causing soil erosion and preventing affected areas from ever being designated as protected wilderness.

Built for the almost exclusive use of the timber industry, the roads represent a hidden subsidy of at least $200 million a year by the U.S. government to the timber interests. By contrast, road building and clearcutting have reduced hiking trails from 150,000 miles to less than 99,000 miles today.

In six Southern Appalachian national forests USFS plans to build 3,000 miles of roads to open more than half of the 3.5 million acres to logging during the next ten years, doubling the present timber harvest. Yet the American Forestry Association has already identified 20 million open acres in the Southeast alone that should be planted to trees.[9]

In all, the Forest Service plans to build or rebuild 580,000 miles of roads in the national forests over the next fifty years – more than enough to reach the moon and back!

Forest Harvesting – There are two main ways to harvest a forest: *selective cutting* and *clearcutting*. Selective cutting or thinning means removing only mature or diseased trees. Because it does not significantly change the look of the forest, it is favored by those who want to use the forest for a variety of purposes and preserve the ecological diversity of the environment. Clearcutting means taking out all the trees from an area and leaving a checkerboard of bald patches that scar the landscape. Timber companies like this method because it enables them to use automated machinery – high-tech chain saws, cable yarders, and mechanical loaders that can handle 300-foot trees, even giant helicopters to get into otherwise inaccessible spots. It saves time and money by cutting down on the labor needed.

Slash-burning– This is exactly what it sounds like – clearing the forest by burning the trees. Although we condemn its use in Brazil, we condone it in the United States. Aside from destroying ecological diversity, slash-burning is the largest source of air pollution in the Pacific Northwest, where much of the timbering is

117

concentrated. In one case the smoke from burning trees on the Olympic Peninsula was so intense that it blanketed the sun in Seattle for five days.

The main purpose of slash-burning is to prepare the forest land for a highly industrialized development known as forest plantation. This is the commercial growing of single species of tree in precisely spaced rows that can be machine harvested at the appropriate time like so many ears of corn.

Continuous-tract Management– A more ecologically oriented approach to managing forest growth is advocated by a team of botanists at the University of Wisconsin, who proposed to the USFS that 140,000 acres of the Chequamegon National Forest be set aside to enable two continuous blocks of woodland to return to true old-growth status.

The proposal is based on the theory that large and continuous parcels of land must be preserved to protect unique ecological communities that are fast disappearing.

One reason for preserving large blocks of land intact is to prevent over-browsing by deer from the forest edges, which prevents growth of old-growth trees that can take 100 years or more to return. Standing dead trees would fall to leave sunlit openings where shrubs and other plants could grow. Rotting logs, sodden with water, would help control soil erosion, protect the forest from fire, and shelter hundreds of species of insects and small mammals. As they decay, the logs release tons of nutrients back into the soil.

The Wisconsin scientists point specifically to the nearby lands of the Menominee Indians, where deer densities are kept under control by year-round subsistence hunting. There, eastern hemlock and other threatened trees are thriving. According to the botanists, the blocks would represent about 20 percent of the forest and have a negligible effect on logging. But the proposal is strongly opposed by the timber industry.[10]

Myths and Realities*

● The first myth is that forests are renewable resources. Perhaps small trees may be grown crop-style in endless rotations to produce a steady flow of pulp and cheap wood fiber. But the clear, dense vertical grain that has made saw timber from the Northwest so valuable in the past is a product of old-growth forests, which take hundreds of years to develop.

● Another myth is that recent job losses in the wood-products industry are the result of environmental set-asides. Nothing could be further from the truth. Since 1983 the timber cut in the Northwest has increased 40 percent while employment per board foot cut has declined by 33 percent. This is the result of exporting large volumes of unprocessed logs which create no manufacturing opportunities for the region.

● The most insidious myth is that the economy and ecology of local areas must compete in the future — that every additional protected wild place or old-growth stand will result in a proportionate loss of jobs. Our perspective is that in the long run the contrary is true: environmental diversity will create economic diversity, and a stable healthy economy will be produced only by a healthy ecology.

---

* From "Lessons from the Ancient Forest," a slide presentation by Lou Gold, the Siskiyou Regional Education Project, Portland, Ore., with permission.

Land of Many Uses – Siskiyou National Park: A Unique Opportunity[11]

Located in southwestern Oregon, the proposed site for a new national park spans a vast wildland from the California border to the town of Grants Pass. The Wild Rogue and Kalmiopsis wilderness areas and the Scenic River corridors of the Illinois and Rogue are already protected for their spectacular values. By including the largely undisturbed timberlands which connect these areas, the largest expanse of unprotected coastal old-growth forest in the Pacific Northwest will be preserved for the benefit of future generations. Park development can occur around a core of nearly 400,000 roadless acres containing the most diverse mixed conifer forest on earth.

For Hiking, Recreation, and Wildlife

For every type of outdoor adventure from a picnic to a remote wilderness trek this is a region of marvels: four wild rivers and cascading white water; a large piece of ancient forest still bearing healthy populations of cougar, bear, osprey, bald eagle, wolverine, and otter; miles of trails winding from rivers to mountaintops; and a paradise for plants and wildflowers, over 1,400 species identified here so far.

Proposal Threatened

As Oregon looks for ways to diversify its economy, a new national park offers ample opportunities for scientific research, watershed restoration, recreation, and tourism. The park's proponents seek to create a sustainable economy based on sound ecology and to preserve clean air and water, salmon-filled rivers, and a heritage of wildlife and stately trees.

The Siskiyou is the largest intact coastal forest in the United States outside of Alaska and the major center of plant evolution on the West Coast. However, the U.S. Forest Service has announced plans for logging and roading 96 percent of the wildest areas within the next fifteen years. This planned liquidation of natural forestland threatens to ruin over half the area proposed for the national park.

What you can do: For more on how to prevent destruction of this national trust, contact Siskiyou Regional Education Project, P.O. Box 13070, Portland, OR 97213; (503) 249-2958.

Nuclear Power May Be Dangerous to Our Trees

Loss of foliage, reduction of growth rate, and dying of trees in forest areas far from heavily industrialized regions are occurring in many parts of Europe and the United States. Although much of this damage is caused by air pollution and acid rain, it may also be due to radioactive gases released from nuclear plants.

A detailed study by a German forestry expert revealed narrow zones of forest damage 30 miles downwind of nuclear reactors located in isolated rural areas in France and Germany, away from other sources of industrial pollutants.[12] This finding was linked by Dr. Ernest Sternglass, professor of radiological physics at the University of Pittsburgh, with similar patterns of damage from nuclear reactors in the southeastern United States. He reported that among the many radioactive gases routinely emitted from these plants was tritium, a type of radioactive hydrogen that combines with oxygen to form water and is taken up by all forms of vegetation. Sternglass added that radioactive carbon-14 was also found in abnormally high concentrations in leaves near nuclear plants such as the one at Wuergassen, Germany, where heavy tree damage has occurred.[13]

As the Spotted Owls Go*

It has become something like a canary in a coal mine – its status signals the health of the old-growth forest as a whole.

Only an estimated 1,600 pairs of northern spotted owls remain and the species faces extinction. Inhabiting Washington's Cascade mountains, they require 1,000 to 4,500 acres of old-growth forest per pair to survive – to provide sufficient shelter, a protective microclimate, and enough prey. The spotted owl avoids clearcuts, burned areas, and younger stands of trees.

Its ecological role is to cull and keep healthy the forest population of flying squirrels, voles, and other small mammals. These animals eat fruit-bearing fungi (truffles) whose spores, vital to the growth of new trees, they deposit at new sites. This relationship between birds, mammals, and plants is what keeps the forests alive. Just as the spotted owl needs the old-growth forest for its survival, so it is most likely that the forest cannot survive without the owl and other medium-sized predators that are vanishing along with the trees.

In 1987 a coalition of conservation groups petitioned the U.S. Fish and Wildlife Service to put the owl on the endangered-species list. They declined, and the groups went to court. In November 1988 a federal district judge ruled that the refusal had been "arbitrary, capricious, and contrary to law." If the spotted owl is formally designated an endangered species, old-growth logging would be affected throughout its range. "This is a major victory," says Jim Pissot, National Audubon Society's Washington, D.C. wildlife specialist. "But it's also an undeniable challenge to the timber industry. We can probably expect them to characterize this battle in terms of the snail darter and the Tellico dam – they'll say we're using the owl to get at the trees. Of course, these issues are interrelated and have common aspects, but we must remember that each is terribly important in its own right, both the owl and the forests."

What you can do:
● Ask your congressional representatives to support legislation to protect the spotted owl and other endangered species.
● Urge your legislators to protect the forests of the Northwest. They are national treasures as important to the people of New York, New England, or New Orleans as to those of the Northwest.

---

* Extracted with permission from "America's Forest Crisis," by Frederick Allen, in *The Urban Audubon*, New York City Audubon Society, January-February 1989.

In response to worldwide destruction of trees is a growing awareness that effective countermeasures must be taken globally before it is too late. There is also virtually unanimous agreement on the need to plant more trees to stabilize soil and water systems seriously damaged by deforestation and to satisfy urgent firewood needs of more than a billion people in India, Africa, and other regions of the Third World.

An estimated 300 million acres of tree planting will be required for these purposes by the turn of the century, plus another 75 million acres to meet the world demand for timber, paper, and other forest products. According to the Worldwatch Institute, the estimated annual cost of the plantings would run from $2.4 billion in 1990 to $6.8 billion in 2000. Because most of the new trees would be grown not on orderly plantations, but in marginal land on hillsides, next to dwellings, and sometimes interplanted with crops, the main resource of this effort would be labor rather than capital.

When farmers and their families plant their own trees, the costs (about $100 an acre) are considerably lower than for commercial plantations ($1,000 or more). Seedlings cost roughly the same in both cases – about $30 an acre. Planting seeds directly into the soil costs even less.[14]

Children of the Green Earth[15]

"I have a vision of the Earth made green again through the efforts of children. I can see the children of all nations holding hands around the globe in celebration of the Earth as their home and all children, all people, as their family." – Richard St. Barbe Baker

In 1922 Dr. Richard St. Barbe Baker, then working for the British Colonial Service, started a society called Men of the Trees, whose first members were Kikuyu tribesmen in Kenya. Each member agreed to plant ten trees a year and to take care of trees everywhere. Over the next six decades St. Barbe became involved in planting and saving trees all over the world, designing "shelter belt" schemes to counter the American Dust Bowl, spearheading a campaign to save the California redwoods, planning reforestation to reclaim erosion in the Sahara Desert, advising the United Nations, expanding Men of the Trees into an international organization, and setting up the organization that carries his vision forward – Children of the Green Earth.

The author of many books, including *My Life, My Trees*, the best overview of his life and work, Richard St. Barbe Baker is said to be responsible for the planting of more than *26 billion trees*!

International Efforts

In 1985 a consortium of international agencies including the United Nations Development Program, the World Resources Institute, and the World Bank released the 8 billion dollar Tropical Forestry Action Plan (TFAP) designed to alleviate tropical deforestation and promote the sustainable use of the world's forests. In the view of many environmentalists, including the highly respected

British magazine *The Ecologist*, the plan is flawed in its analysis of the problem and its proposed solutions. It makes only passing reference to the massive destruction caused by the timber industry, ranching, large-scale dams, and road-building projects which have been responsible for most of the deforestation over the past 40 years. Instead, it lays blame on indigenous people for destroying trees, giving credence to the view that current development policies should continue unabated.

TFAP is seen as less concerned with preserving natural forests than with setting up commercial plantations of fast-growing trees such as eucalyptus, which are not ecologically or environmentally sound. In addition, the type of commercial plantations advocated by TFAP have already proved deeply divisive economically and socially, favoring the rich over the poor, states Nicholas Hildyard, coordinator for the Save the Forests, Save the Planet campaign.[16]

Save the Forests, Save the Planet

In 1987 *The Ecologist* published a plan to save the tropical forests. It proposed:

● exchanging Third World debts for guaranteed protection of the world's remaining tropical forests;

● a massive reforestation program with trees selected for their ecological rather than commercial value;

● phasing out development programs (dams, plantations, roads) which threaten the forests in favor of ecologically sustainable policies to satisfy local needs rather than international markets.

Urging the United Nations to convene a special emergency session to implement its proposals, *The Ecologist* launched a worldwide petition for its Save the Forests, Save the Planet campaign.

What you can do: Add your name to the one million people *The Ecologist* is seeking for its petition and send donations for the campaign to the Ecological Foundation, Lower Bosnieves, Withiel, Bodmin, Cornwall, U.K. PI32 9TT.

Planting Trees

Some of the most successful reforestation programs have come from nongovernmental organizations such as CARE in the United States and Oxfam in Great Britain. In one project the U.S. Agency for International Development contracted with CARE and the Pan American Foundation to encourage agroforestry and tree farming in Haiti – planting more than 27 million seedlings between 1982 and 1986. There have also been successful tree-planting projects in South Korea, India, Ghana, and Lebanon. In Kenya the Greenbelt Movement, sponsored by the National Council of Women of Kenya, has planted more than 2 million trees, involving more than 15,000 farmers and a half a million schoolchildren.[17]

Embracing Trees – Chipko, a legendary forest-protection movement, began in the Garwhal hills of Uttar Pradesh, northern India. In 1973, when a timber company prepared to cut trees near their village, local women, men, and children rushed to the woods, hugged the trees, and dared the loggers to let the axes fall on their backs. An inspiration for many community movements worldwide, Chipko has expanded its work from saving trees to planting them, building soil retainer walls, and other types of ecological management.[18]

"Love Trees, Love Your Country"– In 1973 the South Korean government started a program to protect forests and create new village plantations. Twenty-one thousand village forestry associations were formed with villagers contributing half the costs, mainly in kind. These locally elected bodies are organized like cooperatives and are voluntarily managed by villagers. At the same time a major land reform divided almost 75 percent of the country's forests into private hands, mainly small plots.

Today, forests of pine, larch, cedar, and fruit trees cover two-thirds of South Korea's total land area. The original emphasis was on fast-growing trees; now the Forestry Bureau wants to plant more hardwood trees, which take 75 or more years to mature. This requires low-interest loans from the government, the creation of cooperatives of 200 to 400 acres, and some yielding of power by village associations to the central government. Under the slogan "Love trees, love your country," the process is moving ahead with signal success.

> *"The forest looked like a firm grass sward, and the effect of these lakes in its midst has been well compared. . . to that of a mirror broken into a thousand fragments, and wildly scattered over the grass, reflecting the full blaze of the sun."*
>
> Henry David Thoreau,
> The Maine Woods, 1864

Cashews Reforest Honduras – Clearcutting and abusive exploitation have all but destroyed the once beautiful forests of southern Honduras. Alternating drought and flooding make farming and survival nearly impossible for its people. But reforestation has begun. Poor peasants have organized themselves into cooperatives to plant and raise cashew trees. The nuts provide incomes and the trees help stop erosion and stabilize the soil. A nonprofit organization called Pueblo to People works with the cooperatives to market cashews and other local products. For more information you can contact them at 5218 Chenevert, #5570, Houston, TX 77004; (713) 523-1197.

As Maine Goes . . . "If nothing is done, it will soon be too late to save the Maine woods from the major changes in landscape and land use that have already occurred throughout most of New England." So concludes a 1988 report by the Wilderness Society, a national environmental organization based in Washington, D.C., concerned with saving the northern Maine forests from being converted into subdivisions and vacation homes, a fate that has overtaken much of New England and New York.[19]

Warning that time is running out on saving a priceless heritage, the society proposes creating "an extraordinarily beautiful and diverse 2.7 million-acre forest preserve" surrounding an existing state park in the heart of Maine's North Woods. A protected preserve would assure a continuing balance of uses in the forest which is owned largely by big timber companies. It would continue to provide "a sustainable timber supply," as well as assuring public access for camping, hunting, and fishing and the preservation of pristine lakes, rivers, and other natural areas.

The report suggests a number of ways the preserve could be established, including federal and state land purchases and easements on private property. Generally endorsed by environmental groups, the proposal has met a mixed

Case Study Ghana[*]

World Neighbors, an international humanitarian organization headquartered in Oklahoma City, is an exponent of Community Forestry – growing trees as a way to improve living conditions. Their approach is based on hands-on learning and encouraging local responsibility and self-reliance.

In 1983 they decided to promote tree planting in Garu, a densely populated rural area of northern Ghana that had been denuded of trees. The goal was to help villagers create "a tree rich landscape, where trees play an important role for providing shade and fruit, and individual woodlots for roofing poles and firewood." [20]

The project began modestly by funding two local people with $9,000 a year to set up a nursery that would, it was hoped, inspire their neighbors to start their own plantings. As the first tree seedlings grew, World Neighbors encouraged the formation of village tree committees, composed of other local farmers who began tree nurseries in their own home compounds.

Within three years 35,000 tree seedlings were produced and successfully planted, with a survival rate of about 50 percent (compared with a 30-percent average reported by the World Bank).

When asked what methods they found most useful in promoting tree growing, members of the project replied: "The best method is by example. . . . You have to start planting trees by yourself and the people will see. Do not do too much at once to convince many people. . . just start planting trees and talk to interested people." [21]

The Garu project has attracted the attention of many other groups in Ghana, who come there to buy trees and get advice on how to start their own programs. The greatest accomplishment of the program, says World Neighbors, is that villagers in the region now have a vision of a tree-rich landscape which they are practically making a reality within their limited means and resources: "Even if the Garu program stopped tomorrow, the villagers who have been reached have the motivation and the technical training to continue to plant trees on their own." [22]

Working hand-in-hand with local people and encouraging self sufficiency in rural communities, World Neighbors supports similar programs in other parts of Africa and in Asia and Latin America.

---

[*] Based with permission on *Case Study: Ghana* by Peter A. Gubbels, World Neighbors West Africa representative.

response from government agencies and outright opposition from Maine Forests Products Council, an industry trade association.

Banking on Success[23]

The Amazon rain forest is being destroyed at an increasingly rapid rate – the area cleared has expanded five times between 1980 and 1988 – and will be entirely gone in less than fifty years. In an effort to save what's left, the Environmental Defense Fund has come up with an innovative project.

EDF has targeted the multilateral development banks (MDBs) – particularly the World Bank and the Inter-American Development Bank – as the institutions with the greatest influence over Third World development. The World Bank and other MDBs loan more than $24 billion a year for projects in 100 developing nations. Private banks and local government agencies, acting on this stamp of approval, also loan money for the projects, tripling the amount to over $75 billion a year.

In Brazil the link between MDB-financed development and resource destruction is clear. Undeveloped areas of the Amazon remain intact, but states with MDB-financed roads and mining projects – such as Rondônia, Mato Grosso, Pará, Acre, and Maranhâo – have become "maelstroms" of destruction and vast deforestation.

Rondonia and Mato Grosso, site of the infamous Polonoroeste highway and colonization project, are the worst. Both have lost nearly 25 percent of their forests, mostly since 1980. In Pará and Maranhâo the World Bank's Carajas iron ore project spurred huge, unsustainable schemes, including pig-iron smelters burning native trees as fuel. If carried out, the plan could devastate an area more than twice the size of California.

In one part of the western Amazon, now stripped of trees and sprinkled with cattle, an estimated 10,000 rubber-tapper families have been driven off the land since 1970, when large companies and private speculators first moved in.[24]

EDF has worked closely with Brazilian environmental and indigenous peoples' organizations and community groups to change or halt the most destructive MDB projects and to advance locally supported sustainable alternatives by promoting public discussion of the development process and opening access to developers' plans and methods.

As a result of EDF's efforts, the development banks suspended several projects on environmental and social grounds and the World Bank delayed approval of a $500 million loan supporting gigantic new hydroelectric dams in India that would destroy forests and flood lands.

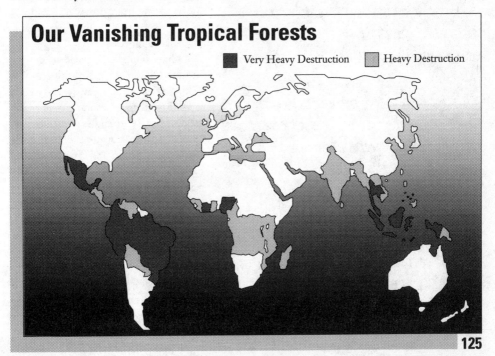

Our Vanishing Tropical Forests

■ Very Heavy Destruction   ■ Heavy Destruction

The banks are beginning to support EDF-backed alternatives such as the "extractive reserves," large forest areas controlled by local rubber-tappers' groups for harvesting rubber, Brazil nuts, resins, and other forest products. With MDB and Brazilian government support, 12 such reserves – totaling roughly the area of New Jersey – are being created.

EDF's collaboration with Brazilian groups has also helped strengthen Brazilian environmental organizations in their efforts to get governmental action to protect the environment.

Swapping Debts for Nature

The idea of exchanging Third World debts for the protection of tropical forests is endorsed by Costa Rica, a small Central American country with a large deforestation problem. At present rates of cutting, it will run out of trees within 25 years, with the leftover land turned into low-quality cattle pasture or scrub too poor to cultivate.

To prevent such a disaster, the Ministry of Natural Resources, under the leadership of Alvaro Umaña, a physicist and ecologist, has acted to preserve one-third of remaining forests, restricting development of another third, and negotiating a "debt for nature" swap in which parts of Costa Rica's foreign debt are converted to conservation endowment.

In January 1989 American Express Bank, a large creditor to Costa Rica, sold $5.6 million in Costa Rican IOUs to the Nature Conservancy, a Washington, D.C.-based environmental group, for $784,000. The conservancy then traded back the paper to the Costa Rican central bank for $1.7 million in local currency bonds, with the interest to be paid to a local conservation group to manage nine projects.

Everyone gained in the deal: AmEx got a tax deduction (as on any bad debt); Costa Rica retired a part of its $1.5 billion debt to foreign banks; Nature Conservancy doubled the purchase power of its cash donation; and the local conservation group got valuable financial support.

> *"If we are to save the Indians' homes and protect the forests, we must prove to the societies that covet these resources that forests are more valuable and productive as forests than they are as cattle pasture or crop land."*
>
> *Cultural Survival*

Other countries – Ecuador, Bolivia, and the Philippines – have done similar debt-for-local-currency swaps with a commitment to environmental preservation. But the trades have all been on a small scale. Larger exchanges are harder to finance and they touch on national sensitivities. In April 1989, responding to worldwide criticism of Brazil's haphazard development of the Amazon, its president, José Sarney, firmly ruled out debt-for-nature swaps. "We accept international aid," he said, "but we don't accept conditions." [25]

Cultural Survival

Because it ignores the needs of indigenous peoples, swapping debts for nature is opposed on humanitarian grounds by many environmental groups, most notably *Cultural Survival* (CS), a nonprofit organization based in Cambridge, Mass. CS's answer is to establish markets in the U.S. and Europe for sustainably harvested rain forest products that will increase the income of forest residents without destroying either the forests or the indigenous cultures. For example, CS supplied the Vermont ice cream company Ben and Jerry's with 100,000 pounds of Brazil and cashew nuts. The Brazil nuts can be harvested directly off the forest floor without doing any damage to the trees. This kind of natural harvesting, CS has shown, could generate five times more income per acre to local residents than the same land would to raise cattle.

A Bad Investment

The idea of saving rain forests in order to protect the environment has carried little weight with Brazil and other countries saddled with heavy national debts. However, a major study reported in *Nature* magazine in 1989 shows deforestation to be a bad investment economically as well as ecologically. For example, revenues generated by harvesting edible fruits, rubber, oils, and cocoa from 2.5 acres of tropical rain forest are nearly two times greater than the return on timber or the value of the land if used for grazing cattle.[26]

The study showed that 12 products, mainly edible fruits and latex rubber, found in 2.5 acres of a forest in northeastern Peru near the Brazilian border, were worth $6,330 if sold in local markets over 50 years (with the cost of harvesting deducted from the market price). By comparison, the same land would produce $3,184 if used as a timber plantation, or $2,960 if converted to cattle pasture. "It appears that keeping it as managed forests has greater economic value [than deforestation]," said Lester B. Lave, an economist and environmental expert at Carnegie Mellon University in Pittsburgh, commenting on the report.[27]

Trading Trees

Trees for Carbon – In the belief that the carbon dioxide emitted by U.S. power plants could be absorbed by 10 million acres of new forest, a Connecticut electric utility company decided in late 1988 to contribute $2 million towards the planting of 52 million trees over 385 square miles in Guatemala.

Concerned that its new coal-burning power plant will add significantly to global warming, Applied Energy Services Thames, a Connecticut utility company, acted on the principle that trees will absorb CO_2 from all over the world, no matter where they are planted.

According to Roger Sant, AES's chief executive, the trees planted in Guatemala will absorb at least as much CO_2 as will be emitted by the new generating plant at Uncasville, Conn. In addition to the $2 million from AES, the same amount in cash or services will be contributed by CARE, $1.2 million by the Guatemalan government, $3.6 million by the U.S. Agency for International Development, and $7.5 million by the Peace Corps.[28]

Trees for Life – In 1983 Balbir Mathur, a naturalized American citizen from India, set up Trees for Life (TFL), a people-to-people organization in Wichita, Kans., to feed the hungry people of the world with the fruit of trees they plant and to share their know-how with others. Since then TFL has planted more than a million trees and distributed millions of seedlings at festivals in India.

Mathur began by planting fruit trees in his mother's village and persuading the inhabitants to plant 18 more trees from their seeds each year. On his return to Wichita, he inspired a class of eighth-grade students to start a fund drive to send 103 fruit trees to India. Many others joined the campaign, including two local bakeries (that made donations based on the number of loaves they sold during the drive), an outdoor advertising agency, and several grocery stores.

In the United States TFL has a Grow-a-Tree division, distributing packets of materials, seeds and instructions in schools and summer camps for student projects. Mathur's most ambitious project is a petition drive calling on the leaders of the United States and the Soviet Union to join in a move to plant more than 100 million fruit trees in developing countries. To help farmers become self-sufficient, TFL provides them with technical know-how, program management, good quality tree saplings or seed, and, where needed, soil improvement help. In return, the farmers provide land to grow trees, farmyard manure, labor, and a commitment to follow instructions and to help at least two more people as they were helped by TFL.

Farmers provide 61 percent of the cost of planting and taking care of the trees. TFL pays the rest. For a village to be selected for the program, a majority of farmers must participate. Mathur says that even though farmers reap the benefits of working on their own land, the spirit of cooperative effort and sharing are the keys to the program's success.

Global Releaf Takes Root– On Arbor Day 1989 hundreds of American communities joined in *Global Releaf*, a nationwide campaign sponsored by the American Forestry Association (AFA) to plant 100 million trees by 1992.

The program focuses on urban "hot spots" – factories, power plants, large buildings, and highways – where heavy concentrations of carbon dioxide are released into the air. Trees give "releaf" by:

● using up excess CO_2 in the atmosphere and turning it into life-giving oxygen;

● conserving energy (three properly planted trees around your home can cut your air-conditioning bill by 10 to 50 percent (See chapter 9, p. 218, for more on this);

● turning urban "heat islands" into cool and comfortable oases, making the concrete jungle more livable.

As the Global Releaf action guide states, there are 100 million energy-efficient tree planting sites available around our homes and in our towns and cities. Planting 100 million trees, they say, could offset America's CO_2 emissions by 18 million tons a year and save $4 billion a year in cleanup costs of air pollution into the bargain.

What You Can Do to Save the Trees

Here are 16 things you can do that will make a difference:

1. *Plant and care for trees* in your own yard and in your town. Greener is more beautiful, is energy-efficient, and helps clean the environment. (See box on next page for how to find best-quality seeds, seedlings, and trees.)

2. *Share your tree knowledge* with your neighbors and help them plant new trees or replace missing ones.

3. *Join or form a neighborhood or block association*, one of whose main purposes will be tree care and planting.

4. *Involve schoolchildren* in tree-planting groups at their schools with a contest to see which one has the most trees growing after one year.

5. *With children's help, clean up* vacant lots and small parks, and replant with trees.

6. *Get local businesses and utilities to plant trees* on their property.

7. *Identify new commercial and residential developments* that need trees and get developers to finance plantings to improve their property.

8. *Invite local tree nurseries to participate* in these and other projects, offering special discounts on Arbor Days, and donating trees for raffles and other events.

Eight Tips on How to Plant Healthy Trees

1. Get your seeds or seedlings from unhybridized, natural, old-fashioned seed lines that are not sprayed, dusted, fumigated, or radiated. Good sources include:

- Abundant Life Seed Foundation, P.O. Box 772, Port Townsend, WA 98368.
- Johnny's Selected Seeds, Foss Hill Road, Albion, ME 04910.
- Living Tree Center, P.O. Box 797, Bolinas, CA 94924; (415) 868-2224.
- Native Seed Foundation, Star Route, Moyie Springs, ID, 83845; (208) 267-7938.
- St. Lawrence Nurseries, R.D. 2, Potsdam, NY 13676; (315) 265-6739.

2. Any tree you buy should be grown to nursery standards developed by the American Association of Nurserymen. Check roots and main stem to make sure they are strong. Container-grown trees should be well established so that roots will retain their shape and hold soil together when removed.

3. Before planting, cover the roots with a black plastic bag to keep them damp and away from sun.

4. Dig a big hole — at least 2 feet deep and 2 to 3 feet wide. Pack the richest soil around the roots. Don't put peat moss or other light material in the hole; tree roots need a structure of real soil to function best. Avoid leaving large air pockets, which prevent water and nutrients from reaching the roots. Fill in around the tree with topsoil first, then subsoil. Use compost and mulch as top dressing spread in a 4-foot-diameter "dish" around the base of the tree so water will flow toward it.

5. Water the tree generously — 5 to 10 gallons a day for the first month, 2 to 3 times a week until midsummer.

6. Cover the base of the trunk with hardware cloth at least 2 feet high to prevent nibbling by mice, rabbits, and other small animals. Fence off the tree, if deer or cattle are nearby.

7. Check yellow pages for technical assistance from county cooperative extension services, state forestry or soil conservation departments, or local parks and public works departments. A nearby community college or university can also be helpful.

8. For a good source of information on plant species and propagation consult the *1988 International Green Front Report*, pp. 160-173, available from Friends of the Trees, P.O. Box 1466, Chelan, WA 98816.

9. *Invite your local library, community college, or university to hold a public symposium* on trees and climate (the greenhouse effect is a hot topic – see next chapter, pp. 139-147).

10. *Support and join* national or local chapters of tree saving/planting organizations such as the Wilderness Society, the American Forestry Association (Global Releaf), Trees for Life, the Rainforest Action Network, Greenpeace, Earth First, and EDF (see "Resources", pp. 130-132).

11. With the help of these groups, *organize special tree-related events* for local press, radio, and television coverage. These events could include saving endangered trees from being cut down, tree-growing demonstrations, special plantings, or food sales with products from trees – apple pies, nut breads, cherry and plum tarts and jams, berry and leaf teas.

12. *Recycle newspapers and other paper products.* This can save enormous quantities of trees from being cut down. (See chapter 1, p. 26 for further details.)

13. *Boycott fast-food restaurants that serve beef raised in tropical rain forests.* Under popular pressure McDonald's and some other chains have given up importing this kind of meat. Check with your local restaurants, to make sure that they are honoring this pledge. The package containing the frozen hamburger products usually states the country of origin.

14. *Support the growing movement to stop the sale of woods from rain forests,* notably mahogany and teak. Use only "good woods," which include beech, birch, oak, pine, larch, and spruce.

15. Read and give these inspiring books: *The Man Who Planted Hope and Grew Happiness,* by Jean Giono; *Trees – Guardians of the Earth,* by Don Nichol; and *My Life, My Trees,* the autobiography of Richard St. Barbe Baker, the initiator of major tree-planting projects on five continents. All of these books can be ordered from the Abundant Life Seed Foundation, P.O. Box 772, Port Townsend, WA 98368.

16. Send for the Recycled Paper Catalog of the *Earth Care Paper Co.,* P.O. Box 3335, Madison, WI 53704, which sells products made from recycled paper – greetings cards, gift wrapping, stationery, cellulose food-storage bags – as well as books and educational materials on recycling and other environmental topics.

RESOURCES

The following is provided to help you locate additional resources on the topics covered in this chapter.

1. International Agencies and Organizations

— *Food and Agricultural Organization (FAO),* Via delle Terme di Caracalla, 00100, Rome, Italy. An agency of the United Nations specializing in the development of world food and agriculture.

— *International Tree Crops Institute,* P.O. Box 4460, Davis, CA 95617.

— *United Nations Environment Program (UNEP),* headquarters, P.O. Box 4704, Nairobi, Kenya; United Nations office, 2 U.N. Plaza, New York, NY 10022; (212) 963-8139.

— *World Rainforest Movement,* Third World Network, 87 Cantonment Road, Penang, Malaysia.

2. U.S. Government

— *Department of Agriculture,* Independence Avenue SW, Washington, DC 20250:

    National Forest Service, Office of Information, P.O. Box 2417, Washington, DC 20013; (202) 447-3760.

— *Department of the Interior,* 18th and C Streets NW, Washington, DC 20240; (202) 343-3171:

    Bureau of Land Management
    Bureau of Wildlife and Fisheries
    National Park Service

3. Associations and Environmental Groups

— *Alaska Conservation Foundation,* 430 West 7th Avenue, Suite 215, Anchorage, AK 99501; (907) 276-1917. Coordinates the efforts of 30 grassroots organizations in the state to protect Alaskan National Parks, the Tongass National Forest, the Arctic National Wildlife Refuge, and the Outer Continental Shelf.

— *American Forestry Association*, 1516 P Street NW, Washington, DC 20005; (202) 667-3300. Dedicated to protect U.S. forests and related resources, AFA runs many programs including Global Releaf and Urban Forest Forum. Publishes *American Forests* bimonthly.

— *Catalyst*, 64 Main Street, Montpelier, VT 05602; (802) 223-7943. Its work includes the New England Tropical Forest Project offering workshops, consultations, and networking help for all concerned with saving the rain forests. It also publishes the quarterly newsletter *Catalyst* devoted to investing for social change. (see also chapter 12, p. 306-308).

— *Chipko*, P.O. Silyara via Ghansale, Tehri-Garwhal, Uttar Pradesh, 249155 India. Born in 1973, the Chipko movement is one of India's (and the world's) most effective groups in creating awareness of the need for trees, forests, and ecological preservation.

— *Conservation Foundation*, 1255 Twenty-third Street NW, Washington, DC 20037; (202) 293-4800. Conducts research on environmental and resource management. Publishes in-depth environmental studies and the newsletter *Resolve*.

— *Cultural Survival*, 11 Divinity Avenue, Cambridge, MA 02138; (617) 495-2562. Sponsors direct assistance projects designed and run by indigenous peoples, and researches and reports on their problems, particularly with regard to tropical rain forests.

— *Earth First!*, 305 N. Sixth Street, Madison, WI 53704; (606) 241-9426. Has no formal organization or "members." Promotes a philosophy of Deep Ecology, an uncompromising defense of natural diversity, and visionary wilderness proposals. Organizes task-force actions and "road shows" to gain media attention. (For further details on their work, see chapter 10, pp. 279-281). Publishes *Earth First! Journal* eight times a year.

— *Earth Island Institute*, 300 Broadway, Suite 28, San Francisco, CA 94133; (415) 788-7324. An international action group whose projects include environmental litigation, rain-forest health alliance, appropriate technology, climate protection. Publishes the quarterly *Earth Island Journal*.

— *Environmental Defense Fund*, 257 Park Avenue South, New York, NY 10010; (212) 505-2100. EDF's many programs include research and lobbying on tropical rain-forest destruction.

— *Friends of the Earth*, 530 Seventh Street SE, Washington, DC 20003; (202) 543-4312. An international environmental organization, it is active in fighting for many world issues including rain-forest protection, preservation and restoration of ecosystems, and renewable energy development.

— *Friends of the Trees*, P.O. Box 1466, Chelan, WA 98816. Promotes reforestation and earth-healing activities worldwide. Distributes seeds, plants, and horticultural information. Acts as a network center for information on the international Green Front. Publishes the *1988 International Green Front Report*.

— *Greenpeace*, 1436 U Street NW, Washington, DC 20009; (202) 462-1177. International direct action and lobbying on rain forests, toxic waste, ocean and air pollution, whales, nuclear radiation. Publishes bimonthly magazine *Greenpeace*.

— *LightHawk — The Wings of Conservation*, Box 8163, Santa Fe, NM 87504; (505) 982-9656. Lighthawk planes fly missions to map rain forest destruction from Costa Rica to Alaska. Focuses on the "chainsaw massacre" of the USFS and other important deforestation issues.

— *National Audubon Society*, 833 Third Avenue, New York, NY 10022; (212) 832-3200. Research, education, and lobbying on wildlife, forests, wilderness, public lands, endangered species, water and energy policy. Publishes bimonthly *Audubon* magazine and *Audubon Activist* newsletter.

— *National Wildlife Federation*, 1412 Sixteenth Street NW, Washington, DC 20036; (202) 737-2024. With a network of 51 state and territorial affiliates, NWF promotes the wise use of natural resources. Sponsors National Wildlife Week and many other educational and demonstration programs. Publishes *National Wildlife* (bimonthly), *NatureScope* (for classrooms), the *Environmental Quality Index*, and *Legislative Hotline*.

— *Nitrogen Fixing Tree Association*, P.O. Box 680, Waimanalo, HI 96795.

— *Permaculture Institute of North America*, 4649 Sunnyside Avenue N. Seattle, WA 98103. Devoted to the design of land-use systems that are sustainable and environmentally sound.

— *Rainforest Action Network*, 301 Broadway, Suite A, San Francisco, CA 94133; (415) 398-4404. Uses direct action to sound the alarm on rain-forest issues. Works internationally

with developing nations to preserve the rain forest as a renewable resource. Publishes the quarterly *World Rainforest Report*.
— *Rainforest Alliance*, 270 Lafayette Street, New York, NY 10012; (212) 941-1900. A non-profit national organization promoting policies and actions that encourage forest conservation and research on the medicinal use of tropical plants.
— *Sierra Club*, 530 Bush Street, San Francisco, CA 94108; (415) 981 8634. Lobbies on wide range of environmental matters including deforestation, wilderness, public lands, toxics, energy, and nuclear waste. Publishes the bimonthly *Sierra* magazine.
— *Siskiyou Regional Education Project*, P.O. Box 13070, Portland, OR 97213; (503) 249-2958. Promotes the conservation of natural resources and sustainable local energies in the Klamath-Siskiyou bioregion.
— *Trees for Life*, 1103 Jefferson, Wichita, KS 67203; (316) 263-7294. Provides funding, management, and know-how to people in developing countries to plant and care for food and fuel trees. Runs a program to educate U.S. children about the importance of trees.
— *Wilderness Society*, 1400 Eye Street NW, Washington, DC 20005; (202) 842-3200. With 13 regional offices, the society educates citizens, public officials, and media on the need to protect and carefully manage public lands. Testifies at congressional hearings; sponsors meetings on public land management; and publishes wilderness-related reports.
— *World Neighbors*, 5116 N. Portland Avenue, Oklahoma City, OK 73112; (405) 946-3333. An international organization working in Asia, Africa, and Latin America to encourage self-sufficiency in rural communities, it has a wide variety of excellent training materials available in English, Spanish, or French to anyone in the world upon request .
— *World Wildlife Fund*, 1250 Twenty-fourth Street NW, Washington, DC 20037; (202) 293-4800. With 23 affiliates in five continents, WWF directs some 500 projects involving habitat protection, rain-forest destruction, and the effects of deforestation on migratory birds.

4. Further Reading

— "America's Forest Crisis," Frederick Allen, *The Urban Audubon*, January-February 1989.
— "The Decadent Forest," David Kelly and Gary Braasch, *Audubon*, March 1986.
— *End of the Ancient Forests*, Washington, D.C.: Wilderness Society, 1988.
— *Indigenous Peoples and Tropical Forests*, Jason W. Clay. Cambridge, Mass.: Cultural Survival, 1988.
— *In the Rainforest*, Catherine Caulfield. New York: Knopf, 1984.
— *Man of the Trees – Richard St. Barbe Baker*, edited by Hugh Locke. Toronto: Richard St. Barbe Baker Foundation, 1984.
— *Mountain Treasures at Risk*, Washington, D.C.: Wilderness Society, 1988.
— *My Life, My Trees*, Richard St. Barbe Baker. Available from Friends of the Trees, Chelan, WA 98816.
— *National Forests*, vol. 2: *Protecting Biological Diversity*, David S. Wilcove. Washington, D.C.: Wilderness Society, 1988.
— *National Forests*, vol. 4: *Pacific Northwest Lumber and Wood Products*, Jeffrey T. Olson. Washington, D.C.: Wilderness Society and National Wildlife Federation, 1988.
— *A New Maine Woods Reserve*, Michael J. Kellett. Washington, D.C.: Wilderness Society, 1989.
— *Primary Source: Tropical Forests and Our Future*, Norman Myers. New York: Norton, 1984.
— *Trees for City Streets*. New York City Parks and Recreation Department (The Arsenal, Central Park, New York, NY 10012).
— *Tree Growing by Rural People*, Forestry Paper No. 64. Rome: FAO, Italy, 1986.
— *Tropical Deforestation*, special issue of *American Forests*, November-December 1988.
— *The Woodland Steward — A Practical Guide to the Management of Small Private Forests*, James R. Fazio. Woodland Steward (Box 3524, University Station, Moscow, ID 83843).
— *Secrets of the Old Growth Forest*, David Kelly and Gary Braasch. Layton, Utah: Peregrine Smith, 1987.

ENDNOTES

1. Dr. Jerry Franklin, USFS scientist and professor of forest ecosystems, University of Washington, quoted in Timothy Egan, "With Fate of the Forests at Stake, Power Saws and Arguments Echo," *New York Times*, March 20, 1989.

2. For further information on biogas digesters, see chapter 9, p. 209.

3. Peter H. Raven, "The Cause and Impact of Deforestation," in *Earth '88: Changing Geographic Perspectives*, Proceedings of the Centennial Symposium, (Washington, D.C.: National Geographic, 1988), pp. 224-225.

4. "Roots of Destruction," *Sunday Times* (London), September 11, 1988.

5. *The Wasting of the Forests*. Washington, D.C.: Wilderness Society, 1988, p.7.

6. Karen Franklin, "Deforestation Hits Home: U.S. Forest Service Levels Our Landscape," *New Republic*, January 2, 1989.

7. Quoted in David Kelly, "The Decadent Forest," *Audubon*, March 1986, p. 60.

8. *The Wasting of the Forests*, p.3.

9. Tom Wicker, "Forests Are Still Vanishing," *New York Times*, March 24, 1989.

10. Jon R. Luoma, "In Wisconsin, a Debate Over Ways to Manage Modern National Forest Growth," *New York Times*, October 18, 1988.

11. Based on information provided by Siskiyou Regional Education Project, Portland, Ore..

12. Reported in a letter to the *New York Times*, March 13, 1984, by Dr. Ernest J. Sternglass.

13. Ibid.

14. Lester R. Brown and Edward C. Wolf, "Reclaiming the Future," in *State of the World 1988* (Washington, D.C.: Worldwatch Institute, 1988), pp. 175-177.

15. Based on information from *1988 International Green Front Report* (Chelan, Wash.: Friends of the Trees, 1988).

16. "Tropical Forests: A Plan for Action," (editorial) *The Ecologist*, vol 17, no. 1, 1987.

17. "The Greening of Kenya," *Christian Science Monitor*, October 7, 1986.

18. Alan B. Durning, "Mobilizing at the Grassroots," in *State of the World 1989* (Washington, D.C.: Worldwatch Institute, 1989) p. 167; *Smithsonian*, February 1988.

19. *A New Maine Woods Reserve*, Michael J. Kellett. Washington, D.C.: Wilderness Society, March 1989.

20. *1988 International Green Front Report*, published by Friends of the Trees, P.O. Box 98816, Chelan, WA 98816.

21. Ibid., p. 24.

22. *Case study: Ghana*, Peter A. Gubbels (Oklahoma City, Okla.: World Neighbors), p. 11.

23. Based on "Protecting the Amazon Rainforest, A Global Resource," by Dr. Stephan Schwartzman, an anthropologist with EDF's international project, in *EDF Letter*, February 1989.

24. Marlise Simons, "Where Back to Nature Is Wave of Future," *New York Times*, April 1, 1989.

25. James Brooke, "Brazil Announces Plan to Protect the Amazon," *New York Times*, April 7, 1989.

26. "Rain Forest Worth More if Uncut, Study Says," *New York Times*, July 4, 1989.

27. Ibid.

28. Philip Shabecoff, "U.S. Utility Planting 52 Million Trees," *New York Times*, October 12, 1988.

7

GLOBAL WARMING

Turning Down the Heat

*"The greenhouse effect has been detected and
is changing our climate now."
– Dr. James E. Hansen, director of NASA's
Goddard Institute for Space Studies.*[1]

The earth is getting warmer. Glaciers are melting.
Ocean levels are rising. The world's climates are
changing. But it took a long, hot summer and a devastating drought in 1988 to fix public attention on
what scientists had been noting for many years: the
atmospheric buildup of carbon dioxide (CO_2), the
greenhouse effect, and global warming. In the last
decade of the 20th century global warming has
become a looming crisis of potentially catastrophic
proportions.

The Effects of the Effect

According to many leading scientists, greenhouse gases have already committed the earth to an average warming of between 1 and 4 degrees Fahrenheit above that of 150 years ago, before the industrial era began.

Up until now only a fraction of this increase has been felt because much of it has been absorbed by the oceans. However, if the current rate of buildup of the gases continues, the effects are likely to be dramatic. The following scenario resulting from a doubling of the earth's CO_2 – a foregone conclusion unless there is an immediate worldwide effort to reduce greenhouse gases – was presented by the EPA at the Forum on Renewable Energy and Climate Change in Washington, D.C. in June 1989:[2]

Will Climate Change Due to "Greenhouse Gases"?

	Likely in long run	Probable	Very probable	Virtually certain
Large Stratospheric Cooling	○○◐◑●●●●●●●●			
Global Mean Surface Warming	○○◐◑●●●●●			
Global Mean Rain Increase	○○◐●●●●●			
Reduction of Sea Ice	○○○◐●●●●●			
Polar Winter Surface Warming	○○◐●●●●●			
High-latitude Rain Increase	○○◐●●●			
Rise in Global Mean Sea Level	○○◐●●			
Summer Continental Dryness	○○◐			

The climate changes are not expected to be geographically uniform. For example, temperature increases are expected to be greater in the northern latitudes, reaching perhaps as much as 20° higher in Siberia, Alaska, and northern Canada than in other parts of the world.

The Greenhouse Effect –
A Brief Explanation

The temperature of the earth's atmosphere is maintained by a process in which the amount of energy the earth absorbs from the sun (mainly as high-energy ultraviolet radiation) is balanced by the amount radiated back into space as lower-energy infrared radiation. Playing a key part in regulating this temperature are the greenhouse gases, primarily CO_2, water vapor, nitrous oxide, and methane, so-called because, like a pane of glass in a greenhouse, they let in visible light from the sun but prevent some of the resulting infrared radiation from escaping and reradiate it back to the earth's surface.

The buildup of heat that results from this reradiation raises the temperature of the earth's lower atmosphere, a natural process commonly known as the greenhouse effect. Without it the atmosphere would be 60 degrees Fahrenheit colder than it is.

Over the past few decades human activity, especially the burning of fossil fuels and the use of chlorofluorocarbons (CFCs), has increasingly overloaded the earth's natural greenhouse system, slowing down the escape of heat into space and increasing the average temperature of the earth's atmosphere. The additional heat is now beginning to affect global climate, with far-reaching impact on food growing and on the earth's life-support systems.

If we continue to consume coal and oil at the present rate, a global temperature rise of 3 to 10 degrees Fahrenheit within fifty years seems virtually certain.[3] Such an increase is guaranteed to trigger immense ecological, economic, and social upheaval.

Global WarNing
Scenario 2050[4]

Unless we reverse the greenhouse effect, these are the prospects we face in less than 60 years:

● Higher global temperatures heat up the oceans, melting glaciers and polar ice, pushing up sea levels by one to four feet, submerging an area larger than the United States or China, mostly in the Northern Hemisphere.

● Virtually the entire East Coast of the U.S. is flooded, forcing evacuation of New Orleans, and requiring levees to hold back rising tides at Boston, New York, Philadelphia, Charleston, S.C., and other cities.

● Salt water intruding into water supplies makes aquifers in Florida and Long Island useless.

● Fighting the effects of rising seas on heavily developed U.S. coastlines (where over half the population lives) costs more than $100 billion.

● Rivers that provide water to California diminish sharply, creating acrimonious competition for water rights.

● Ocean currents shift, altering the climates of many regions and upsetting fisheries; resulting drought causes rapid evaporation of inland waters, draining the Great Lakes.

● Lake Michigan dries up completely, leaving acres of reeking mud around Chicago.

- Rainfall and soil moisture change dramatically with disastrous impact on agriculture worldwide.
- Rising sea levels and floodwaters in Egypt's Nile Valley and Bangladesh's Ganges Delta drive millions of farmers from their land.

Scenario 2050 is no science-fiction fantasy. Consider what has *already* happened:

- Seventy percent of the global temperature rise over the past century has taken place since 1950.
- The six hottest years since recordkeeping began have been, in descending order, 1988, 1987, 1983, 1981, 1980, and 1986.
- Fossil-fuel combustion that gives rise to the greenhouses gases also produces acid rain, smog, and other life-destroying forms of pollution.

Even at the lowest temperature increase projected by scientists, the world climate will change more during our children's lives than at any time since the Ice Age.

At the higher projection, our grandchildren will face a world warmer than at any time in human existence, experiencing average global temperatures as they were 13 million years ago.[5]

The writing is on the wall, or at least in the sky. As Norway's prime minister, Gro Harlem Brundtland, warned at the Toronto conference: *"For too long we have been playing lethal games with vital life-support systems. The time has come to start the process of change."* [6]

Reversing the Process

Unlike other forms of pollution which affect specific areas and regions, the greenhouse effect touches everybody, everywhere. By changing the atmosphere and inducing global warming, humankind is threatening its own existence, a fact that is beginning to permeate public awareness. *In changing the climate, we unleash the first planetary emergency in human history.*

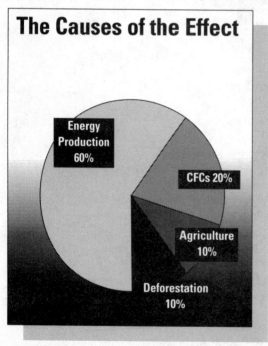

The Causes of the Effect

Energy Production 60%

CFCs 20%

Agriculture 10%

Deforestation 10%

The causes of the emergency are known, as are the essential ways to remedy it. What is lacking is the concerted will to effect the cure. It is a challenge of the greatest magnitude, far exceeding that of building the atomic bomb in 1944 or putting a man in space in 1961.

Finding the Answers

In response to the oft-heard suggestion that we need more time to study the greenhouse problem, Senator Chafee raised a poignant question: Do we have the right to pollute the atmosphere today in a manner that will destroy our grandchildren's future? Although no one measure by itself can solve the multitude of problems involved, he said, we must not let the enormity of the task keep us from taking important first steps. [7]

Carbon Dioxide (CO₂)

Almost 20 billion tons of CO_2 a year are spewed into the atmosphere, accounting for half of the greenhouse gases. Electric utilities burning coal and oil produce a quarter of this amount. Cars, trucks, and buses contribute another quarter. Deforestation is estimated to release between a quarter and a third, with the remainder coming from industry, residential and office buildings, and agriculture.

CO_2 is not a simple pollutant that can be cleaned up, it is a basic by-product of the process of combustion – burning coal, oil, natural gas, or trees.

Geographically, the largest single emitter of CO_2 is the United States, with almost a quarter of the world's total, followed by the Soviet Union (20 percent), Western Europe (17 percent), and China (11 percent).

What Must Be Done to Reduce CO₂

With 5 percent of the world's population, the U.S. produces 23 percent of the world's carbon dioxide. On a per capita basis we are each responsible for 18 tons a year. As Rhode Island Representative Claudine Schneider points out, Americans must send a clear signal to the world that we intend to reduce CO_2 emissions.

How this can be done is spelled out in her *Global Warming Prevention Act* (HR 1078) which mandates a 20-percent cut in 1988 CO_2 emissions levels in the U.S. by 2000 and an international agreement on the atmosphere by 1992 for a 20-percent global reduction by the same date. Energy efficiency, energy conservation, and the increased use of solar and renewable energy resources are the keys to cutting not only CO_2 but carbon monoxide, nitrogen oxides, sulfur dioxide, volatile organic compounds, and methane emissions, the bill emphasizes. (The implications of HR 1078 and the measures it proposes are examined in chapter 9, p. 195 and p. 222.) Other important legislation on global warming has been proposed by Senators Albert Gore (Tenn.) and Timothy Wirth (Colo.).

CO₂ Emissions from fossil fuels, 1987[1]

	CO₂ (millions of tons)	per Capita (tons)
U.S.	4,480	18.37
USSR	3,711	13.07
W. Europe	2,899	7.61
China	2,031	1.90
Japan	908	7.43
India	549	.7
Canada	388	14.93
World	19,438	3.88

CFCs and the Hole in the Sky

There is a natural ozone layer about 15 miles above the earth's surface. It is a thin sheet that envelops the planet and shields it from the sun's harmful ultraviolet rays. In 1982 a British scientific team discovered a gaping hole in this layer of the sky above Antarctica[9]: the ozone had been destroyed by chlorofluorocarbons (CFCs) – industrial chemicals widely used in spray cans, refrigerators, air conditioners, insulator foam, food packaging, and the electronics industry. When CFCs rise into the atmosphere, they react with the sun's ultraviolet (UV) radiation and release ozone-destroying chlorine that swirling winds carry toward the polar regions. The chlorine sticks to crystalline clouds that form there in winter. When released by the summer sun, the chlorine atoms attack ozone molecules, destroying them at the rate of 10,000 for each chlorine atom. In 1988 another scientific expedition found "incredible perturbation" in the stratosphere above the North Pole.[10]

> *"Humanity is conducting an unintended, uncontrolled, globally pervasive experiment whose ultimate consequence could be second only to nuclear war. The Earth's atmosphere is being changed at an unprecedented rate by pollutants resulting from human activities, inefficient and wasteful fossil-fuel use, and the effects of rapid population growth."*
>
> World Conference on Changing Atmosphere, Toronto, June 1988 [12]

As the ozone shield thins out, increased UV radiation from the sun has far-reaching ecological impact. Human and animal immune systems become damaged. UV radiation already causes half a million skin cancers diagnosed each year in the United States. If ozone depletion continues to grow at its present rate, 60 million more skin cancer cases, with 1 million more deaths among Americans, are projected by 2075.[11] UV exposure contributes to many forms of eye disease and EPA projects some 17 million additional cases of cataracts in the future resulting from CFC damage to the ozone layer.

In addition to destroying the ozone layer, CFCs are responsible for 15 percent of global warming. *When they escape into the atmosphere, most CFC molecules trap 20,000 times more heat than CO_2 molecules. They increase the greenhouse effect out of all proportion to their small concentration in the air.*

CFCs and Halons

They are used in about $135 billion worth of equipment in the United States. The main types of ozone-destroying products that use CFCs and halons are:

- aerosols – deodorants, hair sprays, insecticides;
- rigid (closed-cell) foams – packaging, insulation;
- flexible (open-cell) foams – mattresses, furniture, car seats, carpet underlays;
- refrigerators, freezers – home (100 million units in the U.S.) and commercial;
- air conditioners, chillers, heat pumps – in automobiles (90 million air-conditioned cars in the U.S.), large buildings (100,000 have air conditioning), and the food industry (home air conditioners do not use ozone-destroying chemicals);
- cleaning agents, solvents – industrial and electronics degreasing and cleaning, dry cleaning;
- sterilizing agents – hospitals, pharmaceutical industry;
- fire extinguishers (halon).

Household and retail-store refrigerators and industrial and automotive cooling represent almost half the use of CFCs in the U.S., Canada, and Latin America, but only 20 percent worldwide. Aerosol cans represent 35 percent of CFC use worldwide, but less than 2 percent in the U.S. Cleaning applications, particularly for electronics, are 20 percent of use worldwide, but 35 percent in Asia and the Pacific. Foams account for about 30 percent of use worldwide and in the U.S.

CFCs: International Ozone Protection Efforts

Under strong public pressure the U.S., Canada, Norway, and Sweden in 1978 banned the use of CFCs in hair sprays, deodorants, and other nonessential aerosols. However, since then the use of CFCs and halon in nonaerosol applications – refrigerators, automobile air conditioners, solvents, and foams – has increased significantly.

The abundance of trace gases from these sources is primarily responsible for a decrease in the protective ozone layer of as much as 6.2 percent.[13]

In 1985 an effort to protect the ozone layer was formalized in a United Nations convention held in Vienna, Austria. The discovery of the ozone hole in the Antarctic stimulated an international agreement two years later in Montreal calling for a 50-percent reduction of CFCs by the end of the century. Thirty-one nations, including the U.S., ratified the agreement.

In March 1989 even stronger steps were taken when the 12 nations of the European Community (EC), in a move endorsed by the U.S., agreed to halt by 2000 their production and use of chemicals that harm the atmosphere's ozone shield. Together with the U.S., the EC nations produce more than three-quarters of the world's CFCs and halons.

Enlisting Third World Support

The phase-out of CFCs and other chemicals harmful to the atmosphere could be achieved by 1996 or 1997.[14] However, if the worldwide ban is to be effective, it will be necessary to enlist the cooperation of the developing world, most of which did not support the EC agreement.

India, China, and other nations that are industrializing rapidly are using increasing amounts of CFCs in refrigerators, electronics equipment, and many industrial applications. Why, ask these countries, should they be denied the use of products vital to their growth? From their perspective, destruction of the ozone layer is a problem created by the U.S., Western Europe, and Japan.

China says it cannot afford the high cost of substituting alternatives for CFCs. Unless they are helped by developed countries to switch to alternatives, the Chinese will continue making the ozone-destructive gases at a rate that could make them a major producer in the next decade. And even if China's and India's leaders agreed to limit CFCs, they would have trouble controlling the growing number of companies that manufacture and sell refrigerators, plastic foam, hair sprays, and other CFC-containing products.

Sadly, the amount of CFCs and other pollutants that these two giant countries could produce in the next decade would probably offset savings achieved by the U.S. and other industrial nations.

Curtailing CFCs

As the international community moves toward a ban on ozone-destroying chemicals, some progress has been achieved in finding alternatives and in reducing emissions. In 1988 Du Pont, manufacturer of one-quarter of the world's yearly output of 2 billion pounds of CFCs, began phasing out the most harmful CFCs – CFC-11, -12, and -113 – while developing nontoxic substitutes for propellants, refrigerants, cleaning fluids, and plastics.

British and French chemical manufacturers are also developing CFC alternatives, but until they can be mass-produced, their prices are about twice that of conventional CFCs. One promising alternative for the widely used CFCs -11 and -12 is HCF-22. Although technically a CFC, it is considered environmentally safer because most of it is destroyed by sunlight before reaching the ozone layer. In early 1989 most of the American foam-polystyrene packaging industry switched from CFC-12 to HCF-22, but its stability and long-term safety are not certain.[15]

The critical question remains: can CFC production be phased out soon enough to prevent further depletion of the ozone layer?

Ways to Reduce Use of CFCs[16]

Aerosols – The use of CFCs in nonessential aerosols was banned in the U.S. in the late 1970s and is now dropping sharply in Western Europe as a result of pressure from environmentally concerned consumers. A CFC-free aerosol that works by squeezing a rubber sleeve wrapped around a plastic bottle is marketed by Exxel in the U.S. and Osmond Aerosols in the U.K.

Rigid-foam packaging products are very often "throwaways" such as styrofoam trays sold for meats, poultry, and produce in supermarkets or fast-food containers, plastic plates, cups, bowls, and egg cartons. In addition to giving off CFC gases in their manufacture, these items are, as we saw in chapter 1, very hard to recycle and produce dioxin when incinerated.

What You Can Do about CFC Alternatives

- Find retailers who use molded (recycled) cardboard or paper-pulp packaging.
- Protect meats, fish, and other foods with butcher paper or other paper wrapping.
- Buy eggs in molded-pulp, not styrofoam, cartons.
- Contact the *Pro-Environment Packaging Council of New York*, (919 Third Avenue, New York, NY 10022; (212) 753-1690). It represents manufacturers of paper goods and packaging that can easily be substituted for foam .
- Use wood shavings or shredded newsprint as substitutes for foam packaging chips.
- Replace home insulation (ceiling, blown, sprayed, or poured) with cellulose fiber, a flame-retardant, recycled wood product made from newsprint. Although less effective *per inch* as an insulator than foam, it can be applied more thickly to achieve the same result. Other alternatives to foam wall sheathing are fiberglass, fiberboard, gypsum, foil-faced laminated board, and asphalt board.

What Industry Is Doing to Find CFC Alternatives

- A new approach to insulating refrigerators and freezers is vacuum insulation, the type used in thermos bottles. Tests at the Solar Energy Research Institute in Golden, Colo., indicate that vacuum panels take up less space than foams and are more energy efficient.
- Flexible foams presently require large quantities of CFC-11 in their manufacture and most of it gets released into the atmosphere. Capturing these emissions is relatively simple but requires investment in new ventilation systems. Recent technologies developed in Europe recover up to 85 percent of the CFCs for future use.[17]
- Refrigerators and freezers are kept cool by a compressed gas, R-12, known under its market name as Freon, which contains ozone-depleting CFC-12. This

gas leaks into the atmosphere mainly during servicing or when the appliance is discarded. A typical home refrigerator now has 2 1/2 pounds of CFC-11 in its insulation and 8 ounces of CFC-12 in its cooling system. Considerable amounts of the latter can be sucked out of old units by "vampire" machines and then recycled. To make this process economically attractive to salvagers, special incentives should be encouraged through local or state laws.

● Alternative technologies include "hybrid evaporation" – using different cooling gases for the refrigerator and the freezer – which limits the use of CFC-12 to the freezer compartment. Another system, being tested at the University of Maine, is a two-stage, two-temperature, single-compressor refrigerator with thermal ice storage. Using less harmful R-22 gas, this unit is said to be more energy efficient than standard refrigerators. A retail food refrigerator based on the same system has been developed by the United Energy company in Farmington, Maine.

● The imminent phasing out of CFCs -11 and -12 and tougher energy-efficiency rules from the federal government will, it is hoped, stimulate the $3-billion-a-year refrigerator and freezer industry to reexamine the basic design of its products with a greater sense of concern for public health than it has shown up until now.

● Air-conditioning systems are similar to those used in refrigeration. Most chillers, large industrial, commercial, and room units now use R-22, but automobile air conditioners use the dangerous R-12 exclusively, accounting for nearly 40 percent of all its use in the U.S. Recovery of CFCs from junked automobiles is another way to control emissions and would be encouraged by enacting similar incentives as for refrigerators.

● Alternative air-conditioning systems that run on helium or hydrocarbons instead of R-12 have been developed by several manufacturers, including Rovac Corporation of Rochdale, Maine, and Cryodynamics of Mountainside, N.J. Although the auto, refrigerator, and air-conditioning industries have shown some interest, non-CFC cooling systems do not appear likely to be adopted widely without regulatory prodding of these industries by the government.

Solvents emit large quantities of ozone-depleting CFC-113 and methyl chloroform in highly volatile vapors. In some applications – industrial and dry cleaning, for example – equipment filters can be installed to prevent gas releases. Since CFC-113 costs twice as much as other CFCs, investments in recovery and recycling pay off faster. An IBM plant that I visited near Stuttgart, West Germany, recovers up to 90 percent of its solvents. But response by industry in North America has been slow.

Substitutes include a biodegradable solvent made from terpenes found in citrus fruit rinds and marketed as BioAct EC-7. It is manufactured by Petroferm, a small company in Fernandina Beach, Fla., and has been tested by AT&T at several of their plants and found effective and economically competitive. It could replace as much as half the total projected use of CFC-113 in the U.S. electronics industry.[18]

Sterilants such as CFC-12 are a major source for use in gas sterilization of medical and surgical equipment. A promising, long-term substitute is the less toxic FC134a, which is being developed and tested by the chemical industry. Other options include using steam instead of gas sterilization, centralizing gas sterilization in urban areas to improve efficiency and reduce its use, and a chlorine dioxide device developed by Scopas Technology Company, New York, N.Y.

Halons are similar in chemical structure to CFCs and are used primarily in fire extinguishers to minimize damage by water or chemicals in delicate computer equipment, museums, libraries, airlines, and engine rooms. Most home fire extinguishers use dry chemicals, not halons.

The Halon Research Institute and the National Association of Fire Equipment Distributors are investigating other types of gas-propelled extinguishers less harmful to the ozone layer. For firefighter training, a large source of halon emissions, the U.S. military has introduced fire extinguisher simulators that do not need chemical release.

Other Greenhouse Gases

Nitrous oxides, responsible for 6 percent of greenhouse buildup, are created by coal burning, automotive exhaust, and the breakdown of petrochemical pesticides and fertilizers in the soil.

Ground-level ozone. In the stratosphere where it occurs naturally, ozone protects the earth from ultraviolet radiation. But at ground level – produced by motor vehicles, oil refineries, and power plants – it is a pollutant gas which makes up some 10 percent of the greenhouse problem.

Methane gas, the product of decomposing organic material (especially from animal wastes, wetlands and marshes, rice cultivation, mining, garbage landfills, and burning biomass) contributes another 18 percent to the greenhouse effect.

> *"The sudden destruction of forests by air pollution, now being experienced in northern and central Europe and in the eastern mountains of North America, is but a sample of the destruction that appears to be in store."*

Rural Pollution

Growing food and cutting down trees generate large amounts of CO_2, methane, and nitrous oxide. World agricultural output has increased two and a half times since 1950 with a sevenfold increase in oil for machinery and petrochemical fertilizers and pesticides.

The large growth in livestock populations, especially in former rainforest regions, has correspondingly increased the amount of methane gas going into the atmosphere. Each cow produces about 300 quarts of methane a day. And there are more than a billion of them worldwide!

Additional carbon emissions come from the extensive soil erosion caused by "factory farming" practiced by agribusiness in North America and in many other parts of the world. If U.S. farmers switched to organic methods, using natural fertilizers and pesticides, less mechanization, and renewable energy sources such as biomass, solar, and wind power, it would remove as much carbon from the atmosphere as the total emissions from all the cars in the U.S.[19] (For more on organic farming, see chapter 9, pp. 210-211.)

As we have seen, harvesting or clearing trees releases the carbon they contain and from the underlying soil into the air. At present, deforestation is estimated to add 3 billion tons of carbon to the atmosphere yearly, or about half as much as fossil-fuel combustion. Most of the total comes from the tropical regions of Central America, Brazil, Asia, and Africa.[20]

No one knows for sure how remaining forests will respond to the buildup of CO_2 and other greenhouse gases, but there is one ominous possibility suggested by the eminent ecologist George Woodwell. The rising temperatures from the gases would substantially increase the respiration rate of the trees, causing them to release more carbon into the atmosphere than they take in. This would further increase the greenhouse effect and could cause large-scale forest die-off, which in turn would release enormous amounts of CO_2 – perhaps hundreds of billions of tons. As Woodwell puts it, "The sudden destruction of forests by air pollution, now being experienced in northern and central Europe and in the eastern mountains of North America, is but a sample of the destruction that appears to be in store."[21]

The loss of forests contributes heavily to the buildup of greenhouse gases. We need massive efforts to protect existing forests and plant millions of new trees as a way to slow down, if not stop, the greenhouse effect before it reaches the point of no return.

Taking Responsibility

As Representative Schneider and many others have urged, it must be a top priority of the United States to press for international agreement to control greenhouse gases. This involves cooperating with the United Nations and other international agencies and working out joint programs with Soviet, Chinese, Japanese, and European governments. It is also vital that projects sponsored by the World Bank and other multilateral development agencies, and the U.S. Agency for International Development (AID), promote technologies that are more sensitive to global environmental concerns.

The cost of implementing the kind of program seen by Schneider and others as necessary to halt global warming could total $50 billion a year for the next ten years – a large amount of money, but actually much less than 20 percent of the projected military expenditure of the U.S. over the same period of time. The brutal fact is that if we do not put massive environmental protection programs into effect now, the cost we will be forced to pay eventually is sure to be even higher.

Changing Our Priorities

The long series of environmental disasters – Love Canal, Three Mile Island, Bhopal, Chernobyl, the Exxon *Valdez*, to mention but a few – combined with the steady erosion of public health from pesticides, toxic waste, radiation, and air and water pollution have stimulated people everywhere to press for basic changes in their national priorities, away from the preoccupation with war toward protection of the environment and, along with it, of human survival.

> *"Controlling the greenhouse effect requires an enormous shift in economic, military, and political priorities – a shift so extraordinary that it will require a worldwide mobilization effort on a scale never before experienced."*
>
> Jeremy Rifkin, Global Greenhouse Network[22]

The new ecological consciousness is finding expression in a new politics that, like the greenhouse crisis, knows no frontiers. Political leaders who pay mere lip service to this awareness will be held accountable for what they do (or don't do) to clean up pollution and prevent irreversible destruction of life systems.

What You Can Do about Global Warming

The Personal Factor. *"We need to take personal responsibility for bringing about the change."* – U.S. Representative Claudine Schneider

In today's world the rate of change is so rapid that many politicians are out of touch with what their constituents think and need. Yet never were there better opportunities for making our thoughts and concerns known to those who govern. Now indeed is the time for us to take personal responsibility for bringing about the changes urgently needed to halt the greenhouse effect, to clean up the environment, and to build a new leadership from the grass roots up, rather than waiting for it to come down from above.

> *"If every American cut her or his home energy consumption in half, each would keep 7,000 pounds of carbon out of the atmosphere annually."*
>
> *Worldwatch Institute*

1. *Conservation* is a first priority. Examine your own lifestyle and focus sharply on how you can reduce the use of fossil fuels and petrochemicals. This will help slow down global warming and also save you money.

2. *Save energy* at home and work. Seventy-five ways to do this are given in chapter 9, pp. 216-220. See also "Heaters: Care and Maintenance of Gas, Oil, and Wood-burning Systems," chapter 4, pp. 88-89.

3. *Automobiles.* Transportation accounts for 30 percent of U.S. carbon dioxide emissions. For ways to save fuel and cut down on CO_2 emissions and other pollutants, see chapter 5, pp. 107-108.

4. *Recycle.* Increasing your own recycling effort is one of the most important contributions you can make to halting the greenhouse effect. For 28 ways you can do this, see chapter 1, pp. 26-28.

5. *Help phase out CFCs.* See box adjacent.

6. *Plant trees.* You can do this on your own property, in community projects, or by supporting one of the many tree-planting groups listed in chapter 6.

7. *Lobby.* Put pressure on your local power utility to conserve energy and to switch to renewable sources of energy that do not produce greenhouse gases. Lobby your legislators to support HR 1078 and other measures aimed at protecting the ozone layer and reducing the greenhouse effect. (For more information on lobbying, see chapter 11.)

8. *More is better.* Work with community, citizen action, and environmental groups. In particular, contact The Global Greenhouse Network (GGN), 1130 Seventeenth Street NW, Washington, DC 20036, (202) 466-2823. GGN represents a wide range of constituencies: environmentalists, scientists, church organizations, consumer groups, food and health advocates, farm organizations, animal welfare groups, wilderness and wildlife preservation groups, and artists and entertainers.

For information on other groups engaged in combating global warming, see "Resources" at the end of this chapter (see also chapter 11).

9. Appreciate that YOUR contribution does make a difference. It is not only important, it is vital.

Ten Ways to Cut Down on CFCs[23]

1. *Set up CFC recycling centers.* To be done by state and local governments in conjunction with industrial producers and users.

2. *Encourage mandatory CFC recovery* from junked refrigerators and cars. This should be done by an authorized salvager or local sanitation department. A bounty system for old units and a deposit refund for new car air conditioners and refrigerators would provide economic incentives.

3. *Promote better servicing standards* for air conditioners and refrigerators. Preventing ventilation of CFCs during repairs would eliminate needless emissions and cut costs. Service centers should be required to use refrigerant recovery systems and adhere to service standards mandated by local and state governments.

4. *Improve automobile air-conditioner rechargers.* Cans of Freon (R-12) should be sold only with high-quality shutoff valves to prevent leakage, or their sale should be banned. Air conditioners should preferably be recharged only by licensed service centers with CFC recovery and recycling equipment.

5. *Prevent car air-conditioner leaks.* Replace worn-out hoses to prevent coolant leaks. When you get your car air conditioner serviced, do not go to a service station that drains the coolant and lets it evaporate – a widespread practice – but find one that uses a "vampire" (vacuum pump) to recycle it. If Detroit does not develop quality standards for recycling coolants by 1992, the EPA is scheduled to make the practice mandatory.

6. *Use alternative home insulation.* In place of rigid foam materials, use fiberglass, fiberboard, gypsum, and foil-laminated board. This will significantly reduce long-term CFC emissions.

7. *Encourage hospitals to stop using CFC sterilants.* Urge use of steam or centralized sterilization, wherever possible.

8. *Find alternatives to polystyrene foam.* Many states, municipalities, institutions, and consumers are limiting their purchase of these products. This has encouraged the plastic foam manufacturing industry to stop using CFC-11 and -12 – a major step in reducing release of the most damaging ozone-depleting gases.

Minimizing the use any foam plastic product is important for saving the ozone layer. Foam packaging has already been banned in Maine, Vermont, Suffolk County, N.Y., Berkeley, Calif., and other localities.

9. *Work for a ban of polystyrene* and other CFC-containing materials in your own community. (See chapter 11 for details on how to organize for environmental action.)

10. *Promote use of alternative testing agents in fire extinguishers* – i.e. those that don't contain Halon-1301 or -1211.

RESOURCES

The following is provided to help you locate additional resources on the topics covered in this chapter.

1. International Agencies and Organizations

— *United Nations Environment Program* (UNEP), headquarters, P.O. Box 4704, Nairobi, Kenya; United Nations office, 2 U.N. Plaza, New York, NY 10022; (212) 963-8139. Has taken world initiative on ozone layer protection and global warming.

— *World Meteorological Organization* (WMO), Case Postale No. 5, CH-1211, Geneva 20, Switzerland. Its World Climate Program is researching basic issues of global warming and climatic change.

2. U.S. Government

— *NASA Goddard Institute for Space Studies,* 2880 Broadway, New York, NY 10025. Atmospheric and climate research.

— *National Advisory Committee on Oceans and Atmosphere,* 3300 Whitehaven Street NW, Washington, DC 20235.

— *National Center for Atmospheric Research,* P.O. Box 3000, Boulder, CO 80307. Research on climate change.

— *U.S. Congress — Key Figures:*
    Senator Max Baucus (D-Mont.)
    Senator John H. Chafee (R-R.I.)
    Senator Albert Gore (D-Tenn.)
    Senator John Heinz (R-Pa.)
    Senator James Jeffords (R-Vt.)
    Senator Patrick Leahy (R-Vt.)
    Senator Timothy Wirth (D-Colo.)
    Representative Claudine Schneider (R-R.I.)
    Representative Henry A. Waxman (D-Calif.)

3. Environmental and Research Groups

— *Climate Institute,* 316 Pennsylvania Avenue SE, Washington, DC 20003. Promotes public understanding of global warming and strategies to avert stratospheric ozone depletion. Publishes the quarterly newsletter *Climate Alert.*

— *Environmental Action,* 1525 New Hampshire Avenue NW, Washington, DC 20036. Research, lobbying, and citizen action, organized Energy Conservation Coalition of 20 national groups with prevention of global warming as a top priority.

— *Earth Island Institute* 300 Broadway, San Francisco, CA 94133. Very active environmental group including a Climate Protection Network; its outstanding quarterly *Earth Island Journal* devoted its Summer 1988 issue to global warming and reforestation.

— *Environmental Defense Fund,* 275 Park Avenue South, New York, NY 10010. EDF pioneered research on the greenhouse effect, including cosponsoring international meetings in Austria and Italy. In 1988 EDF negotiated an agreement with the fast-food industry to halt use of most harmful CFCs. Its scientists and economists testify at congressional hearings on global warming.

— *Global Greenhouse Network,* 1130 Seventh Street NW, Washington, DC 20036. An "umbrella" coalition of grass-roots groups in 35 countries, whose goal is to halve global CO_2 emissions by the year 2030; raises public awareness through the media and arts, organizes conferences and demonstrations.

— *Natural Resources Defense Council,* 40 West 20th Street, New York, NY 10011. NRDC has launched a ten-point Atmospheric Protection Initiative which includes suing the EPA to end production and use of harmful CFCs.

— *Sierra Club*, 730 Polk Street, San Francisco, CA 94109. Has a Climate Campaign focusing on local, state, federal, and international action.

— *Woods Hole Research Center*, P.O. Box 296, Woods Hole, MA 02543. An independent, non-profit scientific group, investigating global warming, organizing major international meetings on the greenhouse crisis.

4. Further Reading

— *Abating Global Warming*. Special issue, *Rocky Mountain Institute Newsletter*, Fall 1989.

— "The Antarctic Ozone Hole," Richard S. Stolarski, *Scientific American*, January 1988.

— "An Atmosphere of Uncertainty," *National Geographic*, April 1987.

— *The Challenge of Global Warming*, edited by Dean Edwin Abrahamson. Washington, D.C.: NRDC, Island Press, 1989.

— *The Changing Atmosphere*, UNEP Environmental Brief No. 1. Nairobi, 1987.

— *Changing Climate: A Guide to the Greenhouse Effect*. Washington, D.C.: World Resources Institute, 1989.

— *Climate Alert*, newsletter of Climate Institute, 316 Pennsylvania Avenue SE, Washington, DC 20003.

— *CO₂/Climate Report*. Climate Program Office, Environment Canada, 4905 Dufferin Street, Downsview, Ontario M3H 5T4, Canada.

— "The Efficient Response to Global Warming," Bill Keepin and Gregory Katz, *Rocky Mountain Institute Newsletter* (Snowmass, Colo.), August 1988.

— "Global Climate Change: Toward a Greenhouse Policy," Jessica T. Mathews, *Issues in Science and Technology*, vol 3. no.3, 1987.

— "Global Climatic Change," Richard A. Houghton and George M. Woodwell, *Scientific American*, April 1989.

— *Global Greenhouse Network Information Packet*. Washington, D.C.: Foundation on Economic Trends, 1989.

— *Global Lessons from the Ozone Hole*, Michael Oppenheimer. New York: Environmental Defense Fund, 1988.

— *The Greenhouse Crisis — 101 Ways to Save the Earth*. Washington, D.C.: Greenhouse Crisis Foundation, 1989.

— *"The Greenhouse Effect"* (3-part series), Dick Russell. *In These Times*, January 11-17, January 25-31, and February 8-14, 1989.

— *The Greenhouse Effect. The Need for California Leadership*. San Francisco: Sierra Club, 1989.

— *Greenhouse Effect Review*. Business Publishers, 951 Pershing Drive, Silver Spring, MD 20910.

— *The Greenhouse Gases*. Nairobi: UNEP/GEMS Environment Library No.1, 1987.

— *The Hole in the Sky*, John Gribbin. London: Corgi Books, 1988.

— "Hothouse Politics of Greenhouse Effect," Dick Russell, *In These Times*, February 15, 1989.

— "Inside the Greenhouse" (special report), *Newsweek*, July 11, 1988.

— *A Matter of Degrees: The Potential for Controlling the Greenhouse Effect*, Irving M. Mintzer. Washington, D.C.: World Resources Institute, 1987.

— *Montreal Protocol on Substances that Deplete the Ozone Layer, Final Act*. Nairobi: UNEP Na.87-6106, 1987.

— "Our Fragile Atmosphere: The Greenhouse Effect and Ozone Depletion" (13 articles), *EPA Journal*, December 1986.

— "Ozone Depletion and Cancer Risk," Robin Russell Jones, *Lancet*, August 22, 1987.

— *Ozone Crisis: The 15 Year Evolution of a Sudden Global Emergency*. Sharon L. Roan. New York: John Wiley, 1989.

— *The Ozone Layer*. Nairobi: UNEP/GEMS Environment Library No. 2, 1987.

— *Ozone Trends Panel Report*. Washington, D.C.: NASA, 1988.

— *Present State of Knowledge of the Upper Atmosphere*, R.T. Watson, M.A. Geller, R.S. Stolarski, and R.F. Hampson (publication 1162), Washington, D.C.: NASA, 1986.

— "Protecting the Ozone Layer," Cynthia Pollock Shea, chapter 5 of *State of the World 1989*. Washington, D.C.: Worldwatch Institute, 1989.
— *Protecting the Ozone Layer: What You Can Do*, Sarah l. Clark. New York: Environmental Defense Fund, 1988.
— *Report of the International Conference on the Assessment of the Role of Carbon Dioxide and of Other Greenhouses Gases in Climate Variations and Associated Impacts* (Villach, Austria, October 1985). Geneva: International Council of Scientific Unions, UNEP, and World Meteorological Organization, 1986.
— *The Sky Is the Limit: Strategies for Protecting the Ozone Layer*, Irving M. Mintzer. Washington, D.C.: World Resources Institute, 1986.
— *Turning Down the Heat: Solutions to Global Warming*. Washington, D.C.: Public Citizen's Critical Mass Energy Project, 1988.

ENDNOTES

1. At a U.S. Senate hearing in June 1988; quoted in "Endless Summer," *Newsweek*, July 11, 1988, p. 19.
2. "The Potential Effects of Global Climate Change on the United States," report by Joel Smith, U.S. EPA, Forum on Renewable Energy and Climate Change, Washington, D.C., June 14, 1989.
3. Dr. James Hansen, "Scientific Evidence on the Greenhouse Effect & Climate Change," report given at Forum on Renewable Energy and Climate Change, Washington, D.C., June 14-15, 1989.
4. Based on information supplied by the World Meteorological Organization, the U.N. Environmental Program, the World Resources Institute, the National Academy of Sciences, and NASA.
5. Jessica T. Mathews, "Global Climate Change: Toward a Greenhouse Policy," *Issues in Science and Technology*, vol. 3, no. 3, 1987, p. 58.
6. "Endless Summer," p.19.
7. "Finding Answers," *EPA Journal*, December 1986, p. 23.
8. Oak Ridge National Laboratory/Worldwatch, cited in James R. Udall, "Turning Down the Heat," *Sierra*, July/August 1989, p. 32.
9. The background of scientific investigation of the threat to the ozone layer is well told in John Gribbin, *The Hole in the Sky* (London: Corgi Books, 1988).
10. Philip Shabecoff, "Arctic Expedition Finds Chemical Threat to Ozone," *New York Times*, February 18, 1989.
11. "Can We Repair the Sky?", *Consumer Reports*, May 1989, p. 323.
12. Statement of the World Conference on the Changing Atmosphere, Toronto, Canada, June 27-30, 1988.
13. *Ozone Trends Panel Report* (NASA, 1988), cited in *Protecting the Ozone Layer: What You Can Do*, New York: Environmental Defense Fund, 1988.
14. Craig R. Whitney, "12 European Nations to Ban Chemicals That Harm Ozone," *New York Times*, March 3, 1989.
15. "Industrial users face a difficult quest for replacement materials," *London Financial Times*, March 4, 1989; also, Malcolm W. Browne, "Protecting the Atmosphere Choices Are Costly and Complex," *New York Times*, March 7, 1989.
16. Material in this section is based on two main sources: "Protecting the Ozone Layer: What You Can Do"; and "Protecting the Ozone Layer", Cynthia Pollock Shea, *State of the World 1989*, Washington, D.C.: Worldwatch Institute, 1989.
17. Shea, "Protecting the Ozone Layer," p. 90.
18. Ibid. p. 91.
19. Dick Russell, "Earth Needs You," part 3 of "The Greenhouse Effect," *In These Times*, February 8-14, 1989, p. 8.

20. Sandra Postel and Lori Heise, "Reforesting the Earth" in *State of the World 1988*, Washington, D.C.: Worldwatch Institute, 1988, pp. 93-94.

21. Ibid. pp. 95-96.

22. Speech at Earth Day, New York City, April 22, 1989.

23. Based on recommendations in the Environmental Defense Fund booklet *Protecting the Ozone Layer*.

8

RADIATION

Reducing the Threat

"We can expect to see another serious [nuclear]
accident in this country during the next 20 years"
– James Asseltine,
NRC Commissioner, May 1986[1]

On April 23, 1986, a powerful explosion destroyed
the number-4 reactor at Chernobyl power station in
the U.S.S.R. It was the world's worst nuclear-power
disaster and the greatest single release of radioactivity
in history. Thirty-one workers and emergency personnel on-site died from burns and sickness following
exposure to gamma and beta radiation. (For an explanation of different types of radiation and other technical terms used in this chapter, see "Nuclear Glossary,"
on next page.) A thousand more who received large but

Nuclear Glossary

Alpha rays: A stream of charged particles made up of two neutrons and two protons from the nucleus of an atom.

Beta rays: Charged particles emitted from the nucleus of an atom with mass and charge equal to an electron.

Carcinogenic: Cancer-producing.

Collective dose: The average dose of absorbed radiation multiplied by the number of people exposed. It is usually expressed in person-rems. In *Radiation and Human Health*, Dr. John Gofman estimates that 3,771 fatal cancers will occur for every million people exposed to 1 rem of radiation. This means that exposure to one rem of radiation imparts a 1 in 250 lethal contraction chance. An exposure of ten rems (singly or cumulatively) would pose a 1 in 25 risk.

Critical mass: The amount of a radioactive substance great enough so that exactly one neutron from each reaction causes a further reaction.

Cumulative dose: The total dose resulting from repeated exposure to radiation.

Curie: A unit of radioactivity giving off 37 billion disintegrations per second (see also "Measuring Radioactivity," p. 157).

Fallout: Airborne radioactive particles reaching the ground after nuclear fission or explosion.

Fission: The splitting of a nucleus with resultant release of substantial amounts of energy.

Gamma rays: Electromagnetic radiation of short wavelength and high energy. Although similar to x-rays, gamma rays are of nuclear origin, while x-rays are formed by the excitation of orbital electrons.

Half-life: The time needed for the disintegration of one half of the radioactive atoms that were originally present in an element.

Ions: Atoms or groups of atoms carrying positive or negative charges, due to loss or gain of 1 or more electrons. Ionization is the process by which a neutral atom or molecule acquires a positive or negative charge.

Isotope: Any of two or more species of atoms that have the same atomic number (number of protons in the nucleus), but different numbers of neutrons and, therefore, different mass and physical properties.

Meltdown: A nuclear-reactor accident in which excessive heat dissolves the reactor's case and housing, releasing large amounts of radiation.

Nuclear reactor: A device in which a nuclear-fission chain reaction can be started, maintained, and controlled to generate useful energy.

Radiation: The process whereby atoms and molecules undergo internal change, emitting energy as streams of fast-moving particles (alpha, beta, or gamma) or light. It is also the process by which the particles are taken up (absorbed) by living organisms.

Radioactive: Capable of emitting ionizing radiation through spontaneous disintegration of atomic nuclei.

X-ray: Electromagnetic radiation of extremely short wavelength capable of penetrating solid or opaque tissue.

not immediately fatal doses suffered horribly. Some 135,000 people were evacuated from 179 villages within 20 miles of the plant. Thousands of cancer deaths are expected over the next 20-30 years.[2] Widespread birth defects and genetic mutations are predicted.

Toxic fallout from Chernobyl spread over most of the Northern Hemisphere. In Sweden and Norway plants and animals that ate the plants were contaminated by the radioactivity. Milk, meat, and vegetables were particularly affected by radioactive iodine and cesium, threatening public health. The Laplanders in northern Scandinavia were devastated when reindeer – their main source of food and livelihood – were declared unfit for human consumption.[3] In Britain hundreds of thousands of contaminated lambs had to be destroyed. Three years after the disaster, the sheep on 758 farms in Britain's western uplands were still contaminated.[4] In July 1989 the Soviet news agency Tass reported that efforts to reduce the high radiation levels caused by the Chernobyl explosion had failed and that "another 100,000 people may have to be relocated" from the area.[5]

Direct financial losses from Chernobyl total $13 billion, including lost agricultural output and the cost of replacing the 1,400-megawatt plant, but not the cancer cases and inherited disorders to come in later generations.[6] The political, social, and psychological costs of the disaster are incalculable.

Chernobyl was not the world's first nuclear disaster. In 1957 a highly toxic fire at England's Windscale reactor released huge quantities of radioactivity including polonium and iodine-131, causing an estimated several hundred cancers.[7] In the same year there was a devastating explosion at a Soviet nuclear-weapons factory near Kyshtym in the Ural Mountains, causing hundreds of fatal contaminations and evacuating more than 10,000 people from the area.[8] In 1979 a near-meltdown occurred at Three Mile Island (TMI), Pa. Even after ten years and $1 billion in cleanup costs, the lower reaches of the reactor there are so radioactive that workers must use remote-controlled equipment to remove the remaining fragments of the fuel core.[9]

Since 1979 the Nuclear Regulatory Commission (NRC) has documented 33,000 nuclear power-plant mishaps in the U.S. – 1,000 of them regarded as "particularly significant."[10] The large number of mishaps underscores the likelihood of another accident on the scale of TMI, Chernobyl, or worse. In fact, *the NRC itself has projected that the chance of a major core-melt accident in the United States may be as high as 45 percent over the next twenty years.*[11]

Types of Radiation

In the 1960s and '70s, when nuclear-power plants were first built near large cities, the United States government tried to soothe the public's anxiety by saying there was nothing to worry about because radiation is a part of natural life. This was a misleading half-truth. That a substance comes from a natural source doesn't necessarily guarantee its safety. The poisons arsenic and hemlock are cases in point. What matters is not the origin of toxicity, but how much of it you are exposed to.

To understand the dangers of radiation it is important to distinguish between two main forms – *ionizing* and *nonionizing*. (See chart on following page.)

Ionizing Radiation

Radiation is energy transmitted by electromagnetic waves of varying wavelengths produced when energy is released from an atom. It takes many forms – light, heat, radio and TV waves, and radioactivity. When its energy level is high enough to break a living cell, the radiation, called ionizing, is radioactive. Ionizing radiation, found at the high-frequency end of the electromagnetic spectrum, travels in waves (x-rays, gamma rays) or as particles (alpha, beta). In the middle- and lower-frequency ends of the spectrum are nonionizing forms of radiation – light, heat, radar, TV and radio waves – carrying enough energy to excite atoms, but not enough to produce ions.

In high doses ionizing radiation is deadly – Hiroshima, Nagasaki, and Chernobyl are grim reminders of that. In lower doses it is used for medical and dental x-rays and irradiating food. *It is dangerous at all levels.*

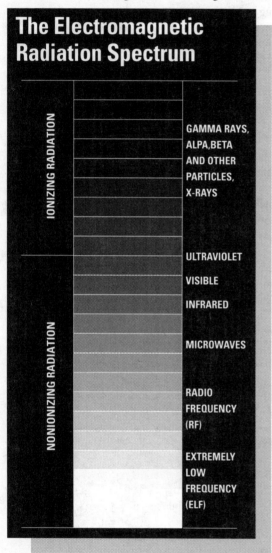

The Electromagnetic Radiation Spectrum

IONIZING RADIATION

GAMMA RAYS, ALPA,BETA AND OTHER PARTICLES, X-RAYS

ULTRAVIOLET

VISIBLE

INFRARED

MICROWAVES

RADIO FREQUENCY (RF)

EXTREMELY LOW FREQUENCY (ELF)

NONIONIZING RADIATION

Nonionizing Radiation

We encounter nonionizing radiation at every turn of our daily lives – from radios and TVs when we get up (even if we don't switch them on), sunlight we step into as we leave home, video-display terminals at work, overhead electric-power lines, and even the electric blanket we use at night. Ultraviolet light, at the most energetic end of the spectrum, is obviously harmful, causing painful sunburn and an estimated 10,000 deaths from skin cancer deaths a year. Although we take many other forms of electromagnetic radiation for granted, they may, as we shall discuss below, be more dangerous than we often realize.

How Safe Is Safe?

The term *low-level radiation* has led many people to believe it is safe, even though it may be ionizing. To compound the confusion, the government and the nuclear industry use the term "permissible" levels of radiation, giving the faulty impression that doses lower than the "permissible limit" are safe.[12]

The fact is: all forms of radiation produce an excess of *free radicals*,[13] highly reactive electrons which interfere with your body metabolism and can cause many types of sickness including cancer.

According to Dr. Ernest Sternglass, professor emeritus of radiological physics at the University of Pittsburgh Medical School, *radiation absorbed into the body is more harmful than chemical poisons like pesticides or lead because each electron emitted by a radioactive nucleus is powerful enough to disrupt millions of organic molecules in living cells.* Other scientists suggest that some low-level, free-radical processes cause more damage to living cells over a long period of time than the same dose given instantly, as in an x-ray.

Measuring Radioactivity

Radioactivity is measured according to (1) the amount and type to which a person has been exposed or (2) the actual amount absorbed by the body.

Exposed radiation: The most common measure is the *curie* (Ci), named after Marie Curie and her husband Pierre who discovered radium. It is the amount of radioactivity present in one gram of radium or a material that undergoes 37 billion radioactive disintegrations per second. In measuring radon, for example, the unit used is a *picocurie* (pCi) – one trillionth of a curie – per liter of air or water. A rule of thumb of the EPA Office of Radiation Programs is that breathing 10 pCi of radon per liter each day carries about the same lung cancer risk as smoking one pack of cigarettes a day. The EPA action level – when they advise remedial action – is 4 pCi per liter.

Rad (radiation absorbed dose) is the amount of ionizing radiation received by living matter in terms of the energy deposited in a given time.

Rem (radiation equivalent man) is used because different types of radiation cause different damage to human tissue for the same amount of rads; it describes the *relative* biological impact of the radiation absorbed.

The effects of radiation depend on which part of the body is exposed – the sex organs, brain, and lungs are the most sensitive – and the type of radiation you are exposed to. For example, one rad of alpha-particle radiation can be ten times more harmful to sensitive organs than one rad of x-radiation. In terms of biological damage, the one rad of alpha radiation would be equivalent to ten rems.

As a point of reference, 400 rems delivered to a body at one time will cause death in 50 percent of exposed cases. Exposure in the 100 to 400-rem range causes radiation sickness and in some cases death. At lower rem levels cell damage occurs, but the exact consequences are hard to predict. The current limit set by the EPA for the general population is a 25 millirem whole-body dose from all sources a year. A millirem (mrem) is one thousandth of a rem.

Roentgens, named after Wilhelm Roentgen, the discoverer of x-rays, measure the amount of energy given off by ionization that is absorbed by a specific quantity of air; it is used primarily to measure and gamma radiation.

Natural Radiation

The earth is continuously bombarded with cosmic rays whose penetration increases three times with every 10,000 feet in altitude. For example, airline crews absorb so much radiation that they are limited to 1,000 hours of flying time a year, during which they absorb about 1,000 millirems (mrem) – one rem. The yearly exposure to your body from cosmic rays varies from a low of 35 mrem in Florida to a high of 130 in Wyoming or Colorado.

A second source of natural radiation is the earth itself, from primordial radionuclides (uranium-238, thorium-232, and potassium-40 for example,) found in rocks, beaches, and other predominantly dry locations. Radiation also occurs in materials made from these sources – bricks and concrete – and in water or air contaminated with radioactive gas such as radon.[14]

Because the soil gives off natural radiation, food and water coming from it contain some radioactivity. An extreme case are Brazil nuts. They are grown in Brazil, a country with high gamma radiation in its soil, and therefore, they can be several thousand times more radioactive than other nuts. Cereals generally have about 500 times more natural radioactivity than fruit. Radiation in fruits, vegetables, and grains is taken up in food eaten by cattle and passed on to consumers of meat and dairy products. Especially "hot" are organ meats (liver, kidney), cheese, and milk. Although the levels are not alarming in themselves, they can be dangerous *when added to other environmental radiation you may get from nuclear reactors, toxic-waste dumps, or deliberately irradiated food.*

The Effects of Radiation

The public-health impact from radiation is hard to assess because it can take up to twenty years for a cancer to appear, longer for a genetic mutation. Also, in cases relating to nuclear radiation, it isn't easy to get the facts. Government agencies and the nuclear industry are generally reluctant to release information harmful to the image of nuclear power as a safe, clean form of energy.

Another important factor is the *cumulative* buildup of radiation. Whatever amount you receive is added to other doses accumulated in your body from natural radiation, medical and dental x-rays, and numerous other sources to which you have been exposed throughout your life.

Further, the impact of radiation varies considerably in different parts of the body and with the age of the recipient. For example, the mouth can absorb with relatively small risk radiation levels that are extremely harmful to the thyroid gland, eyes, or reproductive organs.

The splitting of atoms (fission) by nuclear reactors and bomb testing produces isotopes that are dangerous because they emit radioactive by-products as they decay and concentrate in certain parts of the body. When an isotope decays inside a "target" organ it damages cells, producing toxins, abnormal cell division, and genetic mutations. Iodine-131, for example, concentrates in the thyroid gland and ovaries, and is particularly harmful to young children. Strontium-90 is deposited in the bones, where it irradiates bone marrow and increases the risk of blood diseases, including leukemia. Cesium-137, like strontium a common by-product of nuclear plants, is absorbed by the liver, kidney, and reproductive organs.

What You Don't Know Can't Hurt You?

The levels of radiation "permitted"[15] by the United States government have been lowered from 170 millirads (mrads) per person a year in 1970 to 25 mrads today. Yet many experts consider even this amount too high. In the words of the Nobel Prize-winning biologist Dr. George Wald: *"Any dose of radiation is an overdose."* [16]

Radiation from Nuclear-power Plants

The safety record of nuclear plants throughout the world is alarming. In addition to the headline-making Three Mile Island and Chernobyl accidents, there are regularly occurring events and mishaps – radioactive leaks, fires, water spills – that threaten public health, yet get scant media attention.

If you work or live near a nuclear plant, you are likely to be exposed to radioactive dumping – accidental or intentional release of radioactive substances into the air or water. Although the nuclear industry claims the radioactive concentrations are harmless, the actual effect is to spread out risk of cancers and mutations over a wide and unsuspecting population.[17] Independent physicians, epidemiologists, public-health experts, and concerned consumer groups have long been frustrated by an official policy of barring outside researchers from reviewing the records of people exposed to radiation at or near nuclear plants since the 1940s. It took nine years of legal efforts by a Pennsylvania group, the *Three Mile Island Health Fund*, to get the U.S. Department of Energy to yield such information.

The federal government's immediate reaction to a nuclear accident is to downplay its importance in the hope that the public will forget about it. Only later (and then infrequently) will Washington reveal, as in March 1989, that an accident three months earlier at the Savannah River, S.C., nuclear-weapons plant "may have caused significantly more damage than engineers first thought."[18]

> *"Radiation leaks from nuclear weapons plants might be causing unusually high rates of cancers and birth defects in people who work at or live near these plants."*

Radiation from Military Reactors

In late 1988, reports by scientists under DOE contract indicated that radiation leaks from nuclear-weapons plants might be causing unusually high rates of cancers and birth defects in people who work at or live near these plants.[19] As far back as 1944-1956 large quantities[20] of iodine-131 were released in the air from the Hanford, Wash. Reservation, possibly causing serious thyroid problems.[21] An independent panel investigating one of Hanford's 46-year-old reactors concluded, "The similarities between Chernobyl and Hanford are substantial and make a Chernobyl-type accident at Hanford a distinct possibility, while the differences tend in general to make [Hanford] more, rather than less, dangerous than its Soviet counterpart."[22]

Earlier studies on nuclear workers at Oak Ridge, Savannah River, and Hanford indicated at least a 25 percent higher cancer rate than among the general population.[23]

In December 1988 DOE admitted there had been 155 cases of contamination from 16 nuclear-weapons plants in Ohio, Colorado, and Texas and from two national atomic laboratories in Northern California, as well as radioactive pollution of an underground reservoir at the Rocky Flats Plant near Denver, posing serious threats to public health and the environment.[24] By early 1989 the four largest nuclear-weapons plants in the U.S. – Hanford, Savannah River, Fernald, Ohio, and Rocky Flats, Colo. – had to be shut down because of inadequate safety.

Mishaps at U.S. Civilian Reactors

As mentioned above, there were 33,000 nuclear power plant mishaps in the U.S. in the ten years between the Three Mile Island accident and March 1989. In 1987 alone 2,940 recorded mishaps occurred at the nation's 110 nuclear plants – an average of almost 27 at each site – categorized as Licensee Event Reports (LERs) that a utility must file with the NRC each time a mishap occurs.[25]

According to Public Citizen's *Nuclear Power Safety Report*, human error was involved in 74 percent of these mishaps, and "many other mishaps including some of the most serious accidents of 1987 apparently were not reported."[26]

In February 1988 Senator Edward Kennedy revealed that the National Institutes of Health were investigating evidence of leukemia clusters among people living near the Pilgrim 1 nuclear power plant in Plymouth, Mass., and more than 100 other plants in the U.S. and the United Kingdom.[28] The Pilgrim evi-

Reactors with Most Licensee Event Reports (LERs) in 1987

(from Public Citizen's *Nuclear Power Safety Report*, 1988)[27]

Reactor	Location	Number of LERs
9 Mile Point-2	Scriba, N.Y.	79
Perry-1*	North Perry, Ohio	77
Vogtle-1	Waynesboro, Ga.	75
Sequoyah-1*	Daisy, Tenn.	71
Clinton-1	Clinton, Il.	70
Limerick-1*	Pottstown, Pa.	68
Braidwood-1	Braidwood, Il.	62
Shearon Harris-1	New Hill, N.C.	62
Wolf Creek-1*	Burlington, Ks.	57
Fermi-2*	Newport, Mich.	51
Hope Creek-1	Salem, N.J.	51
Millstone-3	Waterford, Conn.	51
Oyster Creek-1	Forked River, N.J.	45
Rancho Seco	Clay Station, Calif.	45
Catawba-1*	Clover, S.C.	44
	Industry Average	**27**

* Also on Public Citizen's list in 1986

dence was based in part on the testimony of Sidney Cobb, M.D. showing that "this excess leukemia [in five coastal towns north from Plymouth to Scituate] might be attributable to airborne radioactive effluents from Pilgrim 1." [29]

Radioactive Waste – Nowhere to Go

One millionth of a gram of plutonium is too small to be seen by the naked eye. Yet, if inhaled, it can cause cancer. One thousandth of a gram, barely visible, will cause fibrosis in the lungs and death within a few years. Ten pounds is enough to build an atomic bomb. A 1,000-megawatt nuclear-power plant produces about 450 pounds of plutonium a year. Multiply this by 350 plants operating around the world and we have 70 tons of a lethal substance with a half-life of 24,300 years – that is, it will remain a danger to human health for over 16,000 generations or half a million years.[30] According to the pioneering nuclear scientist Dr. John Gofman, past weapons tests have put so much plutonium into our lungs in the Northern Hemisphere that 116,000 people in the United States and one million elsewhere "have been committed to plutonium-induced lung cancer."[31] Up until the mid-1960s – twenty years after the development of U.S. atomic power – it was generally assumed that an acceptable solution to the problem of radioactive waste disposal could be worked out. Today, with millions of tons of lethal material accumulated from this country's military, commercial, and research programs, there is no proven system to remove nuclear waste from the environment.

Types of Nuclear Waste

Nuclear wastes are by-products of nuclear fission and consist either of *fission products* formed by the splitting of uranium or other atoms (e.g., strontium, cesium, krypton) or of *transuranic elements* formed when uranium atoms absorb free neutrons. Although less radioactive than fission products, these elements are more dangerous because many of them, including plutonium, remain radioactive for hundreds of thousands of years.

Irradiated fuel, often called spent fuel, is high-level nuclear waste usually in the form of 12-foot-long rods that are used in the reactor's uranium fuel core. Each nuclear power plant produces 30 tons of spent uranium fuel a year — waste that remains radioactive for thousands of years.

High-level radioactive waste is the liquid or sludge which results from reprocessing irradiated nuclear fuel.

Low-level waste is any other waste that is not legally high-level or transuranic. Even low-level reactor waste contains extremely high concentrations of long-lived radioactivity; it includes reactor hardware and piping that are in constant contact with highly radioactive water for the 20 to 30 year life of the reactor as well as toxic resins, sludge, and water left over from the reactor vessel and fuel pool. Plutonium is the most lethal, but only one of many radioactive substances accumulating at an increasing rate every year as waste products of nuclear energy and weapons production. Less deadly, but vastly more abundant, is uranium ore, 5 million cubic feet of which (enough to build a four-lane highway, 1 foot deep, for 27 miles) are needed to fuel a single 1,000-megawatt nuclear power plant for one year. By the year 2000 the U.S. will have accumulated one *ton* of uranium tailings (a fine gray radioactive sand left over when uranium oxide is extracted from the ore) for every inhabitant in the country. These are often left unprotected in the open where they are easily dispersed by the wind.

Nuclear Waste – Cleanup or Cover-up?

The U.S. government and industry have an appalling record in nuclear-waste management in the military, power, and research sectors. The extent of the problem is almost beyond comprehension. The General Accounting Office says that some atomic weapons plants are so polluted they will never be cleaned up. Congress estimates the costs of cleaning up the waste at the nation's nuclear-weapons installations to run between $100 billion and $200 billion over the next hundred years.[32]

Most of the spent fuel generated by the 110 operable nuclear plants in the United States has been left for ten or more years in water-filled pools at the plant sites awaiting permanent disposal by 1998, as mandated by the Nuclear Waste Policy Act of 1982.

The ultimate repository proposed by the U.S. Congress is Yucca Mountain in Nevada, 85 miles northwest of Las Vegas, on land owned by the Shoshone Native Americans. Originally chosen for its underlying layer of volcanic ash, the site has now been found liable to fault shifting accompanied by volcanic eruption.[33]

As they operate, nuclear reactors produce huge amounts of low-level waste, ranging from extremely radioactive metals from inside the reactor to slightly contaminated workers' clothing.[34] Most of this waste has been stored in steel drums and buried haphazardly in shallow landfills at sites across the country. Three of them – Maxey Flats, Ky., West Valley, N.Y., and Sheffield, Il. – are now closed because of serious problems including leaking of radioactive water into the ground. Another, at Barnwell, N.C., is located in a high rainfall region and has had some radioactive leaking, which is expected to get worse over time. The Beatty, Nev. landfill also has had problems including radioactive drums buried outside the site boundary. Richland, Wash., near the Oregon border, is the main commercial landfill for the United States and is adjacent to the huge nuclear military complex at Hanford, home of one of North America's worst nuclear-waste problems.

Veil of Secrecy

Vital information on these sites, including testing of water in the landfills, has been either withheld or simply not gathered. The U.S. General Accounting Office does not know how much radioactive water has leaked at Hanford nor the extent of its seepage into ground water since 450,000 gallons of high-level waste were spilled there in 1956.[35] In December 1988 the DOE revealed that liquid radioactive and toxic wastes at Hanford have contaminated large underground reservoirs used for drinking water and irrigation.[36]

At the Oak Ridge National Laboratory millions of cubic feet of radioactive wastes are buried in shallow pits, contaminating nearby streams. Hundreds of thousands of gallons have also leaked into ground water from tanks at federal bomb sites in Savannah River and Fernald.[37]

Silent Holocaust*

In May 1984 Bill Houff, resident minister at the Unitarian Church in Spokane, Wash., delivered a sermon that became the opening salvo in a statewide debate over the role of bomb plants at Hanford Nuclear Reservation, encompassing 570 square miles and 14,000 employees.

Titled "Silent Holocaust," the sermon asserted that radiation released by nuclear radiation weapons production was taking a grim though silent toll in the form of latent human cancers and widespread environmental contamination. Houff, who has a doctorate in chemistry and a prior career as an industrial chemist, hit hard on the matter of ethics, attacking the scientific community's reluctance to challenge secrecy and deceit, and the blackballing of critics within its ranks. He concluded with a powerful warning on the dangers of Hanford's plutonium mills that was reported in the local newspaper.

* By Tim Connor, director of the Hanford Education Action League

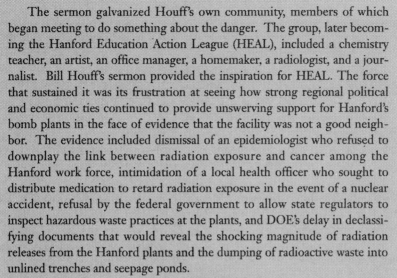

The sermon galvanized Houff's own community, members of which began meeting to do something about the danger. The group, later becoming the Hanford Education Action League (HEAL), included a chemistry teacher, an artist, an office manager, a homemaker, a radiologist, and a journalist. Bill Houff's sermon provided the inspiration for HEAL. The force that sustained it was its frustration at seeing how strong regional political and economic ties continued to provide unswerving support for Hanford's bomb plants in the face of evidence that the facility was not a good neighbor. The evidence included dismissal of an epidemiologist who refused to downplay the link between radiation exposure and cancer among the Hanford work force, intimidation of a local health officer who sought to distribute medication to retard radiation exposure in the event of a nuclear accident, refusal by the federal government to allow state regulators to inspect hazardous waste practices at the plants, and DOE's delay in declassifying documents that would reveal the shocking magnitude of radiation releases from the Hanford plants and the dumping of radioactive waste into unlined trenches and seepage ponds.

Although the *New York Times* and other national news organizations subsequently reported on the alarming environmental and safety revelations at Hanford and other nuclear facilities, the reports by and large have neglected examination of how local attitudes about weapons production are affecting the larger debate over U.S. nuclear policy, and how growing disaffection with the DOE may be radically changing public attitudes towards the continuing production of nuclear weaponry.

It was public pressure after the Chernobyl accident in 1986 that led to closer scrutiny of DOE weapons plants, the subsequent closing of some plants, the suspension of operations at others, and formidable questions about those on the drawing board. At the same time local groups like HEAL and the Energy Research Foundation in South Carolina joined forces with national organizations such as the Natural Resources Defense Council and the Environmental Policy Institute to expose the mind-numbing legacy of radioactive and hazardous chemical wastes at Hanford and other nuclear weapons production sites.

The work of HEAL forced officials and scientists at Hanford not only to defend environmental and safety practices that are essentially indefensible, but to address the ethics of secrecy and sovereign immunity which is the prevailing government legal defense for its nuclear-weapons production and testing.

An important consequence of citizen group action in opening discussion and debate with the nuclear establishment is to *demystify* the processes, policies, and human costs of weapons production. The debate opened by HEAL in eastern Washington is now being focused on other nuclear plants nationwide and is reaching into Congressional hearings and other national forums. It is hoped that it will persuade the framers of national defense and energy policies to defer more to *public involvement* and *accountability* than to ideological totems and the nuclear-weapons industry.

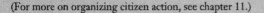

(For more on organizing citizen action, see chapter 11.)

Nuclear Waste – The Long-Term Threat

The search for a long-term solution has revealed no satisfactory answers. In its effort to clean up radioactive and toxic wastes at weapons installations, the DOE is exploring such new technologies as high-voltage devices that can melt contaminated soil, steel drums, and other materials into glassy block (a process known as vitrification), and using microbes to produce polymers to which radioactive particles and toxic metals can stick.

The former process is risky and difficult because it requires extensive digging up of buried waste. The experiments with microbes are at an early stage and not being used to deal with radioactive material. According to a *New York Times* report in early 1989, the DOE may simply "wait out" some of the waste problems.[38]

The DOE's mismanagement of nuclear waste has been criticized by the Nuclear Regulatory Commission, the General Accounting Office, and the National Association of Regulatory Utility Commissioners. In June 1989 a study of radioactive-waste disposal by Dr. Arjun Makhijani, a nuclear physicist and independent researcher, concluded that 100 years of storage at reactor sites would be safer than burying waste in southern Nevada where geologic and climatic conditions are poorly understood. According to the report, delaying permanent storage would allow radiation in older reactors to die down, making it easier eventually to dismantle them.[39]

Worldwide, there are now 30 countries with operating nuclear-power plants. Although situations vary from country to country, no permanent disposal system for high-level waste has been developed, much less carried out, anywhere. Standard procedures for low-level waste include the unsatisfactory shallow-land burial method practiced in the U.S., underground storage in abandoned mines, and dumping it in the ocean!

A pilot vitrification plant is operating in France,[40] but has not yet tackled highly radioactive wastes. Some researchers are critical of this process because of the danger that the glass blocks would eventually disintegrate. Even if it did work, it fails to solve the problem of a permanent repository for high-level wastes. As in the U.S., many experts believe the use of deep underground burial sites to be inadvisable because of the uncertainty of earthquakes and geological movement.[41]

Hard Choices for Nuclear Hardware

Decommissioning Nuclear Reactors

As many nuclear plants in the U.S. and abroad approach the end of their useful life span (30 years or less), we face the grim prospect of closing them down, a problem that was overlooked during the heady rush to put them up in the 1950s and '60s. According to the International Atomic Energy Agency, 71 nuclear-power plants may be shut down worldwide by 2,000.[42]

Unlike ordinary power plants, reactors cannot be simply left standing or demolished. Because of radioactivity, the entire structure must be carefully taken apart and permanently safeguarded. This requires either immediate dismantling, "mothballing" (waiting several decades for some of the more short-lived radioactive materials to decay before cleaning up and dismantling), or "entombment" – erecting a permanent tomb around the reactor. The latter method is effectively ruled out because many radioactive substances would outlive any structure that could be built around a reactor.

Even if high-level radioactivity can be removed, a huge amount of low-level waste is left in place, half as much as the reactor has produced in its entire operating lifetime. As we have seen, there is no indication that future storage systems will be better able to cope with this extra waste than present ones can.

Best estimates for the cost of decommissioning a single reactor range from $175 million to $750 million or more.[43] The Long Island Lighting Company said that decommissioning its Shoreham plant (which has only run for 30 hours and at low

> *"The Long Island Lighting Company said that decommissioning its Shoreham plant will now cost at least $400 million."*

power) will now cost at least $400 million.[44] The cost of cleaning up an aging nuclear recycling plant at West Valley, N.Y., closed down since 1972, was estimated at $400 million in 1982, had risen to $890 million seven years later, and might total twice that amount before the job can be finished.[45]

In late 1988 DOE indicated it was considering permanently closing several of the 17 principal nuclear-weapons factories in a 12-state production complex. The estimated costs of cleaning up and decommissioning these plants range from $50 billion to $175 billion over the next fifty years. However, Senator John Glenn (D-Ohio), chairperson of the Government Affairs Committee, and other lawmakers who have studied the problem fear costs will run so much higher that the task may never be completed.[46]

DOE also faces cleaning up huge piles of radioactive waste at 24 inactive uranium mills in 11 states, disposing of "dozens" of decommissioned nuclear submarines at the cost of "millions of dollars" for each vessel, as well as "more than a thousand" other nuclear cleanup projects.[47]

Considering the abysmal track record of the government and the nuclear power industry to date, the price of dismantling, decommissioning, and cleaning up the aging nuclear civilian and military reactors and nuclear-waste sites will total several hundred billion dollars over the next twenty years or more.

Nukes in Space

As if the hazards of nuclear radiation on land and sea were not enough, there is also the threat of nuclear-powered satellites and space shuttles showering us with radionuclides. In 1978 the Soviet *Cosmos 954* splattered radioactive debris over 40,000 square miles of northern Canada. Ten years later *Cosmos 1900* began falling out of orbit and its reactor, containing 70 pounds of radioactive fuel, was automatically separated from the satellite and shot into higher orbit.

Despite opposition to nuclear projects in earth orbit, the U.S. and the U.S.S.R. are experimenting with satellites that are powered by uranium and the even more deadly plutonium-238. With the aim of banning nuclear power in orbit, California Representative George E. Brown, Jr., introduced a bill in Congress in late 1988. "A major catastrophe has been avoided in large part because only a few percent of today's spacecraft have a nuclear power source on board," he stated. "But *there could well be hundreds of nuclear reactors circling the globe in the 21st century. How lucky will we be then?*"[48]

In the future, space reactors will be larger. In the fall of 1989 a U.S. space shuttle launched the space probe *Galileo* on a two-year voyage to Jupiter. It is powered by 50 pounds of plutonium, which, if accidentally detached from its housing, would release about ten times the radioactivity of *Cosmos 954*. Although NASA claims that there is no alternative to plutonium-powered generators, government studies released under the Freedom of Information Act show solar energy to be a safe alternative for *Galileo* and other space probes.

However, according to Michio Kaku, professor of nuclear physics at the City University of New York, NASA prefers plutonium generators because solar collectors would be easily detected by enemy radar. *"The military wants all kinds of nuclear power packs up there, included those energized by hydrogen bombs,"* he said.[49]

> *"A major catastrophe has been avoided . . . because only a few percent of today's spacecraft have a nuclear-power source on board . . . ."*

A part of the Strategic Defense Initiative (SDI) program, NASA and DOE commissioned the General Electric Company to build a $700 million prototype nuclear reactor to be test-orbited in the mid-1990s. According to Nicholas Johnson of Teledyne Brown Engineering, there are an estimated 50 radioactive satellites – some no more than exposed reactor cores – in relatively low orbits. Each is a potential space mine capable of raining down radiation on our heads.[50]

Let Sleeping Nukes Lie

The sinking of a Soviet nuclear-powered submarine, the explosion aboard the *USS Iowa*, and the fire on another Soviet nuclear submarine in the spring of 1989 have raised concern about the perilous nature of maritime military activities. The accidents also raise the question about the wisdom of leaving reactor-carrying wrecks or nuclear weapons on the seabed.

In the case of two sunken U.S. submarines in the Atlantic, the U.S. Navy says that no more than trace amounts of radioactivity have been detected in their vicinity. But a technical study commissioned by Greenpeace from Large and Associates, a British engineering firm, disputes claims like these. "Significant" amounts of highly radioactive and toxic materials would eventually disperse to the marine environment unless the vessel were recovered intact, the study concluded in its report on the sinking of the Soviet submarine.[51] The two Soviet accidents in the spring of 1989 are only the most recent in a long line of nuclear sea disasters, Greenpeace reports in an investigation it carried out in cooperation with the Institute for Policy Studies.[52] Using public documents and Freedom of Information Act requests, they discovered that the world's navies have experienced at least 1,200 accidents, which have resulted in dozens of ship sinkings, hundreds of explosions and fires, costly repairs, and loss of life. And they have left an astounding record: 50 nuclear warheads and nine reactors lying on the ocean floor. In the report's words, *"It could be said that the world's sixth largest 'power' after the United States, the Soviet Union, France, the U.K. and China, is the deep blue sea."*

Among the U.S. disasters were those of the aircraft carrier *John F. Kennedy* and the cruiser *Belknap* (collided off southern Italy in 1975), the aircraft carrier *Ticonderoga* (dropped a plutonium warhead in the sea 80 miles from Japan in 1965), the nuclear-powered attack submarine *Guardfish* (leaked its primary coolant

370 miles southwest of Puget Sound, Wash. in 1973), and the nuclear submarine *Thresher* (imploded and sank 100 miles east of Cape Cod, Mass., in 1963).

As the Greenpeace report concludes, a full accounting of the accidents, the nuclear-weapons testing and research, and of the radioactive materials and waste strewn about land and sea would "significantly shift the public's tolerance for business as usual in the nuclear age."[53]

What You Can Do about Nuclear Radiation

Because nuclear radiation is so pervasive, many people believe there's nothing they can do to fight it. Yet, as we saw in the example of HEAL above, individuals can influence and change policies and programs even at state and federal levels. Public Citizen's Critical Mass Energy Project estimates that the efforts of environmental and citizens' groups helped force cancellation of more than 100 reactors between 1972 and 1987.

Nor is the struggle simply "us against them." The campaign to clean up nuclear waste was joined in late 1988 by a coalition of three Western governors in what the *New York Times* termed "an extraordinary confrontation" between the federal government and the states of Idaho, Utah, and Colorado, which "demanded federal money and environmental cleanups as their price for allowing a nuclear weapons plant to stay open."[54]

Whatever steps you decide to take, it is important to know you are not acting alone. Over the years the public has become increasingly critical of nuclear power. A Washington Post/ABC News poll in 1986 found 78 percent of the United States population opposed to building new reactors, compared with under 20 percent in 1975.[55] Responding to public apprehension, virtually every environmental group in the world has strategies to fight the spread of nuclear power and to offer safe alternatives in its place.

Antinuclear Groups

In the U.S. one of the most active groups opposing nuclear power is the Critical Mass Energy Project, an arm of the Washington, D.C.-based Public Citizen,[56] a nonprofit research and advocacy organization founded by Ralph Nader.

Critical Mass runs an extensive series of projects devoted to closing down nuclear reactors and proposing safe, non-polluting alternatives. Its 1988 report *Shutdown Strategies* documents 47 case studies of citizen groups working to close nuclear reactors. The strategies include economics (defining the costs of closing reactors), health, safety, and environment (issues of waste, emergency planning, and increasing local authority over nuclear safety), and political action (ballot measures and public ownership of nuclear utilities). Among the nuclear plants targeted by Critical Mass are Diablo Canyon, San Onofre, and Rancho Seco, Calif., Braidwood and LaSalle, Il., Indian Point and Shoreham, N.Y., Davis-Besse, Ohio, Trojan, Ore., Robinson 2, S.C., Point Beach, Wis., Palo Verde, Ariz., Shearon Harris, N.C., Fort St. Vrain, Colo., Seabrook, N.H., and Pilgrim and Yankee, Mass.

Critical Mass also publishes numerous studies on nuclear power and related issues, including *Nuclear Power Safety Report* and the *National Directory of Safe Energy Organizations*; it also organizes workshops and conferences and works

Voters Shut Down Reactor

In June 1989 residents of Sacramento, Calif. voted to shut down the Rancho Seco nuclear power plant, after a $580,000 campaign by the nuclear industry failed to overcome arguments based less on environment and safety than on economics. A majority of the voters were convinced that the plant could not provide electricity at a cost competitive with other fuels. In 1988, for example, Rancho Seco's electricity cost more than twice that generated by natural gas.[57]

Built at a cost of $375 million in 1974, the reactor produced less than 40 percent of the electricity that would have resulted from continuous year-round operation, requiring its owner to double its rates over the last four years to pay for $400 million worth of improvements. Opponents of the plant argued successfully to retire the plant halfway through its expected life span and buy power from neighboring utilities in California, which is glutted with electricity.

Although the Sacramento vote focused on the economic issue, it took place in the context of local and nationwide concern over the safety of nuclear-power plants. Public opposition has, for example, prevented the opening of the Shoreham nuclear plant on Long Island, N.Y., and influenced the decision of the Public Service company of Colorado to shut down its poorly running Fort St. Vrain reactor. Opponents of nuclear power were heartened by the vote to close Rancho Seco. "This revitalizes and reinvigorates the whole consumer and rate-payer movement with regard to [opposing] nuclear power," said Scott Denman, director of the Safe Energy Communication Council.[58]

Although Rancho Seco has been shut down, its future remains uncertain because the plant cannot be dismantled until a place is found for its highly radioactive spent fuel. No such repository is likely to be ready until the early years of the 21st century.

(For more on the disposal of radioactive wastes, see p. 161 and p. 164.)

closely with Public Citizen's litigation group on nuclear-related lawsuits.

Working closely with Critical Mass (as well as independently on other projects) at the grass-roots level are the **Public Interest Research Groups** (PIRGs) in California, New York, and 18 other states. (For more on their impressive work, see chapter 11, pp. 269-275.)

The Nuclear Information and Resource Service (NIRS) is an information clearinghouse for grass-roots safe energy activists, based in Washington, D.C. It issues Legislative Regulatory Alerts, and testifies before Congress and state legislatures and at conferences and rallies nationwide. NIRS has also been involved in lawsuits to release secret NRC documents and to overturn NRC rules that benefit the nuclear industry at the expense of public safety. It publishes nuclear-energy fact sheets and other reports.

Radioactive Waste Campaign, based in New York City, promotes public awareness of the dangers to human health and to the biosphere from the production, storage, and transportation of radioactive waste. The campaign conducts research and public education as well as publishing books, fact sheets, videos, and a quarterly newsletter, *The Waste Paper*. (See also "The Rad Dirt Victory," p. 170.)

The Committee for Nuclear Responsibility, directed by Dr. John Gofman, addresses dangers from all sources of radiation including x-ray treatments and other medical procedures.

The Union of Concerned Scientists, with headquarters in Cambridge, Mass., investigates unsafe reactor design, construction and regulation and carries out important research studies in this field and frequently testifies at government and public hearings. It publishes a newsletter and reports on nuclear-power issues.

Environmental Action, now merged with the Environmental Task Force, is a research and advocacy group that helped persuade Congress in 1988 to delay building a new $1 billion plutonium refinery near Idaho Falls, Idaho.

Important educational work on nuclear issues is done by the **League of Women Voters**, which organizes debates and in 1985 published *The Nuclear Waste Primer: A Handbook for Citizens*.

(For addresses of these groups, see "Resources" at the end of this chapter.)

In addition to these organizations there are many regional citizens groups including the **Clamshell Alliance**, covering the New England states, the **Safe Energy Alternatives Alliance** in New Jersey, Delaware, and Eastern Pennsylvania, the **Abalone Alliance** in California, the **Cactus Alliance** in New Mexico, Nevada, and Colorado, and the **Coalition for Peace and Justice** in Florida.

How You Can Defeat Nuclear Power

1. *Practice individual energy conservation* and alert friends, neighbors, work colleagues, and local contacts to the many opportunities to reduce energy use. (For examples on how you can do this, see chapter 9, pp. 216-220.)

2. *Join one or more of the above-mentioned groups* or the many environmental organizations listed throughout this book, most of which have antinuclear programs.

3. *Specifically, work with an antinuclear group by:*

● writing a letter or making a phone call requesting an economic or environmental impact study (or helping with the study itself);

● attending hearings of your local planning board or state public-utility commission;

● demonstrating against nuclear plants, nuclear-waste landfills, and nuclear harbors;

● focusing on emergency plans for nuclear plants;

● helping increase local authority over nuclear safety;

● influencing the U.S. Congress to be more supportive of safer energy alternatives to nuclear power (it is amazing how much response you can sometimes get with a single postcard, phone call, or telegram to your local, state, and national representatives);

● drafting and supporting state initiatives, ballot measures, and statutes to close existing nuclear plants or ban new ones;

● working to elect candidates who oppose nuclear power to the boards of directors of local utilities, to local councils, and to other bodies that have jurisdiction over nuclear energy.[59]

Such strategies are discussed at greater length in chapter 11.

Radiation at Home and Work

Where to Look for Radiation

Outside of nuclear reactors and nuclear-waste dumps, the most pervasive form of radiation that you will encounter is *radon*, a threat to health that has been seriously underestimated until quite recently. Fortunately, *once it is diagnosed*, the radon problem can be solved with relatively simple measures.

Radon: Natural but Deadly

Radon is an invisible, odorless gas released when uranium in soil and rocks (especially granite, shale, or phosphate) decays into radioactive particles. When inhaled, the particles can lodge in the lungs and cause lung cancer. The risk is particularly great among cigarette smokers, but applies to nonsmokers as well.

When radon gas rises into the open air, it dissipates quickly and presents no risk. However, when it rises into a confined space, it accumulates and can reach dangerous concentrations, especially in tightly insulated buildings.

The Rad Dirt Victory*

In July 1986 the state of New Jersey planned to dump radioactive waste that had been inadvertently used in building foundations in Montclair and other towns into a proposed site less than 4 miles from my home in Warwick, N.Y., which is close to the Jersey border. I contacted Dr. Marvin Resnikoff, staff scientist for the Radioactive Waste Campaign, who was living in New Jersey at the time. Within a week we had a meeting in my home attended by 22 people from New Jersey and New York. It was the first time most of us had an opportunity to hear a scientist explain the issues.

The proposal, he said, was based on two basic flaws: wrong site selection and an undesirable process of dilution, which meant making a small mountain containing 4 million cubic yards of radioactive dirt mixed with sand and gravel. Under the leadership of Jed Bark, we started a protest committee called WARD (Warwick Against Radioactive Dump). Before long thousands of people had made a commitment to block any trucks bringing in radioactive dirt.

Mina Hamilton helped train people in civil disobedience and nonviolent action. Jean Fazzino worked with the affinity groups that provided a corps of several hundred disciplined activists.

Suits brought by the town of Warwick, WARD, and the New York/New Jersey Trail Conference used expert testimony provided by Marvin Resnikoff; he shared information with the Atlantic chapter of the Sierra Club, which also opposed the proposal. The effort was sustained for five months until we learned that New Jersey no longer planned to dump on us. It was a bittersweet victory. We succeeded in protecting our own town, but relief for the people living in Montclair and the other towns was no closer than it had been before.

*By Betty Quick, secretary, Radioactive Waste Campaign, with permission from *Radioactive Waste Campaign – The First Ten Years*

Widespread concern about radon arose in 1984 when the home of a Pennsylvania nuclear plant worker was found to be exposing each member of his family to the equivalent of 400,000 chest x-rays a year. Although such a level of radon concentration is unusually high, considerably lower levels also present *a serious health threat to as many as 10 million households in North America.*[60]

Radon enters a building from the ground. Porous soil and poorly sealed foundations permit more of the gas to penetrate. It can also come in through the water system (especially if you have a private well dug near radioactive deposits), escaping into the house through faucets and shower-heads.

> *"From all the evidence, radon in the home is the most deadly environmental hazard in America today."*
>
> Robert E. Yuhnke, radon specialist for the Environmental Defense Fund

Although older, airy houses are not immune, airtight, energy-efficient structures are more liable to retain high levels of radon indoors. Brick or concrete structures are likely to have higher levels than wooden ones due to radon released from these building materials.

Concentrations of radon can vary widely from day to day due to the moisture content of soil, atmospheric pressure, and changes in ventilation. Contrary to earlier belief, levels of radon gas in the soil may be as much as ten times higher in summer than in winter.[61] In cold weather hot-air furnaces can blow up radon from cellars, crawlspaces, and other high-concentration areas.

What You Can Do about Radon[62]

1. *Ask neighbors and local health officials* if there are dangerous radon levels in your region. Originally thought to be confined to areas where high concentrations of radon-producing materials are found naturally in the ground (such as the Reading Prong, which runs from eastern Pennsylvania through northern New Jersey into New York), relatively high levels of radon have been detected in every part of the United States.

2. *If houses in your immediate area have high radon levels, act fast to have your home tested.* Because of daily variables, have what is known as "track etch" testing done over a period of 60 to 90 days *in summer and winter.* A 3 to 4 day test in the lowest livable area of your home (basement, if you have one) will give a preliminary idea of the radon level during that period.

3. *Work with radon professionals* who use EPA-approved laboratories. Don't rely on do-it-yourself kits available at the local hardware store. A study by the consumer group Public Citizen showed that their findings might be misleading or false because of poor quality control in the evaluating laboratories.[63]

4. *Short-term steps:* Ban smoking in your home. Radon gas attaches itself to smoke, increasing the risk of inhaling radioactive particles. Reduce time spent in areas where radon is concentrated, such as basement, dens, and workshops. Whenever feasible, open windows and turn on fans to increase airflow into and through the house. Keep crawlspace vents fully open all year.

5. *Long-term action:* Try to prevent radon from getting into to your house, but, if it has, you must take steps to remove it. Because poorly designed remedies can actually increase the level in your home, get professional advice from your local radon agency or from a contractor or consultant recommended by the agency. (See "Resources" at the end of this chapter for further information.)

For houses with low levels of contamination there are inexpensive ways to ventilate bottom floors and to seal areas in contact with the ground. Houses with greater amounts of radon may require a combination of both measures. Very high radon levels may call for more complex solutions such as *block-wall ventilation* or *drain-tile or subslab suction*.

The following options are offered only as guidelines for use in contacting the local radon agency:

● *Cover exposed earth* in basement, cellar, storage and drain areas, and crawlspaces; it will help block main entries of radon into your home. Other than opening windows to increase natural ventilation, it is the least expensive option, often costing less than $150.

● *Sealing cracks and openings* with mortar or urethane foam is usually more effective when done in conjunction with other methods. Costing around $350 for labor and materials, it must be done by a trained contractor.

● *Heat-recovery ventilation* uses heat in exhaust air to warm incoming air in the winter, reversing the process with cold air in air-conditioned houses in summer. It requires professionally installing an air-to-air heat exchanger or a heat-recovery ventilator at an average cost of about $1,000.

● *Drain-tile suction* works only in homes built with drain tiles connected in a continuous loop around the building. It requires professionally attaching an exhaust fan to the collection pipe or sealed sump to help pull radon away from the building. Labor and materials cost approximately $1,500 with annual operating costs of no more than $150.

● *Subslab suction* involves installing fans and pipes to pull away radon that accumulates under the foundations. Professional installation is needed; cost and maintenance are about the same as for drain-tile suction.

● *Block-wall ventilation* effectively reduces high radon levels in houses with hollow-block basement walls. It requires either pulling radon from the space within concrete-block walls before it enters the upper part of the home or preventing it from coming in by blowing air into the walls. This must be done by a contractor at a typical cost of between $5,000 and $6,000.

Radon Information

There are two primary sources of information on radon testing and remedial measures: the ten regional offices of the EPA listed in "Resources," p. 30 , or the fifty state radon contacts that these EPA offices will give you on request. For information on the leading state radon programs contact:

Illinois Department of Nuclear Safety, Office of Environmental Safety, 1035 Outer Park Drive, Springfield, IL 62704; (217) 546-8100 or, in state, (800) 255-1245.

Maine Division of Human Engineering, Department of Human Services, State House, Augusta, ME 04333; (207) 289-3826. Has a program to deal with radon-contaminated water.

New Jersey Department of Environmental Protection, 380 Scotch Road, Trenton, NJ 08625; (609) 530-4000.

New York Bureau of Environmental Radiation Protection, Empire State Plaza, Corning Tower, Albany, NY 12237; (518) 458-6451 or, in state, (800) 342-3722.

Pennsylvania Radon Monitoring Program Office, 1100 Grosser Road, Gilbertsville, PA 19525; (215) 369-3590 or, in state, (800) 23-RADON. The

One Community's "Quintessential" Fight against Radon[64]

In March 1986 the 2,000 inhabitants of Clinton, N.J., discovered that their one-square-mile village was the worst residential radon hot spot in the United States. In some homes built on a limestone cliff that is laced with uranium, radon contamination was 250 times the safety limit, the equivalent of smoking twenty packs of cigarettes a day.

Federal and state government experts were brought in. Their answer: design and install ventilating systems to suck the radon gas from beneath the homes and exhaust it before it could seep into houses through basement or cellar cracks. The solution, developed with EPA help, was to place four-inch-diameter pipes through the cellar floors into gravel below the houses, or laid in the gravel around the foundations and run through the cellar walls. Radon-contaminated air was then sucked out by a fan and blown out at roof-top level where it was dissipated by the wind.

By the end of 1988 virtually all the homes in Clinton had been brought down to or near permissible safety levels,[65] according to Alfred B. Craig, head of radon research at the EPA Air and Energy Laboratory in Research Triangle Park, N.C. No health problems linked to the high radon levels have yet been detected, but it could take many years for the lung cancers to show up. The lessons learned at Clinton are now being applied elsewhere in New Jersey and in Pennsylvania, New York, Maryland, Ohio, Tennessee, Florida, and Alabama. "I don't think there's any house made that can't be remediated (sic.), mostly at a cost between $500 and $2,000," Craig said. A fitting tribute came from Clinton's mayor, Robert A. Nulman: "We are the quintessential success story that you can beat radon. You test your house to see if there's a problem and, if there is. . . you fix it, just like a roof leak or termites."

program includes giving away more than 20,000 radon testers to state residents, detailed information on remedial action, and special loans of up to $7,000 to fix radon levels higher than 2 pCi per liter. For further information on a loan application, check with a local Pennsylvania bank.

Radon Testing Services. The best sources are the EPA Office of Radiation Programs, Washington D.C., your state department of health, your local board of health, or as a last resort your local yellow pages. Three mail-order companies are: Key Technology, P.O. Box 562, Jonestown, PA 17038, (800) 523-4964; TCS Industries, 380 Paxton Street, Harrisburg, PA 17111, (717) 657-7032; and Terradex Corporation, 3 Science Road, Glenwood, IL 60425, (800) 528-8237. In all cases, make sure that the service you are considering has been recently approved by the EPA.

Nuclear Medicine

The medical profession, including chiropractors, osteopaths, and dentists, exposes more people to ionizing radiation than any other human source. Although efforts have been made to reduce the amount of exposure, many experts believe that the diagnostic use of x-rays, which goes back to Roentgen's first experiments in 1895, has created more disease than it has uncovered. *An* estimated *300 million Americans a year are exposed to medical and dental x-rays alone.*[66] There is also widespread use of radioisotopes in the diagnosis and treatment of diseases – iodine-131 in thyroid cases, barium to scan the gastrointestinal tract, cobalt-60 to treat cancer. In the 1970s mammograms, used to detect breast cancer in women, exposed each person to a dose of 10 rads per test. When the medical literature began to show breast cancer in women after mammography, the dose was lowered. It is now 0.1 rad.

If administered carefully, nuclear medicine can offer many benefits including the saving of life. However, it can carry considerable hazards. According to Gofman's calculation, a 25-year-old man undergoing a barium meal exam has a cancer risk of between 1 in 2,000 and 1 in 50, depending on the machine and the x-ray technician administering the dose.[67] In 1987 the *Los Angeles Times* reported more than 8,400 medical and dental x-ray machines overdue for inspection in California alone, *excluding* at least an equal number of uninspected units that were never registered with the state.[68]

What You Can Do about Nuclear Medicine

● Whenever you are considering any form of x-ray or radioisotope use for yourself or your family, check first whether there are other noninvasive options available.
● If you decide to go ahead with radiation, find out how many rads of exposure are being used and how carefully your doctor or dentist controls the administration.
● It is wise to avoid any form of radiation given by someone whose equipment is unlikely to be subject to state inspection.
● Be *extra* cautious if you are pregnant or with small children.

Nuking Your Food

In addition to natural radiation, there are three main ways food can become contaminated through radioactivity: from *intentional irradiation, leaking nuclear plants or dumps,* and *microwaves.*

Food Irradiation: Using ionizing radiation to extend the shelf life of food, long promoted by the nuclear industry as a means of using radioactive waste, was approved by the Food and Drug Administration (FDA) in 1986 for grains, vegetables, fruits, spices, and pork. Irradiation is believed by many scientists and consumer groups to threaten public health because it depletes the nutritional value of our diet, masks the bacterial contamination of rotting food, and exposes the consumer to cesium-137, cobalt 60, and other carcinogens.[69]

Gamma radiation causes the formation of little-understood chemical compounds in food known as *unique radiolytic products.* Tests on rats have shown that irradiated food causes cancer, mutations, and chromosomal disorders.[70] Exposing food to ionizing radiation to slow the ripening process and kill insects and bacteria is viewed with suspicion by many scientists and public health experts as well as concerned consumers. In March 1987 the Parliament of the European Economic Community refused to allow irradiated food in its member countries. Banned in the state of Maine, sales of irradiated foods have been made illegal in New York and New Jersey until 1991 pending further study and funding from Congress.

What You Can Do about Irradiated Food

● Check with your neighborhood supermarket, grocery store, and produce market to see if they carry irradiated food and how it is identified. According to FDA rules, labeling is not required, but a flower symbol called the "Radura" must be used.

● Ask the owner/manager if she/he is aware of the dangers of food irradiation. Explain that irradiation treatment can damage fresh produce, creating brown spots and turning it mushy, and in many cases does not extend shelf life more than a few days.

● Encourage your grocer to carry organic food. (See also chapter 12, pp. 288-290.)

● Write or telephone the National Coalition to Stop Food Irradiation, Box 590488, San Francisco, CA 94159; (415) 566-2734, for information on an anti-irradiation group in your area that you can work with.

● Support companies like Nature's Way, 10 Mountain Springs Parkway, Springville, UT 84663, whose organically certified herbs are guaranteed to be free from irradiation.

● Work through elected officials and local and national organizations (see "Resources,"at end of chapter) against introducing irradiated foods.

● Write to the Secretary of Agriculture, U.S. Department of Agriculture, 14th Street and Independence Avenue SW, Washington, DC 20250, demanding that your tax dollars not be used to subsidize food irradiation.

Nuclear energy-contaminated food

This can be caused by iodine-131, strontium-90, cesium-137, and other radionuclides released accidentally or intentionally from nuclear-power stations and atomic bomb test fallout. Radiation is taken up in the food chain, concentrating in fish that eat large amounts of contaminated plankton, and milk (and meat) of cows that eat radioactive grass, and settling on vegetables and grains. When larger animals eat smaller ones the concentration effect increases. Some animals are more vulnerable than others – pigs take up six times more radioactivity than cows. Nuclear contamination of food is increasingly being detected in the vicinity of reactors. It is claimed that cranberries and other foods growing within 30 miles of the Pilgrim 2 reactor at Plymouth, Mass. (which had a serious radiation release in 1982) have been found radioactive.[71] Radiation in food appears to remove basic minerals from the body, causing fatigue, headaches, appetite loss, and other symptoms.[72]

What You Can Also Do

● If possible, live and work at least 30 miles from a nuclear reactor.

● Switch to a diet low in meat (especially pork) and high in organic grains, vegetables, and fruits.[73]

● Thoroughly wash vegetables and grains to remove possible radioactive dust (and pesticides).

● Work with your local antinuclear alliance for phasing out nuclear power through energy conservation and switching to renewable energy sources. (See chapter 9 for details.)

Radiation and Tobacco

High concentrations of radioactive lead and polonium have been found on tobacco leaves, possibly caused by phosphate-based fertilizers used by growers. Radioactive lead is also found in tobacco-smoke particles, which are insoluble. When inhaled (by smokers or nonsmokers) they enter the lungs and eventually move through the cardiovascular system to other parts of the body.

High levels of radioactive lead and polonium have been found in tumors of smokers and in fatty arterial deposits in atherosclerosis. Smoking is also known to amplify the effects of low-level radiation.[74]

What You Can Do about Tobacco Smoke

- Avoid exposure to tobacco smoke in any form. Do not allow it in your own home.
- Help enforce existing no-smoking regulations and work for new ones. (One polite phone call to my local bank manager was enough to have her post No Smoking signs.)
- Ask your congressional representatives to oppose government subsidies for the tobacco industry.

Miscellaneous Sources of Radiation

Smoke detectors Many of these devices contain radioactive materials to ionize the air so that an alarm will be triggered when smoke enters the chamber. Originally radium-226 was used for this purpose, but, as a result of consumer pressure, the less dangerous americium-241 has been substituted.

What you can do: Buy smoke detectors that work (just as effectively) with photoelectric-cell triggers.

Ceramic Tableware and Glassware Until banned in 1978, uranium oxides were used in ceramic glazes for dishes, plates, and glasses. Eating from these three times a day would give radiation doses above the regulatory limit for exposure to nonmedical sources and may cause skin cancer. You can identify these glazes by a shiny orange-red or yellow surface. Suspect brands include *Fiesta, Red Wing, yellow and pink Franciscan, Green Catalina, and Harlequin, Vistosa, Caliente, Riviera, Stangl, and Poppytrail,* as well as decorative glassware and earthenware from Mexico, China, Italy, Portugal, or Spain, whose lead glaze coating may not be properly fired.[75]

The Hazards of Electromagnetic Fields

Although some radios, TVs, and other appliances produce x-rays, they usually do it at voltages low enough to be contained within the unit. One exception is color TV sets manufactured before the early 1970s, which emit x-ray dosages above the regulatory limit (0.5 milliroentgens per hour measured 2 inches from the screen). There is, however, another form of radiation risk over which concern is growing – the hazards of exposure to nonionizing radiation in the form of electric and magnetic fields. Such radiation comes from a wide variety of sources that include radar, power lines, video display terminals (VDTs), electric blankets and many other appliances.

The health hazards of electromagnetic fields have been long disputed by the military establishment, the utility industry, and manufacturers of the now more than 30 million VDTs that have found their way into offices, schools, and homes in North America. Ironically, the downplaying of these hazards was often accompanied by claims that home appliances such as vacuum cleaners or electric razors represented a greater health risk than say radar, power lines, or VDTs. It was, however, never pointed out that exposure to most home appliances is a matter of a few minutes a day compared with perhaps 12 hours a day to radar or power lines or 7 or more a day to VDTs.

Those who the downplay dangers of electromagnetic fields also use the misleading arguments that there is no "smoking gun" to prove that these fields actually cause cancer and that the statistical evidence of increased cancers and birth abnormalities, especially in women and children exposed to the fields, may be due to other hazards such as toxic waste or pesticides. Although nonionizing radiation may not *initiate* cancer, it has been confirmed in repeated laboratory tests that both extra-low- frequency fields (similar to those produced by high-current electrical distribution wires) and very-high-frequency fields (produced by electrical transmission lines) *promote* the growth of cancer. Long-term exposure to this type of radiation has also been linked to high blood pressure, headaches, loss of memory, and brain damage.[76]

Power Lines

There are almost a million miles of overhead high-voltage power transmission lines crisscrossing North America, with many more being built or planned. These high-voltage lines generate electric and magnetic fields, which may be linked with cancer and other harmful effects. According to the *New York Power Line Report, 1987*, there is "an excess risk for childhood cancer, particularly leukemias, associated with high-current wiring configuration near the home."[78]

A study of 450,000 male workers in Canada found that those vocationally exposed to high-voltage and high-strength magnetic fields run three times the average risk of dying of leukemia.[79]

> *"We have evidence that man-made electromagnetic fields from power lines are far more productive of serious health effects than cigarette smoking."*
> Dr. Robert O. Becker,
> author of The Body Electric[77]

What You Can Do about Electromagnetic Fields

- Choose home sites at least a half mile away from actual or proposed power lines.
- Join local organizations that oppose the construction of new power lines near populated areas.
- Persuade your local utilities and government representatives to encourage energy efficiency and conservation measures that will reduce the need to build additional power lines.
- Support research on this important (but neglected) health hazard.

Video Display Terminals (VDTs)

More than ten million office workers in North America work in front of VDTs on a daily basis. Many VDT workers report having eyestrain, sore necks, headaches, "technostress," and other symptoms, the origin of which is not fully understood. However, recent findings of clusters of miscarriages and birth defects among women who work at or near VDTs during pregnancy point to the possibility of a radiation connection. In addition to emitting x-rays (most of which are absorbed by the cathode-ray tube glass), VDTs give off several types of nonionizing radiation – ultraviolet, infrared, microwave, radio-wave, extremely low-frequency, and static electric fields. Some scientists believe that the threat from VDTs (and TV sets) comes from their giving off "pulsating fields" of energy, which cause atoms and molecules in the skin to become excited. This creates friction and heat which the body transfers to the bloodstream and then back to the skin. If exposure to this form of energy is prolonged, the process of molecule vibration can lead to tissue destruction, altered immune function, cell breakdown, and possible chromosomal damage.[80]

An extensive study by the Kaiser-Permanente Medical Care Program found a doubling of miscarriage rates for women working more than twenty hours a week at VDTs compared with those who did not use them.[81] Since 1979 there have been reports of miscarriage clusters in companies as diverse as Sears Roebuck, the *Toronto Star*, and *USA Today*. These have prompted a major investigation by the National Institute of Occupational Safety and Health (NIOSH), Cincinnati, Ohio. "Because so many women use VDTs every day – 10 million or more – we felt we had to find an answer." said Dr. Teresa Schnorr, who is conducting the study.[82]

What You Can Do about VDT Exposure

- If pregnant, avoid all exposure to VDTs.
- Sit at least 12 inches from VDT and TV screens.
- Ask employers to ensure that all VDTs have lead-impregnated glass for the envelope of the cathode-ray tube or, for added protection, acrylic radiation shields to place over the computer screen.
- If in doubt, ask your employer to get VDTs tested for radioactivity and electromagnetic fields.[83]
- Contact your local chapter of the Communications Workers of America AFL-CIO or their headquarters, 80 Pine Street, New York, NY 10005, (212) 344-2515, for the latest findings on VDT hazards in the workplace. (See case history adjacent.)
- Read the independent newsletter *Microwave News*, published by Louis Slesin, 155 East 77th Street, New York, NY 10021.
- Get your congressional representatives to press government regulatory agencies to start discussions with manufacturers on the feasibility of shielding all sources of pulsed electromagnetic field in new and existing VDTs.
- Contact the U.S. Occupational Safety and Health Administration (OSHA).[84]
- Support VDT hazard research by private enterprise and government agencies.

Home Computers, Video Games, and TV Sets

Home computers and video games can present a hazard to children (who are more sensitive to radiation than adults and tend to sit closer to the screen and for longer periods). Video games in public arcades leak more radiation at waist level from the sides and back than from the front, exposing the habitual viewer to the risk of genetic damage.

What You Can Do

- Avoid older TV sets.
- Discourage viewers, especially children, from sitting close to the screen.
- Do all you can to dissuade children from hanging out in video-game arcades.

Local Union Gets Legislature to Pass VDT Law

Thanks to a campaign by the Communications Workers of America local branch in Suffolk County, N.Y., the county legislature in 1988 approved a law requiring properly designed office furniture, work stations, and lighting for all employees working more than 26 hours a week in firms with 20 or more terminals. In addition, those VDT users are entitled to regular 15-minute rest breaks, annual eye examinations, and eyeglasses, if necessary, at the employers' expense. Suffolk County employers had opposed the bill by threatening to leave the county, and after it had passed, by filing suit to stop its implementation. In October 1988 the New York Supreme Court upheld the injunction, but it blocks only the eye-care provisions while the suit is pending.

Microwaves

Microwave frequencies are short wavelengths of electromagnetic radiation that fall just below human perception. They are used extensively by air-traffic controllers and the air force to monitor every plane in the sky, as well as in 20 million CB radio transmitters and in marine navigation, weather forecasting, astronomy, telephone and telecommunications systems, and in law enforcement (to catch highway speeders, shoplifters, and burglars). They are also used in microwave ovens.

Between 1971 and 1986 women living in four towns on Cape Cod, Mass. who were exposed to a nearby U.S. Air Force radar system died from leukemia at a rate that was 23 percent higher than that of other women in Massachusetts; they also developed liver, bladder, and kidney cancers at a rate almost four times that of women in eleven other towns on Cape Cod not exposed to the radar.[85]

What You Can Do

- Be alert to any major radar installations within ten miles of where you live or work.
- Join with neighbors and colleagues to have the installations moved a safe distance away from homes, schools, and workplaces.
- Enlist support of your local and congressional representatives.

Microwave Ovens

Microwave ovens use high levels of nonionizing radiation to cook food by exposing it to electromagnetic microwaves. Although they don't make the food radioactive, these ovens can leak radiation, particularly at the door seal. U.S.

regulations permit microwave ovens to use up to 5 milliwatts of energy per square centimeter. It doesn't sound like very much, but it's five times the amount allowed in Canada.

What You Can Do

- Locate microwave oven away from heavily trafficked areas in the house, workplace, or restaurant.
- Keep the door seal clean to reduce leakage.
- Don't let children look through the oven window to watch what is cooking.
- Buy a microwave leakage tester from your local hardware or electronics store.
- If you don't have a microwave oven, seriously consider slightly less convenient but safer electric or gas units.

Lamps

Sunlamps cause an estimated 10,000 skin burns a year severe enough to require emergency hospital treatment. They also emit sufficient energy to destroy eye tissue. Mercury vapor lamps, used in street lighting, gymnasiums, sports arenas, supermarkets, banks, and parking lots also produce ultraviolet radiation which leaks out dangerously if the lamp's special protective glass barrier is broken. Fluorescent tubes, which have great value as energy savers, emit ultraviolet light that some researchers believe may be responsible for melanomas and other skin cancers. Studies by the photobiologist Dr. John Nash Ott suggest that hyperactivity in young children may be another effect of fluorescent lighting. Research at the Massachusetts General Hospital, Boston, found that calcium absorption of men living under fluorescents fell by 25 percent in the winter.[86] (For more on fluorescent lighting, see chapter 9, p. 218.)

What You Can Do

- Use extreme caution with sunlamps. Remember that exposing yourself to one for 60 seconds is equivalent to spending an hour in the sun.
- If you detect a malfunctioning mercury vapor lamp, report it immediately and make sure it is switched off.
- Get the new broad-spectrum fluorescent lamps that are closer to natural daylight in color temperature and more energy-efficient than older fluorescents and incandescent lighting.
- Check that the ends of fluorescent tubes are shielded with metal to reduce radiation leakage.
- For close work, use daylight or incandescent task lights.
- If you have doubts, check with the manufacturer or contact your local health department on how to have the products tested.

Pagers and Beepers

Used by physicians, emergency medical technicians, firefighters, guards, salespeople, business executives, and some parents who want to keep in constant touch with their infants, these electronic devices create electromagnetic fields which, in prolonged close contact with the body, can upset biological cycles and lead to weight loss, changes in brain function, and diminished resistance to cancers.

What You Can Do

- Keep beepers away from children and from sensitive parts of body, especially ovaries and gonads.
- Avoid wearing beeper for an extended time on your belt by carrying it in a briefcase or bag.

Radioprotective Foods

As we have seen above, certain foods – organ meats and irradiated products – attract or contain radioactivity that could affect our immune systems. Other kinds of food, it is believed, can *protect* our bodies from radioactive fallout, irradiated food, and different forms of radiation. According to this theory, there are many ways "of enhancing the immune system so that radiation protection can be feasible."[87]

In addition to a balanced diet of natural, organic foods, "green" foods such as wheat grass and barley grass are recommended. Other important protectors include raw fermented foods – miso and lactic-acid-cultured milk products – yellow, green-leafy, root, and sea vegetables, high-fiber foods, raw nuts, bee and flower pollens, and certain herbal teas such as Pau d'Arco (also known as bowstick tea).

What You Can Do

- Read: *Fighting Radiation with Foods, Herbs, & Vitamins*, by Steven R. Schechter, and *Radiation Protection Manual*, by Lita Lee, Ph.D. (See "Further Reading," p. 183, for more information). They both cite recent scientific studies showing how foods and nutrients can prevent or treat the toxic side effects of radiation and chemical pollution.

Radiation Risk: Long-Term Considerations

As we have shown throughout this chapter, radiation touches our lives at many points, some of which we can deal with by taking specific courses of action described above. However, because any dose of radiation is an overdose, we must do all we can to reduce the sources of this form of invisible pollution, especially the widespread use of nuclear power in civilian and military applications. Because we are all exposed to radiation in our daily lives, it is important to keep in mind:

1. There is *no known safe level* of exposure to radiation or other carcinogens.

2. There is a *buildup factor* – even the most minute doses can add significantly to amounts of radiation and contamination you have received elsewhere, often without your being aware of prior exposure.

3. *Pregnant mothers, fetuses, and children are many times more vulnerable than others to the effects of radiation and contamination.*[88]

The next chapter focuses on energy conservation and the many forms of environmentally sound, renewable energy that can replace nuclear power within the next ten years, if we persuade our political leaders of the urgency of such an objective. The ways that this goal can be achieved are set forth in chapter 11.

RESOURCES

The following is provided to help you locate additional resources on the topics covered in this chapter.

1. International Agencies and Organizations

— *International Atomic Energy Association* (IAEA), Vienna International Center, Wagramerstrasse 5, P.O. Box 100, A-1400, Vienna, Austria.

— *United Nations Scientific Community on the Effects of Atomic Radiation* (UNSCEAR), at same address as IAEA but P.O. Box 500.

2. U.S. Government

— *Department of Energy*, 1000 Independence Avenue SW, Washington, DC 20585.

— *Nuclear Regulatory Commission* (NRC), 1717 H Street NW, Washington, DC 20555.

— *Occupational Safety and Health Administration*, Department of Labor, 200 Constitution Avenue NW, Washington, DC 20210.

3. Professional and Trade Associations

— *American Council on Science and Health*, 47 Maple Street, Summit, NJ 07901.

— *American Nuclear Society*, 555 North Kensington Avenue, La Grange Park, IL 60525.

— *Committee on Interagency Radiation Research and Policy Coordination*, 1019 Nineteenth Street NW, Washington, DC 20036.

— *National Council on Radiation Protection and Measurements*, 7910 Woodmont Avenue, Bethesda, MD 20814.

— *Society of Nuclear Medicine*, Committee on Biologic Effects of Radiation, 136 Madison Avenue, New York, NY 10016.

— *Union of Concerned Scientists*, 26 Church Street, Cambridge, MA 02238.

— *U.S. Council for Energy Awareness*, 1776 Eye Street NW, Washington, DC 20006-2495. Represents the nuclear-power industry.

4. Environmental and Citizens' Groups

— *Abalone Alliance*, 452 Higuera, San Luis Obispo, CA 93401.

— *Americans for Safe Food*, P.O. Box 66300, Washington, DC 20035.

— *Clamshell Alliance*, P.O. Box 734, Concord, NH 03302.

— *Committee for Nuclear Responsibility*, P.O. Box 11207, San Francisco, CA.

— *Consumers United for Food Safety*, P.O. Box 22928, Seattle, WA 98122.

— *Environmental Action Inc.*, 1346 Connecticut Avenue NW, Washington, DC 20036; (202) 833-1845.

— *Environmental Action Foundation*, (merged with Environmental Task Force), 1525 New Hampshire Avenue NW, Washington, DC 200036.

— *Environmental Defense Fund*, 257 Park Avenue South, New York, NY 10010; (212) 505-2100.

— *Food and Water*, 3 Whitman Drive, Denville, NJ 07834.

— *Food Irradiation Response Newsletter*, Box 5183, Santa Cruz, CA 95063.

— *Health and Energy Institute*, 236 Massachusetts Avenue NE, Washington, DC 20002.

— *League of Women Voters*, 1730 M Street NW, Washington, DC 20036; (202) 429-1965.

— *National Coalition to Stop Food Irradiation*, Box 590488, San Francisco, CA, 94159.

— *Natural Resources Defense Council*, 40 West 20th Street, New York, NY 10011; (212) 727-2700.

— *Nuclear Information and Resource Service*, 1616 P Street NW, Suite 160, Washington, DC 20036.

— *Nuke Watch*, 315 W. Gorham Street, Madison, WI 53703.

— *Public Citizen Critical Mass Energy Project*, 215 Pennsylvania Avenue SE, Washington, DC 20003.

— *Radioactive Waste Campaign*, 625 Broadway, New York, NY 10012.

— *Sierra Club*, 730 Polk Street, San Francisco, CA 94109; (415) 776-2211.

— *USPIRG*, 215 Pennsylvania Avenue SE, Washington, DC 20003.

5. *Further Reading*

— *The Body Electric: Electromagnetism and the Foundation of Life*, Robert O. Becker, M.D., and Gary Selden. New York: William Morrow, 1985.

— *A Citizen's Guide To Radon*, Washington, D.C.: EPA, OPA-86-004, 1986.

— *Deadly Defense: Military Radioactive Landfills*. New York: Radioactive Waste Campaign, 1988.

— *The Effects on Populations of Exposure to Low Levels of Ionizing Radiation*, Washington, D.C.: National Academy of Sciences, 1972.

— *Fighting Radiation with Foods, Herbs, and Vitamins*, Steven R. Schechter. Brookline, Mass.: East West Health Books, 1988.

— *Food Irradiation: Who Wants It?*, Tony Webb, Tim Lang, and Kathleen Tucker. Rochester, Vt.: Thorsons, 1987.

— "How Many Chernobyls," Christopher Flavin, *World Watch Magazine*, January/February 1988.

— *Living with Radiation*, Henry N. Wagner, M.D., and Linda E. Ketchum. Baltimore: Johns Hopkins, 1989.

— *Living without Landfills*, New York: Radioactive Waste Campaign, 1987.

— *Low-level Radiation*, Ernest J. Sternglass, New York: Ballantine Books, 1972.

— *Low-level Radiation Effects: A Fact Book*, edited by A. Bertrand Brill, M.D. New York: Society of Nuclear Medicine, 1985.

— *Multiple Exposures: Chronicles of the Radiation Age*, Catherine Caufield, New York: Harper & Row, 1989.

— *No Nukes*, Anna Gyorgy. Boston: South End Press, 1979.

— "Nuclear Power: The Market Test," Christopher Flavin. Washington, D.C.: Worldwatch Paper 57, 1986.

— *Nuclear Power Safety: 1979-89*, Kenneth Boley. Washington, D.C.: Public Citizen, 1989.

— *Nuclear Power Safety Report: 1979-1987*. Washington, D.C.: Critical Mass Energy Project, 1988.

— *The Nuclear Waste Primer*, League of Women Voters Education Fund. New York: Nick Lyons Books, 1985.

— *Radiation and Health*, edited by R. Russell Jones and R. Southwood. Contains "Childhood Cancers in the U.K. and Their Relation to Background Radiation," G. W. Neale and A. M. Stewart, New York: John Wiley, 1987.

— *Radiation and Human Health*, John W. Gofman, M.D., Ph.D. San Francisco: Sierra Club, 1981.

— *Radiation and the War on Cancer*, Senator Mike Gravel. Washington, D.C.: Congressional Record, vol. 118, no. 6, January 26, 1972, pp. 403-414.

— *Radiation Alert*, David I. Puch. New York: Doubleday, 1985.

— *Radiation Protection Manual*, Lita Lee, Ph.D. Self-published (2061 Hampton Avenue, Redwood City, CA 94061), 1987.

— *Radioactive Waste Campaign — The First Ten Years*, Marvin Resnikoff, Ph.D. New York: Radioactive Waste Campaign, 1988.

— *Radon: The Citizens' Guide*. New York: Environmental Defense Fund, 1987.

— *Radon: The Invisible Threat*, Michael Lafavore. Emmaus, Pa.: Rodale Press, 1987.

— *Radon Reduction Methods: A Homeowner's Guide*, OPA 87-010. Washington, D.C.: EPA, September 1987.

— *Radon Reduction Techniques for Detached Houses*, EPA/625/5-86/019. Cincinnati, Ohio: EPA, 1986.

— *Radon Risk and Remedy*, David J. Brenner, Ph.D. New York: W. H. Freeman, 1989.

— *Shutdown Strategies: Citizen Efforts to Close Nuclear Power Plants*. Washington, D.C.: Critical Mass Energy Project, 1987.

— *The X-Ray Information Book – A Consumer's Guide to Avoiding Unnecessary Medical and Dental X-Rays*, Priscilla Laws, Ph.D. New York: Farrar, Strauss, Giroux, 1983.

ENDNOTES

1. Testimony before the Energy and Power Subcommittee of the House of Representatives Committee on Energy and Commerce, Washington, D.C., May 22, 1986.

2. "Recalculating the Cost of Chernobyl" (*Science*, May 8, 1987) cites a U.S. DOE study that "anticipates 39,000 extra cancer deaths because of the accident, most of them outside the Soviet Union."

3. Francis X. Clines, "Chernobyl Shakes Reindeer Culture of Lapps," *New York Times*, September 14, 1986.

4. *Farmers Weekly*, April 28, 1989, cited in *Environment Digest*, no. 24, May 1989.

5. Cited in *Environmental Digest*, no. 28, September 1989, p. 10.

6. Charles Komanoff Associates, New York; see also Peter Bunyard, "Nuclear Energy After Chernobyl" in *Earth Report* (London: Mitchell Beazley, 1988), p. 39.

7. Edward Goldsmith and Nicholas Hildyard, eds., *The Earth Report*, London: Mitchell Beazley, 1988, pp. 232-233.

8. Francis X. Clines, "Soviets Now Admit '57 Blast," *New York Times*, June 18, 1989.

9. Christopher Flavin, "Ten Years of Fallout," *World Watch*, March/April 1989, p. 30.

10. "Nuclear Power's Worsening Record," section 5D (pp. 32-35) in *Turning Down the Heat*, Washington, D.C.: Public Citizen, 1988; see also Kenneth Boley, *Nuclear Power Safety: 1979-89* (Washington, D.C.: Public Citizen, 1989).

11. *Critical Mass Energy Bulletin*, June/August 1989, p.6.

12. The "permissible" level has been steadily lowered over the past 20 years. In December 1989 the conservative National Research Council reported that the risk of getting cancer from low levels of radiation appeared to be *four* times as high as previous estimates (Philip J. Hilts, "Higher Cancer Risk Found in Radiation," *New York Times*, December 20, 1989).

13. Free radicals are formed in your body during normal body metabolism. They form in excess when your immune system is weakened by radioactive and chemical pollutants in food, water, and air.

14. See special section on radon, pp. 170-173.

15. A "permitted dose" is an arbitrary level which the EPA says should not be exceeded. Since any amount of radiation is potentially harmful, there is no such thing as a truly "safe dose."

16. Quoted in Dr. Lita Lee's *Radiation Protection Manual* (1987), which may be ordered directly from Dr. Lee, 2061 Hampton Avenue, Redwood City, CA 94061. For a detailed discussion of radiation exposure standards, see Catherine Caufield, *Multiple Exposures* (New York: Harper and Row, 1989), pp. 179-189.

17. David I. Puch, *Radiation Alert* (New York: Doubleday, 1985), p. 103.

18. Keith Schneider, "Damage Estimate at Nuclear Plant Rises," *New York Times*, March 7, 1989.

19. Keith Schneider, "U.S. May Yield Health Data on Nuclear Weapon Workers," *New York Times*, October 28, 1988.

20. Over 1 million curies, reported in a public statement by the Peace Development Fund in the *New York Times*, July 27, 1986.

A curie is a unit of radioactivity giving off 37 billion disintegrations per second. According to the same statement, on December 2, 1949, Hanford officials intentionally released 5,000 curies of iodine-131 in a "planned experiment," details of which were withheld from the public at least until 1988. By comparison, the Three Mile Island accident released an estimated 15 curies.

21. Harold M. Schmeck, Jr., "Major New Studies Near Nuclear Plants Seek Health Effects of Radiation Leaks," *New York Times*, November 1, 1988.

22. "Are Nuclear Weapons Killing Us Already?," advertisement, Peace Development Fund, Amherst, Mass., in *New York Times*, July 27, 1986.

23. Goldsmith and Hilyard, eds. *Earth Report*, pp. 202-203; Anna Gyorgy, *No Nukes* (Boston: South End Press, 1979), pp. 90-95.

24. Keith Schneider, "Wide Threat Seen in Contamination at Nuclear Units," *New York Times*, December 7, 1988.

25. *Critical Mass Energy Bulletin*, June/August 1989, vol.1, no. 1, p. 6; see also Kenneth Boley, *Public Citizen's Nuclear Power Safety Report* (Washington, D.C.: Critical Mass Energy Project, December 1988), p. v-1, and Appendix A.

26. Ibid., pp. i-1.

27. *Public Citizen's Nuclear Power Safety Report*, pp. v-3.

28. "Cancer Clusters Prompt U.S. Study," *New York Times*, February 5, 1988.

29. Sidney Cobb, testimony before the Commonwealth of Massachusetts, Joint Committee on Energy, March 24, 1987.

30. *Cousteau Almanac*, New York: Doubleday, 1981, p. 408.

31. John Gofman, *Estimated Production of Human Lung Cancers from Worldwide Fallout*, Committee for Nuclear Responsibility Report, summary of conclusions, July 10, 1975, cited in Gyorgy, *No Nukes*, p.82.

32. Jon R. Luoma, "U.S. Turning to New Technologies to Clean Up Arms Plants," *New York Times*, January 3, 1989; "Rise in Cleanup Cost Seen," (Associated Press report), *New York Times*, February 24, 1989.

33. Nevada Bureau of Mines and Geology, *Comments on DOE/RW-0012 Draft Environmental Assessment, Yucca Mountain Site*, December 1984, quoted in *Turning Down the Heat*.

34. Marvin Resnikoff, *Living without Landfills*, New York: Radioactive Waste Campaign, 1987, p. 9.

35. Reported in *Living without Landfills*, p. 41. This is an authoritative documentation of the history of nuclear landfills in the U.S. and should be read in conjunction with Resnikoff's *Deadly Defense*, a guide to military radioactive landfills (New York: Radioactive Waste Campaign, 1988).

36. Schneider, "Wide Threat Seen," *New York Times*, December 7, 1988.

37. Keith Schneider, "Suddenly, Nuclear Waste Looks Very Visible Again," *New York Times*, September 18, 1988.

38. Jon R. Luoma, "U.S. Turning to New Technologies to Clean Up Arms Plants," *New York Times*, January 3, 1989.

39. Matthew L. Wald, "Storing Nuclear Waste Called Safer than Burial," *New York Times*, June 1, 1989.

40. For further information on the French nuclear industry, see chapter 9, p. 213.

41. Goldsmith and Hilyard, eds., *Earth Report*, pp. 188-189.

42. Cynthia Pollock Shea, "Breaking Up Is Hard To Do," *World Watch*, July/August 1989, p. 11.

43. Ibid., p. 10.

44. *Turning Down the Heat*, p. 30.

45. Matthew L. Wald, "Costly Task of a Nuclear Recycling Plant Cleanup," *New York Times*, October 29, 1989.

46. Keith Schneider, "Candor on Nuclear Peril," *New York Times*, October 14, 1989.

47. Keith Schneider, "Nuclear Plants' Deaths: The Birth of New Problems," *New York Times*, October 31, 1988.

48. William J. Broad, "New Plans for Space Reactors Raise Fears of Nuclear Debris," *New York Times*, October 18, 1988.

49. Karl Grossman and Judith Long, "Plutonium Con," *The Nation*, November 20, 1989.

50. Joseph Treen, "Nuclear Crash?," *The Nation*, October 3, 1988.

51. Rachel Johnson, "Deep Dilemma over Raising Sleeping Dogs," *Financial Times* (London), July 4, 1989.

52. William M. Arkin and Joshua Handler, "Naval Nuclear Accidents: The Secret History," *Greenpeace Magazine*, July/August 1989.

53. Ibid. pp. 15-18.

54. Matthew L. Wald, "3 States Ask Waste Cleanup as Price of Atomic Operation," *New York Times*, December 17, 1988.

55. "78% of Americans Balk at New Nuclear Reactors: Poll Finds Rise in Support for Closing Plants," *Washington Post*, May 26, 1986.

56. For addresses and other details on these organizations, see pp. 182-183.

57. Rancho Seco's electricity cost 5.4 cents a kilowatt hour in 1988 compared with 2.3 cents for natural gas, according to a report in the *New York Times*, June 8, 1989, "Voters, in a First, Shut Down Nuclear Reactor."

58. Ibid.

59. A comprehensive outline of citizen efforts to close nuclear plants is to be found in *Shutdown Strategies* by Joseph Kriesberg (Washington, D.C.: Public Citizen Critical Mass Energy Project, 1988).

60. Robert E. Yuhnke, Ellen K. Silbergeld, and Janice E. Caswell, *Radon: The Citizens' Guide* (New York: Environmental Defense Fund, 1987).

61. Professor Arthur W. Rose, Pennsylvania State University, study of radon levels in central Pennsylvania, presented at joint meeting of the American Geophysical Society and the Mineralogical Society of America, reported in *New York Times*, May 23, 1989.

62. Based on recommendations by EPA and EDF.

63. *Radon Testing Report* (Washington, D.C.: Public Citizen, January, 1989).

64. Information from EPA and Robert Hanley, "The Jersey Village that Fought Radon and Won," *New York Times*, September 15, 1988.

65. For details on how radioactivity is measured, see p. 157.

66. Steven R. Schechter, *Fighting Radiation* (Brookline, Mass.: East West Books, 1988), p. 29.

67. Ibid., p. 30.

68. Ibid., p. 31.

69. Richard Piccioni, "Food Irradiation: Contaminating Our Food," *EPA Journal*, November 1986. Dr. Piccioni is senior staff scientist with Accord Research and Educational Associates, 314 W. 91st Street, New York, NY 10024.

70. Goldsmith and Hildyard, eds., *Earth Report*, pp. 150-151.

71. Reported on Gary Null's "Natural Living," radio program, WBAI, New York, December 29, 1988.

72. Anna Gyorgy, *No Nukes*, pp. 88-89.

73. For further information see Linda Clark, *Secrets of Health and Beauty*, (Old Greenwich, Conn.: Devin-Adair, 1979), p. 88 and passim.

74. Martin D. Becker and Norton J. Bramesco, *Radiation* (New York: Vintage, 1981), p. 46 and p. 161; Schechter, *Fighting Radiation*, pp. 23-26.

75. See "Hidden Hazards of Lead in the Home," *Consumer Reports*, September 1988, p. 542.

76. These findings are extensively documented in part 2 of "Annals of Radiation," a three-part series by Paul Brodeur in the *New Yorker*, June 12, 19, and 26, 1989.

77. Ibid.

78. *New York Power Line Report, 1987*, quoted in Jillie Collings, "Lines of Anguish," *Guardian* (U.K.), September 1, 1988.

79. Puch, *Radiation Alert*, p. 65.

80. Ibid., p.33; see also Brodeur, "Annals of Radiation," Part 3, pp. 40 and 52.

81. Mark A. Pinsky, "VDT Radiation," *The Nation*, January 9-16, 1989.

82. Tim Friend, "Miscarriage 'Clusters' Worry in the Workplace" (cover story), *USA Today*, December 15, 1988.

83. Home-testing kits can be obtained from electronic and scientific supply houses and other sources.

84. See "Resources," p. 182.

85. Brodeur, "Annals of Radiation," part 2, p. 56.

86. Puch, *Radiation Alert*.

87. Lee, *Radiation Protection Manual*, pp. 30-68.

88. Children and fetuses are particularly susceptible to cancers from radiation (and other sources) because at early stages of growth their body cells are in the process of much more rapid division than in later life.

9

RENEWABLE ENERGY

Rethinking Our Options

*"Up to 75 percent of the electricity produced in
the U.S. is wasted through the use of inefficient motors,
lights, and appliances."*
*– David H. Moskovitz, former commissioner,
Maine Public Utilities Commission*[1]

Pollution, growing dependence on imported fuels,
increasing radiation risk, and inefficiency are the shaky
cornerstones of the energy policy our government has
pursued since the election of Ronald Reagan in 1980.
Our obsessive reliance on fossil fuels is a major contributor to the global environmental crisis:

● Oil and coal combustion by cars, factories, power
plants, and buildings produces air pollution and acid rain,
and contributes half of all greenhouse-gas emissions.

● Pesticides and other petrochemicals in our food, water,

and air cause cancer and many more environmental diseases.

● Accidents and "routine" spills from oil-storage tanks, factories, mines, tankers, ships, aircraft, and toxic-waste dumps contaminate earth, lakes, rivers, oceans, and drinking water.

There must be a better way to move people from one place to another, to run our factories and power plants, and to heat and light our homes. There must be a way to break our dependence on fossil fuels, to free ourselves from the fear of nuclear disasters, and to live in the world without polluting it to death.

There is. Or more to the point, there *are*.

This chapter spells out how we can move to a cleaner, more sustainable future by renewing our sources of energy and using them wisely. It also describes many things you can do to help bring about the necessary changes by the year 2000.

Is There Life after Oil?

If curbing pollution isn't reason enough to reduce our use of fossil fuels, there is the law of diminishing returns – depleting accessibility of petroleum. Oil, which provides 30 percent of the world's energy – mainly for transportation and chemicals – is projected to run dry in about fifty years. As it runs out, it is getting more and more expensive to extract from the last remaining sites, most of which are located in the politically unstable Middle East, or in ecologically fragile regions like Alaska.[2] In 1973 we imported 35 percent of our petroleum. Today it's more than 40 percent. If we maintain our current rate of consumption, imports will supply 50 percent by the mid-1990s, and over 60 percent by 2000.[3]

Depletion and waste are costly. The 1989 Exxon *Valdez* spill – 11 million gallons of crude oil – was less than 10 percent of what we import daily. Yet it triggered a rise of 10 to 15 cents a gallon of gas. If you include the $50 billion annual cost of protecting the American oil supply in the Persian Gulf,[4] you'd be paying another 50 cents a gallon at the pump instead of in your income tax.

The future of coal is equally clouded. Although its reserves are considerably larger than those of petroleum, the regions that have coal in abundance – China, the Soviet Union, Poland, and Appalachia – suffer the greatest damage from air pollution and acid rain. The cost of making coal pollution-free is high, although clean new processes such as gasification might be developed in conjunction with solar-energy systems. (For one promising approach, see pp. 205-206.)

Energy Conservation and Efficiency

Moving Beyond Coal and Oil

Giving up our dependence on fossil fuels means switching to other sources of energy. Some of these options are immediately available (conservation and efficiency), many can be implemented in the near future (photovoltaics and wind power), others have longer-term potential (tidal power and hydrogen). The global warming threat makes our choice of options urgent and critical. Let's look at them and see what they have to offer.

Doing More with Less

Saving energy and using it more efficiently are such simple answers to our continuing dependency on fossil fuels that they are often overlooked in favor of more exotic and costly solutions. *By shifting to less energy-wasteful activities in the way we live and work and using energy more efficiently, it is technically and economically feasible to cut per-capita energy use in half while doubling our gross national product.*[5]

Incredible as it may seem, as much as 75 percent of the energy produced in the United States each year is wasted through the use of inefficient motors, lights, and appliances.

The Vital Statistics of Energy

● Total world energy use in 1989 was about 375 quadrillion British thermal units (BTUs). A quadrillion is a million billion and is also known as a quad.

● One BTU is the amount of energy required to raise the temperature of a pound of water one degree Fahrenheit. It is roughly the amount of heat provided by burning a kitchen match from end to end (watch your fingers!).

● Three hundred seventy-five quads is the equivalent of 65.25 billion barrels of oil, or 16.5 billion tons of coal, or what it takes to make 36 trillion kilowatt-hours (KWH) of electricity.

● One kilowatt (KW) is 1,000 watts (equal to the power of ten 100-watt light bulbs). 1,000 KW = 1 megawatt (MW) = enough energy to power about 500 households. 1,000 MW = 1 gigawatt (GW) = the power of a large electric power plant.

● One KWH is the amount of energy ten 100-watt light bulbs burn in one hour.

● One gallon of gas or its energy equivalent could: supply your body with enough fuel for 10 days' worth of metabolic activity, or drive a fuel-efficient car for one hour, or drive a limousine for 12 minutes, or fly a B-1 bomber for 1/10th of a second.

● The comparative costs of building a 1,000-megawatt base-load power plant or equivalent (enough to supply the electricity needs of 500,000 Americans) are:

Fuel Source	Cost to Build (in billions of dollars)
Cogeneration*	1.2
Hydropower	2
Wind energy	0.9[†]
Coal	1.0[‡]
Oil	1.5[‡]
Solar thermal	1.75[†]
Photovoltaics	2†
Nuclear power	5-6[§]
Negawatts (conservation, efficiency)	0.2

*Cogeneration is the production of two useful forms of energy from the same process, as when the excess steam from a factory boiler is used to generate electricity for the factory or sold to a power company.

[‡] Does not include cost of air-pollution cleanup devices required by current laws.

[†] Cost will decline throughout 1990s.

[§] Does not include cost of hidden subsidies and nuclear-waste disposal.

Right after the OPEC crisis, when oil prices rose dramatically, serious efforts were initiated in the United States to save energy and improve its energy efficiency. For about a decade progress was impressive. However, by late 1985 there was a glut of oil on the market and the price dropped to $10 a barrel. Although this did not lead to a return to the extravagantly wasteful days of the 1960s, it gave the Reagan administration an excuse to slash federal energy conservation programs, including the all-important automobile mileage standards.

Home Savings

Appliances consume a quarter of U.S. electricity. *The largest single user in most American homes is the refrigerator, which nationally uses the equivalent of half the output of all nuclear power plants.*[6] Faced with the prospect of having to build a huge number of power plants to meet the demands of domestic appliances, California (which accounts for one-fifth of the nation's refrigerator market) in 1978-80 adopted refrigerator standards requiring 20 percent less energy use than their 1975 counterparts. This paved the way for national legislation cutting these standards by another 15 to 20 percent.

> *"Each 1-percent improvement in lighting efficiency replaces the need for a power plant."*
>
> Arthur Rosenfeld, lighting consultant[7]

In 1987 the U.S. Congress, over the objections of the Department of Energy but with the backing of utilities, appliance manufacturers, and environmental groups, passed the National Appliance Energy Conservation Act. The law sets minimum efficiency criteria for refrigerators, freezers, and other appliances as well as home heating and cooling systems. The standards mandated in the 1987 act would by 2000 save consumers $30 billion on their energy bills, eliminate the need for 20 multibillion dollar new power plants, and reduce the pollutants that cause acid rain, global warming, and other environmental hazards. However, the DOE, which has responsibility for implementing the legislation, is setting the standards too low. It ignored several proven energy-saving measures for refrigerators, freezers, small gas furnaces, and TV sets and rejected others on the dubious grounds that efficiency measures, however much energy they save, must pay back within 3 years.[8]

Buying an energy-efficient appliance is only one of the many ways you can save energy. For a list of 74 other things you can do, see the special section *75 Ways You Can Save Energy and the Earth*, pp. 216-220.

Industry Savings

A major share of industrial energy goes into powering large motors (above 100 horsepower). Although more efficient than smaller ones, larger units are inefficient when run below optimal speed. In anticipation of expanding loads, many users buy oversized motors and waste considerable energy. If the U.S. equipped all of its industrial motors with available speed controls that match motor output to load demand, the nation's electricity demand would drop by 7 percent.[9]

Important energy savings can also be made by recycling materials that have already been processed. For example, using recycled aluminum to produce a die-cast part requires 95 percent less energy than if it is made from primary metal. Although U.S. use of recycled aluminum has grown steadily to about 60 percent today, there is ample room for further savings by recycling.

Cogenerating

Cogeneration saves considerable amounts of energy because it uses energy that would otherwise be wasted. *In fact, it could supply as much power as 100 nuclear plants by the year 2000.* Cogeneration systems can be fueled with any number of materials – fossil fuels, wood and other biofuels including agricultural waste products, even solar energy. They range in size from 20 kilowatt (KW) units in restaurants and apartment buildings to 500,000 KW systems in large industrial facilities. They are widely used in Europe for municipal district heating systems and in most new power plants.

In North America the forest-products industry now gets about three-quarters of its energy from its own wastes; most paper mills, for example, use the same steam to run the pulping process and to generate electricity. Producing both together takes only half as much fuel and money as making heat and electricity separately.

By the end of 1988 there were 20,000 MW of cogeneration capacity in the U.S., producing about 4 percent of the electricity supply at costs usually lower than those of conventional power. Most energy experts agree that this capacity could comfortably be expanded fivefold by 2000.[10]

How to Use a Negawatt

The "Negawatt" is a simple but far-reaching concept popularized by Amory Lovins, director of the Rocky Mountain Institute (RMI). Essentially, it means generating power not by building a power plant and burning fossil fuels or nuclear energy, but by *conserving the energy we are already producing.*

Negawatts offer the potential for large-scale energy savings at a cost significantly lower than supplying electricity from existing power plants. For example, RMI found that Commonwealth Edison, a Chicago utility which runs 12 nuclear plants, could reduce their customers' demand by more than 5,000 MW – the amount generated by 5 of the plants – at a cost below 2 cents per kilowatt-hour (KWH) for energy efficiency and conservation measures. This is far less than it costs to run an existing nuclear or oil plant.

The negawatt principle was successfully applied in a landmark decision by the California Public Utilities Commission in 1979 as a result of a brilliantly fought action by the Environmental Defense Fund against two giant power companies – Pacific Gas & Electric and Southern California Edison. Instead of building six new nuclear- and coal-power plants, the utilities were ordered by the Commission to invest in efficiency, conservation, and renewable energy programs.[11]

On the face of it, telling a privately owned power company to produce *less* energy sounds as futile as telling a supermarket to encourage its customers to eat less food. Yet when forced to spend $250 million on *saving* energy, PG&E was able to avoid spending seven times that amount ($1.75 billion) on additional but unneeded energy supplies.

EDF's success had important repercussions nationwide. In 1988 the Connecticut Department of Public Utility Control ordered Northeast Utilities (NU), New England's largest electric company, to implement a comprehensive

Clean, Quiet, Reliable

Electric vehicles (EVs) have been around for years in Europe, where they are popular as vans for delivering milk and other goods in residential neighborhoods because they make no noise. A one-ton van, called the GM Griffon in the U.S. and the Bedford C11 in other countries, has logged over 5 1/2 million miles for customer service calls, carpools, shuttles, and other runs. Since 1985 Griffons have been used in the service fleets of 11 electric utilities and 11 other companies in North America.

In addition to being quiet and reliable, electric vehicles are clean. Running off batteries that can be recharged at low off-peak night rates, EVs give off no pollution whatsoever while they are running. Two new types of battery are under development – a lithium sulfide battery which is expected to deliver three times more range-per-charge (RPC), better acceleration, and longer life than currently used lead-acid batteries, and a sodium-sulfur unit being tested in the U.K., Canada, and Germany (East Germany makes considerable use of EVs).

Also under development is an alternating-current (AC) engine to replace the heavier direct-current (DC) power trains presently in use. Much of the research and development in this country is done by the Electric Power Research Institute's electric transportation program in cooperation with the Department of Energy, General Motors, Ford, and Chrysler.

In January 1990 GM displayed "the most advanced EV yet developed," saying that it could be on the market as soon as 1995. According to a GM videotape, the prototype model outraced a Nissan 300ZX from a standing start to 60 mph.

The basic engineering of GM's G-Van (successor to the Griffon) is completed and the vehicle is due for manufacture in the U.S. in 1990. Chrysler is field-testing its TEVan, with production scheduled for 1991, and Ford is testing passenger cars and lightweight vans fitted with AC engines and sodium-sulfur batteries. As can be seen from the following table, performance of these vehicles is impressive. The widespread introduction of EVs would give such enormous benefits in terms of environmental health that one wonders why their development is not given the same kind of attention (and funding) by our government as the *Stealth* bomber, for example, for which there is no need whatsoever.

Performance Specifications, Weight, and Space Capacities
(Based on material supplied by Electric Power Research Institute)

	Griffon	G-Van	TEVan*
Top Speed	53 mph	53 mph	65 mph
Range between charges	60 miles	60 miles	110 miles
Acceleration (0-30 mph)	11 sec.	12.5 sec.	7 sec.
Payload capacity	1,900 lb.	1,800 lb.	1,200 lb.
Cargo space	208 cu. ft.	256 cu. ft.	120 cu. ft.

* Projected

energy conservation program at a cost of 2 to 3 cents per KWH saved.

Inspired by EDF's breakthrough, the Boston-based Conservation Law Foundation (CLF) achieved another important negawatt victory. CLF had shown how New England power companies could save between a third and half of their electricity by using it more efficiently to accomplish the same task. In a test case charging that NU was failing in its public duty to save as much energy as possible, CLF won a Massachusetts state decision ordering the power company to launch a major energy-saving campaign, using CLF's power-saving experts to help design the programs.

The decision prevented revival of a plan to build a second reactor at the controversial Seabrook, N.H. nuclear plant and it opened the way for another negawatt action, initiated by NU.

Now convinced that conservation pays, the utility in early 1989 approached one of its largest customers, the aircraft-engine company Pratt and Whitney, with a startling proposal. According to Bob Samuelson, senior electrical engineer at the latter company, "NU said we were wasting a lot of energy but if we would make some simple changes in one part of the factory – replacing old-fashioned machinery and changing light bulbs, for instance – it would save Pratt and Whitney $300,000 a year. When we told them we didn't want to pay the $1 million up front needed to make the changes, NU said they wanted to save the energy so much that they would invest $500,000 of their own money." [12]

Least-Cost Planning

The results of negawatt use have been dramatic. Utilities in California, the Pacific Northwest, and, more recently, New England have deferred building new large-scale electricity generators. And the principle that a kilowatt-hour saved by an efficient appliance or conservation is indistinguishable from one delivered to customers from a new power plant is beginning to figure in national energy policy.

The techniques for meeting future electric power needs by considering less costly energy savings and alternatives have evolved into what is now called least-cost planning. It is a key feature, for example, of the Global Warming Prevention Act (HR 1078) proposed by Congresswoman Claudine Schneider. Title 1 of this bill mandates DOE to prioritize its policies in accord with least-cost options and with the process defined in the Pacific Northwest Electric Power Conservation Act of 1980.

Getting More Mileage

Motor vehicles, a major source of air pollution, consume over 60 percent of the oil used in the U.S., which is about the same as our total domestic production. Better fuel economy is an obvious way of reducing auto emissions – doubling mileage per gallon would cut CO_2 emissions in half – slowing oil reserve depletion and keeping gas prices down.

In 1990 the fuel economy standard set by the U.S. Department of Transportation for passenger cars is 27.5 miles per gallon. In Japan and Europe the mpg level is 30 to 40 percent higher. Yet we live in a world where 70 miles per gallon is eminently feasible. At present the most fuel-efficient car on the U.S. market averages 58 miles per gallon on the highway. Greater economies are being achieved in prototypes with existing technologies such as weight reduction and fuel injection – the Toyota AXV gets 98 mpg, the Volkswagen

E80 averages 85 mpg, the Peugeot ECO 73 mpg. Volvo has built a multifuel car with a 70 mpg average in combined city and highway driving that, the company claims, would cost in mass production the same as today's average compact. There are also promising new technologies such as the Orbital two-stroke engine under development in Australia (bought under license by General Motors in 1989).[13]

If the new cars of the mid-1990s attain efficiencies in the 60 to 65 mpg range, the average for all 533 million cars estimated to be on the road by the turn of the century would be approximately 48 mpg. This would result in 3 million barrels of oil a day less than the 319 million cars on the road in 1982 used.[14]

Renewable Energy: Ready and Willing

By "renewable" we refer to those sources of energy that, unlike oil, coal, or uranium, derive their energy directly from the sun. Solar energy, wind energy, biomass, and photovoltaics are not subject to depletion as are oil, coal, and uranium; they are constantly renewed by the sun and are not inherently harmful to the environment.

The sun is our greatest energy resource, providing the earth with roughly 100,000 times more power than all the utility plants combined. Two days of solar radiation falling on the earth equals the world's total fossil-fuel reserves. As we search for ways to displace polluting and hazardous fuels, the natural energy sources, if appropriately applied, take on tremendous importance as a cost effective and environmentally sound answer.

Water Power
Hydropower

Hydropower converts the kinetic energy of flowing water into mechanical power or electricity. Compared with other sources, it is the most efficient and economical supplier of electricity, with an end-user cost ranging from 3 to 6 cents per KWH, not including capital costs.[15]

Producing no carbon dioxide, hydropower supplies more than 20 percent of the world's electricity, more than nuclear energy but less than coal and oil.[16] Present hydro capacity in the U.S. is close to 90,000 MW – 13 percent of total electricity generation to which can be added available Canadian resources of 60,000 MW, including one 10,000-MW plant that sells large amounts of electricity to power companies in New England.

Outside of North America (which accounts for 30 percent of world output), hydropower's potential for expansion is vast. The World Bank projects that 223 gigawatts of large hydropower capacity (equivalent to 223 large nuclear plants) will have been installed in developing countries by 1995, more than half of them in Brazil, China, and India.[17] In 1986 Venezuela completed the largest hydropower dam in the world with 10-GW capacity. Brazil is building a 12-GW plant, and China is considering a 13-GW project on the Chang Jiang (Yangtze River).

Monster dams such as these pose serious ecological problems – the flooding of natural areas the size of Long Island and larger, displacement of thousands, even (in the case of China's Three Gorges dam) millions of people, the erosion of farmland, and the destruction of untold numbers of wildlife and ecosystems. Moreover, as was discovered at Egypt's Aswan dam, blocking a river's natural course radically changes the surrounding environment. Silt, containing vital nutrients, accumulates behind turbines and dams instead of providing food for fish downstream and being deposited on agricultural flood plains. In tropical regions reservoirs act as breeding grounds for carriers of malaria, schistosomiasis, and river blindness.[18] *Widespread anxiety over the ecological and social impact of large dams has led to pressure on the World Bank and other development agencies to stop funding large-scale water-power projects.*

The most judicious use of hydropower is not in a few gigantic projects but in medium-sized (10 to 100 MW) and small (100 KW to 10 MW) systems, which run on the natural flow of rivers. In the United States there is a great number of small and medium-sized dams ready for refurbishment. A comparison of the Rhone River in France and the Ohio in the U.S. – rivers with similar power potential – shows that there were 21 dams producing 3000 MW of power on the Rhone while the Ohio produced only 180 MW.[19] Less than 5 percent of U.S. dams produce electricity. Estimates of power available at small dams vary from 6,000 to 25,000 MW, a significant source of untapped energy that could be developed under the "limited power producer" section of the Public Utility Regulatory Policies Act (see chapter 10, p. 240).

Many countries in Europe and the developing world are now building "stand-alone" hydroelectric systems. These include ground-water dams built into riverbeds either below or above the ground to store ground water when rivers and aquifers beneath them dry up. They are relatively cheap to build and have low impact on the environment. In Africa, India, and Brazil these small dams are also used for drinking water in rural areas.

Ocean Energy

Ocean energy from waves and tides is being developed as a source of electricity in several experimental and a few commercial systems. They consist of tidal ponds or dams built across the mouth of a river or cove that fills up with the incoming tide. After high tide, sluice gates are closed and the water is returned back to the sea through an electricity-generating turbine.

For twenty years a 240-MW tidal power installation has operated successfully at La Rance in Brittany, France, and 10- to 20-MW units are on line in Canada, the U.K., and China. In 1986 Norway began operating the world's first two wave-power plant prototypes, one with a sea-level reservoir, the other with an oscillating water column that generates electricity from both the rise and fall of individual waves. The water-column prototype, built for less than $2,000 per KW, generates electricity at the competitive rate of 5 cents per KWH, prompting Norway to invest in larger plants and to sell the technology to Portugal, Indonesia, and other countries.[20] Although capital costs of tidal-power projects are high, operating costs are very low. They have long-term potential for generating considerable amounts of electricity with less ecological impact than large-scale dams.

Wind Energy

The power of the wind has been used for thousands of years to propel sailing ships and turn the "sails" of windmills – grinding wheat, pumping water, and performing other tasks. In ancient China, the Middle East, and preindustrial Europe and North America the windmill was an integral part of the landscape. In the mid-nineteenth century wind-driven water pumpers made possible the building of the railroads and the irrigation of new territories across the U.S.

By 1900 there were 5 million wind-water pumpers on farms in the U.S. and Canada, and many of them are still working. Today myriad variations of the classic American farm windmill serve as the basic source of water throughout the world. Often costing less than $1,000, a metal-bladed water pumper, if properly maintained – it must be lubricated once a year – will run for decades without major repairs. With windmills the fuel is free and nonpolluting. It's blowing in the wind.

Wind-electric Power

The widespread generation of electricity by wind power began after World War I, when many farmers living without electricity fitted out army surplus aircraft propellers with simple electric-generator rigs to power a few light bulbs or charge batteries for their new radio sets. In the mid-1920s Marcellus Jacobs, a Minnesota farm youth, using parts from a Model T Ford and his parents' water pumper, developed the prototype of what became known as the Jacobs wind turbine, or more simply "the Jacobs." Between 1928 and 1960 many thousands of these machines were sold throughout the world. Priced at around $1,000, the system included the generator, a 50-foot, self-supporting tower, and a 21-KWH storage battery with a ten-year guarantee. Along with the turbine, Jacobs marketed a comprehensive line of 32-volt DC appliances it could run – refrigerators, radios, frozen-food cabinets, cream separators, electric drills, and "all the electricity you need at 2-3 cents per KWH." [21]

Throughout the 1930s the Jacobs and other wind turbines were the only source of electricity for many thousands of farms and homesteads in North America, Denmark, and other parts of the world. It was the advent of rural electrification powered by cheap coal or hydropower that displaced the early wind generators.

New Wind Power

In the mid-1970s the emergence of a new wind-energy technology was stimulated by the search for "alternative" fuels during the petroleum shortage brought on by the Arab oil embargo. The Carter administration introduced a number of measures that supported energy conservation and solar energy. They included funding for wind-energy research and development, tax credits to manufacturers and consumers, and the Public Utility Regulatory Policies Act (PURPA) of 1978, which opened the way for the generation of electricity by privately owned companies using wind power and other nonfossil fuels. [22]

With this support private-enterprise entrepreneurs built up a fledgling wind industry, manufacturing new-technology wind turbines capable of generating electricity to be sold to utility companies at rates competitive with those of oil or nuclear power. They ranged from tiny 1-KW "windchargers" – suitable for charging batteries on ships and in remote locations – to multimegawatt prototypes with 300-foot-diameter blades, standing 16 stories tall and costing over $4 million each.

Wind Farming

Because the efficient output of many wind-driven turbines depends on a steady supply of wind averaging 10 mph or more, the first areas selected were along the seashore, on islands, or in mountain passes – Hawaii, New England, the Pacific Northwest, and California are most favorable for the creation of "wind farms." These are clusters of as many as 500 or more wind turbines capable of putting out as much electricity as a conventional coal- or oil-fired plant.

After several years of trial-and-error testing, the best machines for wind farming were found to be those in the medium range (each generating between

200 and 500 KW). It was more economical to install greater numbers of these units than fewer large machines which, when they needed repairs, took much more downtime. It was also found that wind turbines imported from Denmark, Belgium, and other European countries operated more reliably than domestic machines.

When the strongly pronuclear Reagan Administration cut back drastically on solar-energy programs in the early 1980s the U.S. wind industry suffered a major blow. The only state to survive the surgery was California.

California Wind Rush

Outside of Hawaii, no state has such easily developable wind resources as California, especially in three mountain areas – Altamont, San Gorgonio, and Tehachapi. It was also fortunate in having a governor, Jerry Brown, who went further than the federal government in encouraging energy conservation and renewable energy. This combination of nature and politics attracted an influx of investors who hoped to cash in on the potentially huge market.

> *The wind turbines in the California windfarms have the equivalent power of two large nuclear plants and were installed in less than half the time and at less than half the cost of conventional power stations.*

California supplemented the federal tax cut by enacting state credits for solar-energy investors and utilities and by permitting accelerated depreciation of an investment in wind-energy. The financial incentives were augmented by a state wind-energy program directed by the California Energy Commission (CEC). In 1978 the state passed legislation requiring CEC to program for 4,000 MW of installed wind power capacity by 2000 – a savings of 25 million barrels of oil a year and a goal which appears to be eminently attainable.

U.S. Wind Energy Today

Wind power is still alive and growing in this country. From 150 wind turbines in 1981 there are today 18,000 wind turbines generating almost 2 billion KWH of electric power, equivalent to 3 million barrels of oil and enough energy to power approximately 300,000 homes.[23]

The wind turbines in the California windfarms have the equivalent power of two large nuclear plants and were installed in less than half the time and at less than half the cost of conventional power stations. Several smaller wind farms, one of which is using Japanese turbines, are operating in Hawaii and New England and there is a growing market for residential wind turbines in the 3-10 KW range, but the funding cutbacks of the Reagan and Bush eras have stunted the growth of this important source of energy in the United States, as well as forgoing an export market for a potential billion-dollar industry.

Wind Energy Abroad

Outside of the U.S. many countries see wind as crucial to their energy future. Denmark, which has no nuclear-energy plants, is the world's leading wind turbine exporter. At home it has more than 2,000 grid-linked turbines on line, with a capacity of 250 MW, including the first sea-based wind installation (on the east coast of Jutland) and a 12-MW wind farm, the largest outside the U.S., under construction near Limfjorden. The U.K. and the Netherlands are also increasing their wind-energy commitments, with the latter planning at least 1,000 MW installed by the year 2000. Wind farms are on line or under way in Italy, Belgium, Greece, West Germany, and the U.S.S.R.

In Asia, India has an ambitious wind-energy program – 5,000 MW by the end of the decade – supplying more electricity than the subcontinent's nuclear energy. The Chinese have initiated a number of important wind-energy projects, mainly in rural areas.

The Technology Is in Place

The cost of wind energy is dropping steadily. At 7 cents per KWH today, it still costs more than hydropower and about the same as coal-fired power, but is competitive with oil and cheaper than power from new nuclear plants, without the hazards of pollution and radiation. *The technology for a major expansion of wind power worldwide is already in place.* If the government were willing to encourage the acceleration of wind development, up to 32,200 MW of wind-generating equipment could be installed in the U.S. by 2000, industry consultant Robert Lynette has projected.[24] If that many wind turbines were installed, the cost of wind-powered electricity would drop to 4 cents per KWH and there would be a yearly reduction of 1.15 million tons of sulfur dioxide and 50.7 million tons of carbon-dioxide emissions, he said.

If other governments, international banks, and multinational industries made the investment in wind power, the world could receive as much as ten percent of its total energy from this source by the first decade of the next century and pay back its investors and the public handsomely in terms of cost savings and environmental protection.

Solar Technologies

The main types of solar technologies are:
- active solar systems (which use mechanical means – solar collectors, pumps and fans – to circulate heat);
- passive solar systems (which rely on design and construction methods to do the same);
- photovoltaics (a direct source of electricity generation); and
- solar-thermal technology (an indirect source of producing electricity).

Active and Passive Systems

Active and passive solar technologies are important because they displace fossil and nuclear fuels in heating and cooling space and water and in lighting buildings, which accounts for more than a third of total U.S. energy consumption. Because they have the potential of supplying up to 80 percent of new buildings' energy requirements, these technologies are critical to our clean energy future.

Active solar collectors contain air, water, or other liquids that absorb the sun's energy to heat space or water for domestic, commercial, and industrial purposes. Their main component is the collector panel – usually placed on the roof of a building, facing south (in the Northern Hemisphere) to get maximum sunlight – consisting of a flat plate and tubes painted black to absorb the most heat. Heated air or liquid is transferred from the tube by gravity or mechanical pump to a storage medium – rocks for air, tanks for liquid. The advantage of air is that it eliminates the risk of damage from freezing in cold climates.

The first commercial solar hot-water systems were introduced in Florida and California in the early 1900s. Today millions of low-cost residential and commercial water-heating solar collectors are in use worldwide – four million of them in Japan. On Cyprus more than 90 percent of homes have installed solar hot-water heaters, in Israel 70 percent. U.S. sales boomed until 1986, when low oil prices and the elimination of residential renewable-energy tax credits dropped the bottom out of the market.

Combined with effective insulation of the space to be heated, active collectors save 50 percent or more of the energy used for that purpose. They are also widely used for heating water for swimming pools, laundries, motels, car washes, and many other commercial and industrial applications. At present there are about a million domestic solar hot-water systems and 100,000 space-heating systems in the United States. Depending on the price of electricity, a well-installed active system should pay back its initial costs in 6 to 10 years.

Passive solar systems use age-old principles of orientation and design of a building to use the sun's energy for heating, cooling, and lighting. Design features include large areas of south-facing windows, building overhangs and awnings (to keep out unwanted heat in summer when the sun is at a high angle), thick stone or masonry walls and floors (to store daytime heat and release it at night), deciduous outdoor vegetation (blocks out summer sun), natural ventilation, heat circulation and lighting, and attached greenhouses or sun spaces. Passive solar systems can be incorporated into new and old buildings of all kinds, from outhouses to 70-story skyscrapers.[25] A well designed passive solar building can reduce energy bills by as much as 85 percent with an added construction cost of only 5 to 10 percent. In North America there are presently an estimated 250,000 fully passive solar homes and more than a million buildings that have some aspect of passive solar design. The payback time is from 3 to 7 years. The U.S. Department of Energy projects conservatively that passive solar power will save (by displacing other fuels) 2.3 quads of energy by 2005. With increased incentives from federal and state governments this could be doubled in the same period of time.

Pipelining Sunlight

You can store solar energy in the form of hydrogen (H_2) which can be burned pollution-free in H_2-powered vehicles, industrial boilers, and home furnaces. The electricity can be generated by photovoltaic cells or other renewable energy sources and then fed into an electrolyzer which breaks up molecules of water into H_2 and oxygen. You can use the H_2 on site or compress it into a liquid that can be sent via pipeline to locations where there is insufficient sunlight locally to produce H_2. The oxygen is a useful industrial by-product. (For more on H_2 see p. 214.)

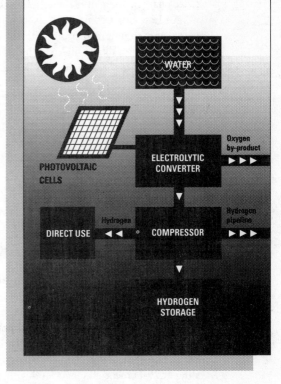

The Photovoltaic Revolution

Generating electricity directly from sunlight is a new technology based on solar – photovoltaic (PV) – cells, most of which are composed of silicon, the second most abundant element in the earth's crust (after oxygen).

When light falls on a PV cell, a transparent wafer thinner than the page you are reading, it releases a flow of electrons, creating an electrical current. The amount of electricity produced depends on the area and efficiency of the cell and the number of them contained in a module. Despite their seeming fragility, PV cells function for many decades with little maintenance. Photovoltaics have little environmental impact, producing neither acid rain nor greenhouse gases.

With PV costs projected to be competitive with other power options by the turn of the century, photovoltaics could displace much of conventional power as the primary source of electricity within a hundred years. If global warming concerns continue to dictate a rapid displacement of fossil fuels regardless of costs, this goal could be reached by 2040 or sooner.[26]

Solar Power to the People

Pocket calculators and watches powered by tiny, thin-film PV cells first appeared in the late 1970s. Since then, as the cost has fallen, the market has expanded into a diverse assortment of consumer products from key-ring lights to roof-top power modules.

One California mail-order house, Solar Electric, sells a wide range of these products including personal stereos, lantern lights, marine modules, an electric-fence charger, and complete home-electricity systems – all run by the sun.

An East Coast company, Chronar, which is a leader in the research, development, and commercial production of PV panels, markets many popular solar items such as walkway lights, windshield- or dashboard-mounted car battery chargers, and tiny flashlights can buy in hardware and discount stores.

Sources of PV Products

For catalogs and other information contact:

West Coast

Solar Electric Engineering, (800) 832-1986, in California (707) 586-1987.

East Coast

For SunEnergy brand products call *Chronar* at (800) 247-6627, or in New Jersey (609) 799-8800; Sunnyside Solar, at (802) 257-1482; or *Talmadge Engineering*, (207) 967-5945.

PV in the Home

As the installed price of photovoltaic modules has dropped from more than $20,000 a kilowatt in 1980 to one-eighth that amount in 1990, solar electricity has become more cost-effective and practical for residential use. A single solar cell measuring 1 inch by 1 inch has enough power to charge a single AA battery or operate a musical greeting-card chip. A 3- by 6-foot panel of PV cells (operating at 20-percent efficiency and with a peak output of 5 kilowatts at midday in the northeastern or northwestern United States) yields an average of more than 1 KW over the entire year, more than enough for the electrical power needs of the average house. For larger houses a correspondingly larger array of panels can be installed. At night or when power demands exceed the capacity of the solar cells, a backup source of electricity is needed either from the power company or from batteries. Costs begin at about $1,000 for a "basic cabin system" (for lighting, black-and-white TV, radio, fan, water pump, and other DC appliances) to $5,000 and up for larger units.

Seeing Is Believing

In 1984 Enersol, a Massachusetts-based nonprofit organization that specializes in developing the renewable solar-energy industry in Latin America and the Caribbean, initiated an ongoing PV project in the Dominican Republic, demonstrating that stand-alone units can be an economical alternative to expanding the electricity grid network. The initial funding was $20,000, with the Dominicans contributing locally available skills and materials. The first unit installed was a $400 system whose 35-watt solar module generated enough electricity for the lighting, radio, and television of one rural home and adjoining market.

The illumination of the market attracted the attention of other villagers, who became interested in getting their own systems. The installation of six more systems by mid-1985 generated even more local interest and stimulated the establishment of a *ferretería* (hardware store) as a source of PV components and service.

Faith in the principle of "seeing is believing" had an important impact on the project, which expanded to other sites in the Dominican Republic and now totals more than 600 installations, with new units going in at the rate of 40 a month. Based on a $500 cost of a typical 35-watt system plus $46 every two years for battery replacement (using locally made car batteries), the payback point is reached within 5 years. Users of the PV systems thus enjoy a reasonable financial return as well as benefitting from increased productivity, convenience, and light quality.[27]
(For further information contact: Richard D. Hansen, Enersol Associates, 1 Summer Street, Somerville, MA 02143; (617) 628-3550.)

As of 1990 there were over 30,000 PV-powered homes with many more being built. In the Laguna Del Mar community of San Diego, Calif., there are 112 solar-electric houses tied into the San Diego Gas and Electric Company line. No storage batteries are required because each house has two electric meters, one to measure electricity consumed (when the PV modules are not generating enough power), the other to record the amount *sold* to the utility (when the PV panels produce more than is needed).

The world's largest PV power plant at present is the 6.5-MW Carissa Plains, Calif. facility run by Arco Solar and Pacific Gas & Electric. Completed in 1985, the plant shows that even larger systems can be excellent sources of peaking* electrical energy with zero fuel costs and minimal environmental impact. In late 1988 agreement was reached between the Chronar Corporation and SeaWest Power Systems of San Diego jointly to develop a 50-MW PV power station to be completed in 1992.

Due to the abundant sunlight in the Southwest, central PV stations are expected to become cost-effective there first, but utilities in all regions of the United States including the Northeast are exploring photovoltaic options in anticipation of continuing reductions in building and running costs of central power plants and home-generating PV modules.

---

*Peak-load plants, which need to start-up fast, burn premium fuels like oil and gas. They cost less to build but more to run than base-load plants

PV's Expanding Market

Chronar, which sold 800,000 of its walkway lights in 1988, has introduced a number of larger products for area illumination and billboard lighting, including a high-efficiency PV-powered metal halide lamp. There is also a fast-growing market for "stand alone" PV equipment for use in areas not supplied by electricity from the utility network – communications, lighting, water pumping, and power for remote communities. The U.S. Coast Guard operates 20,000 PV systems to power lighthouses and various navigational aids. Thousands of similar systems are used by the National Park Service, the Departments of the Interior and Agriculture, and other government agencies, by gas and oil companies, and by a vast array of enterprises in the communications, transportation, and security fields.

PV or not PV

Photovoltaics is a technology whose time has come. Soon to be competitive in price with other forms of energy, it is a simple, nonpolluting source of energy made from readily available materials, fueled at no cost from the sun, and one that can be adapted to a wide variety of situations. The efficiency of the silicon cell is constantly being improved. In 1988 a breakthrough comparable to the four-minute mile was achieved. The U.S. Department of Energy's Sandia National Laboratories in Albuquerque, N.M., built a "mechanically stacked multijunction" PV cell that converts 31 percent of the light striking it into electricity. Until then scientists had considered 30-percent efficiency unattainable. Now it is believed that efficiencies of up to 35 percent or more can be reached with photovoltaics.

Given the potential of photovoltaics, one must ask why the U.S. government is not supporting its development more energetically. Incredibly, the Reagan administration sharply cut back support for PV along with wind and other forms of renewable energy in favor of nuclear and oil subsidies.

It may be significant that a large part of photovoltaics manufacturing in the U.S. has been owned by the oil industry – Mobil, Exxon, and Arco, in particular. One has only to look at Detroit's record in holding back energy-efficient technologies to get a sense of "here we go again." The loss works two ways: slowing development of a new technology that was originated in this country and handing over a lucrative market to Japanese and other competitors. As with automobiles and wind turbines, we shall soon be importing PV systems and components instead of exporting them to an energy-hungry world market.

Solar-Thermal Generation

Solar-thermal (ST) power transforms the radiant energy of the sun into thermal energy (heat) which can be converted to electricity or used for various industrial processes. The main type of ST unit operating commercially in the U.S. is the parabolic trough. In this system, tracking collectors concentrate sunlight onto a receiver tube that runs along its horizontal axis. Inside the tube a heat-transfer fluid (synthetic oil or water) absorbs and carries the thermal energy to a conventional water-to-steam boiler. The steam is then superheated with additional solar energy and used to drive an electric generator.

Solar-thermal Electricity

Luz International, a Los Angeles-based company, designed, built, and now operates seven solar-thermal systems, which together produce nearly 200 megawatts of electricity for Southern California Edison, enough for about 100,000 homes. In 1989 Luz began building the world's largest solar-electric plant – SEGS VIII

– the first of five 80-MW solar plants due for completion in 1994 that will serve the needs of some 200,000 homes. By 1996 Luz expects to have 1,000 MW of electric capacity on line.

Unlike conventional energy, Luz's solar electricity is going down in price. By 1994 Luz expects the electricity coming from their new plants in the Mojave Desert to cost roughly 5 cents per KWH (in 1989 dollars). This is less than the cost of electricity from fossil-fuel plants equipped with air-pollution controls or from new nuclear reactors.

As their tax benefits and fixed-price power contracts with SCE run out, Luz will sell stock to the public. "As of then," says James C. Bazor, the company's chief operating officer, "we expect our system to compete with conventional electricity on pure economics, without any tax breaks." ST power is dependent on large amounts of sun – in the American Southwest, Spain, Brazil, the Middle East, and India, where Luz is discussing future projects. In such places Luz hopes to supply solar-energy systems and hardware, rather than operate power plants. "There is reason for power companies not to own and operate solar equipment the way they do any other power source, says Bazor. "If you can have environmentally benign power on economic terms, why would you go to a nuclear plant or anything else?" [29]

> *"There is something like alchemy in modern solar technology."*
> William E. Rogers, chairman, Power Kinetics, Inc.[28]

Solar + Coal

Even where it is abundant, the sun is an intermittent and diffuse source of energy. In the Luz projects, for example, substantial amounts of natural gas must be used to run a backup system to provide the utility with steady "capacity" when the sun is not shining.

A different approach to the problem is advanced by another solar-thermal company, Power Kinetics, Inc. (PKI), headquartered in Troy, N.Y. PKI manufactures the world's largest point-focusing solar collectors, which generate and deliver steam at very high temperatures. One PKI system uses 18 collectors to power a Saudi Arabian desalinization plant.

Instead of building an expensive thermal-storage system, the company advocates a concept, originated at Lawrence Livermore Laboratory in California, to use sun and coal (in a nonpolluting way) to provide a steady flow of energy and to deliver it to consumers via conventional pipelines.

Using concentrated solar energy to *gasify** coal is the cleanest and most efficient way to convert plentiful coal resources into combustible gas (or syngas).[30] The syngas can be used in many industrial applications to replace limited reserves of natural gas. It can also be converted either into methane and distributed nationwide through natural gas pipelines or into gasoline for transportation.

PKI believes that up to 70 percent of the energy available to a collector in the Southwest can be captured by this process and transported to regions where sun and land (for the collectors) are more limited. According to PKI's chairman, William Rogers, the technology of a solar reactor in a closed system which his company is preparing to develop extends the supply of coal by almost twice and halves the amount of CO_2 exhausted to the atmosphere. Despite the demonstrat-

---

*Coal gasification is a process that uses steam to convert coal to gas.

ed performance of PKI's and other solar-thermal systems, the U.S. Department of Energy remains indifferent. As Rogers points out, *"Their solar thermal budget for the whole of 1989 is equivalent to the amount of oil the U.S. consumes in three hours."* [31]

Going Underground – Geothermal Power

Geothermal energy is heat contained beneath the earth's crust. When it is brought up to the surface in the form of steam or hot water, it can be used directly for water and space heating or to drive an electricity generator. Unaffected by seasonal or daily variations, it emits little CO_2 compared with fossil fuels. Although not strictly renewable, geothermal is included with renewable energies because its sources are virtually unlimited.

The geothermal resource in the upper three miles of the earth's crust is estimated to be greater than all the world's natural gas and crude-oil liquid reserves. Much of it is located in accessible concentrations along North America's western edge and in Hawaii, the Caribbean, East Africa, Central Asia, New Zealand, and other parts of the eastern Pacific.

At present only a tiny fraction of this underground energy is recovered, about half of it in the United States. Worldwide it amounts to 6,000 megawatts of electric capacity and another 12,000 MW of hot water or steam which is tapped for heating.

Geothermal Resources

There are five main types of geothermal reservoir:
- *dry (superheated) steam;*
- *mixed hot water, wet steam, and brine;*
- *hot dry rocks,* where cold water is pumped through one well into intentionally fractured layers of deep hot rocks, converted to steam, then brought to the surface by another well close by;
- *pressurized water fields* containing hot water and natural gas, found deep beneath ocean beds;
- *magma,* molten rock usually found 5 to 30 miles below the earth's crust, but also in or near volcanoes. The first two categories, usually referred to as hydrothermal, are the most accessible for immediate development.

Natural dry-steam wells can be tapped easily and economically with little environmental impact by drilling and piping the superheated, pressurized steam into a nearby turbine. One large system in Italy has been generating electricity since 1904 and is a major source of power for that country's railroads. Other important dry-steam sites are at Matsukawa in Japan, Wairakei in New Zealand, and the Geysers steam field, 90 miles north of San Francisco.

On line since 1960, the Geysers, now with a capacity of more than 2,000 MW, is the largest dry-steam development in the world, generating electricity more cheaply than fossil fuel or nuclear plants. A typical dry-steam plant can be built in about three years, compared with at least three times that for fossil-fuel or nuclear-power plants.

In 1979 the first large *binary* geothermal plant began operating in California's Imperial Valley. This is a closed-loop process which pumps hot fluid out of the reservoir, passes it through heat exchangers (where a second working fluid is evaporated), and then returns the cooled fluid to the reservoir.

The binary system has the ability to use relatively low-temperature fluids, thereby increasing the number of sites that can be used for electric-power generation.

Gas injection is a relatively new process being successfully used to minimize environmental impact at the California Energy Company geothermal plants at Coso, Calif., which increased their capacity from 27 MW in 1987 to more than 200 in 1989.

Geothermal Power and the Greenhouse Effect

In terms of greenhouse gas emissions, geothermal energy has a distinct advantage over fossil fuels. For example, CO_2 emissions from geothermal power plants at the Geysers average less than 4 percent of the emissions from burning gas and coal. Plants using gas-injection technologies have even lower emission rates — less than 0.1 percent of CO_2 emissions from coal and just over 1 percent of the SO_2 emissions from coal and oil.[32]

Removal of CO_2 and other greenhouse gases from fossil-fuel power plant emissions is technologically feasible, but economically prohibitive, whereas geothermal's low production cost and extremely low greenhouse-gas emission make it an attractive source of power in many parts of the world.

Hot-water and Brine Systems

In 1982 a 10-MW prototype plant at Salton Sea in the Imperial Valley began successfully generating electricity from hypersaline brines, demonstrating the feasibility of exploiting a vast geothermal resource estimated at 3,000 MW – equivalent to three large nuclear plants.[33]

Hot-water and brine geothermal wells, more common than dry steam sites, are generating electricity in the U.S.S.R., Mexico, Japan, New Zealand, the Philippines (where geothermal energy accounts for 20 percent of all electricity generation), and Iceland, whose capital is totally heated by underground steam or hot water, as are hundreds of homes in Boise, Idaho, and Klamath Falls, Ore.

Vast Untapped Potential

According to the Electric Power Research Institute, North American capacity could reach 20,000 MW within a decade, perhaps more with the use of new extraction techniques such as the binary cycle system demonstrated in Southern California's Imperial Valley. That region alone has sufficient underground hot-water resources to meet the electricity needs of the entire American Southwest. Newer technologies being developed to capture energy from hot dry rocks and magma are expected to be ready for commercial exploitation by 2000.

There are extensive wet geothermal deposits on the Eastern seaboard, particularly between Florida and New Jersey. Although not hot enough for electricity generation, they could be tapped for space heating and other relatively low-temperature uses. Along the Gulf of Mexico coasts of Texas and Louisiana are substantial underground reserves of pressurized brine capable of supplying both heat and mechanical energy.

Although the potential of geothermal energy development in the United States is virtually untapped, it could be an important adjunct to other forms of renewable energy when a concerted effort is made to move away from fossil fuels and nuclear power.

Biomass

Biomass is a catchall term for anything that grows by photosynthesis. It is a versatile and renewable energy source capable of producing solid, liquid, and gaseous fuels, and electricity. Its main sources include wood and crops (and especially the wastes from them), animal wastes, and organic materials found in garbage. Although less than 1 percent of available biomass is used for energy, it represents 15 percent of energy consumed worldwide and 8 percent of that used in industry in the U.S.[34] Maine is the leading state in percentage of electricity generated by wood – 640 MW, accounting for 23 percent of its electric capacity.

> *... replacing all gasoline with gasohol would reduce United States consumption of gasoline by 10 percent and cut imports by 20 percent.*

Because wood wastes now comprise about a quarter of the volume of our landfills, the resource potential is enormous.

Direct Combustion

Wood and wood wastes are the most common forms of biomass, supplying energy for half the world's population, notably India, China, Brazil, and the New England states. If properly managed, natural forests do not have to be depleted in order to provide fuel wood. However, in India and sub-Saharan Africa, where wood accounts for 80 percent of total energy, the widespread burning of wood for cooking and heating is causing not only deforestation and soil erosion but also dangerous levels of indoor and outdoor air pollution. In the U.S., increasing use of wood stoves that adhere to new emission standards is providing more efficiency and less pollution.

In many industrial countries wood-fired boilers are now economically attractive, especially in cogeneration systems that produce both heat and electricity. These are widely used in the pulp-and-paper and lumber industries of Scandinavia, the Soviet Union, and North America.

Four U.S. utilities have built wood-burning power plants, each with more than 50-MW capacity. Many large industrial energy users, including Proctor & Gamble and Dow Corning, take advantage of regional wood supplies to sell surplus electricity to local utilities.[35]

In Hawaii and other tropical regions cane-sugar residues, rice husks, cotton stalks, coconut shells, and hulls of coffee and other seeds hulls are burned instead of wood. On the island of Kauai 60 percent of electricity is generated by cane-sugar combustion. In the Indian state of Punjab a 10.5-MW plant is planned to burn 20 tons of rice husks an hour. Because India produces almost 20 million tons of husks a year, it has the potential of generating 500 MW of electricity at considerably less cost than fossil-fuel or nuclear power.[36]

Nine hundred tons of cow manure from a local feedlot are burned daily as fuel for an electric-power plant in Imperial Valley, Calif., 110 miles east of San Diego. The 17.5-MW plant went on line in October 1988 and generates enough power for 20,000 homes in the Southern California Edison network, saving 300,000 barrels of oil that otherwise would be burned. It also extends the life of existing landfills. Previously feedlot owners paid to have the manure carted away and dumped. Now they sell it at $1 a ton to the plant which, in addition to selling electricity profitably at 7 cents per KWH, sells 150 tons a day of its residual ash for use as a fertilizer and a paving material.[37]

Biofuels

Biomass can be converted into biofuels such as biogas or methane, methanol, or ethanol, and into raw-material chemical replacements for petrochemicals. The processes to do this have long been known, but were generally too costly compared with fossil fuels. However, as the latter become more expensive economically and environmentally, the interest in biofuels is growing.

Excepting wood, all biomass can be easily converted into biogas, a mixture of methane and CO_2, using a "biogas digester."

Biogas Digesters in China and India

Consisting essentially of a clay or concrete tank dug partially into the ground, the digester can be fueled with varying combinations of organic material, to which water and solar heat are added for fermentation. Costing around $50 including labor, these simple devices produce methane gas for cooking and lighting as well as a slurry which, when mixed with water, serves as a nutrient-rich fertilizer. Another benefit of biogas is its cleanliness compared with fuels such as wood or cow dung, which in many regions are burnt in open fires, causing severe indoor and outdoor air pollution.

Biogas can be used in larger installations, as has been shown in numerous applications in Asia, Europe, and the United States, including the 100,000-gallon plant at the State Prison Honor Farm in Monroe, Wash., and the *Omega-Alpha Recycling Systems* prototype in central West Virginia developed by Robert A. Hamburg.[38]

Alcohol Conversion

Another promising source of biofuels is the conversion of biomass to alcohols. Virtually any kind of biomass that contains starch and cellulose – from cornstalks to cow dung – can be converted by fermentation and distillation into ethanol or grain alcohol. Wood-product waste, coal, and natural gas can be converted into methanol or wood alcohol, a premium fuel long used to power racing cars.

Methanol is considered unsuitable as an alternative to gasoline because mostly it is derived from fossil-based fuels. As it burns, methanol produces highly toxic formaldehyde; it also tends to eat through fuel tanks and other auto parts unless they are made of stainless steel.

Because it is made from plants, ethanol is significantly less polluting than methanol, as well as being more efficient. For the past ten years Brazil has been embarked on a major program of converting half its automobile fuel into gasohol, a blend of gasoline and ethanol made in that country from surplus sugar cane and cassava. Proponents of gasohol state that replacing all gasoline with gasohol would reduce U.S. consumption of gasoline by 10 percent and cut imports by 20 percent. Although ethanol is presently somewhat more expensive to produce than gasoline, it offers the advantage of being produced exclusively from domestic sources. It can be adapted to existing automobiles by a simple modification of their carburetors.

In 1988 the U.S. Alternative Fuels Act gave auto manufacturers incentives to produce cars that burn methanol, ethanol, or natural gas through credits toward their corporate average fuel-economy ratings for the gasoline and diesel fuel that their alternative fuel vehicles save. The credits, which become available in 1993, may result in the manufacture of 100,000 alternative-fuel cars and trucks by that date.

Biofuels also offer an important way to control air pollution. Colorado is the first state to require motorists in Denver and other large cities to use gasohol during the winter, when pollution is at its worst (largely because of the high use of wood-burning stoves). Carbon monoxide emissions are reported to have dropped by 15 to 20 percent.

Biomass and the Greenhouse Effect

Biomass is low in sulfur and generally emits much less carbon dioxide than fossil fuels. The production of biomass as a fuel source creates a carbon cycle, which can increase, decrease, or balance the amount of CO_2 in the atmosphere. As long as trees and plants are not cut faster than they grow back, burning biomass and biofuels does not add to the net amount of CO_2 in the atmosphere.

If properly managed, forests and farming systems can absorb more CO_2 than they emit, thus ameliorating the greenhouse effect. This is particularly true when biomass is used to replace fossil fuels. But when used *in addition to* fossil fuels, atmospheric warming takes place, although to a much lesser degree than if additional fossil fuels are burned.

Organic Farming

Fourteen percent of U.S. energy, most of it fossil fuel, is consumed by agriculture – food growing, processing, and distribution. One-third of the total comes from fertilizers (100 *billion* tons a year) and pesticides (1 *billion* tons), both of which are made from oil and gas. Another third goes into driving the machinery of factory farming – giant irrigation systems, soil cultivators, harvest combines, tractors, trucks, and other vehicles – and the remainder goes into warehousing, processing, and distribution.

The Losing of America

We are eating up more land than food. By 2000 California – yes, California – is projected to become a net *importer* of food. In order to maintain high crop yields and profit margins, agribusiness puts so many chemicals into the soil that they have made it more vulnerable to wind and water erosion than in the 1930s.

Toward a Sustainable Agriculture

The American food system has become a gigantic mining operation that is destroying our health, the economy, and the environment. The answer, prac-

24,000 Tons of Broccoli[39]

Along with widespread environmental pollution created by agribusiness farming is enormous energy wastage caused by its long-distance structure. Instead of growing as much food as possible close to where people live and recycling nutrient-rich wastes back to the soil, we ship in manufactured nitrogen fertilizer from sources thousands of miles away when it can be taken naturally and effortlessly from the air above the farm, if simple crops like peas and beans are grown in the rotation with the desired crop. For example, it takes a million gallons of gas a year to truck 24,000 tons of broccoli 2,700 miles from sunny California to New York City in the cooler East Coast, where the vegetable grows as well, if not better. (It flourishes, without chemicals but with tender loving care, in my own New York State backyard!)

There are dozens of other vegetables and fruits that could and should be grown closer to the people who consume them and raised without unnecessary fertilizers and chemicals – organically.

ticed by increasing numbers of farmers, is an agriculture more respectful of nature – organic farming. It is a time-tested system that involves rotating crops to keep the soil friable and fix the nitrogen content, composting (recycling agricultural wastes as a natural fertilizer), mulching (using leaves and other organic wastes to control weeds and nurture crops without excessive watering), using nonchemical forms of pest management, companion planting (mixing different species of flowers, herbs, and vegetables that enhance each other and keep away harmful insects), and polyculture (growing a wide variety of crops).

More Taste, Less Energy

Unlike the produce of factory farming, which contains chemicals from pesticides and fertilizers, organic grains, fruits, and vegetables are chemical-free, better tasting and more nutritive, partly because natural fertilizers do not increase the water content as much as chemicals.

> *"We are mining the soil of its fertility, and are draining oil and gas fields of their wealth to get the energy to do that . . . We can't afford to let our food system just 'run out' some day."*
>
> *Robert Rodale* [40]

In May 1989 the *Wall Street Journal* published a front-page story reporting that a new movement to farm without chemicals was making "surprising gains." Thousands of farmers, it said, concerned about the environment, rising chemical costs, and soil erosion, are now embracing methods once seen as the province of radical "organic farmers." Sustainable agriculture, as the *Journal* prefers to call it, is gaining momentum among farmers in Illinois, Indiana, Minnesota, Nebraska, and other states who want to reduce use of chemicals in part because of intense pressure from consumer groups.

In September 1989 a return to natural farming was endorsed by the prestigious National Academy of Sciences in a major study finding that farmers who apply little or no chemicals to crops can be as productive as those who use pesticides and synthetic fertilizers.[41]

Although generally associated with small holdings, organic farming can be done on a larger basis. In response to growing demand for their products, many of the 35,000 organic farms in the U.S. are expanding their acreage to 1,500 and more, reaping the benefits of high productivity and economies of scale. On average they require about half as much energy per unit of output as chemical farms and sustain their crop yields much longer because they don't destroy the soil. In fact, they improve it, adding to the value of the land.

The growing interest in the organic approach is reflected in a new U.S. Department of Agriculture educational program called LISA – low-input sustainable agriculture. But with a budget of only $4.5 million in 1989, the project is likely to have only limited effect. More impressive are the track records of the Rodale Research Center in Emmaus, Pa., the Land Institute in Salina, Kans., seven generations of Amish and Mennonites, and the 35 million other organic farmers and gardeners practicing sustainable agriculture in one form or another.

Nuclear Power – Myths and Realities

Although nuclear energy is not renewable – it is fueled by uranium and plutonium, both finite elements – we include it in this chapter because, despite very serious safety and economic disadvantages, it is still put forward by some advocates as an alternative to fossil fuels.

Anxieties about global warming and high-powered lobbying are reviving the hopes of the nuclear industry for a powerful comeback. Let us compare the claims of post-Chernobyl nuclear advocates with the reality.

Claim 1: "Nuclear energy . . . must be revitalized in order to alleviate the greenhouse effect," because, unlike fossil fuels, it doesn't release greenhouse gases into the air..[42]

Reality: Nuclear power adds heat to the earth's atmosphere by liberating energy which otherwise remains in unfissioned uranium and plutonium. It makes a net addition to the greenhouse effect from carbon and sulfur dioxides, because large amounts of fossil fuels are mined and burned to refine uranium, to build nuclear-power plants, to run their backup generators, to clean up radioactive wastes, and, as reactors get older, to decommission them.

Claim 2: The more we use nuclear energy, the less we are dependent on oil, which both pollutes and increasingly "strengthens our ties to the Middle East." [43]

Reality: Although the U.S. has decreased its imports of oil from the Middle East, it has sharply increased its imports from Venezuela, Mexico and Canada. Improving auto mileage and conserving petrochemicals would more dramatically reduce U.S. dependence on imported *and* domestic oil.

Claim 3: Nuclear-generated electricity is "still the fastest growing major energy source in America." [44]

Reality: The "growth" of the U.S. nuclear industry is nonexistent. The last time a nuclear plant was ordered and not subsequently canceled was 1973. In fact, U.S. nuclear capacity will peak in 1992 and slowly decline as aging plants are decommissioned. World nuclear-plant construction has fallen 45 percent since its peak in 1980 and is likely to be much lower by the year 2000, when its share of world electricity will most certainly be less than it was in 1987.[45]

Claim 4: Nuclear power is safe.

Reality: As we saw in chapter 8, there have been over 30,000 mishaps and several near misses at U.S. nuclear utilities since the partial meltdown at Three Mile Island in 1979. The U.S. Nuclear Regulatory Commission estimates that the chances of a Chernobyl-like core-melt accident at a U.S. reactor over the next 20 years may be as high as 45 percent.[46]

Then there is the problem of nuclear waste. The 120 civilian and military nuclear plants in the U.S. produce thousands of tons of long-lived, highly radioactive and toxic waste for which there is no known safe means of permanent disposal or storage.

Also, one-third of the reactors will have to be decommissioned in the next decade. This is an extremely hazardous process that could cost as much as the initial construction.

Claim 5: Nuclear power is reliable.

Reality: U.S. reactors were intended to run at 80 percent of their rated capacity, but they have a long and troublesome history of shutdowns and outages due in large part to extremely poor management.[47] Over the past 15 years they have averaged only 60 percent of capacity. As plants age, capacity factors are likely to drop further.

Claim 6: Nuclear power is cheap, with production costs averaging 2.08 cents per KWH.[48]

Reality: In 1987 the average cost of a new reactor was $3,000 per kilowatt or $3 billion for a 1,000-MW plant. Recent plants including Shoreham, N.Y., Seabrook, N.H., and Comanche Peak, Tex., have cost *double* that amount. To build nuclear reactors costs 15 times as much as energy conservation, five times as much as oil, twice as much as wind power or photovoltaics. (For comparative costs, see p. 191.)

> *The French pay two electric bills, one directly to the power company, the other indirectly for heavy state subsidies of the nuclear program.*

The 2.08-cents "production" figure counts only costs of operation, maintenance, and fuel. It leaves out all construction costs along with repairs, waste disposal, and decommissioning. The last item alone is likely to be over $1 billion per reactor, which, if not funded now by the nuclear industry, will have to be paid later by your rates and taxes.[49] There are also hidden subsidies to the nuclear industry – $9 billion "forgotten" debts to the U.S. Treasury for uranium enrichment and the Price-Anderson Act, which limits the nuclear industry's public liability in the event of an accident. When these expenses are included, the true cost of generating electricity at a new nuclear plant is shown to be between 15 and 20 cents per KWH.[50]

Claim 7: France's nuclear program is generating some of the cheapest electricity in Europe and should be a model for us to follow.

Reality: Although 75 percent of French electricity is nuclear-produced, its price is higher than that in Denmark (which has no nuclear energy) and the Netherlands, which has reduced its nuclear programs. Even more than in the U.S., the price of French nuclear energy does not reflect the cost of producing it. In effect, the French pay two electric bills, one directly to the power company, the other indirectly for heavy state subsidies of the nuclear program. The real cost of generating the French nuclear electricity is believed to be three times the amount claimed by Electricité de France. Moreover, despite her costly nuclear program, France has reduced her dependence on fossil fuels to a *lesser* degree than her European partners.[51]

Claim 8: A "new breed" of reactors – high-temperature, gas-cooled reactors, liquid-metal reactors, "process-inherent, ultimate-safety" reactors, and small-scale units using such small quantites of nuclear fuel that their cores could not achieve meltdown "under any circumstances"[52] – can be designed to correct the cost, safety and environmental problems plaguing the current nuclear generation.

Reality: To date not a single second-generation demonstration reactor has been built, leaving unanswered critical problems of safety and cost that might require two or more decades to resolve. As to long-term environmental hazards, virtually all scientists, physicians, and health experts now agree that no amount of nuclear radiation is safe, either during the life of the reactor or as long-lived waste with no place to go.

Hydrogen – the Almost Perfect Fuel

Hydrogen gas (H_2) is one of the most abundant chemical elements in the world. It can be made out of water and electricity, has the highest energy content of any fuel, and produces only water when burned, emitting virtually no pollutants, not even carbon dioxide. You can burn it much like natural gas for industrial and space heating and to produce steam for electric turbines. It can be shipped in a pipeline for one-third the cost of high-voltage electricity or converted into liquid fuel to replace gasoline (see diagram on p. 201).

H_2 sounds like the perfect fuel, with many advantages over fossil and nuclear fuels; yet at present it is used only to power the space shuttle, but not commercially. The drawbacks of hydrogen are that it is not found "alone" in nature; moreover, it is hard to contain because its molecule is smaller and lighter than natural gas molecules, and it is explosive.

Ways to use and store this potentially perfect fuel are being investigated at several locations, including the Florida Solar Energy Research Center at Cape Canaveral, the Hawaii Natural Energy Institute, Princeton, and Syracuse universities.

Because of the many advantages of hydrogen, its proponents advocate a rapid transition to a worldwide H_2 economy. Other energy experts believe that the improvement of storage technology will take decades. In 1989 DOE funding for hydrogen research was a mere $3 million compared with $350 million for nuclear fusion.[53] According to a study by physicists at Princeton University, recent advances in cells that convert the sun's energy to electricity are increasing the chances of using hydrogen as a practical, low-polluting fuel for motor vehicles. *The declining cost of solar electricity will soon allow hydrogen to be made in the deserts of the Southwest, for example, and then transmitted (via pipeline) to other parts of the country for use as a fuel for automobiles and other purposes.* The anticipated price would be about $2 a gallon – higher than gasoline made from oil but less than other alternative fuels, especially when the environmental benefits of the low pollution are considered.[54]

Fusion Confusion

Since the 1950s scientists have been working on multibillion-dollar projects to find a way to produce a useable net surplus of energy from the fusion process used in thermonuclear bombs and by the sun. In theory, the deuterium (a heavy isotope) contained in one cubic yard of sea water – if fused – releases the energy equivalent of burning 2,000 barrels of crude oil. The U.S. Department of Energy spends four times as much in the effort to control fusion as on its entire renewable energy program. But, as the 1989 turmoil in research laboratories over "cold" fusion* indicated, the solution remains extremely elusive.

A Solution to a Problem We Don't Have

Even if the goal of achieving fusion is reached in the laboratory, the problems of building a viable, economic, and safe fusion reactor are virtually insuperable.

---

*Fusion achieved at room temperature rather than at 150 million degrees Celsius, as in the thermonuclear bomb.

First, fusion is a form of nuclear energy with potentially great risks of radiation and explosion. The energy released in the fusion process would be in the form of neutrons moving 20 times faster than those released in nuclear fission. Second, the power density of a large fusion reactor would probably be a mere one-tenth that of a fission reactor. This would require even larger (and more expensive) power plants than we now have. Third, this would produce what energy expert Amory Lovins calls the biggest turkey on the farm – giant, centralized power plants that make very expensive electricity. Nuclear fusion, Lovins suggests, should remain where we already have it – 93 million miles away, on the sun.[55]

Where Do We Go from Here?

Neither nuclear fission nor fusion are viable means to replace fossil fuels. Hydrogen has promise but is not yet ready for commercial development, which could be more than ten years away – too long to hold up more immediately available options.

For a number of reasons the answer cannot come from a single "fix" that will magically supply us with unlimited amounts of cheap, safe, clean energy (history should teach us that, if nothing else). Technologically, such a source does not exist. And, even if it did, it would be a dangerously one-sided response to a complex problem.

The way to stop energy-caused pollution is to use the energy we already have more wisely and to develop those sources of energy which do least harm to the earth's life-support systems and which are appropriate to the particular regions where they are found, produced, and consumed.

Defining Our Options

By far, the best sources of "new" energy are conservation and efficiency. Simply by not wasting what we have and using it more efficiently we can: (1) *totally eliminate* the need for nuclear fission or fusion and (2) *reduce by 40 percent or more* the amount of fossil fuels we presently burn.

> *"The fault, dear Brutus, is not in our stars, but in ourselves."*
> *Julius Caesar*

The problem with energy conservation and efficiency is not that they don't work but that they don't fire the imagination. Even such a brilliant concept as negawatts has less sex appeal to the media than fusion or the far-fetched idea of beaming down energy from huge solar panels orbiting in space. Part of the difficulty is America's fascination with bigness. *The bigger a project, be it a dam or the ill-fated synthetic-fuel plan to turn coal and oil shale into substitutes for foreign oil, the more likely it is to get the attention of the media and the support of government.*

The crucial role that renewable energy can play similarly has been systematically overlooked. Yet despite this lack of attention and support, despite receiving a mere fraction of the subsidies given to nuclear power, for example, electric capacity from renewable sources has already overtaken that of nuclear power and will almost certainly double by 2000, when it will supply some 20 percent of our projected electricity needs. With better public understanding and government support, this percentage could be much higher. The next move is up to us.

Renewable Energy and National Security

Another reason renewable energies are ignored is that they are not widely used by the military and space establishments. Although photovoltaics are used to power satellites in orbit, they appeal less to governmental decision makers than nuclear fission and fusion whose by-products are used in nuclear weapons' manufacture. As the American Wind Energy Association knows, it is not easy to persuade members of the powerful congressional armed services committees that windmills can play an important role in our defense posture. In point of fact, by *decentralizing* our sources of energy with readily available, small-scale renewable systems we render ourselves less vulnerable to attack from terrorists and military enemies, at much lower cost than our presently grossly inflated arms budget.

Another advantage of renewables is their ability to integrate one or more energy forms together: cogenerating electricity as a byproduct of biomass; producing hydropower from stored water that has been pumped by a windmill; using a solar greenhouse for growing food and heating space; burning wood wastes for steel production, which converts the wood into useful and nonpolluting gas or liquid fuels; hybrid photovoltaic/wind systems that generate energy both when the sun is shining and when it isn't; the combination of photovoltaics and passive solar energy to heat, cool, and light our buildings. The examples could go on indefinitely.

It makes more sense for the U.S. to invest now in the known advantages of energy conservation and efficiency and in those renewable-energy technologies that are significantly cleaner than fossil fuels and increasingly competitive in price with them. Photovoltaics, solar-thermal power, small-scale hydro, geothermal- and wind-energy, biomass, and active and passive solar technologies are all viable options that can mitigate the greenhouse effect *and* provide us with 80 percent of the national demand for energy in 2010, including transportation fuels. Renewables can achieve this goal provided they are backed by aggressive public demand and support by government and industry. Public opinion polls show that most Americans favor energy conservation and solar energy over all other options. The task now is to get government and industry to carry out the mandate. Meanwhile there's a lot you can do to help speed the process.

75 Ways You Can Save Energy – and the Earth

The U.S. uses more energy than Canada, Japan, the United Kingdom, France, Italy, the Netherlands, and West Germany *combined*. This is a startling fact, especially when you consider that as much as half of the energy we use is wasted – that is, it could be saved.

Saving energy is a prime way of cutting down on pollution; it also can save us a good deal of money personally, as well as making the nation more productive in the world market. One major contributor to this waste is energy use in the home, accounting for one-sixth of global energy output. According to the U.S. Department of Energy, the average American home guzzles the energy equivalent of 1,253 gallons of oil a year. Half of this comes from space and water heating, while the rest comes mainly from refrigerators, air conditioners, lighting, and kitchen stoves.

The following are 75 steps you can take to save energy and cut down on pollution.

1. *Check your utility bills.* If they seem high:

2. *Get home energy-conservation information.* There are many publicly and privately published pamphlets and books showing how to save on your utility bills, including some good ones put out by utility companies. Contact DOE's Office of Public Affairs for a free copy of their *Tips for Energy Savers.* (see also "Resources" at the end of the chapter).

3. *Get an energy audit or home-improvement survey.* Many utility companies do this for free or charge a nominal fee; otherwise find an energy consultant through your local yellow pages.

4. *Buy energy-efficient appliances.* Compare Energy Guide Labels on refrigerators, air conditioners, dishwashers, washing machines, and dryers. Buy *Saving Energy and Money with Home Appliances* and *The Most Energy Efficient Appliances* ($2 each) from the American Council for an Energy Efficient Economy, 1001 Connecticut Avenue NW, Washington, DC 20036. Find out if your utility gives a rebate for energy-efficient devices.

5. *RECYCLE.* This is one of the most important things you can do. For details see chapter 1, pp. 26-28.

Keeping Warm

6. *Cut heat loss* from windows and doors. Put storm windows on the outside, weatherstrip and caulk anywhere you can feel cold air coming in. In a new or remodeled building install new "superwindows" that have heat-reflective film applied to or suspended between panes; they insulate 4 to 5 times better than double-glazed windows. Curtains and shades placed one inch from the glass can cut heat loss by one third. Storm doors at about $100 each cut loss by half.

7. *Increase your insulation.* Poor insulation is a major cause of energy waste in most American homes. Going from R-11 to R-30 insulation will save up to 25 percent on your energy use and heating bill. Don't forget the basement, cellar, or crawlspace.

8. *Check walls, floors, and electric outlets* for cracks and openings. Caulk and seal up tight. This can save you 10 percent or more on energy costs.

9. *Cover air conditioners* in winter to stop energy loss.

10. *Close off unused space in your home.* This reduces the load on your heating/cooling systems. Turn off heaters/coolers and block vents in the closed area.

11. *Remove radiator covers during heating season.* They interfere with heating efficiency.

12. *Radiator reflectors* make any radiator more efficient. They are heat-reflecting panels made from insulating material with one face covered by metal foil. They cost about $5, or you can make one by cutting an insulation board and taping aluminum foil to the side facing into the room.

13. *Keep fireplace dampers closed in winter*, unless you have a fire burning (watch that pollution, when you do).

14. *Care and maintenance of heating systems.* See chapter 4, pp. 88-89.

15. *Wear warmer clothing in cooler temperatures.* Jimmy Carter had some good ideas!

16. *Turn down the thermostat.*

17. *Keep windows or doors near your thermostat tightly closed.* Otherwise your furnace will be working overtime.

18. *Insulate your attic* for protection against cold in winter and heat in summer.

Keeping Cool

19. *Wear loose, lightweight clothing.*

20. *Open attic vents* to allow the attic to "breathe." They get rid of moisture and let hot daytime air escape, especially if aided by an attic fan.

21. *Fans use one-tenth the electricity needed by air conditioners.* Whenever there's an outdoor breeze, use your window fan instead of the air conditioner. You can also use your air conditioner's "outside-air" control to bring in fresh air without using the energy-draining cooling section.

22. *Don't open windows when the outdoor temperature is uncomfortably warmer than inside.*

23. *Pull down blinds and draw curtains* when you are away or don't need light from the windows.

24. *When a breeze is blowing, open windows at the bottom on one side of your house or apartment and at the top on the other side.* This sets up cooling crosscurrents of air.

25. *Install ceiling fans* to keep cool in summer and circulate heat in winter.

26. *Set your air-conditioner control so the room temperature is no lower than 78 degrees F.* According to Consolidated Edison of New York, a 75-degree setting costs 18 percent more, a 72-degree setting costs 39 percent more. Because most units don't have degree markings, refer to a thermometer in a part of the room away from the unit's airflow.

27. *Clean air-conditioner filter and coils regularly.* This will make it run more efficiently.

28. *Buy an outdoor thermometer for about $5.* It will help you take advantage of natural cooling.

29. *Plant shade trees next to your home.* They will cut down on summer sun and reduce your air-conditioning costs. They also absorb CO_2 10 to 20 times more effectively than grass or crops.

Lighting

Lighting accounts for one-quarter of U.S. electricity use. Saving lighting at home and work is crucial to cutting down on the emission of greenhouse gases and other forms of pollution.

30. *Switch off lights in any space you are not using.* This simple step can save 10 to 20 percent of electricity use. In many parts of the world they have push-button lights in public areas of the house or apartment that automatically shut off after 3 to 4 minutes, an idea whose implementation is long overdue in this country. Vacant rooms should be kept dark.

31. *Use daylight.* Plan tasks requiring good lighting for the daytime. Place your reading chair near a window.

32. *Locate lamps in places where they can light up specific areas* such as desks, tables, or bedside rather than lighting up the whole room to see what you are doing.

33. *Substitute broad-spectrum, compact fluorescent lamps for incandescents wherever possible.* See box below.

Light Work

A single 18-watt compact fluorescent light bulb produces the same light as a 75-watt incandescent and lasts 13 times as long. Over its lifetime it will save:

- the cost of buying a dozen ordinary bulbs ($20);
- the cost of generating 570 kilowatt-hours of electricity (about $20 worth of fuel);
- approximately $200 to $300 worth of generating capacity at the power station.[56]

34. *Reduce overall lighting.* Replace existing bulbs with lower-wattage lights (especially in areas where no closeup lighting is needed) and take out one bulb from multibulb fixtures.

35. *Keep all lamps clean.* Dust and dirt absorb light, requiring extra wattage you don't need.

36. *Use outdoor lamps only when needed.* Switch them off during daytime.

37. *Solid-state dimmers* use little power and allow you to reduce electricity when you need it only for general or background illumination.

38. *Timers* can turn lamps and appliances on and off when you need them, saving unnecessary electricity. Spring-wound timers are useful for radiant heat bulbs in bathrooms, and for hall and stairway lights.

Kitchen

39. *Reduce your use of hot water, whenever possible:* Turn off faucets all the way. One drop of water a second adds up to more than 700 gallons a year. Don't leave water running when washing dishes by hand. Use a stopper and fill the sink with enough water to do the job. Rinse dishes in cold water.

40. *Save heat and water* by running the dishwasher only when it's full.

41. *Use small electric pans or ovens for small meals.*

42. *Don't boil too much water.* Put in the kettle or pot only what you will use. Turn the heating element or burner on high. Turn it off when the liquid begins to boil.

43. *Keep lids on pots and pans for swifter cooking.*

44. *Watch your oven habits.* Cook as many dishes as possible at one go. Set an average temperature of 350 degrees. If some dishes call for higher or lower heat, adjust the time accordingly.

45. *Use a pressure cooker as often as possible.* It cuts cooking time by one-third.

46. *Buy an oven thermometer.* Many old ovens give out more heat than is set on the dial. For about $5 you can save energy and get better roasting and baking.

47. *Avoid cooling your refrigerator below 38 degrees F, your freezer below 5 degrees.* These are government-recommended temperatures. Anything below is a waste of electricity.

48. *Clean refrigerator coils.* Check the condenser coils at the back or bottom of your refrigerator at least once a year. Clean off dirt and oily residues from cooking.

49. *Leave space around food items in refrigerator* so that air can circulate freely.

50. *Pack freezer contents tightly.* If the compartment is not full, add extra bags of ice to fill it out.

51. *Make sure your refrigerator door gasket is tight.* In the event of a leak, replace the gasket.

52. *Turn off your refrigerator-freezer* if you plan to be away for a week or more. Eat the food or ask a neighbor to store it for you. Clean both compartments and prop all doors open.

53. *Manually defrost.* Check the freezer and be sure no more than one-quarter inch of frost has built up. The thicker the coating, the harder your compressor must work.

54. *Replace your refrigerator-freezer with a new-technology unit that uses less than 500 kilowatt-hours a year.* Depending on the cost of electricity, it will pay back the investment in 5 to 6 years.

Around the House

55. *Use nonpetrochemical soaps, cleaners, and insecticides.* For details on safe alternatives, see chapter 12 pp. 298-304.

56. *Find alternatives to plastic containers and packaging.* For details, see chapter 1, pp. 26-27.

57. *Eat organic food, preferably locally grown.* This saves fossil fuels used for fertilizers, pesticides, processing, preservatives, and transportation.

58. *Grow your own food organically.* This saves even more energy and money. You can even sell the surplus or have the pleasure of giving it away.

59. *Add a solar greenhouse* as a place to grow food and plants and to help heat your house.

60. *Actively support organic gardening and sustainable agriculture.* See "Resources" for more information.

61. *Presoak clothes and other laundry items.* It saves having to wash things twice.

62. *Fill your washer, but don't overload it.* Combining loads saves electricity.

63. *Avoid using too much detergent.* Too many suds make the machine work harder and use more electricity or gas.

64. *Keep your dryer's lint screen clean at all times.*

65. *When ironing, start with low-temperature fabrics first.* Turn off the iron about five minutes before you finish and use heat stored in the plate.

66. *Use a solar dryer whenever possible.* If you don't have an outdoor clothesline, drip-dry some items in laundry or bathroom. This saves electricity and the chore of ironing.

67. *Install a flow-control device in the showerhead.* This is a simple, do-it-yourself device that limits the flow of water and adds up into important energy and money savings. If you can't find one locally, write: Rocky Mountain Institute, 1739 Snowmass Creek Road, Old Snowmass, CO 81654, or 7th Generation Catalog, 10 Farrell Street, South Burlington, VT 05403.

68. *Take showers instead of baths.* A five-minute shower with a 3-gallon-per-minute flow uses 15 gallons of water, half the amount of an average bath. If you bathe once a day, this adds up to 5,475 gallons of hot water a year that you won't have to heat!

69. *Dry your hair with a towel instead of an electric dryer,* which uses as much electric power as a toaster and for longer.

70. *Set your water tank thermostat between 110 and 120 degrees.* Most tanks are set too high, which means you have to dilute the hot water with cold. If you have an electric heater, turn it to the minimum setting when you go on vacation.

Becoming Energy-Self-sufficient

71. *Consider installing a solar system* to provide at least half your hot water.

72. *Build a passive-solar house* or remodel your existing one.

73. *Generate your own electricity with PV panels, a wind turbine, or small-scale hydro,* depending on where you live.

74. *Ride a bicycle* or walk if the distance is not too great.

75. *Save energy when you drive a car.* See chapter 5, pp. 107-108.

Mobilizing Support for Renewable Energy

The need to reduce our dependence on fossil fuels takes on special urgency because their use is so clearly linked to global warming. Translating the need into action is ultimately the responsibility of the federal government, utilities, and other larger consumers of these polluting fuels. It also presupposes considerably more international cooperation than presently exists.

Although the U.S. government is expressing concern over the problems caused by burning oil and coal, it is not yet taking the necessary action to deal

Renewable Pedal Power*

Question: *What mode of transportation is non-polluting, scenic, economical, fun, healthy, and personally liberating? And conveys more people in Asia alone than do all the world's automobiles?*

Answer: the bicycle. Worldwide bicycles outnumber cars by two to one. China alone has 270 million, roughly a third of the world's 800 million bicycle fleet; its 35 million annual bike sales exceed global auto sales.[57]

Bicycles are used for commuting, freight, and recreation not only in the Third World, but in Japan, Denmark, the Netherlands, and other industrial countries. Even in the U.S., where auto is still king, an estimated 3 million people ride bicycles for daily transportation – triple the number a decade ago. In midtown Manhattan, one in every dozen vehicles in motion during midday is a bicycle.[58]

Unfortunately, the bicycle is held back by planners' tunnel vision that builds "modern" transportation systems around the automobile. A 1985 World Bank study of transportation in China didn't even mention the word bicycle, although bikes account for the vast majority of trips in Chinese cities. In the U.S. and other industrial countries, subsidies for high-speed highways, auto parking, and oil development mirror social activities that value short-term comfort over the independence afforded by the bicycle.

This may be changing, however. Polluted air, oil spills and encroaching climate change are heightening the need for environmentally compatible transportation. Bicycling is energy efficiency personified – human solar power, metabolizing organic matter into motion. Like other renewable energy forms, bikes curb acid rain, bypass Alaskan oil, and keep the greenhouse effect at bay.

In the U.S., where half of all commuting trips are five miles or less and most jobs are sedentary, the potential for bicycle commuting is enormous. In Third World countries, the bicycle can provide affordable mobility to the masses. All over the world, bicycles can reduce pollution, conserve fossil fuels and reinforce the traveler's connection to the society she or he is traveling through.

If citizens speak loudly enough for transportation planners to hear, the bicycle can play a critical role in preserving the environment and engendering a more harmonious relationship between humans and the earth.

---

*Contributed by Charles Komanoff, energy economist and president of Transportation Alternatives, a New York City bicycle advocacy organization

with either the symptoms or the causes of the widespread pollution it creates.

Increasing pressure on the government to use energy more wisely and to switch to renewable sources is coming from a coalition of environmental and citizens groups and professional and industry associations, including the American Solar Energy Association, the American Wind Energy Association, Renew America, the Energy Conservation Coalition, and the Solar Energy Industries Association. Also contributing is a growing number of legislators in Congress and state governments, especially California, the Northwest, and the Northeast.

Ten Ways You Can Support Renewable Energy in Congress

1. Find out if your representatives support HR 1078, a bill introduced by Representative Claudine Schneider and its counterpart in the Senate sponsored by Senator Albert Gore, which embody most of the energy options set forth in this chapter. If your representatives do support this proposed legislation, commend their action, but make sure they are *actively* working for its passage. Some legislators put their names on bills they think will get defeated, just in order to claim subsequently that they were "supporters." If they do not support the bills, explain to them that:

2. *Renewable-energy options* are vital to this country's economic health. They create local jobs, build the export industry, and reduce the trade deficit *and* environmental pollution.

3. *Tax breaks and other incentives for renewable-energy production* should match those presently given to oil and nuclear power.

4. *Increased federal research and development funding for renewables* and organic farming will pay off fast in better productivity, profits, and benefits for producers and consumers.

5. *Switching to smaller, decentralized energy and food sources* will significantly enhance the security of the United States.

6. There should be *a federal requirement* that *environmental* costs of energy be factored into the setting of rates for the purchase of electric power or generating capacity. This would put renewable energy on an even "playing field" with fossil-fuel and nuclear power.

7. *All U.S. government and military facilities and installations should switch wherever possible to renewable energy use.*

8. *Congress should increase funding for trade programs to encourage renewable-energy development overseas* and assist the renewable-energy industry in competing in international markets.

9. Your representatives should urge the U.S. president and the administration to take a more aggressive lead on showing how energy conservation and efficiency, renewable energy, and sustainable agriculture can reduce global warming and other environmental hazards.

10. Make sure your representative has received and read *Design for a Livable Planet*, especially this chapter, as well as other publications listed in "Resources" below.

For specifics on how the U.S. legislative process works and how you can become involved in it, see chapter 10, pp. 245-257.

RESOURCES

The following is provided to help you locate resources on the topics covered in this chapter.

1. International Agencies and Organizations

— *United Nations Environment Program* (UNEP), headquarters, P.O. Box 4704, Nairobi, Kenya; United Nations office, 2 U.N. Plaza, New York, NY 10022; (212) 963-8139.

2. U.S. Government

— *Department of Energy*, Office of Conservation and Renewable Energy, 1000 Independence Avenue SW, Washington, DC 20585; (202) 586-9220:

Appropriate Technology Transfer to Rural Areas, Fayetteville, Ark.

Conservation and Renewable Energy Inquiry and Referral Service (CAREIRS), P.O. Box 8900, Silver Spring, MD 20907; (800) 523-2929. Provides information on all aspects of renewable energy, wood heating, alcohol fuels, and municipal waste.

National Appropriate Technology Service (NATAS), P.O. Box 2526, Butte, MT 59702-2525; (800) 428-2525 (in Montana, 800-428-1718). Provides technical information and assistance on energy conservation and renewable-energy technologies.

National Center for Appropriate Technology (NCAT), 3040 Continental Drive, Butte, MT 59701; (800) 346-9140.

Solar Energy Research Institute, 1617 Cole Boulevard, Golden, CO 80401; (303) 231-1000.

— *Federal Energy Regulatory Commission*, 825 N. Capitol Street NE, Washington, DC 20240.

— *Tennessee Valley Authority*, Division of Conservation and Energy Management, 703 Power Building, Chattanooga, TN 37401; (615) 751-2061.

3. State Government

— *California Energy Commission*, 1516 Ninth Street, Sacramento, CA 95814-5512; (916) 324-3298.

— *New York State Energy Office*, 2 Rockefeller Plaza, Albany, NY 12223; energy hotline, (800) 342-3722.

4. Associations

— *American Solar Energy Society*, 2400 Central Avenue, Unit B-1, Boulder, CO 80301; (303) 443-3130.

— *American Wind Energy Association*, 777 North Capital Street, Washington, DC 20005; g19 (703) 276-8334.

— *Canadian Wind Energy Association*, 44A Clarey Avenue, Ottawa, Ontario, KIS 2R7, Canada; (613) 234-9463.

— *Geothermal Resources Council*, P.O. Box 98, Davis, CA 95616; (916) 758-2360.

— *Institute for Alternative Agriculture*, 9200 Edmonton Road, Greenbelt, MD 20770; (301) 411-8777.

— *International Alliance for Sustainable Agriculture*, 1701 University Avenue SE, Minneapolis, MN 55414; (612) 331-1099.

— *National Association of Home Builders/National Research Center*, 400 Prince George Boulevard, Upper Marlboro, MD 20772; (301) 249-4000.

— *National Hydropower Association*, 1133 21st Street NW, Washington, DC 20036; (202) 331-7551.

— *National Wood Energy Association*, 1730 N. Lynn Street, Arlington, VA 22209; (703) 524-6104.

— *Natural Organic Farmers Association*, RFD 2 Sheldon Road, Barre, MA 01005.

— *Northeast Solar Energy Association*, P.O. Box 541, Brattleboro, VT 05301; (802) 254-2386

— *Organic Food Production Association of North America*, P.O. Box 31, Belchertown, MA 01007; (413) 323-6821.
— *Passive Solar Industries Council*, 2836 Duke Street, Alexandria, VA 22314; (703) 832-3356.
— *Renewable Fuels Association*, 201 Massachusetts Avenue NW, Washington, DC 20002, (202) 543-3802.
— *United States Export Council for Renewable Energy*, P.O. Box 10095, Arlington, VA 22210-9998; (703) 524-6104.

5. *Environmental and Citizen Groups*

The vast majority of the environmental groups listed in "Resources" in other chapters promote the use of renewable energy. Those that have special energy-related programs and initiatives include:

— *Conservation Law Foundation*, 3 Joy Street, Boston, MA 02108-1497. A public interest group that works with state agencies, utility commissions, and other groups to implement energy efficiency and conservation in New England.
— *Public Citizen Critical Mass Energy Project*, 215 Pennsylvania Avenue SE, Washington, DC 20003; (202) 546- 4996.
— *Renew America*, 1001 Connecticut Avenue NW, Washington, DC 20036; (202) 466-6880.

6. *Research and Consulting Groups*

— *Florida Solar Energy Society*, 300 State Road 401, Cape Canaveral, FL 32920; (407) 783-0300.
— *Land Institute*, Route 3, Salina, KS 67401.
— *R. Lynette & Associates*, 15042 NE 40th Street, Redmond, WA 98052; (206) 885-0206.
— *North Carolina Solar Center*, Box 7401, NC State University, Raleigh, NC 27695-7401; (919) 737-3480.
— *Rocky Mountain Institute*, 1739 Snowmass Creek Road, Old Snowmass, CO 81654; (303) 927-3851.
— *Worldwatch Institute*, 1776 Massachusetts Avenue NW, Washington, DC 20036; (202) 452-1999.

7. *Renewable Energy Manufacturers*
Geothermal

— *California Energy Company*, 601 California, San Francisco, CA 94108-9835; (415) 391-7700.

Photovoltaics

— *Alpha Solarco*, 600 Vine Street, Cincinnati, OH 45202; (513) 621-1243.
— *Arco Solar*, 9351 Deering Avenue, Chatsworth, CA 91313; (818) 700-7000.
— *Chronar Corp.*, P.O. Box 177, Princeton, NJ 08542; (609) 799-8800.
— *Energy Conversion Devices/Sovonics Solar Systems*, 1675 West Maple Road, Troy, MI 48084; (313) 280-1900.
— *Intersol Power*, 11901 West Cedar Avenue, Lakewood, CO 80228; (303) 989-8718.
— *Mobil Solar Energy*, 16 Hickory Drive, Waltham, MA 02254; (617) 466-1286.
— *Solarex*, 1335 Piccard Drive, Rockville, MD 20850; (301) 948-0202.
— *Spire Corp.*, Patriots Park, Bedford, MA 01730; (617) 275-6000.

Solar Thermal

— *Coyne Solar*, P.O. Box 1120, San Juan Pueblo, NM 87566; (505) 852-2622.
— *FAFCO Inc.*, 235 Constitution Drive, Menlo Park, CA 94025; (415) 321-3650.
— *Hansolar*, River Road, Newcastle, ME 04553; (207) 563-3884.
— *Luz International*, 924 Westwood Boulevard, Los Angeles, CA 90024; (213) 208-7444.
— *Ramada Energy Systems*, 1421 South McClintock Drive, Tempe, AZ 85281; (602) 829-0009.
— *Power Kinetics Inc.*, 415 River Street, Troy, NY 12180; (518) 271-0782.
— *Sunsteam*, 998 San Antonio Road, Palo Alto, CA 94303; (415) 494-9144.

— *U.S. Solar Corp.*, P.O. Drawer K, Hampton, FL 32044; (904) 468-1517.

Wind Energy

— *Bergey Windpower*, 2001 Priestley, Norman, OK 73069.
— *Northern Power Systems*, 1 North Wind Road, Moretown, VT 05660.
— *Southwest Wind Power*, Rte 8, Box 52 LRB, Flagstaff, AZ 86004.
— *U.S. Windpower*, 6952 Preston Avenue, Livermore, CA 94550.

8. Further Reading

— *Beyond Oil*, John Gever, Robert Kaufmann, David Skole, and Charles Vorosmarty. Cambridge, Mass.: Ballinger, 1986.
— *Brittle Power: Energy Strategy for National Security*, Amory B. Lovins and L. Hunter Lovins. Andover, Mass.: Brick House, 1982.
— *Design for a Limited Planet*, Norma Skurka and Jon Naar. New York: Ballantine Books, 1978.
— *Direct Use of the Sun's Energy*, Farrington Daniels. New York: Ballantine Books, 1964. The classic book on solar energy
— "Energy-Efficient Buildings," Arthur H. Rosenfeld and David Hafemeister, *Scientific American*, April 1988.
— *Energy Unbound*, L. Hunter Lovins, Amory B. Lovins, and Seth Zuckerman. San Francisco: Sierra Club, 1986.
— *Farmland, a Community Issue*. Washington, D.C.: Concern, Inc., 1987.
— *Farmland or Wasteland*, R. Neil Sampson. Emmaus, Pa.: Rodale Press, 1981.
— "International Developments in Geothermal Power Production," Ronald DiPippo, Geothermal Resources Council *Bulletin* (Davis, Calif.), May 1988.
— *The Little Green Book*, John Lobell. Boulder, Colo.: Shambala, 1981.
— *Meeting the Expectations of the Land*, Wes Jackson, Wendell Berry, and Bruce Colman. San Francisco: North Point Press, 1984.
— "The Myth of France's Cheap Nuclear Electricity," Peter Bunyard, *The Ecologist*, January/February 1988.
— *The New Wind Power*, Jon Naar. New York: Penguin Books, 1982.
— *Northeast Sun* (bimonthly), Northeast Solar Energy Association, Greenfield, Mass.
— *The Passive Solar Energy Book*, Edward Mazria. Emmaus, Pa.: Rodale, 1979.
— *Photovoltaics: Solar Electricity in the 1990s*. Arlington, VA.: Photovoltaics Division, Solar Energy Industries Association, November 1988.
— *Power Surge, Nancy Rader*. Washington, D.C.: Public Citizen, 1989.
— *Soil and Survival*, Joe Paddock, Nancy Paddock, and Carol Bly. San Francisco: Sierra Club, 1986.
— *The Solar Electric Book – How to Save $$$ through Clean Solar Power*, Gary Starr. Lower Lake, Calif.: Integral Publishing, 1987
— *Solar Today* (bimonthly), American Solar Energy Society, Boulder, Colo.
— *Too Costly to Continue: the Economic Feasibility of a Nuclear Phase-Out*, Joseph Kriesberg. Washington, D.C.: Public Citizen, 1987.
— *The Unsettling of America – Culture and Agriculture*, Wendell Berry. San Francisco: Sierra Club, 1977
— *Wind Energy Weekly*, American Wind Energy Association, Arlington, VA, 22209.
— *Wind Power Monthly*, P.O. Box 6007, Redding, CA 96099.

1. David H. Moskovitz, "Cutting the Nation's Electric Bill," *Issues in Science and Technology*, Vol. 5, No. 3, 1989, p.88.

2. Christopher Flavin, "Moving Beyond Oil," *State of the World 1986* (Washington, D.C.: Worldwatch Institute, 1986).

3. Richard J. Stegemeier, "Get Ready for Longer Gasoline Lines," *New York Times*, January 22, 1989; Matthew L. Wald, "Oil Lobby Warns of New Crisis," *New York Times*, November 16, 1988.

4. Nancy Rader, *Power Surge* (Washington, D.C.: Public Citizen, 1989) p. iv-1.

5. Robert H. Williams, "A Low-Energy Future for the United States," *Energy 12* (10/11), 1987, pp. 929-955.

6. Quoted in Craig Canine, "Generating Negawatts," *Harrowsmith*, March/April 1989.

7. L. Hunter Lovins, Amory B. Lovins, and Seth Zuckerman, *Energy Unbound* (San Francisco: Sierra Club, 1986) p. 26.

8. Michael Shepard, "DOE Squanders Chance to Help Economy and Environment," *Rocky Mountain Institute* press release, January 3, 1989, Snowmass, Colo.

9. Howard S. Geller, *Improving End-Use Electricity* (Washington, D.C.: World Bank, 1986), pp.10 and 14.

10. Christopher Flavin and Alan Durning, "Raising Energy Efficiency," in *State of the World 1988* (Washington, D.C.: Worldwatch Institute, 1988), pp. 55-56.

11. The blow-by-blow account of EDF's successful test case against Pacific Gas & Electric is detailed in David Roe's *Dynamos and Virgins*, (New York: Random House, 1984), available from EDF, 257 Park Avenue South, New York, NY 10010.

12. Reported on "Morning Edition," *National Public Radio*, April 17, 1989.

13. Philip E. Ross, "A Promising Design for a Deficient Engine," *New York Times*, December 28, 1988.

14. World Resources Institute, *World Resources 1988-89*, (New York: Basic Books, 1988).

15. Rader, *Power Surge*, p.ii-29.

16. *World Resources 1988-89*, p. 111.

17. Ibid.

18. Cynthia Pollock Shea, *Renewable Energy: Today's Contribution, Tomorrow's Promise*, Worldwatch Paper 81 (Washington, D.C.: Worldwatch Institute, 1988), pp. 12-13.

19. *Hydropower — An Energy Source Whose Time Has Come Again* (Washington, D.C.: U.S. General Accounting Office, 1980).

20. Shea, *Renewable Energy*, p.17.

21. Jon Naar, *The New Wind Power* (New York: Penguin Books, 1982), p. 48.

22. For further information on PURPA, see chapter 10, p.240.

23. Robert Lynette, "Wind Energy Systems," report to *Forum on Renewable Energy and Climate Change*, Washington D.C., June 1989.

24. Ibid.; see also American Wind Energy Association, *Windletter*, August 1989.

25. The first passive solar skyscraper, designed by New York architect William McDonough, is planned for Warsaw, Poland and is due for completion in 1992. See also *When Working Is Good for Your Health*, a report on the EDF national headquarters in New York designed by the same architect, in chapter 4, pp. 90-91.

26. H. M. Hubbard, "Photovoltaics Today and Tomorrow," *Science*, April 21, 1989.

27. Richard D. Hansen and Jose G. Martin, "Photovoltaics for Rural Electrification in the Dominican Republic," report to the Natural Resources Forum, May 1988, United Nations, New York.

28. William E. Rogers, position paper, "Power Kinetics, Inc.," Troy, N.Y., 1988, p. 3.

29. James Cook, "Warming Trend," *Forbes*, February 20, 1989.

30. Mike Ross, "Lawrence Livermore Laboratory Studies Solar Coal Gasification," *American Gas Association Monthly*, November 1979, pp. 10-13, cited in Rogers, PKI position paper, p. 4.

31. "A Solar Energy Future for the United States," in Rogers, PKI position paper, p. 11.

32. David W. McClain, manager of project development, California Energy Company, personal communication to author.

33. Ronald DiPippo, "International Development in Geothermal Power Production," *Geothermal Resources Council Bulletin*, May 1988, pp. 11-12.

34. International Energy Association *Renewable Sources* cited in Shea, *Renewable Energy*, p. 19.

35. Shea, "Shifting to Renewable Energy," *State of the World 1988*, pp. 67-72.

36. Ibid. p. 70.

37. "Cow Manure Fuels a California Power Plant" (AP report), *New York Times*, February 14, 1989.

38. For further information contact Robert A. Hamburg, Omega-Alpha Recycling Systems, Rt. 1, Box 51, Orma, WV 25268.

39. Based on an institutional advertisement by Rodale Press, reprinted in *Empty Breadbasket*, (Emmaus, Pa.: Rodale Press, 1981), p. 158.

40. Robert Rodale in *Organic Gardening*, September 1980.

41. Keith Schneider, "Science Academy Recommends Resumption of Natural Farming," *New York Times*, September 8, 1989.

42. Edward Davis, president, American Nuclear Energy Council, testimony before U.S. House of Representatives Subcommittee on Science, Research, and Technology, June 29, 1988.

43. "Imported Oil Strengthens Our Ties to the Middle East," title of a 1989 full-page advertisement in national magazines by the U.S. Council for Energy Awareness, Washington, D.C.

44. "How Nuclear Energy Can Help Defuse the Next Oil Crisis," national advertisement, U.S. Council for Energy Awareness, 1987.

45. Christopher Flavin, "Reassessing Nuclear Power," in *State of the World 1987* (Washington, D.C.: Worldwatch Institute, 1987), pp. 68-74.

46. Kenneth Boley, *Nuclear Power Safety* (Washington, D.C.: Public Citizen, 1989) cited in *Critical Masss Energy Bulletin*, June/August 1989, p. 6.

47. "Where Nuclear Power Works," *Technology Review*, February/March 1989, pp. 30-40.

48. *Atomic Industrial Forum Survey*, September 25, 1986, cited in *Turning Down the Heat*, (Washington, D.C.: Public Citizen, September 1988), p. 20.

49. Rader, *Power Surge*, p. iv-2.

50. Joseph Kriesberg, *Too Costly to Continue* (Washington, D.C.: Public Citizen Critical Mass Energy Project, November 1987), pp. 28-31.

51. Peter Bunyard, "The Myth of France's Cheap Nuclear Electricity," *The Ecologist*, January/February 1988.

52. Philip Elmer-Dewitt, "Nuclear Power Plots a Comeback," *Time*, January 2, 1989, p. 41.

53. Rader, *Power Surge*, p. ii-57.

54. Matthew L. Wald, "Hydrogen Pushed as Motor Fuel," *New York Times*, September 28, 1989.

55. Lovins, Lovins, and Zuckerman, *Energy Unbound*, p. 161.

56. "Light Bulbs Have Global Reach," *Rocky Mountain Institute Newsletter* (Snowmass, Colo.), November 1988, p. 7.

57. Marcia D. Lowe, "Pedaling Into the Future," *World Watch*, July/August 1988, p.11.

58. *City Cyclist*, May-June 1988, p.3, and July-August 1988, p.2, Transportation Alternatives, NY (based on surveys of over 20,000 vehicles).

10

ENVIRONMENTAL LAW

"There ought to be a law. . ."
maybe there already is

*"Next to personal example, law is
the most powerful teaching tool in society."
– J. William Futrell, president,
the Environmental Law Institute*

In the last twenty years, environmental protection has become entwined in a legal and regulatory maze of extraordinary complexity. Writing on a practically blank slate, the federal and state governments have drawn up sweeping new legislation aimed at almost all environmental concerns. It is impossible to grasp or to try to correct any pollution problem without an understanding of its legal setting. The aim of this chapter is to show in general terms how you can use the law to best advantage in the fight for a healthier environment.

The Background of Environmental Law

There have been "environmental laws" for much of human history. In 2000 B.C., Babylonian laws prohibited adulteration of grain, and the first ordinance limiting coal burning was enacted in England in 1273 (records show that at least one London violator was put to death). In this country, several cities adopted smoke-abatement ordinances in the late 18th century.

Yet until 1970, the only legal remedies for environmental problems were those provided by "common law," that is, judge-made law developed through private lawsuits. Many environmental cases will support a common-law "nuisance" action, a claim by the plaintiff that the defendant is interfering with the use and enjoyment of the plaintiff's property. Noise, odors, smoke, and water contamination might all cause such interference. In addition, the common law provides a remedy, in general, where you or your property has been injured by the negligence of another. Thus, if you fail to exercise due care in disposing of certain wastes, dumping them in a stream from which my horse drinks, and my horse dies, I can sue you for damages.

> *Environmental concern has deep historical roots in this country, dating at least to the nature preservation ethic articulated and exemplified by John Muir...*

These common-law remedies are important. Indeed, they are now starting to come back into vogue after a two-decade hiatus. The well-publicized "toxic tort" lawsuits are all common-law actions. But they are also incomplete. By the late 1960s, many viewed them as hopelessly so. The narrow focus on physical harm, the requirement of proof of actual rather than probable harm or increased risk, strict causation requirements, the burden on a private plaintiff to initiate and pursue the lawsuit, and the unlikelihood that enough lawsuits will be brought to make an appreciable difference in environmental quality all called for a whole new body of law, based on statutory limits on pollution.

The Social Cost of Pollution

Such legislation involves a significant intrusion on the operation of the free market. By the late 1960s, however, it was clear that the market economy was not going to protect the environment. The view that environmental degradation was the necessary and appropriate consequence of a bustling economy had fallen out of favor not only with the general public, which saw a few big corporations as the villains, but even with economists. The reason is this: Historically, pollution was unlimited because it was free; no one sent a power plant a bill for its use of the (formerly) clean air as a dump. But such pollution has a cost, and society at large was picking up the tab. (It's because the *individual* harm from *individual* polluters tends to be slight that the common-law remedies are inadequate.) The market gives a polluter the wrong signal if, as is usually the case, his or her individual benefit from the pollution is greater than his or her individual cost in the form of environmental degradation, but the societal cost is greater than the polluter's benefit. In the language of the economists, the societal costs of pollution are "externalities"; only through some regulatory intervention (e.g., emission limits) will they be borne by, or "internalized" by, the polluter. This insight, which received its most famous expression in Garret Hardin's classic 1968 article in *Science*, "The Tragedy of the Commons,"[1] forms the basic theoretical justification for environmental regulation.

New Ecological Awareness

There is one last piece in the explosion of environmental legislation in the 1970s: the new ecological awareness. Environmental concern has deep historical roots in this country, dating at least to the nature-preservation ethic articulated and exemplified by John Muir, "St. John of the Mountains," who founded the Sierra Club in 1892. Yet for most of this century, the *preservation* ethic was subordinate to a philosophy of *conservation*, which stressed intelligent use and development of natural resources, welcoming human intervention into and domination of natural processes.

In the late 1960s the longstanding preservationist ethic blossomed into a movement of political protest demanding action by the federal government.[2] Finally, it *mattered* that we cannot trust the market economy, scattered municipal pollution ordinances, and the occasional nuisance suit to protect the environment. During the 1970s, the conviction that "there ought to be a law" was embodied in an extraordinary and unprecedented flurry of major federal legislation.

Federal Environmental Legislation

We summarize only the highlights of this output below. Thousands of pages of the U.S. Code have been reduced to thumbnail sketches, and many important laws are not mentioned at all. But you should get some sense of the complexity, the comprehensiveness, and, unfortunately, the inadequacy of the legislative effort to protect the environment.[3]

The National Environmental Policy Act of 1969 (NEPA)[4]

Signed into law on the first day of 1970, this *Magna Carta* of environmental legislation ushered in an era of environmental awareness. NEPA requires federal agencies to take into account the environmental consequences of all their plans and activities. *Whenever the federal government plans to initiate, finance, or permit a "major" action, it must prepare an "environmental impact statement" (EIS) assessing the project's environmental effects.* In 1987, federal agencies filed 455 EISs. As part of this process, the appropriate agency must hold hearings to take public comment and provide a public review period of a draft EIS. The project cannot proceed until a complete, final EIS is released.

Among other things, the EIS must review alternatives to the proposal that would have less impact on the environment, including forgoing the project altogether ("the no-action alternative"). For example, more environmentally benign alternatives to building a new highway might include a smaller highway, slight expansion or improvement of existing roadways, or development of new mass-transit facilities that would eliminate the need for any highway. All these would have to be explored in an EIS before work got under way on the proposed highway.

NEPA has proved a powerful tool. It is, of course, impossible to say how many projects have been changed or abandoned outright because the EIS process revealed (or would have revealed) intolerable environmental harms; the act has certainly had some effect in that regard. In addition, lawsuits challenging the adequacy of an EIS, or the decision not to prepare one, have become a staple of environmental litigation. In the decade from 1974 to 1983, over 100 such suits were filed every year. The number has decreased slightly in more recent years, but remains significant. These suits have often held things up long enough to allow for legislative intervention or to cause the project to fall of its own weight.

Nonetheless, NEPA is hardly a complete environmental-protection statute. It applies only to actions of the federal government, not the states or private parties, and it creates no substantive duties. In theory, the government could write a complete EIS detailing devastating environmental impacts and, having duly noted their existence, still go ahead with the project. Efforts to give NEPA more teeth have been shot down by the Supreme Court. Thus, NEPA requires the feds to stop and think, but never simply to stop. Substantive limits on pollution (which generally apply to both governmental and private polluters) were to follow in the antipollution legislation of the 1970s.

Major Pollution and Hazardous-Substances Statutes

NEPA was followed by a series of major antipollution statutes. These address the problem of "residuals" – that is, waste. Pollution, whether from a smokestack, a sewage pipe, or a leaking landfill, is at bottom simply the improper disposal of waste. Beginning with the 1970 Clean Air Act, Congress began to impose actual limits on permissible pollution.

The Clean Air Act (CAA)[5] was first enacted in 1955 and rewritten in 1963, 1965, and 1967. In these early versions, the federal government remained in the background, providing dollars and information, but leaving most regulatory responsibilities to the states – which generally ignored them. The current act was born in 1970 and significantly amended in 1977. Now well over 100 pages long, with accompanying regulations many times longer, the Clean Air Act is the environmental law par excellence. Somewhere or other in this complex and controversial legislation is an example of every approach to environmental regulation that the mind of Congress has been able to conceive.

At the heart of the CAA are National Ambient Air-Quality Standards (NAAQS), which establish maximum allowable concentrations for the pollutants that EPA deems to be particularly widespread and dangerous. EPA has established NAAQS for carbon monoxide, sulfur dioxide, particulate matter, ozone, nitrogen oxide, and (as the result of a lawsuit) lead. These are of two sorts. *Primary standards* must be set at the level allowing an adequate margin of safety, adequate to protect public health, including sensitive groups such as asthmatics. *Secondary standards* – which are generally equal to or more stringent than the primary standards – are supposed to protect the public welfare by preventing injury to crops and livestock, decreased visibility, deterioration of materials and property or other environmental harm. Not surprisingly, whether EPA's standards are sufficiently (or excessively) stringent is a matter of dispute.

While EPA sets these nationally applicable air-quality standards, it is up to the states to meet them. Each state is to develop a State Implementation Plan (SIP) setting out the various pollution-control programs and requirements that will result in compliance. Congress set specific deadlines – all extended more than once, and all now expired – for attainment of the primary standards; secondary standards are to be achieved within a "reasonable" time.

The act also imposes various performance standards on factories, power plants, and other so-called "stationary sources" of air pollution. First, new stationary sources are subject to "new source performance standards" that reflect what can be achieved using the best demonstrated pollution-control technology. EPA has issued such standards for about 60 sorts of facilities and is slowly continuing to issue more. Second, any new stationary source over a certain size, whether subject to a new source performance standard or not, must obtain a permit and employ the "best available control technology," or, if it's in a dirty-air area, do even better than that. Third, *existing* facilities, if located in areas where the air does not meet the NAAQS, must add "reasonably available control technology" – a requirement that in practice has tended to be rather lax. Fourth, EPA is to set emission limits for hazardous air pollutants. These are based on health protection rather than technological feasibility; they apply to both new and existing facilities. EPA has managed to produce only a handful of hazardous air-pollutant standards.

Somewhere [in the Clean Air Act] is an example of every approach to environmental regulation that the mind of Congress has been able to conceive.

Finally, the act addresses automobile emissions. It required a 90-percent reduction of emissions of carbon monoxide and hydrocarbons and a 75-percent reduction in nitrogen oxides per car, from 1970 levels. These reductions have been accomplished, although it took twice as long as the act mandated. Unfortunately, the resulting air-quality benefits have been offset (and may in the future be defeated altogether) by a huge growth in the number of cars and miles driven. The act also gives EPA exclusive authority to regulate automotive fuels and additives; it is under this section that EPA has required the almost total elimination of leaded gasoline.

How well is all this working? Air quality is undeniably better than it would have been but for the act; on the other hand, it is not that much better than it was 20 years ago. The one huge exception is lead, which has been all but eliminated from the ambient air as a result of the ban on leaded gasoline. The other pollutants for which there are NAAQS remain at approximately their 1970 levels or slightly below.

This means that while most of the country meets the standards for lead, nitrogen oxide, and sulfur dioxide (which is not necessarily the same, remember, as having healthy air), many areas violate the particulate-matter standard, and *three out of five* Americans live in the more than 100 urban areas that violate the carbon monoxide and/or ozone standards. In addition, the act has been utterly ineffectual in controlling acid rain, and has left most toxic air pollutants untouched.

These obvious problems are dominating the current political agenda. As this is written, Congress is debating much-needed amendments that would require a 10-million-ton-per-year (about 40-percent) reduction in sulfur-dioxide emissions, the primary cause of acid rain, and would impose a new scheme for attaining the ozone standard and finally grapple with the air toxics problem.

Like the CAA, the **Clean Water Act** (CWA)[6] had limited, nonregulatory predecessors. Only in 1972 did Congress develop the present far-reaching federal regulatory program. The 1972 act set a goal of fishable, swimmable waters nationwide by 1983. Congress also anticipated (but did not require) an end to all discharges of pollutants into waterways by 1985. Not only were these goals not met, it has been some time since anyone in Washington has even taken them seriously.

The 1972 CWA took aim at two targets: municipal sewage and industrial discharges. First, it ordered that all municipal waste be treated before being discharged into waterways. To help make this command a reality, it initiated a $5-billion-a-year federal grants program to finance construction of local sewage treatment systems. Second, the act required that all facilities discharging into waters, new and old, obtain a permit. The permit sets specific effluent limitations for relevant pollutants, including toxics, based on industry-specific EPA regulations reflecting the best available technology. New facilities must also meet additional EPA performance standards. Every facility must monitor its discharges and file monthly reports with the state or federal environmental agency. CWA also calls for states to develop water quality standards (the counterpart to the CAA's federally imposed NAAQS), but the heart of the act is the best-available-technology discharge limits implemented through the permit program.

> *Not only were these goals [of the Clean Water Act] not met, it has been some time since anyone in Washington has even taken them seriously.*

Two defects in the act were addressed by 1987 amendments, passed overwhelmingly after a presidential veto. First, Congress was concerned with the many "hot spots" where concentrations of toxic pollutants are unacceptably high. The amendments require the states to identify such spots, determine their specific sources, and develop individualized control strategies that will eliminate the problem within three years. EPA's narrow interpretation of what constitutes a hot spot has brought its implementation of this provision under attack.

Second, the amendments attempt to fill the act's one gigantic gap. Roughly half of all water pollution does not come from specific discharges but from so-called "nonpoint sources" – runoff from agricultural and mining operations, road salting, construction sites, city streets, and so on. The permit program does not apply to these sources and for all intents and purposes they are unregulated. The 1972 act made a halfhearted effort to address this problem, requiring local areas to write plans that would identify such sources and describe means of controlling them (e.g., land-use controls). This effort never really got off the ground. The 1987 amendments include a renewed effort to attack nonpoint sources. Again, this is largely a planning effort; each state was to submit a plan addressing nonpoint sources by August 1988 for EPA approval. As yet, it is too early to say whether this new effort will be effective.

Section 404 of the CWA requires a permit to place any dredged or fill material into "waters of the United States." "Waters" are defined broadly, and include wetlands. Permitting authority lies with the U.S. Army Corps of Engineers, which is hardly known for its commitment to environmental protection; EPA can veto a Corps permit. EPA has been reluctant to use its veto authority, though in recent years it seems to be doing so with slightly more frequency. The key requirement for the grant of a permit is a showing that no practicable alternative is available that would not involve filling in waters. The Section 404 permit program has been the source of many pitched battles over permits for subdivisions, shopping malls, marinas, and the like in swamps and coastal wetlands.

The Safe Drinking Water Act (SDWA),[7] adopted in 1974 and substantially amended in 1986, requires EPA to set standards, known as *Maximum Contaminant Levels* (MCLs), for contaminants in public drinking-water supplies.

MCLs are health-based, but adjusted to reflect economic and technological feasibility. Primary enforcement responsibility lies with the states; if a state fails to act within 30 days of being notified of a violation, EPA must step in.

The SDWA also takes minor steps toward protection of underground drinking water supplies. It requires EPA to set standards and issue permits for underground injection of liquid wastes, and it offers some federal funding and guidance to states that set up special programs to protect particularly valuable underground drinking-water sources.

The very limited ground-water protection provisions of the SDWA point out that ground water is the last major unregulated environmental medium. A number of proposals for comprehensive federal ground-water protection legislation have appeared in recent years. None is presently high on the agenda, but it seems likely that Congress will eventually enact such legislation.

The Resource Conservation and Recovery Act (RCRA)[8] addresses the disposal of solid waste. Though it has some applicability to ordinary garbage, primarily in the form of EPA regulations for landfills, the act for the most part leaves that problem to state and local governments. What it does do is set up a comprehensive regulatory scheme for the handling and disposal of hazardous wastes.

First, generators of a solid waste must determine whether it is hazardous. The success of the whole system depends on the generator doing so honestly and correctly. EPA has developed a list of hazardous wastes and also identified certain tests that must be performed to determine if an unlisted waste still counts as hazardous. Any hazardous waste must be sent to a permitted treatment, storage, or disposal (TSD) facility, via a licensed hazardous waste transporter. The generator must keep careful records of the shipment and of the amount of waste generated. *Generators of less than 100 kilograms of hazardous waste per month are exempt; their hazardous waste is disposed of just like ordinary garbage.*

EPA has developed extensive design, operating, and financial responsibility requirements for TSD facilities. It is illegal to dispose of hazardous waste other than at a TSD facility that meets these requirements and has a permit. Also, under amendments adopted in 1984, EPA is slowly implementing a ban on simply burying hazardous wastes; treatment or incineration are its preferred options.

However sound this system may be for handling and disposing of hazardous waste, it would still be better to cause such waste not to be produced in the first place. The latter task has, unfortunately, proved to be a far greater legislative and technological challenge. The expense and poor public relations associated with hazardous-waste generation create an incentive to produce less waste. RCRA also nods several times to the principle of waste reduction, but the act contributes nothing that attacks the hazardous waste problem at its source.

Whereas RCRA regulates the management of hazardous waste we generate now, the **Comprehensive Environmental Response, Compensation, and Liability Act (CERCLA or Superfund)**[9] attempts to remedy the improper disposal of such substances in the past. Enacted in 1980 and substantially amended in 1986, CERCLA creates a scheme for identifying and cleaning up chemical spills and inactive toxic-waste sites that threaten human health or the environment. Any site where there has been a release of a hazardous substance is a potential Superfund site; EPA is charged with identifying the most serious sites and ranking them on its National Priorities List (NPL). As of mid-1989, EPA had identified more than 26,000 Superfund sites, of which 1,224 were on the NPL (849 final and 335 proposed).

CERCLA in essence invites anyone and everyone to clean up Superfund sites (though it usually the government that initiates the cleanup), then makes various private parties responsible for the costs. CERCLA casts the net of liability widely. Anyone who has any involvement with a Superfund site – the generator of the waste, the transporter, the operator of the facility, its current or prior owner – regardless of fault, can be stuck with the whole bill for cleanup. Not surprisingly, this has kept the lawyers busy in massive lawsuits between potentially responsible private parties trying to get each other to pay.

If no solvent private party can be found to foot the bill, the Superfund is available. Under the 1986 amendments, $8.5 billion (generated by taxes on industry generally and the chemical and oil industries in particular) is available for cleanups over the next five years. Eight and a half billion dollars doesn't go far, however, and the expectation is that private parties will pay for most of the cleanups (either directly or by reimbursing EPA).

Cleanups are of two sorts. *Removal actions* involve short-term containment and damage control; *remedial actions* are designed to solve the problem permanently (for example by removing, solidifying, incinerating, or capping the hazardous substances). Superfund monies can only be used for remedial action if the site is on the NPL. Before the adoption of any remedial plan, extensive investigations are required. Among other things, the public must be given an opportunity to comment on the cleanup proposed for their community. Crucial to effective public participation in the investigation and cleanup process are technical-assistance grants to citizens to hire experts. Grants are limited to $50,000 per site and depend on a 20-percent contribution from the recipient. EPA may, however, waive both of these requirements.

The Emergency Planning and Community Right-to-Know Act of 1986,[10] a freestanding portion of the 1986 Superfund amendments, requires federal, state, and local governments and industry to work together in developing plans to deal with chemical emergencies and community right-to-know reporting on hazardous chemicals. State governors are to designate state emergency-response commissions, which in turn set up local emergency-planning committees. These must include elected state and local officials; police, fire, and public health officials; environmental, hospital, and transportation officials; community groups; and members of the media.

The local committee's primary responsibility is to develop an emergency plan on how to deal with a potential chemical accident. The plan must identify the facilities that produce, transport, store, use, or release any of 402 extremely hazardous substances identified by EPA. In perhaps its most important provision, the act requires such facilities to provide information on its use and handling of these chemicals to the local committee, the state commission, and the local fire department.

The Surface Mining Control and Reclamation Act (SMCRA)[11] attempts to limit the scarring of the landscape, erosion, and widespread water pollution associated with surface mining. Through regulations developed by the Department of the Interior (DOI), the act adopts a program of nationwide minimum environmental standards for all surface-mining operations. The regulations emphasize restoration of the land to its original condition, contour, and vegetation. With certain exceptions, no person can conduct surface mining without a permit from DOI or the state.

The SMCRA has always been viewed by the environmental community as halfhearted and incomplete, and its implementation has been plagued by a lack of commitment at DOI. During the tenure of James Watt, the department did all it could to get out of the mine-regulation business altogether; regulations were loosened and almost all enforcement responsibilities were handed over to the states. These efforts were rebuffed by Congress and the courts, but the SMCRA program has never fully recovered.

The act's history also provides a classic example of the unintended loophole. The act originally exempted surface mines of two acres or less, the reasoning being that such small operations have negligible environmental effect and that the exemption would allow private coal users to extract coal for their own use. What happened was that many coal companies completely escaped the act's permit and reclamation requirements by mining "strings of pearls" (series of two-acre sites, with a few feet of unmined land between them) or by setting up numerous dummy corporations, each of which worked a two-acre mine. By the mid-1980s, half the coal mined in Kentucky came from exempt mines. Congress eliminated the two-acre exemption in 1987. It is an object lesson in the difficulty of writing a statute that does what you want it to. Congress's aim is rarely perfect.

The Toxic Substances Control Act (TSCA)[12] attacks the toxics problem at its source, regulating the entry of toxic substances into the product stream. The key provisions of TSCA concern testing, premanufacture clearance, and regulation of the manufacture and distribution of toxic substances.

The act seeks to develop information about toxic substances. EPA is to develop rules requiring manufacturers to test the substances they produce to determine the risk, if any, they pose to human health.

The act also requires manufacturers to notify EPA before they begin to produce a new chemical substance. The notification must include any data the manufacturer knows of or has developed concerning the substance's toxicity. EPA has the authority to block the proposed manufacture if it deems the substance too dangerous or if it finds there is inadequate information on which to base a determination of safety.

Finally, the act provides that EPA may restrict or forbid use of any substance, old or new, that it has "a reasonable basis to conclude . . . presents or will present an unreasonable risk of injury to health or the environment."

Thus far, TSCA has been a sleeping giant. It has generated mountains of paper – EPA receives over 200 premanufacture notices a month – but little else. Nonetheless, it is potentially one of the most powerful weapons in EPA's arsenal.

The Federal Insecticide, Fungicide, and Rodenticide Act of 1972 (FIFRA)[13] regulates the registration, marketing, and use of pesticides. No manufacturer or importer may make or sell a pesticide unless it is registered with the EPA; all pesticides registered before 1972 must be reregistered with EPA; all registrations are automatically reviewed every five years. If a pesticide would have "unreasonable adverse effects on the environment," EPA is to deny or cancel its registration. If EPA does cancel a registration, it will often allow the sale and use of whatever has already been produced; if it does not, the federal government will purchase and dispose of the manufacturer's unsold stock.

Like so much legislation, FIFRA looks better on paper than in reality. The "unreasonable adverse effects" standard leaves a good deal to EPA's judgment and the reregistration program has been notoriously slow. More than 600 ingredients are now in use in almost 50,000 different pesticides presently on the market. EPA has completed review of only a fraction of these; the five-year automatic review has been, in practice, a five-year automatic renewal; the scientific bases for EPA's evaluation of safe levels of pesticide residue have been seriously challenged; and only a handful of registrations has ever been canceled (perhaps in part because the cost of indemnifying manufacturers is a tremendous disincentive to cancellation).

> *The five-year automatic review [of 50,000 pesticides] has been, in practice, a five-year automatic renewal.*

The foregoing are the main federal laws relating to pollution; in less detail we now turn to federal laws designed to protect wildlife and their habitat.

Wildlife and Habitat Protection

The distinction between pollution laws and those designed to protect wildlife and their habitat is somewhat arbitrary. Bear in mind that the pollution laws are in part an effort to protect wildlife, and that the following "wildlife" laws are in part an effort to eliminate pollution.

The Endangered Species Act,[14] passed in 1973, rests on congressional recognition that endangered species of wildlife and plants "are of aesthetic, ecological, educational, historical, recreational, and scientific value to the Nation and its people." The secretary of the interior is to identify species that are endangered; once he has done so, no person may in any way harass, harm, pursue, trap, collect, or kill a member of that species. The secretary may also identify "threatened" species and develop such regulations as may be necessary to protect them. In addition, federal agencies may not take any action that would jeopardize the continued existence of an endangered species. It was this provision that led to the famous snail darter case, in which the courts enjoined completion of the Tellico Dam (only to be overruled, with far less publicity, by Congress).

Numerous statutes regarding public lands have tremendous environmental importance. The United States government owns approximately one-third of the nation's land. Management of all the public lands, which is the responsibility of the secretary of the interior, is plainly a vital environmental concern. Some federal lands – notably wildlife refuges – are specifically and exclusively dedicated to the protection of wildlife habitat. Wildlife protection is also to be taken into account, to a greater or lesser extent, in the administration of other types of federal land: the national forests, the national parks, national resource lands (essentially everything that's left over), specially designated wilderness areas within each of these, and the outer continental shelf. The relevant statutory provisions are varied and numerous.[15] There is a continuing battle, which ebbs and flows and no doubt will forever continue to do so, between those, both inside and outside the Interior Department, who see federal lands as a resource to be developed and those who see them as ecological treasures that should be left alone.

The Marine Mammal Protection Act[16] is intended to protect, conserve, and encourage research on marine animals. The essential feature of the act is a moratorium on any "taking" ("take" is broadly defined to mean "to harass, hunt, capture, or kill") and importation of marine mammals. This moratorium is subject to exceptions (for example, it does not apply to subsistence hunting by Eskimos), but the basic idea is that marine mammals are off limits.

The Marine Protection, Research, and Sanctuaries Act,[17] also known as the **Ocean Dumping Act**, regulates the dumping of material in U.S. waters to protect the marine environment. It forbids outright the ocean dumping of radiological, chemical, and biological warfare agents and high-level radioactive waste, and requires an EPA permit to dump any other material in the ocean. EPA can issue such a permit only if the need for the dumping (taking into account possible alternative disposal methods) outweighs the harm to human health and welfare (including economic, aesthetic, and recreational values) and to marine ecosystems.

In 1977, Congress amended the act to eliminate the then common East Coast practice of dumping sewage sludge in the ocean. New York City and neighboring New York and New Jersey counties ignored the prohibition and continued to dump tons of sewage sludge each day. EPA tried to stop this practice but lost in federal court because it was unable conclusively to show environmental harm. In 1988, over vociferous protest from New York City, Congress imposed a flat ban on ocean dumping of sewage sludge after 1991. Whether New York will (or is able to) comply is unclear; it has said that it will.

The Port and Tanker Safety Act of 1978[18] empowers the U.S. Coast Guard to supervise vessel and port operations and to set standards for the handling of dangerous substances. The act and the regulations cover the design, construction, alteration, repair, maintenance, operation, equipping, personnel, and manning of vessels and set minimum standards for ballast tanks, oil-washing systems, and cargo-protection systems. The act also mandates a national program for annual inspection of vessels.

The Intervention on the High Seas Act[19] authorizes the Coast Guard to take measures on the high seas to prevent, mitigate, or eliminate the danger of harm from any oil spill on the high seas that poses "a grave and imminent danger to the coastline or related interests of the United States." The determination of whether such a danger exists must be based in part on consideration of threats to human health, to fish and other marine resources, and to wildlife.

The Marine Plastic Pollution Research and Control Act of 1987,[20] implementing Annex V of the International Convention for the Prevention of Pollution from Ships (known as MARPOL, for marine pollution), prohibits the dumping of plastics at sea, severely restricts the dumping of other ship-generated garbage in the open ocean or in the waters of the United States, and requires all ports to have adequate garbage-disposal facilities for incoming vessels. The act applies to all watercraft, including small recreational vessels.

Nuclear Power Legislation

One particular area of environmental concern is the use and misuse of nuclear power. In the Atomic Energy act of 1954, Congress established a central federal regulatory role very early on, long before it got to work on the environmental laws described above. But not until the 1980s did Congress finally attempt to deal with the intractable problem of nuclear waste.

The much-amended **Atomic Energy Act**[21] establishes exclusive federal authority over nuclear-power facilities with regard to health, safety, and environmental concerns. The Nuclear Regulatory Commission (successor to the Atomic Energy Commission) grants permits for new power plants and has adopted extensive requirements for their operation. In contrast to most of the pollution statutes, which envision a joint state-federal effort, the act leaves little room for state regulation.

The Price-Anderson Indemnity Act[22] limits the nuclear industry's liability for reactor accidents. It provides that a utility's liability in the case of a nuclear accident shall not exceed $560 million; above that amount the government (i.e., the taxpayer) pays the bill. At today's prices, total liability resulting from a major nuclear accident could exceed $50 billion, 100 times the amount the utility would have to pay.

The Nuclear Waste Policy Act of 1982[23] is intended to solve the problem of high-level radioactive waste, primarily the spent reactor fuel now in temporary storage around the country. It charges the Department of Energy with development of a permanent high-level waste repository by 1998. DOE must consult with state governments on the siting of a nuclear-waste dump within its borders. A state can veto DOE's plans, but the state veto can in turn be overruled by Congress. By 1985, DOE had narrowed its selection process down to a few sites, which provoked enormous, almost paralyzing, controversy and local opposition. In late 1987, Congress stepped in, instructing DOE to investigate a particular site in Nevada and to report back if that site did not work out. There seems little or no possibility that DOE will in fact have sited and constructed a depository by the statutory deadline or indeed in the foreseeable future.

> *It's EPA, not Congress, that decides which pollutants will be regulated and what the permissable concentrations will be. . .*

Whereas the federal government is taking charge (though unsuccessfully) of finding a place to dispose of high-level radioactive waste, the **Low-Level Radioactive Waste Policy Act of 1980**[24] places responsibility for disposal of low-level radioactive waste squarely with the state in which it is generated. The act encourages development of regional, multistate compacts, under which a group of states could develop a disposal site within the region and keep out all wastes from other states. Nine such compacts have been formed, comprising all states except California and Texas, which have chosen to go it alone.

Energy-related Legislation

Energy conservation, with its concomitant savings of pollution and nonrenewable resources, has been an important part of the environmental agenda for years. With recent concern over the greenhouse effect, the need to limit our consumption of fossil fuels has taken on a new dimension. A wide variety of federal laws, taxes, and policies affect energy consumption. A few pieces of legislation directly aimed at energy conservation are summarized below.

The Public Utility Regulatory Policies Act (PURPA)[25] encourages the development of renewable energy and small-scale power production. It requires electric utilities to buy power at "just" rates from small power producers using sources such as wind, water, sun, biomass, and cogeneration. If a small power producer offers the utility electricity, the utility has to buy it, whether it wants it or not. PURPA is administered by the Federal Energy Regulatory Commission, which is also charged with establishing conditions under which independent power producers may easily interconnect their electricity into the public-utility grid.

The National Appliance Energy Conservation Act,[26] passed in 1987, eliminates "electricity guzzlers" by setting minimum-efficiency standards for new-home heating and cooling systems, refrigerators, freezers, small gas furnaces, and other appliances. DOE is mandated to review these standards periodically and revise them to reflect technological improvements.

The history of this legislation provides an instructive lesson on the interplay between state and federal regulation. For years, the appliance industry vehemently opposed any federal efficiency standards. Then a handful of states began to adopt such standards, no two of which were exactly the same. Threatened by the prospect of trying to operate in a national marketplace with varying standards (or having, as a practical matter, to comply with the standards of the strictest state), the industry changed its tune about federal standards. As long as the federal requirements would trump any conflicting state standards (which they do under the final legislation) the manufacturers were for them. It was this support that made the federal legislation politically feasible. The story contains an important lesson about the leverage that the states have in trying to solve what look like national problems.

The Motor Vehicle Information and Cost Savings Act,[27] as amended by the 1978 **Energy Policy and Conservation Act**, sets fuel-efficiency standards for automobiles. Each automaker must achieve a Corporate Average Fuel Economy (CAFE) standard set by statute, subject to some tinkering by the National Highway Traffic Safety Administration (NHTSA) within the Department of Transportation. For model year 1988 and thereafter, the CAFE standard is 27.5 miles per gallon. If an automaker's fleet average is below the standard, it must pay a penalty of $5 per car sold for every 1/10 mpg shortfall.

The CAFE standards were a target of particular hostility by the Reagan administration. NHTSA lowered the standards as much as it could, and the administration repeatedly, but unsuccessfully, proposed their complete elimination. Such proposals continue to appear, while environmentalists contend that the 27.5 mpg standard is far too low.

The Alternative Motor Fuels Act of 1988[28] uses the CAFE program to encourage auto companies to make cars that burn methanol, ethanol, or natural gas, which are, as we saw in chapter 9, generally less polluting than gasoline or diesel fuel. In essence, a manufacturer receives CAFE credit for the petroleum fuels that its alternative-fuel vehicles are not burning. Under this formula, for example, a methanol vehicle that gets 15 mpg (about the same efficiency as 26 mpg on gasoline) is deemed a 100-mpg car for CAFE purposes.

Implementation and Enforcement

Just looking at the statutes reveals little about what happens in the real world. Though they are lengthy and detailed, they are also only the tip of the iceberg. Congress has relied heavily on federal agencies, primarily EPA, to flesh out the specific requirements. For example, Congress wants clean air, so it tells the EPA administrator to make a list of "each air pollutant, emissions of which, in his judgment, cause or contribute to air pollution which may reasonably be anticipated to endanger public health,"[29] and then to set an ambient standard that, "allowing an adequate margin of safety," will "protect the public health."[30] It's EPA, not Congress, that decides just which pollutants will be regulated and what the permissible concentrations will be, and it plainly has a good deal of maneuvering room. Or, Congress wants to make sure hazardous waste is disposed safely, so it tells EPA to determine which wastes qualify as "hazardous" and then to write up requirements for handling and disposing such wastes "as may be necessary to protect human health and the environment."[31] Armed with these general instructions, EPA goes off and writes hundreds of pages of specific regulations.

The nuts and bolts of environmental regulation are thus not in the laws, but in the regulations. EPA's regulations are binding, legally enforceable requirements, just as if Congress had enacted them itself. Any serious attempt to determine exact legal requirements has to include review of the regulations.[32]

This is why it matters so much who is in charge at EPA and the other federal agencies. Statutory language that sounds great may be undercut by meaningless regulations; statutory language that doesn't sound like much can translate into very tough regulatory requirements. Reading the surface-mining laws, for example, it seems that they should afford adequate protection to the environment; in practice, the act has been a failure because the Interior Department has shirked its responsibilities from start to finish, not least by writing regulations that fail to do the job. Not surprisingly, a huge amount of environmental litigation consists of suits against federal agencies trying to force them to write overdue regulations or challenging the regulations that have appeared.

> **The Interior Department has shirked its responsibilities from start to finish.**

But only so much can be accomplished by such litigation; what really matters is what the agency chooses to do.

Take the ban on leaded gasoline. The 1970 Clean Air act authorized, but did not require, EPA to prohibit gasoline additives that "will endanger the public health." Such an authorization is plainly only as strong as the agency to which it is given. When EPA began to phase lead out of gasoline under this provision, there was a strong argument that EPA could not show that lead "*will*" endanger the public health," only that it *might*. Both the scientific evidence and the statutory language have changed since then, but at the time it was a bold and somewhat surprising move by EPA which gave real meaning to an empty statutory provision. The regulations withstood industry challenge in the courts by the narrowest of margins. *And had EPA decided instead to leave leaded gasoline alone, there is nothing anyone could have done to force it to do otherwise.*

EPA and all federal agencies have an enforcement role in translating statutory language into environmental protection. Consider the following:

● A 1983 General Accounting Office report found that 3,400 (about half) of the nation's largest plants had violated their Clean Water Act discharge permits for six or more months during the previous year.

● The 1970 Clean Air Act required nationwide compliance with the ambient air-quality standards by 1975; later amendments extended the deadline to 1977, then 1982, then December 31, 1987. Each of these deadlines came and went without compliance. While Congress tries to rethink the deadlines, most Americans breathe air that violates the CO and/or ozone standards.

● In 1986, DOI had a backlog of more than 10,000 cases of Surface Mining Act violations, had failed to collect more than $100 million in assessed fines, had allowed more than half of its 2,400 cessation orders simply to be ignored by mine operators, and had achieved only a fraction of the reclamation projects it anticipated. In the words of a House of Representatives report, it was "floundering."

An account of enforcement failures could take up this entire book. Citizen enforcement suits (on which more later) can take up some of the slack, but they will never wholly substitute for government enforcement. *Although EPA enforcement has improved from the nadir reached during the bad old days of Anne Gorsuch, it is still inadequate and the environmental laws remain as much promise as reality.*

State Laws

The federal government is not the only game in town. Each state has its own set of environmental laws. These vary significantly from state to state in both comprehensiveness and stringency. Most states at least have their own air, water, and hazardous-waste laws. By and large, these track their federal counterparts, but there can be important differences in the specifics.

Obviously, review of legislation from all 50 states is beyond the scope of this book. However, there are a few farsighted and innovative state laws that bear mention.

"Baby NEPAs." Many states have passed statutes modeled on NEPA and imposing similar requirements (applicable, of course, to state actions rather than federal).[33] In some states, the "baby NEPA" reaches much further than its federal counterpart. Not only may the procedural requirements be more extensive or apply to more projects, but some also impose substantive requirements. In New York, for example, the NEPA equivalent, known as SEQRA, requires that the state government and all applicants for state permits minimize or avoid the adverse environmental impacts of their activities. The Michigan Environmental Protection Act, which is in fact separate from the state's EIS requirement, imposes such a responsibility on all persons and entities, across the board. Such an open-ended requirement can be a powerful tool in opposing a particular project.

Solid-waste Laws. Whereas the federal government dominates hazardous-waste regulation, it has pretty much left nonhazardous solid waste to the states. Garbage has rapidly become one of the central environmental challenges of our time; at the local level, it is often far and away the dominant environmental concern. Many states have developed or are developing strict environmental standards for solid-waste facilities such as landfills and incinerators. While as a rule these still do not go as far as they should, they are important steps in the right direction.

In addition, a huge variety of legislation to promote recycling is now being introduced at the state level. Almost a dozen states, including New Jersey, Pennsylvania, and Rhode Island, have mandatory recycling laws; about half the states now require the state government to purchase recycled products; nine states have bottle bills; and a wide variety of packaging taxes, disposal charges, recycling grant programs, bans on the disposal of certain recyclables, and other initiatives have recently been passed or are being examined across the country.

Cleaning Up Hazardous Waste when Selling Property. As one means of identifying and forcing the cleanup of hazardous-waste sites, several states, including New Jersey, Connecticut, and Illinois, have laws that force the cleanup of contaminated property, if and when it is sold. New Jersey's 1983 Environmental Cleanup Responsibility act (ECRA), the first of these laws, forbids the sale of any commercial property until it is inspected for toxic contamination. If the site is contaminated, the sale cannot go through until the property is cleaned up or a state-approved cleanup plan is in place. Investigation and cleanup are the responsibility of the seller, with state oversight. Similar proposals are pending in several states.

Proposition 65. California's Safe Drinking Water and Toxics Enforcement Act, which went into effect in February 1988, is a striking example of a state initiative resulting from public demand. Better known as Proposition 65, this citizen-sponsored initiative passed overwhelmingly despite a multimillion-dollar campaign against it by industry and the governor.

Under this law no business may expose people to chemicals that cause cancer or reproductive problems such as birth defects, sterility, or miscarriage without giving "clear and reasonable warning." Failure to give warning can bring fines of up to $2,500 a day for each exposure. The law also makes it a criminal offense for any business knowingly to discharge toxic chemicals into drinking water. Exceptions are made when "no significant risk" of human cancer (or "no observable effect" on birth defects at a thousand times the level of exposure) can be proven.

Proposition 65 designates a warning list of 29 substances including such common industrial chemicals as benzene, lead, asbestos, chromium, arsenic, and vinyl chloride; later, 150 other carcinogens and birth-defect toxins will be added, including ethyl alcohol in alcoholic beverages. The governor, who is empowered to issue regulations to enforce the law, may also add ambient cigarette smoke.

There is controversy over what constitutes "significant risk." The governor issued interim regulations stating that, temporarily at least, existing federal Food and Drug Administration safety levels would be accepted for food, drugs, and medical devices. But one of the law's coauthors, David Roe of the Environmental Defense Fund, maintains that the existing federal law isn't tough enough, commenting, *The people of California didn't go to all this trouble just to endorse the existing system."*

What You Can Do to Influence Legislation

Opportunities for public involvement in the development and implementation of environmental laws are numerous. Our intent here is to alert you to the overall legal context of citizen participation in environmental cleanup and change. Specific information on how you can work more effectively as an individual or as part of a citizen's or environmental group is provided in the following chapter, "Eco-Action."

New Legislation

Although there are considerable numbers of laws on the books already, the United States Congress is constantly considering new proposals and amendments to the existing legislation. For example, critical amendments to the Clean Air Act are being hotly debated on Capitol Hill, and bills are pending that would set air-pollution limits for incinerators, make the EPA administrator a cabinet post, designate various wilderness areas, eliminate the CAFE standards, label and/or tax various plastics and products made from CFCs, control indoor air pollution, allow tax credits for expenses of preventing radon contamination, create a new compensation and liability scheme for oil spills, and alter the existing environmental laws in a host of other ways.

The message that a senator or representative hears from his or her constituents does make a difference. Congress works for you (though not, unfortunately, only for you). The box adjacent describes how a law is created.

How the U.S. Legislative Process Works[34]

The basic outline of creating a law is simplicity itself: a bill is introduced by a congressional representative, is referred to and then approved by a committee, passed by the House and Senate, and signed into law by the president. In real life, the process is more complicated.

A bill's chance of passing depends on which of several committees it goes to (the chair of one may support it, the chair of another may not) and on when it is introduced (Congress works on a cycle of two one-year sessions; a bill pending at the end of the first session carries over to the second, but one still pending at the close of the second session must be reintroduced and go through the whole process again).

This delay mechanism is sometimes used by members of Congress to please their constituents by appearing to favor bills they know have no chance of passing!

As they take the long path toward enactment, bills change substantially, first in committee, then when considered by the full House and Senate, and then when representatives from both houses meet to reconcile differences between the House version and the Senate version. House and Senate agreement is reached only after a good deal of "horse trading" in the conference committee, usually composed of the chair and the senior members of the committee which originally handled the bill. A conference committee meets in private session — no public or press is allowed, and no minutes are taken.

The resulting compromise is submitted to both houses on an all-or-nothing basis with no amendments allowed.

The bill is still not home free. It must now be reviewed by the Appropriations Committee which can castrate it by authorizing too little money. Even if it gets through this hurdle intact, a bill can be killed by a president who, instead of using his veto power, may quietly refuse to release the funds appropriated by Congress, thus allowing the appearance of being for an issue while not in fact supporting it.

How to Get Involved

● Write a letter to your congressperson, referring to the bill by its name and number, and summarizing your position and how you would like him or her to vote. (For details on writing to legislators, see chapter 11, p. 263.)

● Your best chance of influencing a congressional bill is before it goes to a *conference* committee – either during public hearings at which testimony is given by scientists, representatives of all interested parties, and other witnesses, or at special meetings where the congressional staff consider alternative proposals. Your own representative can give you information on legislation under review, which committees are responsible, and when hearings are going to take place.

● Even if your representative is not a member of the relevant committee, his or her aides can be very helpful in providing information on legislation.

- Find out when the appropriate committee of Congress is holding an *investigative* or an *oversight* hearing. Tell your representative that you want to attend, and (if you have special expertise) would like to testify.
- Your influence can be greater on state legislation than federal because actions taken at the state level usually involve issues of local concern with which you are more familiar. State legislators are generally quite receptive to your input and local media are usually more accessible than national.

New Legislative Regulations

As we have seen, getting a law on the books is only the first step. It falls to an agency, usually EPA, to translate the broad statutory language into specific rules. Federal agencies cannot announce new regulations without first publishing a proposal in the *Federal Register* for public comment. Although the details of many environmental regulations are highly technical, there is room for important contributions from the public.

As a practical matter, it is next to impossible for you as an individual to check every *Federal Register* (they come out daily) to see if it contains proposed regulations that you might be interested in. But the environmental groups do keep track of EPA's regulatory program and the environmental loose-leaf services (the *Environment Reporter* and the *Environmental Law Reporter*) flag proposed environmental regulations weekly. As a member of an environmental group, you can stay in touch with those working full-time on problems of concern to you and you can become aware of what EPA and other government agencies are working on.

Agency Petitions

You can always simply ask EPA (or any other federal or state agency) to do something, whether it's issue a regulation, attack a general problem, or, most likely, go after a polluter. Many of the federal laws specifically reserve the right of a citizen to petition the agency for action – for example, to cancel a pesticide registration, or to review the safety of a chemical under TSCA. In addition, there is a fallback provision of federal law that requires agencies to entertain petitions for rule making.

A request for agency action can be formal or informal. Don't be afraid just to call up or to send off a letter. In any environmental dispute, you are always way ahead of the game if the state or federal authorities are on your side. As a matter of strategy, common sense, fairness, and, in some cases, statutory requirement, you should go there first. You may well hit a brick wall, but it's worth the try. Also, state and federal agencies can be a vital source of information.

Freedom of Information Act

The Freedom of Information Act (FOIA) makes most agency records available to the public. Many individuals and community groups have used FOIA to reach otherwise unavailable evidence. The Critical Mass Energy Project used FOIA to obtain CIA files detailing a nuclear disaster in the Soviet Union which the agency had withheld from the U.S. public. Friends of the Earth used the act to find out from the Nuclear Regulatory Commission that the Three Mile Island nuclear plant had dumped radioactive water into the Susquehanna River.

Any citizen or group can make a FOIA request; processing fees will generally be waived for individuals and nonprofit groups. To file a FOIA request, telephone the appropriate government agency and ask to whom to address your letter, then begin by stating that you are submitting "a request under the Freedom of Information Act, 5 U.S.C. 522." Be as specific as you can about the documents you want. If you are turned down, the decision can be appealed within the agency and ultimately to the courts.

Citizens' Suits

Most of the federal environmental laws have provisions for citizens' suits. These are of two types. First, any citizen can go to federal court to sue a polluter who is violating the relevant federal law or the terms of its permit. The plaintiff cannot recover monetary damages in a citizens' suit. Relief is limited to an order telling the polluter to comply with the law (though not necessarily immediately), and to pay your costs of bringing the suit, including attorney's fees, and, perhaps, fines. Although fines can be quite hefty, they go to the federal government, not the plaintiff. Sometimes, if a suit is settled out of court, the defendant will make a payment to support environmental-protection projects in the affected area.

The second kind of citizens' suit is not against a polluter but against the EPA administrator. If the administrator fails to do something that the law requires the agency to do, you can sue to force compliance with the statutory mandate. Most of these suits are brought when EPA fails to issue regulations that a statute tells it to promulgate. A suit can be brought only if EPA has a nondiscretionary (mandatory) duty; unfortunately, enforcement is generally not considered nondiscretionary. Thus, the fact that EPA is failing to enforce the environmental laws, either generally or in a specific case, does not make it liable in a citizens' suit.

Permits

As the description of federal laws showed, there are numerous permitting schemes. Large new sources of pollution – incinerators, factories, power plants – must obtain permits under the Clean Air Act; any discharge into the water requires a permit; filling up wetlands requires a permit. This is a vital forum for public opposition to new projects. The permitting process is generally handled by the state environmental agency, though EPA has that responsibility for some permits in some states, and the Corps of Engineers issues permits for fill. Permitting is always a public process. At the least, the agency must give public notice of the application and take written comments. Often a public hearing is held; sometimes there is a full-fledged, triallike proceeding, with witnesses, exhibits, and cross-examination, before an administrative law judge.

Part of the problem is learning about permit applications. The agency will notify people it knows might be interested; you can get on the list. Local citizens' and environmental groups keeping tabs on the agency and its activities will also be aware when a permit application comes up for review and public comment.

Environmental Litigation

The history of the environmental movement since the first Earth Day (1970) has been in large measure the history of environmental litigation. As David Sive, the principal attorney in the Storm King litigation described below, has said, "In no other political and social movement has litigation played such an important and dominant role. Not even close."[35] It is through the courts that the environmental movement has achieved many of its victories (or avoided many possible losses) – defeating destructive projects, halting pollution, ensuring that the government does its job.

Bringing Action

Suppose that you are concerned over water pollution from a factory. As long as you are somehow adversely affected by the factory's actions (living near or in one way or another using or enjoying the water into which the factory discharges), you can bring a lawsuit to force compliance with the Clean Water Act and/or the factory's discharge permit.

Before bringing such an action, consider that it is likely to a long-drawn-out affair that will drain your resources of time, energy, and (depending on whether and how you obtain a lawyer or expert witnesses) money. It's not a project to be undertaken lightly.

Your first step is finding out whether the factory is in compliance. Bear in mind that much pollution is considered to be legal. EPA or, more likely, its state counterpart will have copies of the factory's permit and its discharge-monitoring reports. If they show levels of discharge higher than allowed by the permit (or, of course, if the factory does not have a permit) there has been a violation.

If the factory is in violation, draw it to the attention of the agency and find out what it's doing about it. If the response is unsatisfactory, you may undertake enforcement yourself. You'll be much better off with the support of an environmental or citizens' group and/or an attorney, but neither is a legal requirement. You cannot sue if EPA or the state has itself brought an enforcement action, although you can join the government's lawsuit.

Before filing a lawsuit, you must notify, in writing, the proposed defendant, the state agency, and the federal EPA of your intent to do so. Only after 60 days have elapsed can you file the suit. If you file the suit without having given notice, you run a serious risk of being tossed out of court. The suit should be filed in the federal district court for the area where the factory is located. In a case such as this, there is a strong likelihood of prevailing simply on the strength of the factory's own monitoring reports. However, there must be some proof that the violations are continuing or likely to recur. Under a much-criticized 1987 Supreme Court decision, violations that are wholly in the past will not support a citizens' suit.

The same general principles apply to citizens' suits under the other federal laws, though proving the violation is generally easiest in CWA cases because of the ready availability of comprehensive discharge reports. EPA regulations set out specific procedures for citizens' suits under the different statutes.

Please be advised that on no account should you undertake a citizens' suit using this brief description as your legal guide. You must investigate the legal requirements further, preferably with the assistance of an attorney who has had experience in environmental law.

"Getting Away with Bloody Murder"

The following cases, chosen from thousands of decisions that have been handed down, are intended to give a general idea of the role of private litigation in environmental protection.[36]

There are several broad categories of environmental litigation. There are cases in which one private party sues another to compel it to stop polluting. Consider, for example, the case of *Chesapeake Bay Foundation* v. *Bethlehem Steel Corporation*. As of 1983, an enormous Bethlehem Steel wastewater treatment plant, discharging into the Chesapeake Bay, was operating under an outdated permit that allowed it to discharge 500 million gallons per day (mgd) of waste-water, containing up to 11,860 pounds of oil and grease, 990 pounds of zinc, 454 pounds of chromium, and 51,900 pounds of unspecified solids.

> *"In no other political and social movement has litigation played such an important and dominant role. Not even close."*

There were two problems. First, the permit limits were outdated; new limits reflecting "best practicable technology" were supposed to kick in as of 1979, but Bethlehem and the state of Maryland were locked in endless negotiations over the specifics. Second, the plant was not even meeting the antiquated limits in its permit. Between 1979 and 1983, the plant exceeded even these lax requirements on over 700 occasions, often by a factor of two or three. In the words of the Annapolis *Capitol*, "Bethlehem has been getting away with bloody murder."

In 1984, frustrated by the state's refusal to get tough with Bethlehem, the Chesapeake Bay Foundation and the Natural Resources Defense Council finally sued under the Clean Water Act's citizens'-suit provision. The District Court rejected Bethlehem's arguments that the plaintiffs had no right to sue, had filed too late, and had not given adequate notice of their intent to sue (all typical arguments of defendants in such suits). Relying on Bethlehem's own discharge reports, it ruled that the giant company was liable for over 200 excess discharges during the five years before the suit was brought.[37] The decision did not address the question of remedy. In February 1987, Bethlehem settled out of court for a whopping $1.5 million, which will go to local environmental projects. It also agreed to increase treatment levels and step up monitoring.

The Storm King Landmark

A related type of suit involves a challenge to an as yet unbuilt project – a dam, a high-rise, a subdivision. By going to court challenging the validity of permits, the adequacy of EISs, compliance with environmental standards, or procedural errors, citizens' and environmental groups have prevented construction of untold numbers of harmful projects. The case, generally seen as the watershed environmental lawsuit, falls into this category. In the early 1960s the New York utility Consolidated Edison sought to construct a pumped storage facility on the banks of the Hudson River at Storm King Mountain some 40 miles north of New York City. Storm King is located, in the words of the court, "in an area of unique beauty and major historical significance . . . offer[ing] one of the finest pieces of river scenery in the world."[38] Not only would the project have destroyed this pristine natural area, but it raised serious concerns over impacts on fish supplies in the river. All but ignoring the objections of environmentalists, the Federal Power Commission (FPC) granted Con Ed the necessary permit.

249

Led by the Scenic Hudson Preservation Conference, environmentalists challenged the decision in federal court. The court agreed that the FPC had failed to adequately consider environmental impacts – at the time quite a novel proposition – or alternatives.[39] After lengthy administrative proceedings, the FPC again granted the permit, and Scenic Hudson again went to court. This time, it lost, and the Supreme Court refused to hear an appeal.[40] But the fight was not over. Scenic Hudson and a fishermen's group went back to the FPC, arguing that the proceedings had to be reopened because the commission had failed to take into account the project's impacts on fish. The FPC considered the matter closed; again the project's opponents went to court; and again the court ordered the FPC to reconsider.[41]

> *. . . EPA often finds itself defending regulation against industry charges that it is too strict and environmentalist challenges that it is too lax.*

Meanwhile, Scenic Hudson was also contending that the project required a CWA Section 404 permit from the Army Corps of Engineers – a permit it did not have. When both Con Ed and the corps disagreed about the need for a permit, Scenic Hudson went to court again. The district court ruled that the project would need a permit, and the court of appeals affirmed.[42] This meant yet further administrative proceedings.

Finally, with various administrative and judicial matters still pending, all parties agreed to negotiate. With former EPA Administrator Russell Train as mediator, the parties worked out an agreement bringing the long struggle to a close. As part of the December 1980 agreement, Con Ed forfeited its FPC license, and it and other utilities agreed to establish a fish hatchery, reduce summer water withdrawals from the Hudson, endow a river-research organization, and pay their adversaries' attorney's fees. All of this was only possible because of the opponents' extraordinary perseverance and the use of the courts to keep the project at bay. Storm King Mountain remains one of the highlights of the train ride between New York City and Albany, still one of the world's most spectacular.

Coming to the Government's Defense

In the Storm King case, environmentalists challenged the government's decision to let the project go ahead. Sometimes, the government *denies* a permit (often as a result of the public input in the permitting process) and is hauled into court by the disappointed applicant. In this situation, environmental groups will often join the suit to defend the government's decision – as a show of support, to add weight to the government's case, because of doubts as to the conviction with which the government will argue its case, or to offer the court a rationale that may go further than the government wants to go.

Take the efforts of the Pyramid Corporation to pave over 50 acres of wetlands known as Sweedens Swamp to build a million-square-foot shopping mall in Attleboro, Mass. It received the Corps of Engineers' OK. EPA vetoed the permit, however, because Pyramid had passed up an alternative site that would have involved no wetlands loss. Pyramid then sued EPA – not once but three times: first in Washington, trying to prevent EPA from reviewing the permit;[43] then in Boston, arguing that EPA's veto was invalid because of improper procedures;[44] then in upstate New York, challenging EPA's veto on the merits.[45] Each time it filed suit a dozen environmental groups intervened as defendants, filing briefs and arguing in support of EPA. Each time, the court upheld EPA's action. When Pyramid appealed its final defeat, the groups again participated, and again Pyramid lost.[46] In March 1989, the Supreme Court refused Pyramid's request that it hear the case.[47] Sweedens Swamp remains intact.

Challenging Inadequate Regulations

Another important part of the environmental docket consists of challenges to inadequate regulations. During 1988, for example, the courts struck down, among others: certain EPA regulations allowing plants to disperse pollutants by using skyscraper smokestacks rather than reducing the amount of pollution emitted; DOI regulations allowing "flexible" compliance with the surface mining law; performance standards under the CWA that EPA had set without considering no-discharge, in-house recycling technologies; and EPA's decisions to exempt certain hazardous-mining wastes and used oil from regulation under RCRA.

Bear in mind that regulations can be attacked from two sides. Indeed, EPA often finds itself defending regulation against industry charges that it is too strict and environmentalist challenges that it is too lax. In 1989, for example, extensive CWA regulations setting new limits for the discharge of toxics were upheld, almost in their entirety, against challenges by environmental groups and by industry. Each can claim at least partial victory.

Helping Set EPA's Agenda

Many of the government's sins are ones of omission. Frequently, environmental groups sue EPA for just sitting on its hands. Most people would agree that in fact EPA simply does not have the resources to do everything Congress tells it to. As a result, environmental priorities are determined in a somewhat peculiar way: EPA decides to do some of what it is told to do; environmentalists sue it to do another portion; and the rest is left undone. In this roundabout way, the environmental community helps set EPA's agenda. It does so with some care and discretion. For example, in 1977 Congress set limits on the extent to which air quality could deteriorate in areas meeting the national standards for sulfur dioxide and particulate matter. It told EPA to write regulations developing similar limits for the other pollutants for which there are national standards.[48] The regulations were due in 1979; by 1984 EPA still had not produced them. So the Sierra Club and others sued. But the plaintiffs did not argue that EPA had to issue regulations for each of the national standards (which is what the statute says). The suit was limited to the regulations for nitrogen oxides, which the plaintiffs considered the most important. The suit was successful,[49] and pursuant to court order EPA subsequently issued the regulations for NO_x.

Banning DDT

In the NOx suit, there was an explicit congressional command. Where Congress has instead left the agency some discretion, its decisions are much harder to attack. The plaintiff generally has to show that the agency inaction (for example, refusal to regulate a certain toxic substance or denial of a petition to cancel registration of a pesticide) is wholly unjustifiable – to use the legal term of art, "arbitrary, capricious, or an abuse of discretion." This is a difficult but not impossible burden.

Consider the lengthy proceedings that led finally to the banning of DDT. The major focus of Rachel Carson's *Silent Spring*, DDT received increasing attention during the 1960s for its extensive harm to wildlife and threat to human health. In October 1969, the Environmental Defense Fund and others petitioned the secretary of agriculture to take DDT off the market. The secretary began limited proceedings, requested further comment, and ignored EDF's request that all uses of DDT be suspended pending a final decision. In the face of this meager response, EDF went to court. In a precedent-setting 1970 decision,[50] the U.S. Court of Appeals for the D.C. circuit held that (1) environmental groups do have access to the courts to challenge such (in)action by the government and (2) the secretary at least had to explain himself. So the matter returned to the secretary, who said that while DDT was dangerous, further study was needed before he could make a decision. EDF sued

> *It is because the courts have, by and large, taken the environmental laws seriously that they are not just empty words on dusty pages.*

again. This time the court, relying on the Secretary's own findings, ordered EPA (which had since taken over administration of the pesticide program) to begin an administrative proceeding in which the manufacturers would have the burden of showing that DDT was in fact safe.[51] There followed a yearlong proceeding ending in the almost total cancellation of registered uses of DDT.

That was not an end to the matter; again the case returned to court, with EDF arguing that the decision did not go far enough because it allowed some limited use, and industry arguing that it had gone much too far. This time the court, ruling in 1973, upheld the agency's decision.[52] *Without this judicial oversight, who knows when, if ever, the secretary of agriculture or EPA would have acknowledged the force of its own evidence.*[53]

Rewriting the Law

Sometimes, litigation against EPA is in turn translated into statutory requirements. For example, in the early 1970s the Sierra Club, relying entirely on a statement in the preamble to the Clean Air Act to the effect that one of the act's purposes was to "maintain" air quality, successfully sought a federal court order requiring EPA to develop a regulatory program that would prevent the deterioration of air quality in areas that already met the ambient-air standards.[54] Those standards, the club argued, should not become an invitation to pollute. Under the court order, EPA developed the complex "prevention of significant deterioration" program, which is the source, among other things, of the Clean Air Act's Best Available Control Technology (BACT) requirement for new facilities. In the 1977 amendments, Congress wrote the EPA program into the Clean Air Act almost without change.

A similar course of events occurred with regard to the regulation of toxic pollutants under the Clean Water Act. The 1972 act told EPA to develop health-based discharge limits for toxic pollutants. Overwhelmed by the magnitude of the task and the scientific uncertainties it raised, EPA got nowhere, leaving toxics essentially unregulated. NRDC sued. The result was a consent decree requiring EPA to include toxics in the existing-technology-based effluent limitation regulations.[55] EPA was required to develop standards reflecting the best available technology for controlling 65 different toxic pollutants. In the 1977 CWA amendments, Congress essentially codified the decree, and EPA has now developed the regulations, much to industry's dismay.

The Role of the Courts

The above-cited cases indicate the importance and possibilities of environmental litigation. However, lawsuits are not always successful. For example, the northeastern states and several of the major environmental groups have suffered one defeat after another in suits brought to force EPA to use the existing Clean Air Act to control acid rain. And too many times litigants have learned the hard way that there is still many a slip between cup and lip even after a judge has ruled in their favor. The Bethlehem Steel plant that was the subject of the suit described on p. 249, for example, had already been hit with a $250,000 fine and was under a court order to comply with its permit by 1979.

Lawsuits can be expensive and they take a long time. They are certainly not, nor should they be, the only weapon the environmental movement has. And the importance of litigation has perhaps begun to fade somewhat now that a number of important victories have been won, the movement has matured, the issues have become more complex, and the judiciary, by and large, is more hostile to environmental litigants.

Yet in the modern administrative state, with its far-flung bureaucracy, the courts have a vital role to play in overseeing EPA and other agencies. And there are times when it really takes a court order to stop a project or bring a halt to illegal pollution. Resort to the courts, actual or threatened, remains absolutely indispensable to ensure that both the regulators and those they regulate turn square corners, living up to their legal obligations. It is because the courts have, by and large, taken the environmental laws seriously that they are not just empty words on dusty pages.

How You Can Use the Law to Bring about Environmental and Social Change

● Educate yourself on the laws relating to the environment by following up the sources provided in "Resources" on the following page.
● Join one of the environmental or citizens' groups that are most actively engaged in environmental litigation. These include Public Citizen, the Sierra Club, the Environmental Defense fund, the Natural Resources Defense Council, the National Audubon Society, and the National Wildlife Federation.
● Support Earth First!, the Citizen's Clearinghouse for Hazardous Waste, Sea Shepherd, Greenpeace, and other high-profile activist organizations that are frequently the target of harassment (and sometimes legal action) by government and industry.
● Find out about and support single-issue groups that are involved in legal action in your own district or sphere of interest.
● It is important to keep in mind that you should consult with a lawyer at all times when you are thinking of taking legal action.
● For more specifics on how you can use the process of law to effect environmental cleanup and change, see the next chapter, "Eco-Action."

RESOURCES

1. U.S. Government

Distribution of Congressional Publications

Senate bills, reports, and documents are distributed through the Senate Documents Room, B-04, Hart Senate Office Building, Washington, DC 20510. House equivalents can be obtained from the House Documents Room, H-226, U.S. Capitol, Washington, DC 20515. Public laws are distributed by both document rooms.

Telephone inquiries on the status of legislative items may be made by calling the Senate room at (202) 224-7860 or the House room at (202) 225-3456.

— Daily proceedings of Congress are published in the *Congressional Record*.

To find out the status of a House bill, telephone (202) 225-1772; for a Senate bill, (202) 224-2971.

To receive copies of bills, write (enclosing self-addressed mailing label) to either House Documents Room, H-226, or Senate Documents Room, S-325, U.S. Capitol, Washington, DC 20510.

House Appropriations Committee, H-218, U.S. Capitol, Washington, DC 20510.

Senate Appropriations Committee, 118 Dirksen Senate Office Building, U.S. Capitol, Washington, DC 20510.

— *U.S. Government Printing Office*, Superintendent of Documents, Washington, DC 20402; (202) 275-3030. Sells copies of all U.S. laws, treaties, and implementing regulations. Copies of these documents may also be obtained from the main or regional offices of the federal agency responsible for enforcement.

— *The EPA Public Information Center*, 401 M Street SW, Washington, DC 20460; (202) 382-2080. Will provide copies of laws of which EPA is the regulatory agency, as well as a mine of information on all EPA-related activities.

— *The RCRA Hotline* — (800) 424-9346 or (202) 382-800 — provides information about hazardous waste, EPA's regulatory activities, and legal obligations.

2. State Laws

— Documents on state environmental legislation can be obtained from the individual state governments, most of which have departments of environmental protection or natural resources. Most state environmental laws are collected in the *Environmental Reporter*.

3. International

— *Law of the Sea Treaty*, Secretariat, United Nations, Room 1827A, New York, NY 10017.

4. Professional and Environmental Associations

Litigation is undertaken by a wide variety of local, regional, and national organizations, some formed expressly for the purpose of bringing an individual suit. Of the national groups, four have particularly extensive dockets: EDF, NRDC, Sierra Club, and the National Wildlife Federation.

— *Antarctica Project*, 1845 Calvert Street NW, Washington, DC, 20009.

— *Center for Environmental Education*, 1725 De Sales Street NW, Washington, DC 20036; (202) 429-5609. Devoted to marine conservation and the fight against illegal wildlife trading.

— *Center for the Study of Responsive Law*, 2000 P Street NW, Washington, DC 20036.

— *Citizens for Ocean Law*, 1601 Connecticut Avenue NW, Washington, DC 20009.

— *Environmental Defense Fund*, 257 Park Avenue South, New York, NY 10010; (212) 505-2100.

— *Environmental Law Institute*, 1616 P Street NW, Washington, DC 20036. Publishes the *Environmental Law Reporter* and the *National Wetlands Newsletter*, books, and research materials. It also runs a continuing legal-education program.

— *The Environmental Litigation Fund*, P.O. Box 10836, Eugene, OR 97440; (503) 683-1378. The fund is a project of Earth Island Institute.

— *League of Women Voters Education Fund*, 1730 M Street NW, Washington, DC 20036; (202) 429-1965. Concerned with citizens' right-to-know, election laws, voting rights, government processes, and other issues.

— *National Wildlife Federation*, 1400 Sixteenth Street NW, Washington, DC 20036; (202) 797-6800.

— *Natural Resources Defense Council*, 40 West 20th Street, New York, NY 10011; (212) 727-2700.

— *Sierra Club Legal Defense Fund*, 2044 Fillmore Street, San Francisco, CA 94115.

5. Further Reading

— *Clean Coal/Dirty Air, or How the Clean Air Act Became a Multibillion Dollar Bail-Out for the High-Sulfur Coal Producers and What Should Be Done About It*, Bruce Ackerman and William Hassler. New Haven: Yale University Press, 1981.

— *Community Relations in Superfund*, EPA/540/G-88/002. Washington, D.C.: EPA Office of Emergency and Remedial Response, 1988.

— *Crossroads: Environmental Priorities for the Future*, edited by Peter Borrelli (contains "Environmentalists at Law," Frederic P. Sutherland and Vawter Parker; and "Legal Eagles," Tom Turner). Washington, D.C.: Island Press, 1988.

— *Directory of State Environmental Agencies*, edited by Kathryn Hubler and Timothy Henderson. Washington, D.C.: Environmental Law Institute, 1989.

— *Dumpsite Cleanups: A Citizen's Guide to the Superfund Program*. Washington, D.C.: Environmental Defense Fund, 1983.

— *Dynamos and Virgins*, David Roe. New York: Random House, 1984.

— *The Environmental Impact Statement Process*, Neil Orloff. Washington, D.C.: Information Resources Press, 1978.

— *Environmental Law — Twenty Years Later*, J. William Futtrell. Washington, D.C.: Island Press, 1988.

— *Environmental Law in a Nutshell*, Roger Findley and Daniel Farber. St. Paul: West, 1988.

— *Environmental Law Reporter* (monthly reporting service on environmental issues), Environmental Law Institute, Washington, D.C.

— *The Evolution of Wildlife Law*, Michael Bean. New York: Praeger, 1983.

— *Green Justice: The Environment and the Courts*, Thomas More Hoban and Richard Oliver Brooks. Boulder, Colo.: Westview, 1987.

— *A Guide to the Clean Water Act Amendments*, OPA 129/8. Washington, D.C.: EPA Office of Public Awareness, 1988.

— *Handbook on Environmental Law*, William Rodgers. St. Paul: West, 1984.

— *How You Can Influence Congress*, George Anderson and Everett Sentman. New York: E.P. Dutton, 1979.

— *Law of Environmental Protection*, Sheldon Novick, Margaret Mellon, and Donald Stever, editors. New York: Clark Boardman, 1987.

— *Legislative Sourcebook on Toxics*, edited by David Jones and Jeffrey Tryens. Washington, D.C.: National Center for Policy Alternatives, 1986.

— *Managing the Commons*, Garrett Hardin and John Baden. New York: W.H. Freeman, 1977.

— *Resolving Environmental Disputes: A Decade of Experience*, Gail Bingham. Washington, D.C.: Conservation Foundation, 1986.

— *Shutdown Strategies: Citizen Efforts to Close Down Nuclear Power Plants*, Joseph Kriesberg. Washington, D.C.: Public Citizen Critical Mass Energy Project, 1988.

— *U.S. Environmental Laws*. Washington, D.C.: Bureau of National Affairs, 1988. Indispensable 874-page documentation of the major environmental legislation.

ENDNOTES

1. Garret Hardin, "The Tragedy of the Commons," *Science* 162:1243 (1968).
2. For speculation on why environmental protection rose to such sudden political prominence, see Council on Environmental Quality, *Tenth Annual Report* (Washington, D.C.:1979), pp. 1-15.
3. The Acts of Congress are scattered through the United States Code, which is the official compilation of the laws of the United States. There are two annotated versions of the U.S. Code, with citations to commentary and relevant judicial opinions: the *United States Code Annotated* and the *United States Code Service*. All three versions can be found in any law library. The U.S. Code is divided into "titles," and citations of the provisions of the code identify the title and the section number within it. The section numbers in the U.S. Code do not correspond to the section numbers of the acts as passed by Congress. Thus, 304 of the Clean Air Act, the citizens' suit provision, is codified at 7604 of title 42 of the U.S. Code, cited as 42 U.S.C. 7604.

    The federal environmental laws are also reproduced in two one-volume anthologies: *U.S. Environmental Laws* (Washington, DC: Bureau of National Affairs) and *Selected Environmental Law Statutes* (St. Paul: West Publishing Co.). The first of these is both more comprehensive and significantly more expensive. In addition, two loose-leaf services reproduce the text of the federal laws and also include commentary, reports on recent developments, and the text of recent court decisions: *Environment Reporter* (Washington, D.C.: Bureau of National Affairs) (weekly updates) and *Environmental Law Reporter* (Washington, D.C.: Environmental Law Institute; monthly updates, with a one-page weekly newsletter). Most law libraries subscribe to both.
4. 42 U.S.C. §§ 4321-4347.
5. 42 U.S.C. §§ 7401-7642.
6. 33 U.S.C. §§ 1251-1376.
7. 42 U.S.C. §§ 300f to 300j-11.
8. 42 U.S.C. §§ 6901-6987.
9. 42 U.S.C. §§ 9601-9675.
10. 42 U.S.C. §§ 11001-11050.
11. 30 U.S.C. §§ 1201-1328.
12. 15 U.S.C. §§ 2601-2629.
13. 7 U.S.C. §§ 136-136y.
14. 16 U.S.C. §§ 1531-1542.
15. Among others, see the Wilderness Act of 1964, 16 U.S.C. §§ 1131-1136; Wild Free-Roaming Horses and Burros Act, 16 U.S.C. §§ 1331-1340; Outer Continental Shelf Lands Act, 43 U.S.C. §§ 1331-1343; National Wildlife Refuge System Administration Act, 16 U.S.C. §§ 668dd-668ee; and National Forest Management Act, 16 U.S.C. §§ 1601-1614.
16. 16 U.S.C. §§ 1361-1407.
17. 33 U.S.C. §§ 1401-1434.
18. 33 U.S.C. §§ 1221-1236.
19. 33 U.S.C. §§ 1371-1387.
20. 33 U.S.C. §§ 1901-1912.
21. 42 U.S.C. §§ 2011-2296.
22. 42 U.S.C. § 2210.
23. 42 U.S.C. §§ 10101-10270.
24. 42 U.S.C. §§ 2021a-2021j.
25. 16 U.S.C. §§ 824a-1 to 824a-3, 2701-2708.
26. 42 U.S.C. § 6201.
27. 18 U.S.C. §§ 2001-20__.
28. 18 U.S.C. § 2013, and elsewhere.
29. Clean Air Act § 108(a)(1), 42 U.S.C. § 7408(a)(1).
30. Clean Air Act § 109(b), 42 U.S.C. § 7409(b).

31. Resource Conservation and Recovery Act § 3004(a), 42 U.S.C. § 6924(a).

32. Regulations are officially published in the *Code of Federal Regulations* and most environmental regulations are also collected in the *Environment Reporter*. The annotated versions of the U.S. Code include cross references to relevant regulations.

33. For a summary of the state baby NEPAs, with references to legal authorities, significant cases, and state contacts, see the Special Report in appendix C of the 18th and 19th annual report of the Council on Environmental Quality, *Environmental Quality 1987-1988*, Washington, D.C., 1989.

34. Based on "How Does the Legislative Process Work ?" in G. Tyler Miller, *Living in the Environment*, Belmont, Calif.: Wadsworth, 1979, pp. E138-139, and *The Citizen's Guide to the Ocean*, Washington, D.C.: Center for Environmental Education, 1985, pp. 129-141.

35. Tom Turner, "The Legal Eagles," in Peter Borrelli, ed., *Crossroads: Environmental Priorities for the Future* (Washington, D.C.: Island Press, 1988), p. 53.

36. We do not address lawsuits by the government. As the previous discussion on enforcement suggested, such litigation is extraordinarily important. In general, EPA has the authority to order compliance, and under some statutes it can impose fines. If these are ignored or are insufficient to compel compliance, EPA must go to court. If it thinks a lawsuit is in order, it refers the matter to the Department of Justice which decides whether or not to bring a case.

Most of the environmental laws have provisions for both civil and criminal penalties. Civil-enforcement actions lead (if successful) to an injunction ordering the polluter to obey the law and perhaps to pay some fines. These cases are handled by the Justice Department, with assistance from EPA attorneys. Criminal prosecutions are handled solely by the Justice Department. Although they remain the exception, criminal prosecutions are slowly increasing. Certainly a lot of people sat up and took notice when, in April 1989, a Halley, Fla. father and son were each sentenced to 21 months in prison without possibility of parole for filling wetlands without a permit and in July 1989, when a Bucks County, Pa. developer was sentenced to 3 years in prison and a $202,000 fine for the same crime.

37. *Chesapeake Bay Foundation* v. *Bethlehem Steel Corp.*, 608 F. Supp. 440 (D. Md. 1985).

38. *Scenic Hudson Preservation Conference* v. *Federal Power Commission*, 354 F.2d 608 (2d Cir. 1965).

39. Ibid.

40. *Scenic Hudson Preservation Conference* v. *Federal Power Commission*, 453 F.2d 463 (2d Cir. 1971), reh'g en banc denied by an equally divided court, 453 F.2d 494, cert. denied, 407 U.S. 926 (1972).

41. *Hudson River Fisherman's Assn* v. *Federal Power Commission*, 498 F.2d 827 (2d Cir. 1974).

42. *Scenic Hudson Preservation Conference* v. *Calloway*, 370 F. Supp. 162 (S.D.N.Y. 1973), aff'd, 499 F.2d 127 (2d Cir. 1974).

43. *Newport Galleria Group* v. *Deland*, 618 F. Supp. 1179 (D.D.C. 1985).

44. *Bersani* v. *Deland*, 640 F. Supp. 716 (D. Mass. 1986).

45. *Bersani* v. *EPA*, 674 F. Supp. 405 (N.D.N.Y. 1987).

46. *Bersani* v. *Robichaud*, 850 F.2d 36 (2d Cir. 1988).

47. *Bersani* v. *USEPA*, __ U.S. __, 109 S.Ct. 1556 (1989).

48. Clean Air Act § 166, 42 U.S.C. § 7476.

49. *Sierra Club* v. *Thomas*, 658 F. Supp. 165 (N.D. Cal. 1985).

50. *Environmental Defense Fund* v. *Hardin*, 428 F.2d 1093 (D.C. Cir. 1970).

51. *Environmental Defense Fund* v. *Ruckelshaus*, 439 F.2d 584 (D.C. Cir. 1971).

52. *Environmental Defense Fund* v. *EPA*, 489 F.2d 1247 (D.C. Cir. 1973).

53. The foregoing gives just the outlines of a lengthy and multifaceted effort. For the full story, see Dunlop, *DDT*.

54. *Sierra Club* v. *Ruckelshaus*, 344 F. Supp. 253 (D.D.C. 1972), affirmed by an equally divided Court, 412 U.S. 541 (1973).

55. *NRDC* v. *Train*, 8 Envt. Rep. Cases (BNA) 2120 (D.D.C. 1976), reversed in part on other grounds, 561 F.2d 904 (D.C. Cir. 1977).

11

ECO-ACTION

Organizing for Environmental Change

"The flow from knowledge to action draws upon the complete person with his or her catalyst and synergistic potential." – Ralph Nader

On May 15, 1989, the American apple industry announced it would stop using Alar, a chemical sprayed on apples (and other produce) to enhance color and prolong shelf life. The action came as a consequence not of government intervention but of consumer power in the marketplace – people refusing to buy produce they consider harmful to their health – and pressure by environmental and activist organizations.

The Natural Resources Defense Council, Public Citizen, Consumers Union, Americans for Safe Food, the National Coalition against Misuse of Pesticides, and other groups alerted the media and the public to the threat of Alar and other dangerous chemicals in our food. It was this initiative (and the widespread public response) that brought about the apple industry's decision. As the following case history shows, it involved a long and complex process.

Alar Chronology

1963: Initial registration by Uniroyal.

1964: Registered for use on apples.

1973 to 1984: Five separate studies, including National Cancer Institute, U.S. Air Force, and University of Nebraska, find link between Alar and cancers in laboratory animals.

1980: EPA notifies Uniroyal that a "special review" of Alar may be conducted, but this is delayed after six closed-door meetings of the two parties. Delay is challenged in litigation by NRDC.

July 1984: EPA finally initiates "special review." Uniroyal challenges tests by others as invalid.

December 1984: Welch's Grape Juices refuses to accept Alar-treated grapes.

September 1985: EPA says it is "conducting an expedited cancellation for food uses of daminozide." Federal Insecticide, Fungicide, and Rodenticide Act Science Advisory Board concludes Alar data were flawed. Still no testing done by Uniroyal.

1986: January – EPA reverses position, deciding not to ban Alar, but requires Uniroyal to conduct studies.

April – EPA proposes reduction in Alar residue level in apples.

May – American Academy of Pediatrics urges EPA to ban Alar. Massachusetts and Maine act to ban Alar in baby foods and other apple products.

July – NRDC, Public Citizen, et al. petition EPA to ban Alar.

October – Reviewing samples of apples collected by Uniroyal, EPA finds 87 percent have Alar residues, 73 percent have UDMH.

November – EPA study finds UDMH in most processed products sampled.

Summer/fall – In response to public concern some supermarkets and food manufacturers stop accepting Alar-treated apples.

1987: January – EPA classifies Alar as a probable human carcinogen.

March – NRDC et al. file suit against EPA in U.S. Court of Appeals on the grounds that EPA was violating the Food and Cosmetic Act by allowing residues of Alar in food.

1988: February – Independent lab survey finds 30 percent of apples tested from one supermarket chain contain Alar, despite chain's claim they had not accepted Alar-treated apples.

October – Court of Appeals dismisses NRDC case on jurisdictional grounds.

1989: January – EPA finds "inescapable and direct correlation" between UDMH and "life-threatening tumors," but delays action for 18 more months.

February – NRDC publishes *Intolerable Risk: Pesticides in our Children's Food*, identifying that average exposure to UDMH may cause one cancer case for every 4,200 children exposed by the age of six – *240 times* the cancer risk considered "acceptable" by EPA – after a full lifetime of exposure.

May – U.S. apple industry says it will stop using Alar by fall 1989.

June – Uniroyal agrees to stop marketing Alar in the U.S., but continues manufacture for sales internationally.

Cause for Alar(m)

Alar is the trade name of daminozide, a "plant growth regulator" manufactured by Uniroyal and used on apples as well as peanuts, cherries, and other fruits and vegetables. It contains a chemical contaminant, UDMH, which has been shown in numerous studies to be a potent carcinogen.

Formation of UDMH is accelerated when apples sprayed with Alar are heated or processed, as, for example, in apple juice and apple sauce – products particularly consumed by pre-school children, who are 240 times more likely than adults to get cancer from the chemical.[1]

The Food-Chain Gang

As the Alar story shows, there's no quick, easy way to get the harmful chemicals out of our food. Any effort faces determined resistance from a combination of powerful interests and bureaucratic inertia.

The main opposition comes from manufacturers, who sell $7 billion worth of farm chemicals annually, from agribusinesses that buy the chemicals, and from processors and distributors who supply us with our daily bread – and apples.[2] Sometimes called the "food-chain gang," these include giant corporations whose names you associate with food (Sunkist, Kraft-General Foods, Nestle) and others you don't (Exxon, Union Carbide, Du Pont, Dow Chemical, and Uniroyal). Publication of NRDC's *Intolerable Risk* in February 1989 threatened the huge profits made by Uniroyal and other pesticide makers. Their immediate response was a multi-million-dollar media campaign to discredit the report.

More insidious is the ongoing strategy of the food industry to foil every attempt at overhauling pesticide regulation and to keep EPA as weak as possible. This includes product and institutional advertising, funding of public TV and radio programs, political-campaign contributions, financing propesticide research programs, expense-paid lobbying trips, and, when necessary, good old-fashioned arm twisting.

Your Eco-Action Guide

Beyond Bandaids

Presenting your case in the face of formidable opposition from the food industry and other powerful interests may at first look like David taking on Goliath. However, your chances of winning are greatly enhanced if you know the basics of environmental judo, how to turn apparent weakness into a strategy of winning. It involves two important rules:

1. Get to the roots of the problem. The symptoms of pollution are what we first perceive and often focus on (putting scrubbers on smokestacks to clean up coal smoke), instead of getting to the cause (burning coal) and eliminating it (by switching to clean fuel or, better still, using conservation to make the power plant unnecessary).

2. Be prepared to make changes. The health of a system depends on its ability to change. So long as a biological, political, or energy system responds to its environment, it stays healthy. When it doesn't respond, it gets sick – that is, it pollutes. To bring a sick system back to health, we must get it back in harmony with the environment. If we want clean air, clean water, safe food, or accountable politics, we have to remove the underlying causes of the pollution. This means changing unhealthy systems and institutions and, in so doing, we will change ourselves. Like charity, the process of protecting and cleaning up the environment begins at home.

The following is a short, do-it-yourself manual for starting the process – ECO-ACTION. The key principles of eco-action are: *get the facts; join forces; use the law; then take action*.

A. Getting the Facts

Reliable information is the starting point of any effective action. Here are seven ways you can develop your own investigative power:

1.   Begin at home. Firsthand observation is your best source. Look out for signs of pollution and unexpected changes in the local environment. You can often see or smell bad air. Unseasonable yellowing of trees and plants usually means ecological disturbance. Unexplained ailments – coughing, eye watering, intestinal upsets – are often environmentally induced.

2.   Connect symptoms with causes. Foul-tasting water can come from a leaking gasoline tank, a toxic-waste dump, or other outside contaminants. The persistent noise of helicopters overhead might mean pesticide spraying in your area.

3.   Keep a diary of events you may need to know about later in a bound composition book. Keep notes on everything, from phone conversations to minutes of meetings. If possible, document evidence with photographs (Polaroids are easy). Tape conversations, interviews, and meetings. Start an *Eco-Action* file on your word processor.

4.   Start local. There's a mine of information in your library, town hall, public-health department, and other local agencies. In most cases officials are glad to help, especially if you offer to do some of the legwork. They will also get you information from other libraries or from state and federal agencies.

5.   Diversify your sources. Use newspapers, magazines, TV, and radio to get a general picture and for leads to other sources. These include public documents – court transcripts, congressional hearings, state legislative findings, utility reports – and corporate data such as annual reports, technical papers, periodicals, brochures, even press releases.

By piecing together information from all these sources you can find out what is and what is not known about a subject.

6.   Compare findings. Share your concerns and findings with friends and neighbors. They may have additional facts that will give a different perspective or reinforce your position.

7.   Reach out. If you think you have a case, speak out in your community – at PTA meetings and other events. Ask questions.

B. Joining Forces

A one-person band can make only so much music. Joining with others – in an existing group or forming a new one makes your voice count for more, and begins the process of building a network.

Pay your dues in money and time. The act of joining an organization is a commitment to support its program and a necessary financial contribution in the

How to Write an Effective Letter to a Legislator

The right to participate in the political process is one of the most important freedoms we have. One easy way to do this is by communicating your position on issues with your elected officials.

1. Address it correctly:

a.
> *The President*
> *The White House*
> *1600 Pennsylvania Avenue NW*
> *Washington, DC 20500*
>
> *Dear Mr. President:*

b.
> *The Honorable............*
> *U.S. Senate*
> *Washington, DC 20515*
>
> *Dear Senator............:*

c.
> *The Honorable............*
> *U.S. House of Representatives*
> *Washington, DC 20515*
>
> *Dear Representative...............:*

2. Write first to your own representative and then to the chair or members of the committee dealing with the legislation you are interested in.

3. Identify by name and number the bill that deals with the subject you are writing about – e.g., *Global Warming Prevention Act* (HR 1078) proposed by Representative Claudine Schneider, Republican of Rhode Island.

4. Keep it brief. Politicians have short attention spans. Summarize your points and try to confine them to one page.

5. Be personal. Identify yourself. Write in your own words. Don't send a form letter. Give your own reasons for supporting or opposing a piece of legislation.

6. Follow up. You will almost always get a reply, but it most likely will be a form letter. If you are not satisfied with it, write another letter or, if time is short, send a telegram or make a phone call.

7. Be courteous. Don't threaten. When appropriate, thank your legislator for taking positive action.

8. Phone numbers: The President: (202) 456-1414; U.S. Senate; (202) 224-3121; House of Representatives (202) 456-1414.

9. For details on how legislation gets passed, see chapter 10, p. 245.

10. Get others to write as well; there is strength in numbers.

costly fight against corporations that spend billions of dollars to protect *their* interests. The joint contributions of the food industries to congressional candidates for 1985-86, for instance, came to $6,533,937 compared with $361,524 of political-action contributions from the leading environmental organizations.[3] However, doing something for the environment doesn't just mean writing a check, it means getting involved with other people to undertake a specific task or project. It can be as simple as stuffing envelopes for a mailing, as complex as working on a lawsuit against a major polluter.

> *Join, support, and volunteer your time to organizations, groups, and publications working on issues that are important to you.*

Increase your clout. In joining a citizens' or environmental group, you gain access to larger resources of research, education, and organizational know-how. Your membership is a commitment to the group's goals. It also helps the group to grow. As you'll see below, the group can often strengthen its clout by forming coalitions with other ones.

Main Types of Citizen and Environmental Organizations

The kind of group(s) you join depends on your interests and concerns. Here are some of the options:

Community Groups: PTAs, work and trade associations, and church groups are all good places to start. Most are now environmentally minded or will respond to your concerns about Alar, lead in water, radon, toxic-waste dumps, and other issues.

Single-issue Groups: They range from large national and regional organizations such as the *Citizen's Clearinghouse for Hazardous Waste*, the *Rainforest Action Network* (whose action on Burger King forced its owner, the Pillsbury Corporation, to sever its contracts for Central American beef raised on land cleared from rain forests), and the *Northwest Coalition for Alternatives to Pesticides* to small local committees like WARD (Warwick Against Radioactive Dump), reported in "The Rad Dirt Victory," p. 170).

Multi-issue Groups: In terms of membership size the leading environmental groups are: *World Wildlife Fund,* 6 million worldwide (of which 680,000 in the U.S.); *National Wildlife Federation,* 5.8 million members; *Greenpeace,* 2.5 million members worldwide (1 million in the U.S.); *U.S. Public Interest Research Group,* 1 million members; *National Audubon Society,* 550,000 members; *Sierra Club,* and *Nature Conservancy* – 440,000 members each; *Environmental Defense Fund, Natural Resources Defence Council, Wilderness Society,* the *Cousteau Society,* and *Public Citizen* – all about 100,000 members each.

How They Work: Generally speaking, the *World Wildlife Fund,* the *National Wildlife Federation,* the *Audubon Society,* the *Wilderness Society,* and the *Nature Conservancy* appeal to a broad constituency of nature conservation and wildlife lovers. They put out excellent publications, run educational programs, initiate litigation, and support research projects on important environmental and ecological issues, nationally and internationally.

Greenpeace and *Earth First!* (which has no formal membership organization) are the most action-oriented groups. Greenpeace is an international direct-action organization with its U.S. headquarters in Washington, D.C. Its actions, mostly carried out under extremely hazardous conditions, protest nuclear-weapons testing, toxic-waste dumping, illegal whaling, the destruction of Antarctica, and other critical issues. Greenpeace action attracts considerable media attention and often violent reaction from its opponents, as when French secret agents blew up its ship *Rainbow Warrior*. (For more on Greenpeace and Earth First!, see "Ecotage," pp. 278-281.)

U.S. Public Interest Research Group (USPIRG) is an association of 18 state groups directed mainly by college students. They combine research with grass-roots organizing and legislative lobbying to bring about social change through action on important issues such as water pollution, bottle bills, and garbage recycling. (For specifics on how this is done, see pp. 270-277.)

Public Citizen is a hard-hitting, Washington, D.C.-based consumer group founded by Ralph Nader, combining environmental research and educational work (especially through its *Critical Mass Energy Project*, focusing on nuclear energy and its alternatives) with litigation and citizen action at many levels.

EDF and *NRDC* are national organizations that combine top-level scientific and economic research with legal action, as we have seen in the California utilities case (see p. 193) and the Alar campaigns described above.

EDF's origins are in courtroom testimony used in its successful fight to get DDT banned first on Long Island, later from one state to another, and finally nationwide. Its current priorities include work on the greenhouse effect, ocean pollution, wildlife and habitat, recycling, rain forests, acid rain, Antarctica, and toxics.

NRDC also covers most aspects of environmental and ecological concern. In its Atmospheric Protection Initiative it has committed some 20 attorneys and scientists to work together to combat the interacting problems of acid rain, ozone depletion, forestry management, coastal conservation, global warming, nuclear safety, and energy efficiency.

Earth Island Institute (EII), a spin-off from Friends of the Earth, runs 19 projects that include the *Bioregional Institute*, Santa Cruz, Calif., the *Environmental Litigation Fund*, Eugene, Ore., the *Japan Environmental Exchange*, Kyoto, Japan, and the *Nicaraguan Center for Appropriate Technology*, Bellingham, Wash. The quarterly *Earth Island Journal* is one of the best-informed publications in the environmental field.

Citizen's Clearinghouse for Hazardous Wastes, founded by Lois Gibbs, is based in Arlington, Va., with field offices nationwide, especially in the South and Appalachia. CCHW publishes a quarterly newsletter, *Everyone's Backyard*, as well as its regular *Action Bulletin*, and numerous studies on hazardous waste. It also initiates demonstrations, boycotts, and other citizen actions.

The Cousteau Society, with offices in Los Angeles, New York, Norfolk, Va., Paris, and Monaco, renowned for its popular TV series, is a pioneering underwater-research organization whose work covers oceans and rivers, Amazon and Antarctica. Jacques Cousteau and his son Jean-Michel Cousteau have probably done more than any other individuals to educate (and entertain) the world, especially its children, in matters of environment, ecology, and human coexistence with the biosphere.

On a Coalition Course.

Given the large number of environmental groups in North America, it is not surprising that some have joined together formally. In 1988 the *Environmental Action Foundation* merged with the *Environmental Task Force*. With a broader base and more diverse staff expertise, the new group is strengthening its high-visibility "Dirty Dozen" political campaign, which focuses on Congresspeople with the worst environmental voting records, its toxics and solid-waste teams, and legislative action on Capitol Hill.

In 1989 *Friends of the Earth (FOE)*, the *Environmental Policy Institute*, and the *Oceanic Society* combined forces to create a single international advocacy group. Their goal is to carry out campaigns on ozone layer protection, tropical defor-estation, ocean dumping, cleanup of DOE nuclear-weapons plants, and other issues. *Friends of the Earth International*, with 37 associates in Europe, Africa, Asia, and Latin America, includes such far-flung affiliates as the *Polski Klub Ekolgicny* (Polish Ecology Club) and the *Estonian Green Movement*. In October 1988 FOEI hosted the first ever East-West environmental summit with partici-pation from East Germany, Czechoslovakia, and the U.S.S.R.

Less formal coalitions between environmental organizations take place as and when suitable occasions arise. For example, in November 1988 eighteen groups jointly issued a 32-page booklet *Blueprint for the Environment: Advice to the President-Elect from America's Environmental Community.* They included Defenders of Wildlife, Environmental Action, the Environmental Policy Institute, FOE, the Global Tomorrow Coalition, the Izaak Walton League, the National Audubon Society, National Parks and Conservation Association, the National Wildlife Federation, the Natural Resources Council of America, NRDC, the Oceanic Society, Renew America, the Sierra Club, Trout Unlimited, the Union of Concerned Scientists, the Wilderness Society, and Zero Population Growth.

Research, Networking, and Lobbying Organizations

Although most groups do their own research, outreach, and lobbying, the fol-lowing organizations are more specialized and can provide important resources and skills needed for effective longer-term strategies:

The Advocacy Institute, 1730 Rhode Island Avenue NW, Washington, DC 20036. Provides a broad range of services to support public-interest groups, including tactical counseling, strategic planning and coalition building, and advocacy training. Publishes a monthly newsletter, *The Advocate's Advocate.*

CONCERN, 1794 Columbia Road NW, Washington, DC 20009. Publishes reports and community-action guides on key environmental issues such as drinking water, pesticides, hazardous waste, and farmlands. CONCERN has also created a broad-based community-outreach program promoting local and regional citizen action.

Electric Power Research Institute (EPRI), 3412 Hillview Avenue, Palo Alto, CA 94303. Manages a research and development program for the U.S. electric utili-ty industry and its customers. Its environment division covers clean coal tech-nologies, effects of electric and magnetic fields, air, land and water quality, and climatic change. Publishes *EPRI Journal* nine times a year.

INFORM, 381 Park Avenue South, New York, NY 10016. Founded in 1973 by environmental research specialist Joanna Underwood, it has initiated major investigations on air and water pollution, toxic waste, acid rain, and health and safety in the workplace. Its reports have helped win lawsuits, changed regula-tions, and shown many corporations that environmentally sound business prac-tices can also be economically beneficial.

The Learning Alliance, 494 Broadway, New York, NY 10012; (212) 226-7171. A pioneering group that organizes community seminars and workshops on a wide range of issues and provides hands-on strategies for effective environmental action.

Nuclear Information and Resource Service, 1424 16th Street NW, Washington, DC 20036. A national clearinghouse and networking center for nuclear and renewable energy information. Publishes the quarterly journal *Groundswell*, and has a computerized bulletin board (NIRSNET) containing information on every nuclear plant in the country.

Renew America, 1001 Connecticut Avenue NW, Washington, DC 20036. An educational and networking forum dedicated to the efficient use of all natural resources. Publishes the annual *State of the States* report, rating the environmental-protection performance of the 50 states, and the quarterly newsletter *Renew America Report*, which includes "Scorecard" – state-by-state voting records and cosponsorships of members of Congress on key environmental legislation.

Rocky Mountain Institute, 1739 Snowmass Creek Road, Snowmass, CO 81654-9199. Founded in 1982 by Amory and Hunter Lovins, RMI specializes in energy-related research.

> **In 1988 Friends of the Earth International hosted the first ever East-West environmental summit with participation from East Germany, Czechoslovakia, and the U.S.S.R.**

Consults with utilities, corporations, governments, and environmental groups. Publishes the quarterly *RMI Newsletter*, special reports and studies.

TRANET (Transnational Network for Appropriate/Alternative Technologies), Box 567, Rangely, ME 04970. Works as a clearinghouse for its members worldwide. Publishes *TRANET*, a quarterly newsletter-directory.

World Resources Institute, 1735 New York Avenue NW, Washington, DC 20006. Its main programs cover conservation of forests and biological diversity, energy and pollution, economics and institutions, and resource and environmental information. WRI publishes the annual *World Resources*, a comprehensive, authoritative assessment of the world's natural-resource base.

Worldwatch Institute, 1776 Massachusetts Avenue NW, Washington, DC 20036. Since 1984 has been publishing the yearly *State of the World* report on progress toward a sustainable society. It also puts out regular *Worldwatch Papers* and the bimonthly magazine *World Watch*.

C. Using the Law to Effect Change

The main laws affecting the environment were discussed in chapter 10. However, before we can take action on them, we need to understand how they can be applied to the most critical task of all – changing our institutions.

Although the notion of change is inherent in our system of public law, the nature of institutions is to remain static, to resist new ideas, not to rock the boat. For example, immediately after the 1973 OPEC oil crisis, individuals willingly made lifestyle changes, but most government and corporate agencies went on with business as usual.

The combination of outmoded technologies and institutional policies subsidizing waste has led to the pollution of air, land, and water and has overextended our consumption of resources, *in most cases without our knowledge or consent.*

The measures needed to stop pollution – reduction of waste, energy-efficiency, water conservation, reducing fossil-fuel combustion, moving to renewable energy and organic farming – will require, in addition to lifestyle changes, *institutional* changes that will bring about the enforcement of existing standards, regulations, and laws, and where necessary, the creation of new ones.

How We Can Educate Ourselves and Take Action*

A crucial challenge before each of us is to find new ways, individually and collectively, to understand, learn, and act for the environment. The traditional approaches of our society have been to isolate ourselves from the problem and even from each other rather than to see the links. Part of our work to protect the environment and to create a sustainable and just society is to change the way we think, feel, and act in an integrative process which allows us to grow personally and to learn how to participate as an active and responsible member of our society *and* to see ourselves as part of the larger human and natural community.

We need to challenge ourselves and each other to find new ways, tools, means of communication, learning how to act in mutual support of each other and all other species. One way to understand our growth toward becoming environmentally responsible citizens is to understand life as a learning process, extending beyond our formal schooling into a lifestyle that allows us constantly to evaluate and grow with our experiences, feelings, and thoughts. The process of learning about ourselves in turn needs to be connected to our understanding of the natural world and how to find a balance between the two.

Personalizing your involvement with the environment, becoming a critical thinker, envisioning an ecological world, organizing study and action groups, and developing skills and resource exchanges are some of the models that have served as the foundation for our work at the Learning Alliance. Since 1985 the alliance has organized community seminars and workshops on environmental health, energy conservation, household pollutants, food and nutrition, land use, deforestation, water quality, global warming, and many other topics. These programs emphasize local as well as national and international concerns, while providing individual, hands-on strategies for effective environmental action. We have helped form the New York Food and Agriculture Network, an advocacy and educational group for local agriculture, food, and farming concerns. We also helped develop for New York City an environmental platform and organizing effort that focuses political and social attention upon a broad range of issues. Other efforts have included starting recycling programs for community centers, implementing ecological and socially responsible design projects, coordinating an environmental skills exchange for the bioregional movement, and initiating special programs for youth groups, universities, labor unions, and homeless shelters.

(For more information on how the alliance's resources and know-how could benefit your own situation, contact Learning Alliance, 494 Broadway, New York, New York 10012; (212) 226-7171.)

---

*Contributed by David Levine, founder and director of the *Learning Alliance*

The legislative framework for such changes is largely in place at the federal level. However, it needs to be integrated into a top priority, long-range program for environmental and ecological protection that will save resources, protect public health, and significantly reduce costs of pollution cleanup. Such a program can only be worked out with support and cooperation at state and local levels.

The State of the States

Encouraging initiatives are taking place at the state level:[4]

- California passed Proposition 65 on food safety, going beyond federal requirements;
- Massachusetts enacted a law to levy stiff fines against polluters;
- New Jersey, New York, Florida, Iowa, Pennsylvania, Rhode Island, Connecticut, and Oregon introduced comprehensive programs to promote solid-waste recycling;
- Arizona plans to be self-sufficient in water by 2025;
- Iowa has set up the first state center to promote organic-farming alternatives.

> *"We cannot change unless we survive, but we will not survive unless we change."*
> **NYPIRG poster heading**

The advantage of state-sponsored plans is that they can be tailored to regional and local needs. But sometimes they run into conflict with federal policy. When North Carolina tried to introduce water-pollution regulations more stringent than those of EPA, the federal government threatened to cut off its funding to the state.

Federal-State Cooperation

It is vital for the federal government to demonstrate strong environmental leadership and to provide research, technical support, minimum standards for compliance, and national deadlines for action, and to facilitate better communications between states. The federal-state partnership must also enlist the cooperation of industry and shift greater liability to polluters. This will encourage energy efficiency, reduction of waste and recycling at the source rather than trying to control pollution "at the end of the pipe."

Ultimately, the progress of change in our institutions will depend on pressure exerted from below, from the grass roots.

As we see in the cases of pesticide control and garbage incineration, people act when they see a threat to their health and safety. And they find expression for their action in many different ways.

D. Taking Charge

Environmental and citizen organizations do not exist in a vacuum. Their members have many connections in society, through churches, labor unions, business and consumer organizations, professional associations, sports clubs, and senior citizen and many other groups.

If the battle against pollution is to be won, it must be fought with the participation of this wider constituency. In building a coalition our first priority is to have a common goal, which must be clearly defined and easy to understand. The following scenario by NYPIRG is based on an all-too-familiar reality that is taking place in many of our backyards today. Its principles are relevant to a wide variety of situations that you may find in your particular area.

Organizing Guide for Anti-Incineration Pro-Recycling Campaigns*

Step 1 – Getting Your Act Together

Oh no! You've just heard that a 3,000-ton-per-day garbage incinerator is going to be built in your community. You're shocked. The noise, congestion, and pollution problems will be awesome. You're afraid about what could happen to your family's health, your property values, your drinking water, the air. What can you do? You're a schoolteacher, office worker, businessperson, parent, homeowner. Should you sell your property and move before it's too late?

On the contrary, all is not lost. You've just begun to fight. Listen to the radio, watch TV, talk to friends and neighbors. Find out who is supporting the incinerator and who is opposing it. You can't beat an incinerator proposal single-handedly. But you can almost certainly find at least a few people who share your concerns.

If you can't, you won't have much chance of beating the project anyway. If you hear of a meeting about the incinerator, go to it. If no one is fighting the proposal, you'll have to organlze your own group.

Organizing a group is easier than preparing a group to wage a sustained political battle. Keeping it running harmoniously is harder still. Organization needs structure, but it is best to keep it simple. Define your goals and priorities, how you want decisions made, who your leaders will be (if there are to be any at all), where your funding will come from. Then write down ground rules:

● You may want to incorporate as a non-profit or not-for-profit organization to make contributions to your group tax deductible and to lessen your risk of disastrous lawsuits, should one of your members say something that is considered libelous.

● Set up committees to take care of key functions, appoint reliable members whose skills and personalities fit the roles – businesspeople to work on financing and fund-raising, someone with a home computer to be in charge of membership, a journalist to direct publicity, and the most gregarious members to recruit volunteers.

● Share the work load. It makes for harmony and prevents burnout.

● Pick a witty, snappy, recognizable name such as RAGE (Residents against Garbage Expansion), COP (Citizens Opposed to Pollution), or TOMORROW (Town of Midland Opposed to "Resource Recovery" of Waste).

Step 2 – Immediate Priorities

1. *Membership.* To succeed you need members and volunteers.
2. *Funding.* You need money to keep the group alive.
3. *Technical and regulatory implications.* Your group must figure out the technical and regulatory components of the incinerator proposal.
4. *Political considerations.* Get to know your local political lay of the land.
5. *Organizing tactics.* Base your campaign on a sound plan.

Membership – Typically you will need to recruit 6 to 12 key members to carry the main burden of the work and a hundred or more additional members who will pay dues and turn out for public meetings and special events. Here are a few things to keep in mind about membership:

---

* Adapted with permission from *A Citizen Organizing Guide to Anti-incineration Pro-recycling Campaigns*, Walter Liong-Ting Hang (New York: NYPIRG, 1987).

- Keep recruiting new members to replace those who drop out for one reason or another.
- Good prospects for volunteers are generally college students, senior citizens, mothers of small children, and environmentalists.
- Tried and true recruiting methods: door-to-door canvassing, tabling at shopping centers, local schools, college campuses, community events, marching in *Earth Day* and other parades, and appealing to community organizations.
- To help in recruiting, get a copy of the U.S. Geological Survey map of the area containing the proposed incinerator site (you can find these maps in better bookshops and in most camping or bicycle stores). They show local topography, waterways, roads, schools, churches, homes, and other structures.

> *"In general, the closer people live or work to a proposed incinerator site, the greater will be their concerns about its impact."*

First, focus on those who would be *directly affected by the facility*:
- people living or working near the proposed site or the site where the incinerator's ash residues would be disposed of, along the roads servicing the sites, or downwind from the sites;
- people in agriculture whose lands, crops, and livestock might be affected;
- local merchants, developers, banks, chambers of commerce, Rotary clubs, with business interests in the vicinity of the proposed incinerator.

You can get additional support from:
- taxpayer organizations that oppose bond financing or spending on public-works projects (incinerators are almost as expensive as nuclear reactors);
- members of environmental, naturalist, garden, 4-H, and hiking, bicycling, and other sports organizations;
- senior citizens, who often have professional training and abundant time to volunteer;
- expectant mothers and their organizations.

Funding – Start by setting a membership-fee schedule consistent with local economic conditions. For example, $20 a year general membership, $35 family, $50 business or professional, $100 and up patron, with $10 for students and those with low income and $15 for senior citizens. Deposit money in a special bank account. Appoint a treasurer to keep track of expenses. Make sure renewals are made on time.

Devise creative ways to raise money: characterize donations as an insurance policy or an investment in home improvement; get members to invite their friends and neighbors over for coffee and dessert before hearing the pitch; sell T-shirts, bumper stickers, and buttons; canvass door-to-door; hold fund-raising events such as bake sales, raffles, rock-and-roll-against-resource-recovery dances; find local celebrities who can help your cause.

Understanding Technical and Legal Implications – Proposed incinerators require the legal approval of a variety of regulatory authorities. The better you understand the approval procedures, the better your chances of stopping the project.

First, get copies of all available documents on the proposed incinerator, including draft, generic, or final environmental impact statements and all the documents that have been prepared regarding construction or operational permit applications, land-use planning, financing, site purchase, minority hiring requirements, historic preservation, and limitations on bonding authority. Read these documents thoroughly. If you have lawyers, scientists, and engineers at your disposal, the task will be much easier.

Your goal is to understand the approval process to the extent that you can find technical, procedural, and political ways to slow down, frustrate, and thwart the incinerator's progress. Essentially, you should ensure that *every* single regulatory requirement is fulfilled before the project proceeds along each step of the approval pathway. *This can literally add as much as a decade to the development of an incinerator.*

Judging the Political Lay of the Land – Figure out who your political friends and enemies are. Devise strategies and tactics that will reduce the effectiveness of your enemies while building the strength of your friends until the tide of public opinion turns in your favor.

Find out who is the key person proposing to build the facility – the mayor, city manager, town supervisor, county executive, or someone else. What are his/her political affiliation and environmental record? Has the official served well? Which political party is in control of the government body behind the proposal? How can your group exert political pressure to weaken your opposition? You must know the answers to all these and other questions in order to work out a winning political strategy.

Step 3 – Developing a Plan of Action

Based on your review of the undesirable (incinerator) proposal and your new-found knowledge of the political tensions and conflicts surrounding efforts to build or oppose the project, you have probably discovered issues that can be used to delay or kill it. Educating the public about these issues and organizing a political base of support is your goal.

Organizing Tactics – Here is a general hierarchy of actions to consider, in order from least to most ambitious. All can be highly effective under the right circumstances: petitioning, letter writing, phone banking, door-to-door canvassing, leaking stories to the press, writing letters to the editor, writing op-ed articles, testifying at regulatory hearings, face-to-face meetings with local, state, and federal officials, events, rallies, community meetings, legislative lobbying, legal actions, sustained organizing campaigns.

Always transact important business in writing. Oral agreements often turn out to be worthless.

The Art of Lobbying – When lobbying keep these principles in mind:
- the essence of politics is to reward your friends and punish your enemies;
- politicians live by two rules: (l) always get reelected; and (2) never forget the first rule;
- lobby the most powerful public officials and community leaders first;
- if possible, use lobbyists who are personally acquainted with the targets; otherwise lobby in groups;
- keep your pitch short, simple, and polite;
- never make veiled threats you can't fulfill;
- be persistent; don't be intimidated because you don't have an advanced chemistry degree;
- remember, you always have a right to express your opinion;
- never take no for an answer.

Step 4 – Launching the Campaign

A campaign is a unified effort to accomplish specific objectives: systematically attacking the shortcomings of the proposed incinerator until it ceases to be a viable option; winning a majority of the votes of the pubic body that will decide the fate of the proposal. Pacing a campaign to a successful conclusion requires great attention to planning, timeliness, logistics, resources, and fortuitous opportunities. The schedule is often dictated by election days, legislative sessions, or the deadlines of the incinerator approval procedure.

Generally speaking, the best launch time is early September, when people are refreshed from summer vacations and ready for action. But prepare your groundwork in advance so that you can take advantage of unforeseeable events such as political scandals, environmental catastrophes, or a favorable court ruling to catalyze a campaign at short notice. Every tactic you use, whether a special event, a press release, a lawsuit, a meeting with a public official, or a radio/TV appearance, must be designed to put increasing pressure on the approval process of the proposal you are opposing.

When planning to attend events or running your own, keep the following in mind:

● *There's strength in numbers.* Bring out as many of your supporters as possible. A poor turnout can kill your effort.

● *Plan your event well in advance.* Provide enough time to print flyers to publicize your event. Have schoolchildren bring invitations to their parents, make reminder calls to your members, put an ad in the local newspaper, get an announcement or appearance on radio/TV shows, prepare signs and banners, write letters. Above all, involve as many people as possible.

● *Choreograph each event down to the last detail.* Who will speak for your group? (Don't bore the audience to death with long-winded speeches. If possible, negotiate an agenda that lets your group speak first and leaves ample time for questions and answers.) Who will arrange for the room, the chair and platform arrangement, the microphone, the slide projector, and so on? If you are bringing in a speaker, who will make the pickup at the airport, and deal with expenses? There are many such details that have to be anticipated.

Using the Media – Get to know the media in your area and learn how they can help your effort. Develop personal contacts with local newspapers, and radio and TV stations so that they know you as a reliable source; help them arrange interviews with experts representing your viewpoint.

Maximize coverage. Present clearly written press releases at least two days ahead of the event to ensure coverage. Make reminder calls on the day of the event to confirm that a reporter, photographer, or camera crew has been assigned. Make sure your spokesperson knows how to speak slowly in short, to-the-point, quotable phrases that can't be edited. See that the best quote is spoken at the start of the press conference or interview, when the red TV light is on.

Pay close attention to follow-up. Get your group to hold a post mortem review immediately after the event. Each person should say what worked and what didn't. Balance criticism with positive suggestions. Write thank-you letters to media for favorable coverage and to officials who attended, reiterating in writing any promises they made.

Real-life Campaign Scenario

The following is a case history of a hard-fought campaign by NYPIRG that successfully stalled construction of a 3,000-ton-per-day incinerator in New York City, against enormous odds. Although the overall scope and details of this campaign may exceed your particular case, the basic principles are applicable to many environmental situations.

August 1985: Ten thousand New York City citizens march across the Brooklyn Bridge in a last-minute attempt to block a favorable Board of Estimate vote to build an incinerator in Brooklyn Navy Yard. To defuse opposition the City makes a vague promise to recycle 15 percent of its waste. By a vote of six to five funding is approved for at least five incinerators to be built at an estimated cost of $290 million.

September to December 1985: Based in part on a firsthand investigation of recycling plants and incinerators in Norway, Sweden, Denmark, and West Germany, NYPIRG completes a major study of the environmental, health, and financial consequences of the Brooklyn incinerator and devises an alternative recycling proposal to reduce New York City's waste by 60 percent in 1995 and 90 percent in 2005.

January 1986: Community-organizing contacts and recruitment plans are made in preparation of release of NYPIRG's report, *Burning Question: Garbage Incineration Versus Total Recycling in New York City.* A coalition of groups opposed to the incinerator, Citizens for a Safe Environment (CASE), is reactivated.

February 1986: The report is released and receives extensive TV, radio, newspaper, and technical trade-journal coverage. Door-to-door canvassers and volunteers systemically drop thousands of leaflets in the areas around the Navy Yard and other proposed incinerator sites throughout the city urging citizens to call the mayor and the Department of Sanitation to oppose burning in favor of recycling. Presentations of the report's findings are made to the Board of Estimate, New York State attorney general's environmental protection bureau, the State Department of Environmental Conservation (DEC), the state assembly and senate, and to environmental and civic organizations of all descriptions. Efforts are made for a statewide incinerator moratorium and comprehensive recycling initiatives. At first, virtually no support exists for either proposal.

March to June 1986: Citizen-training sessions are held to build support for NYPIRG's campaign. NYPIRG releases a *Lessons from Europe* study. Citizens lobby legislators to thwart incineration. Media coverage continues. Op-ed articles and letters to the editor appear in local newspapers. Door-to-door canvassing expands with nearly 100 people involved. More than 90 groups now support NYPIRG's position. But local and state officials refuse to abandon their pro-burning commitment. Plans to break ground at the Navy Yard are delayed pending approval of construction and other required permits. A major legal challenge brought by residents opposed to the project fails. NYPIRG's legislative efforts are killed, but pro-incineration efforts also are stymied.

July 1986: Contrary to the City's promise, little or no recycling has been accomplished. DEC prepares to hold hearings on the Navy Yard's permit applications.

On the day before the hearing NYPIRG obtains previously unreleased documents revealing that the company applying to build and operate the incinerator (Signal Environmental Systems) signed a contract with DEC agreeing to pay up to $63,000 for the services of an administrative law judge to preside over the permit hearings. According to state finance law, the company is arguably entitled to a refund of those monies if the permit is denied. Working through the night, NYPIRG lawyers prepare a suit seeking to declare the arrangement invalid due to an obvious conflict of interest. The suit is filed virtually at the same time NYPIRG is testifying before the administrative law judge. NYPIRG applies for party status in the permit proceedings before the same judge.

August 1986: A N.Y. State Supreme Court justice agrees with NYPIRG and issues a permanent injunction against all contractual arrangements similar to the one the group identified in its suit. The decision receives widespread news coverage. Unfortunately, the state attorney general appeals the decision and a temporary stay is granted. Nevertheless, the aministrative law judge decides to put the permit hearings on hold.

September to December 1986: NYPIRG files suit to vacate the state's stay, but fails. NYPIRG and many groups in the anti-burn coalition work successfully to pass a $1.45 billion environmental bond issue to clean up toxic dumps, close garbage landfills, and preserve environmentally sensitive lands. NYPIRG also files to support a permit proceeding that may establish an incinerator moratorium until a statewide solid-waste master plan has been adopted.

January 1987: The intervention fails, but N.Y. State finally issues the long-awaited plan. It proposes to recycle 50 percent of the state's waste by 1997 – the most ambitious goal in the nation. An important moral victory is won. Perhaps the tide has turned. Meanwhile NYPIRG's research and advocacy efforts have expanded to six states. Another N.Y. state legislative session unfolds. Budget battles begin to support recycling and oppose incineration. The appellate division of the state supreme court decides unanimously to require the Brooklyn Navy Yard permit hearings to start over again. The campaign enters its second year.

November 1988: DEC temporarily delays final consideration of a city permit to build the Brooklyn Navy Yard incinerator (whose estimated cost is now at least $552 million) because its ash disposal plan and its trash recycling plans are found unacceptable.

March 1989: The city's case to dump the 900 tons-per-day incinerator at the Fresh Kills landfill on Staten Island. N.Y., falls apart when tests at the site show that there is only a 2-foot depth of clay soil . The city says it has an alternative site in Falls Township, Bucks County, Pa.

April 1989: Mayor Koch signs a bill requiring recycling of 25 percent of the city's garbage. NYPIRG's toxic waste coordinator Arthur Kell, discovering that the plan to use the Pennsylvania dump site has been withheld from the inhabitants of Falls Township, breaks the news to the Bucks County *Times Courier*. In an April 7 article in the newspaper the township supervisor calls Waste Management Inc. (the company designated by New York City to carry out the toxic waste dumping) "a cancer on the town." Four days later the city backs out of the Falls Township proposal and asks DEC for a variance to build the incinerator on the dubious grounds that its ash-disposal plans had fallen through.

June 1989: NYPIRG, along with the Environmental Defense Fund, NRDC, the Interstate Sanitary Commission, and the United Jewish Organization (representing the Jewish community of Williamsburg in Brooklyn where the incinerator would be located), files suit to bar construction of the plant.

January 1990: David Dinkins, who pledged a two-to-three-year moratorium on the incinerator, becomes mayor of New York City.

Maryland Burning*

"If the citizens continue to do the lobbying and continue to bring out a lot of facts, the plan could be in trouble." This remark was made in the fall of 1988 by Anthony Cicoria, a Democratic member of the Prince Georges County Council in Maryland, two weeks before the council was to vote on whether to construct a $146 million incinerator.

The plan was enthusiastically backed by the county executive, but Cicoria was one of a handful of council members still undecided as the vote on the controversial proposal grew near. As the debate raged and the trash piled up, the residents of Prince Georges County were faced with the same critical choice as other communities across the country: how to deal with a growing trash problem and inadequate disposal methods.

In the end, when the council voted unanimously against the incinerator, the impetus for that decision was citizen protest. The citizens, in the form of the Prince Georges recycling coalition, had brought out the facts.

The coalition – an impromptu patchwork of middle- and upper-middle-class homeowners – was credited with creating a torrent of protest so loud and so professionally organized, it single-handedly stopped construction of the incinerator. The campaign also left in place a grass-roots movement that has become a local political force in the county.

The coalition was formed after Gary Murray, a business owner, learned that an incinerator capable of burning 1,200 tons of trash a day was being proposed for an area of residential growth near seven schools in Largo, Md., just outside Washington, D.C.

"No one asked our opinion; no one included us in the process," says Murray. *We felt we needed to be part of the process.* It was an ill-advised direction, from both an economic and environmental standpoint. But it would have gone through unless we asked some questions and did some research."

Coalition members wrote to churches and schools to see if local civic leaders were aware of the county's plans and asked if there were people willing to help.

The response from the community was encouraging. Using membership lists of church and civic groups, and later the mailing lists of local environmental groups, the coalition reached 50 citizens who showed up for a preliminary meeting. Some of them placed crudely-written signs announcing a second meeting shortly afterward, and 150 turned up.

At that meeting, the coalition agreed to assemble every week and organized committees to work on research, publicity, legal affairs and outreach. The coalition also arranged town meetings and hearings attended by as many as 500 people, which drew the attention of the county's decision makers.

The coalition showed the council members examples of communities, such as Seattle and Philadelphia, that had already considered incineration but had found it too expensive, and confronted them with environmental data on incinerators that showed high levels of toxic emissions, including

---

* From "Prince Georges Recycling Coalition Trashes the Incineration Myth," By Bob Mentzinger, from the bimonthly magazine *Public Citizen*, March/April 1989, with permission.

sulfur dioxide, one of the major components of acid rain. They also presented data showing the incinerator would produce annually "several hundred thousand tons" of carbon dioxide, one of the major greenhouse gases, as well as vapors containing cancer-causing heavy-metal compounds. In the end, says Murray, the county councilors "just couldn't justify their position."

In the face of such a well-planned opposition, the council voted against the proposal.

County officials expect to continue working with the recycling coalition as debate over waste disposal continues. A county spokesman says that existing landfills will not reach capacity for another 10-15 years, but a goal of recycling 35 percent of the county's trash is planned for 1996 anyway, in order to extend the life of those landfills.

What is clear is that incineration will not be a solution, at least not so long as groups such as the recycling coalition are around to voice the community's opposition. That is a measure of grass-roots organizing. "It took a little effort from a lot of people," according to Murray. *"Whatever you can do. Some people found putting up signs was therapeutic. Some people gave 50 cents, others $500. That was the beauty of the grass-roots effort: people did little things which added up to a lot."*

Ecotage, Monkeywrenching, and Other Stratagems

The United States was forged in the crucible of radical politics and revolution. Civil disobedience and guerrilla tactics represent a tradition that embraces the Boston Tea Party, Harper's Ferry, Walden Pond, and the civil-rights movement. It's all American as apple pie.

As Ralph Nader has said, pollution is violence and environmental pollution is environmental violence, with a seriousness of harm far exceeding that of crime in the streets. To deal with a system of oppression and suppression which characterizes the environmental violence in the U.S., he wrote, "the first priority is to deprive the polluters of their unfounded legitimacy. Too often they assume a conservative, patriotic posture when in reality they are the radical destroyers of a nation's resources and the most fundamental rights of people." [5]

> **"The first priority is to deprive the polluters of their unfounded legitimacy."**

For many environmentalists it was the nuclear-power issue in the early 1960s that pushed them toward a policy of activism. A citizens' group in Cape Cod, Mass. had forced the Atomic Energy Commission to stop illegal dumping of radioactive waste into the nearby Atlantic. In 1962 demonstrators forced the giant utility Consolidated Edison to cancel plans for a nuclear reactor at Ravenswood, Queens, in the heart of New York City. And hundreds of demonstrators have been arrested at Shoreham, N.Y., Bodega Head, Calif., and dozens of other nuclear sites across the country.

Civil Disobedience[6]

On Washington's Birthday, 1974, a Massachusetts organic farmer, Sam Lovejoy, took a crowbar and felled a 550-foot weather-monitoring tower that Northeast Utilities had put up in preparation for a 1,150-megawatt atomic reactor to be built at Montague, Mass. Turning himself over to the local police, Lovejoy took full responsibility. At his trial, he presented expert witnesses to testify to the dangers of nuclear power and the legitimacy of civil disobedience.

The judge dismissed the case on grounds of faulty indictment: the charge should have been a misdemeanor, not a felony, because the tower was "real," not "personal," property. Later, the jury revealed they would have found Lovejoy not guilty because they were convinced his action had not been malicious. The Lovejoy action was one of many in the United States and abroad that showed growing support for civil disobedience in cases where there was a perceived threat to public health and the environment.

Ecotage

An example of ecological protest, cited in *The Cousteau Almanac*[7], tells how one person, "The Fox", of Aurora, Il., took this *nom de guerre* after watching the Fox River he had fished in as a boy become a poisoned stream. He reportedly entered the executive offices of U.S. Steel with a bottle of foul-smelling liquid he had collected from one of the company's drains along the river. Announcing he had an award to the company for their "outstanding contributions to the environment," he dumped the sludge on U.S. Steel's immaculate white carpet. As he departed, he placed a bumper sticker on the company's front entrance. It read "Go Fox, Stop Pollution."

> *The Lovejoy action was one of many in the United States and abroad that showed growing support for civil disobedience in cases where there was a perceived threat to public health and the environment.*

This was one of many similar exploits carried out by the Fox and numerous other individuals and groups. If such tactics sometimes border on the illegal, they can be, nevertheless, highly effective in calling public attention to specific problems.

Action on the High Seas

The Rainbow Warriors. In 1971 a group called "Don't Make a Wave Committee" was started in Vancouver, B.C. It sailed an old fishing boat and a converted minesweeper, christened *Greenpeace I* and *II*, to the Aleutian Islands to protest a United States underwater nuclear test. Although the U.S. Coast Guard and foul weather prevented them from reaching the test site, the subsequent deluge of protests convinced Washington to give up Aleutian testing.

The next year *Greenpeace III* sailed to the Pacific atoll of Moruroa, where the French had been carrying out atmospheric nuclear tests. The three-man crew held position near the atoll throughout the summer, preventing most of the testing. When the ship returned to Moruroa in 1973, French commandos came aboard and severely beat up the crew, although they were in international waters.

One year later the French ceased atmospheric testing. But they didn't forget Greenpeace, as the group was now called. On July 10, 1985, the world was shocked to learn that the French secret service had sunk Greenpeace's *Rainbow Warrior* in a New Zealand harbor, killing a photographer on board.

Greenpeace workers are highly dedicated and highly trained men and women who risk their lives in nonviolent, direct-action protests against toxic waste, sludge dumping, ocean incineration, and the wholesale killing of marine mammals. After they launched their *Save the Whales* campaign, the annual slaughter dropped from 25,000 to 1,000.

The Sea Shepherds. The Sea Shepherd Conservation Society, based in Vancouver, B.C., with offices in Los Angeles, Washington, D.C., and Plymouth, England, describes itself as aggressive, controversial, and effective. Founded in 1977 by Paul Watson (who was a cofounder of Greenpeace), the society is committed to a confrontational role in which they "actively interfere with the killing of marine mammals on the high seas where it occurs." [8]

The group's record includes:

- Sinking the pirate whaling ship *Sierra* in 1979;
- Sinking outlaw Spanish whalers *Isba I* and *Isba II* in 1980;
- Being first to spray harmless, indelible dye onto the white fur of seal pups to protect them by destroying the commercial value of their pelts;
- Landing the *Sea Shepherd* in Siberia to document illegal Soviet whaling activities in 1981;

> *"The Sea Shepherd's crew of Canadians, Australians, Britons, and Americans are front-line soldiers in a war of the whales, environmentalists willing to risk their bodies as well as their time and energies . . . to save the great sea mammals."*
>
> *New York Times*[9]

- Blockading the Canadian sealing fleet, which saved 76,000 seal pups from being clubbed to death;
- Shutting down the gray seal hunt in Scotland by buying two of the islands where the seals were being killed;
- Engineering the sinking of half of Iceland's illegally operated whaling fleet in 1986, thus enforcing the international moratorium protecting whales;
- Forcing the Japanese drift-net fleet to retreat from their killing grounds in the North Pacific, saving thousands of seals, dolphins, whales, sea birds, and sea turtles that would otherwise have drowned in the nets.[10]

Throughout all of these operations, Watson says, *Sea Shepherd* has worked without using weapons and without causing a single injury.

Earth First!

"What?! you say, Another wilderness/environmental group? There are more environmental outfits than plague fleas on a New Mexico prairie dog! I already belong to the Sierra Club, Wilderness Society, Audubon Society, Greenpeace . . . Why another one? Why EARTH FIRST!? Because we are different." [11]

Yes! EF! is different. When phoning them in Tucson, Ariz., to order a copy of their book *Ecodefense*, I (inadvertently) described myself as a member. "Hah!" came the reply, "We don't have members!," implying that I must be working for the FBI. I should have known better, because I had previously sent in $20 to get the *EF! Journal*, a 40-page tabloid put out eight times a year, and it makes abundantly clear that EF! is a *movement*, not an organization. It has no formal leadership, no board of directors, and no hierarchical structure. EF! consists of self-supporting but cooperating elements that include dozens of local groups, a foundation, a direct action fund, *EF! Journal*, and various task forces.

Deep Ecology

The EF! philosophy is based on the concept of *Deep Ecology*, which holds that the earth is not simply a place for human exploitation but instead a living community where all species and all things have intrinsic (and interrelated) value.

In EF!'s view, lobbying, letter writing, research, and lawsuits are important and necessary, but not enough. Thus EF! also uses civil disobedience, confrontation, guerrilla theater, and direct action to fight for wild places and life processes.

Brief Guide to Monkeywrenching[12]

In the book *Ecodefense* the anonymous authors describe in graphic detail many ways that this form of ecological-defense action can be carried out. They include:

● *Tree spiking* – hammering in nails in order to jam the blades of the large saws used to cut-up trees in the sawmill.*

● *Stake pulling* – pulling up survey stakes (to slow up land development in forests and wilderness areas).

● *Incapacitating powerlines* – removing bolts from towers, cutting towers with hacksaws or blow torches, or smashing insulators with shotguns).

● *Spiking roads* – to bar access to loggers and developers.

● *Disabling vehicles* (12 different ways).

● *Sabotaging heavy equipment, smoke bombs, trash return, stink bombs, jamming locks, billboard trashing, burning, and revision.*

The book's final chapter (71 pages) is devoted to security, a most important part of the monkeywrencher's arsenal.

---

* In this operation the nails or spikes must be placed several feet above the area where the fellers will cut in order to avoid the possibility of injuring the chainsaw operator.

A Radical Credo for Radical Times

EF! makes clear that, as a group, it does not advocate or engage in environmental sabotage. However, monkeywrenching is one of the "creative" ideas of opposition it presents in its discussions and literature.

Monkeywrenching is described in the *EF! Journal* as "*the final step in the defense of the wild, the deliberate action taken by the Earth defender when all other measures have failed, the process whereby the wilderness defender becomes the wilderness acting in self-defense.*" [13]

It is no accident that our survey of environmental groups ends with Earth First! Their significance, I believe, stretches far beyond their numbers. EF! is one of the few groups to translate John Muir's philosophy of leaving the wilderness alone into action. If their actions are radical, so is Muir's philosophy. "No compromise in defense of Mother Earth" is a radical credo for dealing with such overriding issues as how can we slow up and reverse global warming and its consequences? As EF!'s Dave Foreman and others point out, there can be no basic solutions without our understanding that nature is not a resource for humankind to use and that we are simply a small part of a living, whole biosphere. As long as we continue to destroy nature by the wasteful way we run our society, and especially by the reckless use of fossil fuels, we continue to destroy ourselves. The catch is that human-induced climate change (global warming) has upped the ante, speeding the rate of destruction toward the point of no return. This is the challenge we face as we approach the 21st century. It is a radical challenge that calls for radical solutions.

A Night on Bald Mountain

How effective is monkeywrenching? Perhaps the best answer is given by the environmental writer Dick Russell in *Crossroads: Environmental Priorities for the Future:*

"*THE SCENE:* A remote wilderness area in the Siskiyou National Forest near Grants Pass, Oregon, May 1983. A construction company has begun bulldozing an access road to about 150,000 acres of old growth trees that the U.S. Forest Service plans to have clear-cut.

> *Human-induced climate change (global warming) has upped the ante, speeding the rate of destruction toward the point of no return. This is the challenge we face as we approach the 21st century. It is a radical challenge that calls for radical solutions.*

It is shortly before dawn when two burly, bearded men arrive and set up a log roadblock, then retreat temporarily into the dark forest. When sheriff's deputies, anticipating another round of confrontation with Earth First!, show up and remove the obstruction, Dave Foreman decides to use his body instead.

As a pickup truck grinds down the narrow dirt road, Foreman steps out and blocks the way. The truck slows down, but keeps coming, hitting him in the chest, knocking him back five feet. This time the driver accelerates, backpedaling Foreman up a hill, faster and faster until he can no longer keep his balance. Falling, desperately he clings to the bumper, his legs trailing under the engine for over 100 yards until the pickup finally stops. As workers pile out and surround him, shouting obscenities, the local police move in and place him under arrest.

Dave Foreman's knees suffered permanent damage, but four years later Bald Mountain Road has yet to be completed. Three more blockades bought time for a lawsuit resulting in a temporary injunction."

The Green Perspective

The wholesale devastation of forests, the contamination of ground water, and the overuse of fragile ecosystems are a form of "ecological insanity" that has brought us to the verge of ecocide and possible suicide as a species. Such is the thesis of *Dwellers in the Land*, an important book by Kirkpatrick Sale. The key to saving our beleaguered species, he urges, is *bioregionalism* – a restructuring of society based on the bioregion, a territory defined by natural characteristics rather than human dictates. In place of centralized, competitive nation-states, bioregional society would be decentralized and cooperative, reflecting a scale where "human potential is unleashed, human potential is magnified, human accomplishment magnified."[14]

Bioregional sensitivity, long the province of Native Americans and other indigenous societies, is now emerging in the industrial countries of the world, most notably West Germany, Austria, Belgium, Sweden, and Australia, where Green politics, as it is known, is scoring important electoral successes. The West German Green Party, for example, has a program of active partnership between nature and human beings and an economic policy "oriented to the necessities of life today and for future generations, to the preservation of nature and a careful management of natural resources."[15] Although still in its infancy in the U.S., the Green movement has representation in California, New York, Vermont, and Massachusetts, with regional outposts across the country and a Green Organizing Committee that can be contacted at P.O. Box 40040, St Paul, MN 55104 or Box 91, Marshfield, VT 05658. As we move into the 1990s, it seems likely that Green politics will play an increasingly influential role at federal, state, and local levels.

Which Side Are You On?

Cleaning up the environment is an idea everyone supports, so much so that some of the worst polluters have taken on positive sounding names like Global Ecology Enterprises and U.S. Waste Disposal, Inc. Before supporting any environmental group, you should find out whose interests they actually represent and who is paying their printing and mailing bills. A case in point is the Council on Energy Awareness, whose innocuous title hides the fact that it is the lobby of the nuclear-power industry.

Throughout this book and particularly in this chapter we describe the work of the leading environmental and citizens' organizations. Although we have tried to be as comprehensive as possible in our listings, there are undoubtedly many other groups and organizations that are active in your area. Faced with a perhaps bewildering choice, you may well ask which one or ones you should join. Clearly, the final answer must be personal, depending on your needs and interests.

As a general principle, however, it is useful to belong to at least one national organization because this will give you the picture of what is happening and what needs to be done at the national and global level. At the same time you can get more involved in grass-roots activities (and in helping build the environmental movement) by joining a local group focused on a single issue or the local chapter of a national organization. To find out which ones are most suited for your needs, compare the literature and programs of, say, six different organizations to whom you can write, requesting such information. (For example, from the listing in the next two pages select two conservation-oriented groups, two multi-issue and two single-issue organizations.) If you are not already a member of an environmental group, join one or two that appeal to you most, support them for at least a year, and then decide how you want to extend your participation, either by doing more work for the groups you belong to or by joining another one.

Whichever course you take, you will be making an important contribution to cleaning up our polluted planet. At the same time you will be taking part in the major force of the 1990s – the realization that, whether you live in East Detroit or East Berlin, *you have the power to change your life and the environment you inhabit.*

RESOURCES

The following is provided to help you locate additional resources on the topics covered in this chapter.

In addition to the listing given here there are a great number of other groups working on specific issues or in local areas. For further information, see the *Directory of Environmental Organizations*, available from U.S. Environmental Directories, Box 65156, St Paul, MN 44165.

1. Organizations

— *ACORN* (Association of Community Organizations for Reform Now), 413 Eighth Street SE, Washington, DC 20003. Focuses on community improvement, health care, taxes, toxics, and utilities.

— *Citizens for a Better Environment*, 59 E. Van Buren, Suite 1600, Chicago, IL 60605; (312) 939-1530. Research, education, litigation on waste management, toxic substances, and air and water quality.

— *Citizen's Clearinghouse for Hazardous Wastes* (CCHW), P.O. Box 926, Arlington, VA 22216; (703) 276-7070. The only national environmental organization started and led by grass-roots leaders. Provides information and resources, organizing help and outreach, and scientific and technical assistance.

— *Clean Water Action Project*, 317 Pennsylvania Avenue SE, Washington, DC 20003; (202) 547-1196. Working in many states, especially in rural areas, CWAP exerts effective pressure on legislators at state and federal levels.

— *CONCERN, Inc.*, 1794 Columbia Road NW, Washington, 20009; (202) 328-8160. Its primary activity is the publication of excellent community-action guides defining major issues, explaining relevant legislation, describing successful local initiatives, and recommending specific action guidelines.

— *Earth First!*, Box 5871, Tucson, AZ, 85703; (607) 622-1371. Has no formal organization or official members. Promotes a philosophy of Deep Ecology, an uncompromising defense of natural diversity, and visionary wilderness proposals. Organizes task-force actions and "road shows" to gain media attention. Publishes *Earth First! Journal* eight times a year.

— *Earth Island Institute*, 300 Broadway, San Francisco, CA 94133; (415) 788-7324. A national and international action group whose projects include environmental litigation, rainforest health alliance, appropriate technology, climate protection. Publishes the quarterly *Earth Island Journal*.

— *Environmental Action Coalition*, 625 Broadway, New York, NY 10012; (212) 677-1601. Education, research, action projects, conferences, workshops, technical assistance: recycling, toxic waste, urban forestry in New York metropolitan area.

— *Environmental Action Foundation*, 1525 New Hampshire Avenue NW, Washington DC, 20036; (202) 745-4879. Information on packaging; helping cities and states to implement recycling.

— *Environmental Defense Fund*, 257 Park Avenue South, New York, NY 10010; (212) 505-2100. Combines outstanding scientific research and legal action on a wide range of subjects including pesticides, recycling, renewable energy, radon, and toxic waste.

— *Environmental Research Foundation*, P.O. Box 3541, Princeton, NJ 08543; (609) 683-0707. Provides assistance to grass-roots environmental groups in fighting landfills and incinerators. Publishes the weekly bulletin *Rachel's Hazardous Waste News*, giving news and resources on fighting toxics.

— *Friends of the Earth*, 530 Seventh Street SE, Washington, DC 20003; (202) 543-4312. A national and international environmental organization, it is active in fighting for many world issues including rain-forest protection, preservation and restoration of ecosystems, and renewable-energy development.

— *Greenpeace*, 1436 U Street NW, Washington, DC 20009; (202) 462-1177. National and international direct action and lobbying on rain forests, toxic waste, ocean and air pollution, whales, nuclear radiation. Publishes bimonthly magazine *Greenpeace*.

— *Green Committees of Correspondence*, Box 30208, Kansas City, MO 64112; (816) 931-9366. The national clearinghouse and contact for all interested in the Green movement.

— *Learning Alliance*, 494 Broadway, New York, NY 10012; (212) 226-7171. Provides education and resources on a wide range of issues, including political action, community involvement, women's leadership, recycling, and urban agriculture and transportation.

— *National Association of Neighborhoods*, 1651 Fuller Street NW, Washington, DC 20009. Neighborhood organizing in context of environmental quality.

— *National Audubon Society*, 833 Third Avenue, New York, NY 10022; (212) 832-3200. Research, education, and lobbying on wildlife, forests, wilderness, public lands, endangered species, water and energy policy. Publishes bimonthly *Audubon* magazine and *Audubon Activist* newsletter.

— *National Wildlife Federation*, 1412 Sixteenth Street NW, Washington, DC 20036; (202) 737-2024. With a network of 51 state and territorial affiliates, NWF promotes the wise use of natural resources. Sponsors National Wildlife Week and many other educational and demonstration programs. Publishes *National Wildlife* (bimonthly), *NatureScope* (for classrooms), the *Environmental Quality Index*, and *Legislative Hotline*.

— *Natural Resources Defense Council*, 40 West 20th Street, New York, NY 10011; (212) 727-2700. A national organization dedicated to protecting the natural and human environment. It combines research, education, advocacy, and litigation on toxic substances, air and water pollution, nuclear safety and other subjects. Publishes a bimonthly newsletter and the quarterly *Amicus Journal*.

— *National Toxics Campaign*, 37 Temple Place, Boston, MA 02111; (617) 482-1477. Makes effective use of public education, citizen pressure, and electoral influence.

— *New York Public Interest Research Group* (NYPIRG), 9 Murray Street, New York, NY 10007; (212) 349-6460. A grass-roots, student oriented, action organization involved in a wide range of environmental issues. (Note: There are PIRGs in California, Connecticut, Illinois, Massachusetts, Michigan, New Jersey, Oregon, Vermont, Washington, and 12 other states. Check your local yellow pages.)

— *Public Citizen*, 2000 P Street NW, Washington, DC 20036; (202) 293-9142. A grass-roots activist group closely associated with Ralph Nader, highlighting the interests of environmentalists, consumer advocates, and other concerned citizens.

— *Rainforest Action Network*, 301 Broadway, San Francisco, CA 94133; (415) 398-4404. Uses direct action to sound the alarm on rain-forest issues. Works with developing nations to preserve the rain forests as renewable resources. Publishes the quarterly *World Rainforest Report*.

— *Rural America*, 1900 M Street NW, Washington, DC 20036. Community development, environmental concerns, and energy in rural areas.

— *Sea Shepherd Conservation Society*, P.O. Box 7000-S, Redondo Beach, CA 90277; one of the most effective direct-action groups.

— *Sierra Club*, 730 Polk Street, San Francisco, CA 94109; (415) 776-2211. The nation's oldest and still very effective voice for the environment. Its work includes lobbying, public eduction, political action, grass-roots organizing, and national and international outings and tours. Publishes the bimonthly magazine *Sierra*.

— *Urban Environmental Conference*, 666 Eleventh Street NW, Washington, DC 20001. Organizes on community, environmental, and other issues.

— *U.S. Public Research Interest Group* (USPIRG), 215 Pennsylvania Avenue SE, Washington, DC 20003; (202) 546-9707. The national office for 21 state PIRGs, providing research and advocacy assistance on environmental protection, consumer rights, safe energy, and open government.

— *Wilderness Society*, 1400 Eye Street NW, Washington, DC 20005; (202) 842-3200. Educates citizens, public officials, and media on need to protect and carefully manage public lands. Testifies at congressional hearings. Sponsors meetings on public-land management. Publishes wilderness-related reports. Has 13 regional offices.

2. *Further Reading*

— *Crossroads: Environmental Priorities for the Future*, edited by Peter Borrelli. Washington, D.C.: Island Press, 1988. Excellent overview of the environmental movement and its perceived priorities for the future by Barry Commoner, Stewart Udall, Lois Marie Gibbs, Gus Speth, William K. Reilly, Jr., and other leading authorities.

— *Cousteau Almanac*, Jacques-Yves Cousteau. New York: Doubleday, 1981. See especially

Part VII, "Making Waves" which deals with organizing and communicating. It also contains Cousteau's classic "Strategy of the Dolphin."

— *Dwellers in the Land: A Bioregional Vision*, Kirkpatrick Sale. San Francisco: Sierra Club, 1985. The most comprehensive book on an important subject.

— *Earth and Other Ethics*, Christopher D. Stone. New York: Harper & Row, 1988. A path-breaking work on environmental ethics.

— *Ecodefense: A Field Guide to Monkeywrenching*, edited by Dave Foreman and Bill Haywood. Tucson, Ariz.: Ned Ludd Books, 1988.

— *Ecotactics: The Sierra Club Handbook for Environment Activists*, edited by John G. Mitchell with Constance L. Stallings. New York: Simon and Schuster, 1970.

— *Giant Killers*, Michael Pertschuk (chairman of the Advocacy Institute). New York: Norton, 1986.

— *The Gift of Good Land*, Wendell Berry. San Francisco: North Point, 1981. Perceptive, beautiful essays on the relationship of humans and the land.

— *How Nature Works: Regenerating Kinship with Planet Earth*, Michael J. Cohen, Walpole, N.H.: Stillpoint, 1988. Explains our deep connection with nature and how, when we oppose the natural order, we oppose ourselves.

— *In Common Cause*, John W. Gardener. New York: Norton, 1972. Excellent book on citizen action by the founder of Common Cause.

— *The Monkey Wrench Gang*, Edward Abbey. New York: Avon, 1986.

— *More Action for a Change*, Kelley Griffin. New York: Dembner Books, 1987. An in-depth documentation of the work of the Public Interest Research Groups (PIRGs).

— *NOT in Our Backyards!*, Nicholas Freudenberg. New York: Monthly Review Press, 1984. One of the best books on community action for health and the environment.

— *Organizing: A Guidebook for Grassroots Leaders*, Si Kahn. New York: McGraw-Hill, 1982.

— *Politics of the Solar Age*, Hazel Henderson. New York: Doubleday, 1981.

— *Shutdown Strategies: Citizen Efforts to Close Nuclear Power Plants*, Joseph Kriesberg. Washington, D.C.: Public Citizen, 1988.

— *Solid Waste ACTION Project Guidebook*, Lois Gibbs and Will Collette. Arlington, Va.: Citizen's Clearinghouse for Hazardous Waste, 1987. Valuable, hands-on tactics and strategies from preeminent grass-roots leaders.

— *When You Write to Washington*, published annually by League of Women Voters, Washington, D.C.

ENDNOTES

1. Anne Witte Garland, *For Our Kids' Sake*. New York: Natural Resources Defense Council, 1989, p. 19.

2. Sheila Kaplan, "The Food-Chain Gang," *Common Cause*, September/October 1987.

3. Ibid.

4. *The State of the States*, published annually by Renew America, Washington, D.C., is an invaluable source of information on state environmental activities.

5. From the introduction to *Ecotactics*, edited by John G. Mitchell with Constance L. Stallings (New York: Simon and Schuster, 1970), p.15.

6. Based on a report in Anna Gyorgy, *No Nukes* (Boston: South End Press, 1979), pp. 393-394.

7. Jacques-Yves Cousteau, *Cousteau Almanac* (New York: Doubleday, 1981), p. 793.

8. Letter to Friends of the Seas from Paul Watson, April 1989.

9. Cited in Sea Shepherd Conservation Society newsletter, April 1989.

10. These operations are graphically described in Dick Russell, "The Monkeywrenchers," chapter 2 in Peter Borrelli, ed., *Crossroads* (Washington, D.C.: Island Press, 1988), pp. 27-48.

11. From the front page of *Earth First!*, a manifesto describing EF! and its activities.

12. The term is taken from the title of the classic book by Edward Abbey, **13.** Ibid., p. 4.

14. Kirkpatrick Sale, *Dwellers in the Land: The Bioregional Vision*, (San Francisco: Sierra Club, 1985), p. 55. **15.** Ibid., pp. 174-175.

12
THE POWER OF GREEN

Shopping for a Better World

*"As consumers, we have real power
to effect change. We can use our ultimate power,
voting with our feet and our wallets."*
– Anita Roddick, founder,
The Body Shop International

It seems that so many everyday decisions we make have a down side on our health or the environment. Give the kids Alar-treated apples, and you increase their risk of getting cancer. Eat a fast-food hamburger, you take a bite out of a tropical rain forest (and increase your chances of heart disease). Use the wrong aerosol hair spray, you help destroy the ozone layer. Drive a big American-made car, you create more air pollution and more acid rain, and accelerate the greenhouse effect. Is there anything we can do, many people ask, that doesn't pollute or otherwise harm the environment?

Yes, there are environmentally sound options but they often mean avoiding much of what we take for granted in our daily living. In this chapter, we offer guidelines to help you decide what's safe and what's dangerous in products you are exposed to every day – foods, cleaning materials, toilet items, clothing, home furnishings, building materials, and office supplies.

Six Basic Principles of Ecological Shopping

1. Use products that don't endanger your and others' health.
2. Avoid products or services that:
- consume disproportionate amounts of energy (incandescent light bulbs, electric can openers, energy-inefficient refrigerators);
- generate unnecessary waste (fast-food packaging);
- are based on materials taken from threatened environments or endangered species (teak, mahogany, redwood);
- cause harm to animals or other parts of the living planet (furs, ivory).
3. Find or create ecologically sound alternatives to petroleum-based packaging and household products.
4. Buy only what you need.
5. Recycle.
6. Remember at all times that, as a consumer, you have real power to bring about change. *You can vote with your pocketbook as well as with your ballot.*

The Pure Food Quest

Food adulteration, chemical additives, pesticides, synthetic fertilizers, irradiation, these are the hazards you face every day you go to the supermarket or grocery store. In theory, the U.S. Food and Drug Administration and the Department of Agriculture are empowered to keep your food safe and free of chemicals. In practice, they do a poor job of protecting the consumer. Although labeling laws have become stricter, most of the foods that are widely promoted in the American media are overrefined, adulterated with insufficiently tested chemicals (some of which are carcinogenic), and low in fiber and nutritional value but high in harmful salt, sugar, and fat.

Caveat emptor – let the buyer beware. Read labels, especially the small print. If you shop carefully, you can find some products that are safe, but by far your best options are:
- Grow as much of your own food as you can.
- Buy from local farmers and green markets.
- Join or form a food co-op.
- Buy organic food.

Going Organic

In fall 1988 a Lou Harris poll found that 84 percent of adults in the U.S. would buy organic if it cost the same as regular produce, and half of them would pay more. In 1989 the produce industry's newspaper *The Packer* reported that 80 percent of respondents were concerned with food safety and 18 percent had already changed their buying habits. Consumer demand for clean, pesticide-free products is changing America's habits of buying food and the system that produces it.[1]

Organic food is not quite the same as "natural" food, which covers a multitude of ambiguities. As the magazine *Organic Gardening* puts it, *organic* means using our understanding of nature as a guide for gardening and living, and growing food without the use of chemical pesticides or synthetic fertilizers.

Pending passage of the Farm Conservation and Water Protection Act of 1989, sponsored by Senator Wyche Fowler (D-Georgia), there is no federal specification of how organic foods must be grown, harvested, and processed. Nor do the FDA or the U.S. Department of Agriculture act as watchdogs over the growing organic industry.

State Support of Organic Food

Supervision varies from state to state: Texas, New Hampshire, and Washington operate state certification programs; Minnesota, New Hampshire, Ohio, and Vermont cooperate with independent certification programs; and 20 other states including California, Massachusetts, Minnesota, New York (pending), Washington, and Wisconsin have organic labeling laws or rules. California requires that land be pesticide-free for twelve months before food grown on it can be certified as organic. Iowa imposes a taxing and fee system on farmers who use chemical fertilizers and pesticides. Massachusetts is helping farmers reduce pesticide use and provides grants to help organic farmers with certification and marketing.

Until Senator Fowler's bill (or similar federal legislation) is enacted, you will have to rely on your own state's regulation of organic food growing and marketing. According to the New England Food Cooperative Organization, 95 percent of growers and packers of organic food are legitimate.[2] One important exception is so-called organic products from Mexico and other foreign countries. They are not subject to rigorous control and often contain large amounts of toxic pesticides and preservatives that are banned in the U.S. *All imported "organic" foods should be treated with caution.*

Independent Testing

At a growing number of supermarkets, shoppers are seeing signs that read, "NutriClean laboratory tests reveal NO detectable pesticide residues." NutriClean is an Oakland, Calif. company started by Stan Rhodes in 1984 to provide "some uniform structure and some quality control" to the growing organic foods industry.[3] The company conducts multiresidue analyses using federal guidelines for more than 100 pesticides. Out of 17,000 food stores in the nation, some 1,000 offer NutriClean-certified products, including such outlets as Ralph's Grocery, Raley's, Petrini's, Quality Plus, and Andronico's in California, Farmer Jack's in Michigan, Farm Fresh in Virginia, Stop & Shop and Bread and Circus in Massachusetts, and Fred Meyer in the Pacific Northwest, many of whom did not handle organic produce until they signed on with the Oakland company.

At present it is companies like NutriClean and not the federal government that are having a positive impact on organic agriculture. Organic food, which could until recently only be bought in health-food stores, is now appearing in many mainstream supermarkets and grocery stores across the U.S. and Canada.

For further information on sources in your area contact:

The Committee for Sustainable Agriculture, P.O. Box 1300, Colfax, CA 95713, supported by California Certified Organic Farmers, and many leading organic farmers and distributors in California and the Pacific Northwest. Publishes the quarterly *Organic Food Matters*; sponsors conferences and educational programs.

The Organic Crop Improvement Organization P.O. Box 729A, New Holland, PA 17557), a farmer-owned group certifying farmers who meet their standards. They will provide their list of approved organic food distributors in your area (enclose a self-addressed, stamped envelope with your request).

The Organic Food Production Association of North America P.O. Box 31, Belchertown, MA 01007, a trade association of organic farmers, processors, and distributors, which should be contacted for information on suppliers of high-quality, authentic organic food.

Read the Fine Print

There are more than 40 nongovernment certifying organizations nationwide. Most certify fresh produce, but processed foods present certification and labeling problems. Next to eating organic, your best bet is eating fresh, unprocessed foods, and if you can't do that regularly, *read labels extremely carefully.*

On average, Americans consume ten pounds of chemical additives a year, mostly without knowing it. Unfortunately, many products such as fruit, vegetables, unwrapped bread, eggs, meat, fish, soft drinks, and beer carry no labels, although most of them contain additives and pesticides. Even when labels are used – in packaged, canned, and bottled foods – the information given is inadequate or misleading.

If a product contains anything labelled "artificial," it is advisable not to buy it, because it probably includes a chemical additive, preservative, or flavoring. If the label says "100-percent natural," there should be no such chemicals in the product. But watch out. Some items such as canned soups or vegetables are called "natural" although they contain bacon or lard (which themselves contain chemicals). The manufacturers get around this misinformation by stating that they have not added any other artificial ingredients.

As Debra Lynn Dadd explains in her invaluable book *Nontoxic and Natural,*[4] there are many types of deceptive advertising used by manufacturers, including:

The Misleading Modifier – "Naturally flavored strawberry ice cream" may contain many artificial ingredients including artificial vanilla flavor, but has a literally accurate label because "natural" modifies "strawberry," not "ice cream."

Assumed Naturalness – "Farm-fresh" granola bars and other "health" foods sometimes contain artificial flavors, chemical additives, sugar, and hydrogenated oil, but lead you to think of them as natural because of the name, the picture on the package, and the descriptions of some natural ingredients they do contain.

Playing Up the Irrelevant – Sometimes a label prominently displays a harmful ingredient the product does *not* contain, hiding the fact that artificial flavors and colors are included in one or more of the ingredients (margarine, for example) that the law does not require to be listed. Many people who use margarine to avoid the saturated fat in butter think they are getting 100 percent corn oil. But if you read the label it might say: Liquid corn oil, partially hydrogenated corn oil, water, salt, whey, vegetable mono- and di-glycerides and lecithin (emulsifiers), sodium benzoate (as a preservative), artificial flavor and color (carotene), vitamins A and D added. Most of these items are undesirable or unnecessary in this particular form.

Is There a Safe Diet?

Given the widespread use of chemical fertilizers, pesticides, artificial additives, preservatives, flavoring, and coloring in our food, what can be considered safe?

Analysis of food by the U.S. Department of Agriculture and the FDA shows that meat and high-fat dairy products are much more heavily contaminated with

Common Food Additives and Their Side Effects[5]

Artificial colors and flavors are used mainly in foods of poor nutritional value. They make foods high in fat, sugar, and fiber-stripped starches more attractive and palatable than they would otherwise be. Cosmetic additives encourage the overconsumption of these types of food and thus contribute to many diet-related diseases (heart disease, cancers of breast, stomach, and colon, diabetes) as well as being harmful in themselves. Although a few (natural) additives, preservatives, and emulsifiers are useful, most are either unnecessary or used in excess. Worse, most have not been adequately tested, especially in the combinations in which they are consumed. Some of the most common harmful additives are:

Aspartame – diet sweetener used in ice cream and many low–calorie soft drinks and desserts. May affect the brain, causing epileptic fits. Banned in France, Netherlands, Austria, and Italy.

Benzoates – found in beer, soft drinks, milk desserts, pizza bases and some cheese products. May cause asthma, rashes, migraine, hyperactivity.

BHT (butylated hydroxytoluene) – antioxidant used in oils, cereals, potato chips, and other products. Concentrates in your body fat. May cause hyperactivity and rashes. Causes cancer and liver damage in lab tests. Not allowed in foods for babies and young children in U.K. Banned in Japan and Austria.

BVO (brominated vegetable oil) – emulsifier of soft drinks. Stores in body fat.

Citrus Red No. 2 – injected into the skin of some Florida oranges. May cause cancer.

Di-, tri- and polyphosphates – used in hamburgers, sausages, processed meats, frozen chicken, frozen pizza, fish fingers, processed cheese, cookies, and cakes. Cause kidney damage in test animals.

MSG (monosodium glutamate) – used in canned and packaged soups and sauces, frozen foods, fish fingers, and in most Chinese restaurants. Causes dizziness, headaches, and palpitations. Not allowed for babies and children in the U.K. and other countries.

Potassium bromate – put in flour to bleach it and accelerate baking. May cause stomach pains, nausea, and diarrhea. May reduce vitamin E in flour. Banned in bread in many European countries.

Red No. 3 – used to color cherries in fruit cocktails, candy, baked goods. May cause cancer.

Red No. 40 – widely used in soft drinks, hot dogs, candy, gelatin desserts, pastry, pet foods. Causes cancer in mice.

Saccharin – synthetic sweetener. Used widely in toothpaste and other products. Causes bladder cancer in test animals.

Sodium nitrite, sodium nitrate – used in cured meats. Lead to formation of cancer-causing nitrosamines, particularly in bacon.

Sulfites – used in hamburgers, hot dogs, mayonnaise, sauces, and soft drinks. (They occur naturally in wine and now must be declared on labels.) Provoke asthma attacks. Destroy vitamin B1. Cause mutations in bacteria.

pesticides than are other foods.[6] These products also contain antibiotics and hormones that farmers use to protect and fatten their animals. And, as we have seen in chapter 8, meat is more likely than grains and produce to take up radioactivity from nuclear reactors and other sources. If you choose to eat meat, poultry, and fish, make sure that they have been organically raised. Venison (wild deer) is ecologically sounder, especially in areas where they have become a pest species. Beware only of lead shot used by many hunters.

In terms of safety (and, many people believe, health), the best diet for avoiding toxic chemicals is vegetarian, based on organic foods including fresh vegetables and fruits, whole grains, legumes, soy milk and soy margarine. Other advisable steps:

● Wash, soak, and cook food in pure water.
● Use cookware made from stainless steel, cast iron and porcelain-coated cast iron, glass, or clay. Utensils, mixing bowls, and other kitchenware should be made of stainless steel, glass, ceramic, wood, or clay.
● Avoid aluminum cookware because it interacts with acid foods to form toxic aluminum salts that may cause brain damage; also avoid plastic because it, too, can contaminate food. Teflon and other "no-stick" finishes on pots and pans scratch easily and can release plastic fragments into what you are cooking. (For no-stick baking, I line the pan with a thin coating of safflower or canola oil.)

How to Have a Healthful Home

As we noted in chapter 4, your home sweet home can be a deadly time bomb with its fuse steadily burning. Contaminated drinking water; toxic fumes from cleaning products; formaldehyde gases from particle board, carpeting, furnishings, and clothing; bacteria and allergens from air conditioners, humidifiers, and heating systems; electromagnetic fields from microwave ovens – these are the main problems. Here is what you can do about them.

How to Find Out If Your Water Is Safe

Regardless of where you live, there is a better than even chance that the water you drink and bathe in is not as safe as it should be.

In 1988 EPA data identified more than 2,000 chemicals in our drinking water. Volatile organic chemicals, including many carcinogens, have been detected in 45 percent of public water systems serving more than 10,000 people.[7] Despite this evidence, EPA tests for fewer than 20 of these chemical pollutants on a regular basis. Some 55 million people in the United States depend on wells for their water, and the odds are that half of them may be polluted.

Here is how you can find out what your own situation may be:

1. Look for the signs. Start with your faucet and sink. An orange-red or brown color in the water or around the sink can result from iron from rusting pipes; greenish stains could mean copper oxidization. Pour the water into a clean glass. Does it foam as it comes out of the tap or when you swish it around? That could be detergent residue. Cloudy (turbid) water might indicate undesirable minerals, heavy metals, or other contaminants. However, well water sometimes gets clouded after a heavy rain when particles of soil percolate into the water table. This is usually a self-correcting condition.

2. Sniff the water. An odor of rotten eggs is probably from sulfur or decaying bacteria. A sweet candylike aroma might indicate vinyl chloride or other organic chemicals in the water. The smell of gasoline or oil could come from a leaking underground storage tank or a defective water pump. If the water smells like a swimming pool, it probably contains too much chlorine. A decaying emanation could come from a leaking septic tank or a small animal fallen into your well.

3. Take the taste test. Swish a small amount of water around in your mouth. Minerals impart flavor, but not odor; they usually taste metallic and are sometimes thought to be healthful. Often they are not. Any chemical or suspicious taste is a signal for further investigation. But, even if so far your water has a clean record, don't think you are home free. *The most dangerous pollutants are those that give off no color, odor, or taste.*

4. Go to the source. If your water comes from a public system, find out if the supplier is a local water company, a municipal board, or a regional authority. Your water bill will provide the answer and the telephone number to call. Ask what tests they have done recently. In towns with more than 10,000 people, any system supplying more than 15 homes is by law required to test for bacteria, organic chemicals, pesticides, and other contaminants at least once a year. *Insist on getting copies of the most recent results.* If pollution levels are higher than those set by EPA, the water company must act to reduce them. Of course, if you have a well, you must do your own testing.

5. Explore the neighborhood. Ask your neighbors, read the local newspapers, check with the town hall and local hospital to see if there has been trouble with the water in your area. If you have any doubt, contact the nearest municipal water supplier, or county or state health or environmental-control department. In many cases these agencies can provide fairly detailed reports on the quality of the water in your district, though probably not in your immediate location.

6. Get tested (primary). According to EPA, a comprehensive testing of your drinking-water quality should include these criteria: general characteristics (color, taste, odor); coliform bacteria count; hardness/softness; pH (degree of acidity/alkalinity); and levels of nitrates and chlorides, heavy metal, pesticides, herbicides, fungicides, and THMs and other organic chemicals. As you will find out, the first five of these tests are relatively simple to have done.

The best place to start is your local or state health or environmental department. Some county health departments do routine bacteriological tests free of charge. If not, they can put you in touch with a lab that will do it for about $25. The general procedure is for them to send you a sterile bottle with instructions, which are usually, to touch the bottle only when you fill and close it; to make sure the faucet is not leaking; to run the water for at least two minutes to clear the pipes; and, if you can't deliver the sample to the lab immediately, to keep it in the refrigerator until you can.

You should receive results within a week, including the coliform bacteria count per 100 milliliters (ml) – 1 ml is about one-fifth of a teaspoon. Since conditions vary seasonally, get the water tested at different times of the year, even if it tests clean the first time. If you like to be self-sufficient, do your own tests, using kits designed for schools and other institutions. They cost about $50 and can be ordered from water-analysis laboratories listed in your local yellow pages.

7. Test for organics. This is more complex (and expensive) because organic chemicals have to be analyzed by specialized laboratory equipment.

If you decide to go this route, call the EPA Safe Drinking Water Hotline toll-free at (800) 426-4791 or write to the EPA Office of Drinking Water

Criteria and Standards, 401 M Street NW, Washington, DC 20460. Ask EPA for recommended maximum contaminant levels (RMCLS) and background information on water contaminants. The data will help you tailor the tests for your situation. But keep in mind that certain states – New Jersey, for example – have *higher* drinking water standards than the EPA. If this is true in your state, use its standards to find out how safe or unsafe your water is.

What to Do If Your Water Tests Unsafe

If your water comes from a well or cistern, it will be relatively easy for you to track down the source of the contamination and take the necessary action. Correcting a high coliform bacterial count could be as simple as removing a dead animal or making sure there is no seepage from a nearby septic tank. (When we bought an old farmhouse a few years ago, we had to remove a very decayed squirrel to get the well water clean.)

Lead, copper, or iron in the water might mean replacing the pipes from the well or storage tank. The presence of oil could come from your own pump or tank. You are unlikely to find chlorine, but you could come across organic chemicals or radon gas (for details on radon see chapter 8, pp. 171-173) .

If you detect organic chemicals in your drinking water, they probably come from the ground water in your area. Check with neighbors to see if they have the same problem – it could originate from pesticide spraying by local farmers or from a leaking landfill. Either way, you will get better results if you act together with your neighbors. Be prepared for a long process, involving private and public meetings, and possibly bringing in outside experts and lawyers.

If your water comes from a public supplier, the contamination probably originates within the system itself, rather than at your home. However, it is still advisable to have primary testing, as outlined on p. 293. Once you have established you are not the culprit, you have two options: short-term remedial action, or long-term cleanup. The latter must be done by the local water company working in conjunction with the relevant government agency.

Quick Fixes

Here are three easy ways to reduce contaminants in your drinking water (but they are not substitutes for removing underlying causes):

● To flush out high levels of lead, iron, or copper that may have built up overnight in the pipes, let cold water run for at least three minutes before using. For hot beverages and infant formulas, draw cold water from the faucet, because hot water dissolves lead and copper solder more readily.

● To get rid of bacteria and volatile organic chemicals (VOCs), use cold water and let it boil for 20 minutes. Don't inhale the steam. You can also remove some VOCs by whipping the water for 15 minutes in a blender with the top off.

● To offset chlorine's effect on red blood cells and get rid of its odor and taste, add a pinch of powdered vitamin C to a glass of water just before drinking.

Long-term action: Step-by-step guidelines are provided in the excellent booklet *Drinking Water... An Endangered Resource*, published by the Citizen's Clearinghouse for Hazardous Waste (see "Resources," p. 310). Topics include knowing your rights, understanding the responsibilities of private and public suppliers and of various governmental agencies, and how to organize your community in the fight to clean up water pollution at the source. The booklet contains tables on the health effects of many contaminants, the traditional parameters of pollution, water-quality criteria, and detailed descriptions of treatment methods for cleaning up contaminated water sources.

Bottled Water

Readily available and ranging from 2 to 35 cents for an eight-ounce glass, bottled water is consumed by one in six American households, who spend two billion dollars a year for the beverage. Assuming, for the moment, that this supplies clean water for your family's drinking and cooking, it still leaves you with using potentially contaminated water for washing up, bathing, and showering, all of which can expose you to pollutants such as carbon tetrachloride or radon gas.

How Safe Is Bottled Water?

As far as the federal government is concerned, the product must meet standards for only 22 pollutants – *two fewer than tap water.* Soda and mineral waters, consumed by millions of people as their prime beverage, are subject to even less stringent controls.

A California study in 1985 found bottled water to contain potentially harmful organic and inorganic substances including arsenic, benzene, chloroform, fluorides, and nitrates. A survey in Massachusetts two years later revealed that 13 of 15 brands of mineral water sold in that state exceeded one or more federal or state guidelines, while a New York state review in 1988 found traces of toluene, carbon tetrachloride, and other solvents in 48 of 93 bottled waters sampled.[8]

Testing by *Consumer Reports* of 28 brands in 1987 revealed excessive sodium levels in two brands, excessive fluoride in three, and arsenic in three.[9] These and other similar findings are not surprising because *many bottlers use tap water as the source for club sodas, seltzers, and "purified" or even "mineral" waters.* "Spring" water, in principle, comes from underground sources, but, as we have seen, this is no guarantee of purity.

If bottled water is stored in a warm place, it is vulnerable to bacterial growth. A British test of bottles taken from store shelves found bacteria, including human staphylococci, presumably due to unhygienic bottling practices. This led the researchers to suggest that bottled water "not be used as an alternative drink for infants."[10]

Home Drinking-Water Treatment

Basically, there are two main types to consider – purifiers and filters:

Purifiers disinfect bacteria and viruses from "raw" or untreated water (e.g., from a well). They usually work by injecting small amounts of chemical disinfectant into the well or other source of supply; some systems employ ultraviolet radiation to kill the microorganisms. Purifiers are expensive to buy (costing several hundred dollars) and maintain.

Filters screen out some contaminants but are not able to remove all disease-causing microbes and should be used only on water that has been previously disinfected – that is, from a public water system. On the next page you will find guidelines on how to compare different systems.

Types of Filters

These are mechanical devices designed to improve the quality of your tap water; they range in price from under ten dollars to several hundred, not including the cost of installation and maintenance. Sales of home-treatment units in the United States are estimated to run at 3 million units a year. Before buying one, you will need to find out how well they work and which ones might be suited to your particular situation.

Basically, there are two main types: activated-carbon filters (ACFs), and reverse-osmosis (RO) systems.

Activated-carbon Filters. Activated carbon, the black stuff you put in your fish-tank filter, has been used as a medicinal purifier for centuries; it contains small porous granules with a large surface area which *adsorbs* organic molecules. This system does not actually take out impurities, but keeps them on the surface of the water at the top of the filter, cleaning the water as it slowly passes down. ACFs can remove as much as 98 percent of chloroform, chlorine, some pesticides, and other organic chemicals. They are *not* effective in removing heavy metals, bacteria, nitrates, or dissolved iron.

In general you get more for your money in a larger filter, but, unless you keep it scrupulously clean, there is a risk of bacterial contamination. This is more likely to occur if your water comes from a private well; public systems are safer in this respect because the water is usually disinfected.

The best way to control bacteria is to replace filters more frequently than recommended by the manufacturer. Try to get a service contract from your dealer that will include this option. Of course, if your well water is contaminated, you should deal with it at the source (in the well or ground water), not by means of a filtration system.

ACFs come in two versions: those that fit on the end of the faucet and those that go under the sink. The former are cheaper and easier to install, but have been found by *Consumer Reports* and other testing agencies to be less effective than under-the-sink units in removing chloroform and other chemicals.

Reverse Osmosis. In this system, water passes through three different filters: a paper cartridge unit to remove particulate matter; then an RO membrane to separate larger contaminant molecules from the water; and finally an activated-carbon filter which removes contaminants, including dissolved gases and lighter-weight organic chemicals, that may have gotten through the first two stages.

RO systems are designed primarily to remove dissolved solids from the water – heavy metals such as cadmium, chromium, and lead, minerals such as calcium, magnesium, and sodium, some organic chemicals, many pesticides, detergents, fluorides, nitrates, dirt particles, asbestos, and bacteria. Alas, they are not effective against arsenic, chloroform, and phenol.

Because they have three filters, reverse-osmosis units are the most expensive systems to buy (the average price is $750 plus installation, which usually has to be done by a plumber) and the most complex to clean and maintain. They also depend on your home having a water pressure between 35 and 200 pounds per square inch.*

Distillers purify your water by heating it into steam and leaving behind a residue of dissolved solids and polluting liquids that have a higher boiling point than water. But they do not usually filter out hazardous volatile gases, like chlo-

---

* Check with your local water board to find out what the pressure is at your location.

roform, that have a lower boiling point. These vaporize with the water, but recondense and end up in the finished product. Some distillers, known as *fractional distillers*, are designed to take care of this problem. They are more expensive, but worth the difference. Keep in mind: distillers are hard to clean because the residue of minerals, chemicals, and other pollutants builds up to form a scale; this also cuts down on the system's efficiency. Check carefully in advance to see how easily the model you are considering can be cleaned.

Because the conversion from liquid to steam removes *all* the minerals from the water, there is with distillers a loss of valuable trace minerals and of the *taste* of the water – a condition you may have to get used to. Most distillers run on electricity and average about 25 cents a gallon of distilled water produced, as well as giving off undesirable residual heat.

WARNING

Any purifying or filtering device that uses a silver screen or filter should not be used in connection with any chlorinated water supply. Chlorine reacts with silver and leaching can damage the filter, reducing its bacteria-killing capabilities.

Which System Is Best?

There is no federal certification program for water filters and treatment devices in the U.S., and only California and Wisconsin maintain state programs. The only central source of performance standards is the National Sanitation Federation, an independent research agency in Ann Arbor, Mich. Its program is confined to manufacturers who volunteer to have their products tested and who pay a fee for the evaluation. Companies authorized to use the federation's health-effects seal include *Amway*, Ada, Mich., *Aqualux Water Systems*, Stamford, Conn., *Culligan International*, Northbrook, Il., *Cuno Inc.*, Meriden, Conn., *Everpure Inc.*, Westmont, Il., *Keystone Filters*, Hatfield, Pa., and *Performance Filters*, Cincinnati, Ohio.

The consensus of those who have tested home filtration systems is: no single type is 100-percent effective for all kinds of water contamination; some units can be useful when there is no reliable supply of clean water or when you want to provide an extra margin of safety for yourself and your family. However, like drinking bottled water, using a filter system is at best a stop-gap measure.[11] It is no substitute for getting at the source of water pollution, a matter that we examined in chapter 3.

Warning: Skin and Waterborne Contaminants

Drinking is not the only way you can be affected by contaminated water. In the section on radon (pp. 171-173) we noted that this toxic gas can enter your home through the shower or bathtub. There are many other waterborne toxic substances that you can absorb through your skin, nose, or mouth when bathing, showering, or swimming.

Particular attention should be paid to exposure to chlorine in unventilated swimming pools. If you swim indoors, try to find a place equipped with heat-recovery ventilators which at least dilute the amount of chlorine in the air.[12]

Before You Buy a Water-filter System

1. Have your water tested to find out what pollutants are present.

2. Check your neighborhood to see if other people have a similar problem; if so, what action are they taking?

3. Pick a filter system best suited for your situation.

4. Buy only the equipment you need. For example, a simple carbon filter will do for improving the taste of your water.

5. Be prepared to add the cost of *frequent* filter replacement to your overall investment.

6. Get a comprehensive service agreement from the dealer – in *writing*.

7. Most importantly, work with local government, community, and environmental groups for *long-term* water-quality improvement.

8. Consult books and articles on this subject in "Resources" at end of this chapter, pp. 310-311, especially those which include material on filter testing.

Common Household Products and Safer Alternatives

Over 55,000 chemicals are contained in everyday "convenience" products and over 1,000 more come on the market each year. Most are untested and unregulated. Many present serious health threats and leave their mark on the environment for several generations. The use of household or garden pesticides, for example, can increase the chance of childhood leukemia sevenfold, according to a study by the National Cancer Institute.[13]

Aerosols

The Problem: Replacing ozone-destroying CFCs, a new generation of propellants contain butane, isobutane, and propane that laboratory studies show to be harmful to the heart and central nervous system.

The Solution: Don't buy aerosol cans. If a spray is necessary, get a pump dispenser. (And you can save old pump dispensers to use when mixing your own cleaners.)

All-purpose Cleaners

The Problem: Many contain ammonia (which attacks your lungs) and chlorine (which forms cancer-causing compounds). Mixed together they form a deadly chloramine gas.

The Solution: You can make your own light-duty cleaner by mixing 1/4 cup of liquid soap (such as Murphy's Oil Soap) or borax in a quart of hot water and adding a tablespoon of white vinegar or lemon juice to cut grease. There are now several ecologically benign cleaners on the market. One is *Con-Lei*, a biodegradable, colloidal fluid that breaks down grease and oil molecules; along with other nontoxic products, it can be ordered from Seventh Generation and other mail-order houses. (See pp. 308-309 for details.) Another long-established, environmentally-minded company is Shaklee, with headquarters at 444 Market Street, San Francisco, CA 94111. Working through distributors nationwide, Shaklee markets a wide range of nontoxic, biodegradable household cleaners, personal-health products, vitamins, and nutritional items which rely on the use of natural and organic ingredients. If you can't locate one of their distributors in your area, call Shaklee at (800) 426-0766 for more information and direct ordering. Other phosphate-free and biodegradable cleaners include *Allen's*, *Golden Lotus*, and *Granny's Old Fashioned Products*, all available from Baubiologie Hardware, 207B Sixteenth Street, Pacific Grove, CA 93950.

Art Materials

The Problem: Children under 12 are particularly susceptible to toxic substances in these products.

The Solution: Use the substitutes as indicated below.

Toxic Substance	Safe Substitute
Permanent felt-tip markers (contain toxic solvents)	Water-based markers
Aerosol spray paints and fixatives	Water-based products
Powdered colors and clay (can cause breathing difficulty)	Liquid colors, crayons; Wet clay is safe
Instant papier mâché (may contain asbestoslike fibers)	Papier mâché made from newspaper and paste
Turpentine, benzene, and other solvents; epoxy glues, rubber cement	Water-based products

Automatic Dishwashing

The Problem: Commercial powders contain harsh detergents with high concentrations of phosphates that, when released into lakes and streams, kill fish and other aquatic life.

The Solution: You can get nontoxic varieties at health-food stores or by mail order. As a last resort, you should choose the dishwashing detergent with the lowest phosphate content listed on the package.

Bleach

The Problem: It contains chlorine, detergents, synthetic dyes and fragrance, and hydrogen peroxide. Particularly dangerous if you mix it with ammonia.

The Solution: There's no single "magic" product. In some cases (such as cleaning wood surfaces) you can use lemon juice or vinegar. In other cases, washing with natural soaps and drying clothes in sunlight make bleaching unnecessary.

Carpets and Rugs

The Problem: Most contain formaldehyde (for finishing), pentachlorophenol (for backing), and pesticides (for mothproofing) as well as often being made of plastics such as acrylon, latex, nylon, polyester, polyurethane, and PVC/vinyl chloride. Even if your wall-to-wall carpet is made of natural fibers, it probably has a polyurethane foam padding underneath which outgasses toxic vapors of formaldehyde and pentachlorophenol.

The Solution: Avoid synthetic rugs and wall-to-wall carpeting. If you have the latter, seriously consider replacing it with area rugs made of natural materials – wool, cotton, sheepskin, sisal – that have not been mothproofed. *Carpet and upholstery cleaners:* Remove small spots with club soda; sprinkle fuller's earth or cornstarch on larger spots for 15 minutes or longer to absorb stains or grease, then wash with a mixture of 3 parts very hot water and 1 part white vinegar. If stains persist, use a soap-based, nonaerosol rug or upholstery shampoo. Test a small area beforehand for colorfastness.

Clothing

The Problem: Much clothing is made of synthetic materials (polyester, acrylic, vinyl chloride, nylon) and contains artificial dyes, mothproofing pesticides, and formaldehyde finishes.

The Solution: Buy clothing made from natural fibers – cotton, wool, linen, silk, mohair – and wash thoroughly before wearing to get rid of harmful dyes and finishes.

Dishwashing Liquids

The Problem: Most are detergents derived from petroleum products, are non-biodegradable, and often contain harmful fragrances and colors. *Detergents cause more child poisonings than any other product.*

The Solution: Use products made from soap (such as *Dr. Bronner's castile*), *Ecover*, or *Shaklee's Basic-H.*

Disinfectants

The Problem: Most contain highly toxic chemicals such as ammonia, chlorine, cresol, and phenol, whose fumes can even leak through the container.

The Solution: Baking soda on a damp sponge will clean most surfaces, nooks, and crannies; an open box in a refrigerator deodorizes the air inside for up to 3 months. Use white vinegar or fresh lemon juice either full strength or diluted half and half with water. Another effective disinfectant is 1/2 cup borax mixed in 1 gallon hot water.

Drain Cleaners

The Problem: They contain lye and hydrochloric and sulfuric acids that can burn human tissue. If not used precisely according to instructions, they can explode. Especially dangerous around children.

The Solution: Install a strainer in the drain to trap hair and food particles. As a preventive measure, pour boiling water down drain once a week. If the water flow is sluggish, pour 2 tablespoons of baking soda and 1/2 cup white vinegar down the drainpipe and cover for 60 seconds. The chemical reaction will build up pressure and unclog most drains. If necessary, repeat the process or use a rubber plunger to build up pressure. As a last resort, use a plumber's "snake" to clear out the pipe.

Floor and Furniture Polish

The Problem: Many polishes contain phenol, which causes cancer in animals. Can also cause severe skin irritation. Residual vapors contaminate long after use.

The Solution: Blend 1 tablespoon lemon oil with 1 pint mineral oil; or blend 1 cup linseed oil, 1/2 cup white vinegar, and 1/2 cup rubbing alcohol. To remove water marks from wood surfaces, rub in a small amount of toothpaste.

Glass Cleaners

The Problem: They contain ammonia, glycol, naphthalene and other toxic substances.

The Solution: Several homemade mixes work well – 1 tablespoon vinegar or lemon juice in 1 quart water; 2 tablespoons washing soda or borax in 3 cups water; 2 tablespoons cornstarch and 1/2 cup white vinegar in 1 gallon warm water. Spray it on the window and clean with a natural linen towel, a clean damp chamois cloth, or a rubber squeegee. Newspapers are not advised because the newsprint gives off fumes when damp.

Insecticides

See *Pesticides*, p. 302.

Interior Finishes and Furnishings

The Problem: Harmful contaminants such as formaldehyde, volatile organic compounds, and plasticizers are outgassed by many materials and products made from synthetic plastic resins that we use in our homes, including particle boards, floor and ceiling tiles, wall coverings, adhesives, paints, waxes, finishes, and upholstery.

The Solution: As much as possible, use natural materials – wood, clay, slate, or marble for floor and wall finishes; wool, cotton, linen, or silk for curtains, upholstery, and rugs. For an example of how natural materials can be used most effectively in interior space, see "When Working is Good for Your Health," pp. 90-91.

Laundry Products

The Problem: They contain ammonia, nonbiodegradable detergents, naphthalene, phenol, and other harmful substances.

The Solution: Use natural soaps boosted with small quantities of borax, baking soda, or washing soda. A drop or two of vinegar in the water will help prevent colors from fading. Replace chlorine bleach with small amount of baking soda or borax to whiten clothes.

Metal Polishes

The Problem: They contain ammonia, ethanol, petroleum distillates, and sulfur compounds, giving off toxic fumes.

The Solution:

Aluminum – Clean with a soft cloth dipped in straight lemon juice or white vinegar.

Brass and copper – Make a paste of lemon juice and salt or baking soda. Leave it on for five minutes. Wash off with warm water and dry with a soft cloth. If copper is tarnished, boil the item for several hours in a pot of water with 1 cup vinegar and 1 tablespoon salt. Then wash with soap and water, rinse, and dry.

Chrome – Rub with lemon peel, rinse, and polish with a soft cloth or wipe with a soft cloth dipped in straight cider vinegar.

Gold – Wash in warm, soapy water, then polish with a chamois cloth.

Silver – Clean with toothpaste applied on a soft rag or cloth. (It's a good way to use up your old widely advertised brands, most of which contain undesirable saccharin!) Wash off with warm water. Another method is to fill a glass jar half full with strips of aluminum foil, add 1 tablespoon rock salt, and top off with cold water. Put silver items in the jar for 3 minutes, then rinse well in plain water.

Oven Cleaners

The Problem: They contain aerosols, detergents, and lye, a powerful caustic that can burn and disfigure human tissue. If you splash lye in your eyes, it can blind you. Keep them away from children.

The Solution: Cook food in proper-sized containers. To catch spills, line the bottom of the oven with aluminum foil. Sprinkle salt on spills while they are still warm, then clean with a paste made of 2 tablespoons of baking soda in 1 cup hot water. For tough spots, use a nontoxic scouring powder and steel-wool pads (be sure to pick up leftover steel slivers with a magnet).

Paints and Paint Thinners

The Problem: More than 300 toxic substances and 150 carcinogens have been found in commercial oil and latex paints. Toxic vapors remain for months after they have dried.

The Solution: Use nontoxic, vegetable-based paints, stains, and lacquers. Finish woods naturally with oil or wax. Use a heat gun, scrapers, and sandpaper to remove paint and other finishes. Beware of inhaling fumes or dust.

Pesticides

The Problem: Pesticides, insecticides, herbicides, fungicides, and rodenticides are used in 90 percent of American households. Commercial brands are highly toxic, especially when released in enclosed space. They pose a hazard to health during application and from continued inhalation of residues.

The Solution:

Ants – sprinkle red chili powder, borax, or dried peppermint where you see them coming in. Plant mint by the back and front doors of your house to help keep them out.

> *Pesticides, insecticides, herbicides, fungicides, and rodenticides are used in 90 percent of American households.*

Beetles and Weevils – Put a bay leaf in each container where you store flour and other grain products.

Cockroaches – Mix equal parts of baking soda and powdered sugar, and spread it around the infested area. Cockroaches can also be controlled with common boric acid powder sprinkled around baseboards, under sinks, and in other infested areas. Do not use in places accessible to children and pets. Pyrethrin (see *Houseplants* below), is an effective and safe all-purpose bug killer, provided that it is not formulated with other, toxic pesticides. Garlic is another natural pest-repellent; you can grow it in your garden to keep harmful bugs away or mix it in your blender with a mild soapy liquid and use as a spray.

Fleas – Feed your pets nutritional or brewer's yeast. The vitamin B supposedly makes them immune. Dips and sprays containing delimonine gas derived from citrus extracts safely repel fleas and other pests. Organic spray repellents made from cedar wood, eucalyptus, and bay leaves are also effective.

Flies – Put screens on windows and doors. Hang clusters of cloves in your rooms. Leave crushed orange or lemon skins in strategic places; the citrus oil repels flies and other insects.

Houseplants can be kept insect free, if you wash or hand-spray leaves and stems frequently with mild soapy water or with pyrethrin, a time-tested insecticide derived from chrysanthemums, marigolds, and other members of the aster family. It is safe as a spray, provided it is not mixed with potentially harmful ingredients such as piperonyl butoxide. To control spider mites, white flies, scale, and mealybugs, wash leaves with lukewarm soapy water or wipe the pests off with a cotton swab dipped in rubbing alcohol.

Mosquitoes – Keep screens on windows and doors. Burn oil of citronella rings. Grow garlic, marigolds, and any flowers that attract birds who eat mosquitoes. Spray with pyrethrin. *Don't use electronic zappers; they attract (and kill) many beneficial insects but not mosquitoes!*

Rats and Mice – One of the most effective nontoxic safeguards against rodents is still the cat. Make sure no food is left in the open, including food in cardboard boxes. Use mechanical traps, but beware of poisoned bait. Stuff up their entry holes with steel wool (they'll eat their way through almost anything else.)

Room Fresheners

The Problem: They contain aerosols, ammonia, synthetic fragrances, and other toxic substances.

The Solution: Aerate your home more frequently. Put out a bowl or two of potpourri, a mixture of dried flowers, herbs, and spices that you can get at many health-food stores or make up yourself. Also, make sachets of fragrant herbs (lavender, rosemary, mint), spices (cinnamon, cloves), and dried flowers (roses, hibiscus, apple blossom).

Scouring Powders

The Problem: They contain chlorine, detergents, and talc.

The Solution: Buy a chlorine-free brand such as *Bon Ami* (made of feldspar and soap) or make your own mix of table salt (or baking soda) sprinkled on a sponge that has been moistened with equal parts of water and vinegar. You can also apply liquid soap to a surface and sprinkle with dolomite powder. Scour with steel wool. For safe bleaching add a pinch of sodium perborate.

Textiles

The Problem: Hundreds of "miracle fibers" are made with phenol, vinyl chloride, and other harmful plastics that may be outgassed or absorbed by the skin. Many are treated with formaldehyde as a finish for easy care (bedsheets, for example) or for flameproofing (nylon curtains). Some "permanent press" products (shirts, blouses, and dresses) combine the formaldehyde resin directly with the fiber so that the formaldehyde becomes irremovable.

The Solution: Be prepared in some cases to give up the convenience of synthetics for the safety (and comfort) of natural materials like cotton, wool, silk, and kapok (a fiber from seed pod of the tropical kapok tree).

Toilet Cleaners

The Problem: They contain chlorine and hydrochloric acid, which can burn your skin and eyes. Swallowing them can cause severe illness or death.

Safe Household Products

Here are a few inexpensive common household basics that are effective and safe for many cleaning needs. They can replace most formulated brand items that are hazardous and overpriced:

Baking Soda: Common baking soda (sodium bicarbonate) is an all-purpose cleaner that removes odors, and can be used as a polish, for cleaning teeth, even as an antacid. It is mildly abrasive, noncorrosive, and safe to ingest.

Beeswax: You can add melted beeswax to mineral oil to make a natural and durable furniture polish.

Borax: Ordinary powdered borax is effective as a light cleaner, and for removing odors and preventing the growth of mold. You can find it in the supermarket laundry section. It is harmful if swallowed, however; keep it out of the reach of children.

Fuller's Earth: A clay powder that can be bought in building-materials and ceramics-supply stores. It useful for absorbing liquids spilled on carpets and upholstery (see p. 299).

Lemon Juice: At full strength or, sometimes, diluted, lemon juice is an excellent cleaner and grease cutter used by itself or in combination with other ingredients.

Mineral Oil: A safe and odor-free petroleum oil, it works well as a wood and furniture polish. Mildly laxative if ingested in small quantities, it can also be used to clean greasy hands. It is available in pharmacies.

Pure Soap: Made without additives, bar or flake soap is a gentle, effective cleaner for many uses.

Vinegar: Common white vinegar is excellent at cutting grease, removing odors, and preventing the growth of mold.

The Solution: Use soap and borax. Remove stubborn rings and lime buildup with white vinegar or a safe scouring powder.

Toilet Paper

The Problem: Many brands that contain dyes and fragrances that contaminate the water system and may cause skin irritation.

The Solution: Switch to unscented, white toilet paper made from recycled paper.

Disposing of Hazardous Materials[14]

Once you know what toxic materials you *don't* want in our homes, the question arises how you can get rid of them safely.

The first step is to take stock of what you have. According to the EPA, there are four main types of dangerous materials found among the 160 pounds of hazardous waste produced by the average household each year: *flammable* – those that can be easily ignited; *corrosive* – those that dissolve metals or burn the skin; *reactive* – materials that dissolve violently with water or other substances; and *toxic* – substances that are poisonous and may contain high concentrations of heavy metals, pesticides, and other toxic chemicals. Of course, some products exhibit more than one of these characteristics.

Here are the most common items you are likely to find and recommended disposal instructions.

Aerosol Cans – Keep away from heat, high pressure, and flames. Make sure the can is completely empty before throwing it in the trash because it could explode when crushed in the garbage truck or compactor.

Ammonia and Ammonia-based Cleaners – Do not throw in the trash. Dilute with *lots* of water and flush slowly down the drain. Do not mix with bleach: deadly gases may result.

Antifreeze, Automotive Fluids (brake and power-steering fluids, engine-radiator flushes) – Do not pour down drains or on the ground. Take these products to a recycling center or a service station.

Auto Waxes and Polishes, Body Fillers, Road Salts – Road salts kill plants and pollute water. Use up the product or take it to a collection program.

Barbecue Lighter Fluid – Do not store in your home. Use it up or give it to a friend. Do not incinerate cans or throw in garbage.

Batteries – Nickel, cadmium, mercury, and alkaline harm people, animals, and fish. If put in wood stoves or open fires, they explode. Recycle auto batteries at a battery retailer, hearing-aid batteries at hospitals. Take mercury batteries to a hazardous-waste center.

Cesspool Cleaners – Prohibited by federal and state law. Do not use! If you have some stored, take it to a hazardous-waste center.

Chlorine Bleach – Never mix chlorine-based products with ammonia. Do not put them in the trash. Dilute with lots of water and pour slowly down the drain or toilet.

Disinfectants and Drain Cleaners – only very small amounts should be put down the drain and only if diluted with large amounts of water. Do not put them down the drain if it is connected to a septic tank. Industrial-strength disinfectants should be taken to a collection center.

Fingernail Polish Remover – Take to a collection center.

Floor and Furniture Waxes/Polishes – If in aerosol cans, see above. Otherwise, use up the product.

Fuels (gasoline, diesel, kerosene) – These are highly dangerous to have in your home. Store in containers approved by the local fire department. Use up soon or give to someone who will.

Glass Cleaners – Rinse the empty container before throwing it in the trash. Take leftover cleaner to a collection center.

Glues – Avoid fumes. Let harden and take them to a collection center.

Insecticides, Herbicides, Pesticides (chemical) – Do *not* risk using them and do *not* throw them in the garbage. Take them carefully to a collection center that handles toxic waste.

Medicines – If you are no longer using them, flush liquids down the toilet. Take other products to a collection center.

Metal Cleaners/Polishes – Let petroleum-based polishes dry out, away from children and pets. Wrap carefully and place in the trash.

Mothballs – Avoid skin contact. Do not put in trash. Take to a collection center.

Oven Cleaners – Take to a collection center.

Paints, Stains, Finishes, Thinners – Leftover oil-based paints are a fire and toxic hazard. Give to a community group, for outside use only. Do not put in the trash or sewers. Take other products to a collection center.

Swimming Pool Chemicals – These products are very dangerous. Use with extreme care or give away to a careful user. Do not put in the trash. Take to a collection center.

Tires – These are among the hardest items to dispose of. They are breeding grounds for rats, mosquitoes, and other pests. They are also a serious fire hazard, and, when burned, a source of heavy air pollution. Do not leave tires lying around. Contact your local collection center for special recycling instructions.

Toilet Bowl Cleaners – If you are connected to a septic tank, do not pour these chemicals down the drain. Take to a collection center. Otherwise, dilute with a lot of water and pour down the drain.

Waste Oil – Probably the most common household waste that is disposed of improperly. Do not pour in sewers or dump on the ground. Call your local auto service station and ask if they will collect it. If not, contact your local collection center for instructions.

Environmental Seals of Approval

Small decisions made by large numbers of consumers every day add up to significant impact on the global environment. Decreasing our use of CFCs in aerosols and plastic foams slows depletion of the ozone layer. Energy-efficient appliances consume less fossil fuels, tempering the greenhouse effect. However, without adequate information to counter conflicting claims of manufacturers and advertisers, we can't always make the best choices of what we buy.

The first major example of an ecological "Good Housekeeping Seal of Approval" comes from West Germany. In 1979 the victorious Green Party was instrumental in initiating a program known as the *Blue Angel*. Today it is a household institution, having given its approval to 2,250 products in 50 different categories. The resulting change in buying habits of German consumers has led to important environmental gains, including an estimated 44,000-ton annual reduction in the use of carcinogenic and ozone-depleting substances.[15]

In October 1988 the British followed suit with a Green Consumer Week which, together with the publication of a *Green Consumer Guide* focused national attention on the power of the Green consumer to push industry in more environmentally aware directions. Encouraged by the German success, the Canadian government initiated an Environmental Choice program in which paints, batteries, paper, plastic, and other products that meet government standards are given a seal of approval – a stamp featuring the maple leaf formed of the tail feathers of three doves. In addition to the logo the product carries information on why it is a good environmental buy, including resources saved in its manufacture and the low level of pollution it creates.

Although the program is voluntary, many manufacturers are willing to pay an annual fee of up to $5,000 to use the seal because they believe it will increase sales of their products. As Canada's environmental Minister explains the program, "Good environmental practice is good business."[16]

In the United States no similar program has been initiated by the federal government, although the need for one is widely acknowledged. In 1988 the Council on Economic Priorities (CEP), a New York-based national research and educational organization, introduced a 146-page guide to socially responsible supermarket shopping called *Shopping for a Better World*. The pocket-size guide rates 1,300 brand-name products from 138 parent companies on ten social issues – environment, women's and minority advancement, animal testing, military contracts, disclosure of information, nuclear power, community outreach, giving to charity, and South Africa. In 1989 CEP, in coalition with the Center for Science in the Public Interest, the Sierra Club, and other nonprofit organizations, formed *The Alliance for Social Responsibility*, designed to improve the social responsibility of corporations and the consumer public through the use of a social seal of approval to be placed on products and used in advertising them. Judging by the success of CEP's guide – it had sold over 350,000 copies by the end of 1989 – the new seal of approval should help shoppers trying to thread their way through the maze of household-name products, many of which (*Alka-Seltzer*, *Aim* toothpaste, and *Old Spice* deodorant, for example) flunk the CEP test. High marks went to Quaker Oats (top ratings in nine categories), *Pledge* by Johnson Wax (the first company to ban CFCs), and *Paul Newman's Own Sockarooni Spaghetti Sauce* (for donating all of its profits to charity, using biodegradable material for packaging, and overall environmental excellence).

Socially Responsible Investing

In this time of increasing environmental awareness, more and more people want to invest their savings in companies that offer social as well as financial benefits. While socially responsible investors earn interest on their principal, their money works to influence corporate and public policies in a number of ways. From a negative viewpoint, not buying stock in, say, Exxon because of their response to the *Valdez* oil spill or in a company that is destroying the rain forests serves notice to the company, investment house, or bank that you (and, one hopes, many others) will not support antiecological (or antihuman) activities. Taking your money out of companies that are environmentally or socially insensitive thus becomes a positive affirmation of your beliefs.

When looking for positive ways in which you can invest, there are several useful places to begin. One practical and comprehensive guide is the book *Economics As If the Earth Really Mattered* by Susan Meeker-Lowery, who also publishes an excellent quarterly newsletter, *Catalyst – Investing in Social Change*. In addition to showing how your investing can affect the corporate world, the book describes different types of investment you can make (for example, in

The Valdez Principles

In the summer of 1989 a coalition of environmentalists and investors, including the National Audubon Society, the Sierra Club, the Franklin Research and Development Corporation, and the Social Investment Forum, drafted guidelines for corporate conduct relating to the environment. Named after the Exxon oil spill, the ten principles include:

- *Protection of the biosphere* – signers will try to eliminate pollutants that damage, the air, water, or earth;
- *Sustainable use of natural resources;*
- *Reduction and disposal of waste;*
- *Wise use of energy;*
- *Risk reduction* – minimizing environmental risks and preparing for environmental accidents;
- *Marketing of safe products and services;*
- *Damage compensation* – restoring the environment from harm caused and compensating persons adversely affected;
- *Disclosure of accidents and hazards and protection of employees who report them;*
- *Environmental directors and managers* – having at least one board member qualified to represent environmental interests and a senior executive for environmental affairs; and
- *Assessment and audit* – conducting annual self-evaluation to determine progress in implementing principles.

As a consumer, investor, or employee you can influence corporate behavior by directing your resources and energy to corporations that subscribe to the Valdez Principles. For further information contact the National Audubon Society, 950 Third Avenue, New York, NY 10022; (212) 832-3200.

housing cooperatives, community land trusts, revolving loan funds, and environmentally responsible companies).

Socially-minded investment funds include:

Affirmative Investments, 59 Temple Place, Boston, MA 02111, (617) 350-0250;

Calvert Social Investment Fund, 1700 Pennsylvania Avenue NW, Washington, DC 20006, (800) 368-2748;

Dreyfus Third Century Fund, 767 Fifth Avenue, New York, NY 10153, (212) 715-6200;

New Alternatives Fund, 295 Northern Boulevard, Great Neck, NY 11021, (516) 466-0808;

Parnassus Fund, 1427 Shrader Street, San Francisco, CA 94117, (415) 664-6812;

Pax World Fund, 224 State Street, Porstmouth, NH 03801, (603) 431-8022;

Social Investment Forum, 711 Atlantic Avenue, Boston, MA 02111, (617) 423-6655;

Social Responsibility Investment Group, 127 Peachtree Street NE, Atlanta, GA 30303, (404) 577-3635;

Socially Responsible Banking Fund, Vermont National Bank, P.O. Box 804, Brattleboro, VT 05301, (800) 544-7108;

Working Assets Money Fund, 230 California Street, San Francisco, CA 94111, (800) 533-FUND.

The Mail-Order Green Consumer

There are increasing numbers of companies that sell ecologically safe products and services. Virtually all of them have catalogs of their products and offer return, exchange, or refund guarantees. They include:

AFM Enterprises, 1140 Stacy Court, Riverside, CA 92507, (714) 781-6860. AFM is a custom formulating and manufacturing company that sells products for people who are chemically sensitive. Although not from 100-percent natural sources, their paints, cleaners, grouts, and adhesives are claimed not to outgas and to be safe to use.

The Allergy Store, P.O. Box 2555, Sebastopol, CA 95473, (800) 824-7163. Offers nonallergenic and nontoxic home products as well as vitamins, skin-care products, respirators, herb teas, and books.

Auro Products, imported from West Germany by Sinan, P.O. Box 181, Suisun, CA 94585, (707) 427-2325. The line includes quality paints, lacquers, thinners, and cleaners, all made from natural ingredients.

Baubiologie Hardware, 207B 16th Street, Pacific Grove, CA 93950. Started by John Banta, a highly respected home and business environmental consultant, this company specializes in healthful alternative building. It is an excellent source for full-spectrum lights, nonionizing smoke detectors, radon monitors, air and water filters, natural pest controls, and many other products. The Baubiologie "Healthful Hardware Catalog" is full of items made from natural, environment-friendly ingredients.

The Body Shop, 485 Madison Avenue, New York, NY 10022, has 350 locations from Brighton, England, where it was founded by Anita Roddick, to Dubai, United Arab Emirates. The company offers a wide range of environmentally safe body products, none of which is tested on animals. Most of the ingredients are derived from plants that the company encourages Third World communities to grow. A percentage of their profits goes to Greenpeace, Friends of the Earth, and other environmental projects.

East West Books by Mail, P.O. Box 1200, Brookline Village, MA 02147. Carries Debra Lynn Dadd's books and many other useful publications on health and well-being.

Ecco Bella (Here is Beautiful), 6 Provost Square, Caldwell, NJ 07006. Markets non-animal-tested items, biodegradable household products, body-care products, soaps, and cleaners (including the *Life Tree* and *Ecover* product lines), also recycled copier, computer, and stationery paper.

Environmental Testing and Technology, P.O. Box 369, Encinitas, CA 92024, (619) 436-5990. Sells detectors for formaldehyde, radon, and electromagnetic pollution, and the *Somashield* video screen. Also does testing and consulting.

Global Village Imports, 195 Second Avenue, San Francisco, CA 94118-1450. Sells hand-loomed cotton clothes, bedding, and other products.

Jim Morris Environmental T-Shirts, P.O. Box 831, Boulder, CO 80306. Offers beautiful T-shirts illustrating clean water, protecting the dolphins, and saving tropical rain forests and endangered species.

Livos Plantchemistry, 2641 Cerrillos Street, Santa Fe, NM 87501. Has developed nontoxic paints, paint thinners, oil finishes, stains, waxes, and cleaners made only from natural ingredients.

Macrobiotic Mall, Gaitersburg, MD 20879, (800) 533-1270. Specializes in whole grains, legumes, sea vegetables and other food items, and kitchenware.

The Nature Company, 1731 4th Street, Berkeley, CA 94710, (415) 525-2879, and 8 Fulton Street, South Street Seaport, New York, NY 10038, (212) 422-

8510. Offers many ways of enjoying nature without exploiting it – e.g., no seashells or mounted butterflies but telescopes, binoculars, audiotapes, scientific games, and many other products. Now affiliated with the Nature Conservancy, the company sponsors free exhibitions and nature discovery events nationwide and organizes ecologically directed safaris all over the world.

Real Goods Trading, 3041 Guidiville Road, Ukiah, CA 95482, (800) 762-7325. Claims to be the largest distributor of alternative-energy products in the world. Its 80-page catalog includes photovoltaic systems, wind generators, energy-efficient refrigerators, low-voltage appliances, tools, and lighting, tankless water heaters, water purifiers and filters, composting toilets, and energy-related books.

Seventh Generation, 10 Farrell Street, Burlington, VT 05403, (802) 862-2999. Their products include solar watches and calculators, pollution test kits (lead paint, formaldehyde, arsenic, chloroform, and radon), books, water savers, health-care products, cleaning materials, and household energy savers.

Shaklee, 444 Market Street, San Francisco, CA 94111, (800) 426-0766. A Fortune 500 company that produces an extensive line of environmentally benign household cleaners and personal health and nutritional items that are sold through distributors. Organizes health programs and conferences.

Sunrise Lane Products, 780 Greenwich Street, New York, NY 10014, (212) 242-7014. Markets the *Life Tree* line, which includes biodegradable, nontoxic cleaning products that do not contain chlorine, ammonia, or phosphates, and premium dishwashing, laundry, and all-purpose liquids containing aloe vera and calendula to prevent hands from becoming chapped.

To Your Health, 2815 Elm Street, Dallas, TX 75226, (800) 233-2606. A fine source for nontoxic household products including heavy gauge stainless-steel pots from Switzerland, *Presto* pressure cookers, and environmentally safe cleaners.

RESOURCES

The following is provided to help you locate additional resources on the topics covered in this chapter.

1. U.S. Government

— *Consumer Information Center*, General Services Administration, Pueblo, CO 81009.

— *Consumer Products Safety Commission* (CPSC), 5401 Westbard Avenue, Bethesda, MD 20207; hotline (800) 638-CPSC.

— *CPSC Regional Offices*:

Eastern Regional Center, 6 World Trade Center, Vesey Street, 3rd Floor, New York, NY 10048; (212) 264-1125.

Central Regional Center, 230 South Dearborn Street, Rm. 2944, Chicago, IL 60604; (312) 353-8260.

Western Regional Center, 555 Battery Street, Rm. 401, San Francisco, CA 9411; (415) 556-1816.

— *EPA*: Office of Public Information and other offices, see p. 30.

— *Food and Drug Administration*, Department of Health and Human Services, 500 Fishers Lane, Rockville, MD 20013.

— *Office of Consumer Affairs*, Department of Commerce, Room 5275, Washington, DC 20230; (202) 377-5001.

— *Office of the Consumer Advisor*, Department of Agriculture, Washington, DC 20250; (202) 382-9681.

2. Consumer and Advocacy Organizations

— *Americans for Safe Food*, 1531 P Street NW, Washington, DC 20036; (202) 332-9110.

— *Center for Science in the Public Interest*, 1501 Sixteenth Street NW, Washington, DC 20036; (202) 332-9110. Publishes *Nutrition Action* newsletter.

— *Center for Study of Responsive Law*, 2000 P Street NW, Washington, DC 20036. Publishes the newsletter, *Buyer's Market*.

— *Consumers Union*, 256 Washington Street, Mount Vernon, NY 10553. Publishes *Consumer Reports* and an annual buying guide.

— *Co-op America*, 2100 M Street NW, Washington, DC 200063; (800) 424-2667.

— *Council on Economic Priorities*, 30 Irving Place, New York, NY 10003; (212) 420-1133. Publishes *Shopping for a Better World*.

— *Public Citizen*, 2000 P Street NW, Washington, DC 20036; (202) 293-9142

— *U.S. PIRG*, 215 Pennsylvania Avenue SE, Washington, DC 20003; (202) 546-9707. There are also 21 state PIRGS; for telephone numbers and addresses check your local yellow pages.

3. Further Reading

— *Consumer Reports Buying Guides*, published annually by Consumers Union (see above for address).

— *Consumer's Resource Handbook* (OCA 582T). Pueblo, Colo.: Consumer Information Center, 1988.

— "Drinking Water," special issue of *Buyer's Market*, 1988.

— *Eating Clean*, Steven Gold and Katherine Isaac. Washington, D.C.: Center for the Study of Responsive Law, 1987.

— *The Green Consumer Guide*, John Elkington and Julia Hailes. London: Gollancz, 1988.

— *Hazardous Waste: What You Should and Shouldn't Do*. Alexandria, Va.: Water Pollution Control Center, n.d.

— *The Healthy Home*, Linda Mason Hunter. Emmaus, Pa.: Rodale, 1989.

— *Healthy House Catalog*. Cleveland, Ohio: Environmental Health Watch and Housing Resource Center, 1988.

— *The Home Book*, Elizabeth Hax. Washington, D.C.: Center for the Study of Responsive Law, 1989.

— *Home Ecology*, Karen Christensen. London: Arlington Books, 1989.

— *Household Waste Safety*. Philadelphia: Clean Air Council, n.d.

— *Nontoxic and Natural*, Debra Lynn Dadd. Los Angeles: Jeremy Tarcher, 1984.

— *Shopping for a Better World – A Quick and Easy Guide to Socially Responsible Supermarket Shopping*. New York: Council on Economic Priorities, 1989.

— *Your Home, Your Health, and Your Well-Being*, David Rousseau, W. J. Rea, M.D., and Jean Enright. Vancouver: Hartley & Marks, 1988.

Drinking Water

— "Bottled Spring Water" (evaluation), *Canadian Consumer*, May 1987.

— "Bottled Waters," *Consumer Reports*, May 1987, January 1988.

— *Citizens Handbook on Groundwater Protection*, Wendy Gordon. New York: NRDC, 1984 (out of print).

— "Clean Water: A Guide to Equipment for Home Treatment," *American Way*, April 1987.

— *Contamination of Ground Water by Toxic Organic Chemicals*. Washington, D.C.: Council on Environmental Quality, 1981.

— "Distilling the Essence: A Trustworthy Guide to Home Water Filters," Greg Canine, *Harrowsmith*, September/October 1989.

— "Drink Up: Putting Bottled Waters to the Test," Linda Greider, *Washingtonian*, February 1988.

— *Drinking Water*. Washington, D.C.: *Buyer's Market*, Center for Study of Responsive Law, 1988.

— *Drinking Water*, special issue, *Resources Magazine*, vol. 7, no. 1, Environmental Task Force, Washington, D.C., 1987.

— *Drinking Water . . . An Endangered Species*, Stephen U. Lester and Brian Lipsett. Arlington, Va.: CCHW, 1988.

— *Drinking Water Filters*. Arlington, Va.: Citizen's Clearinghouse for Hazardous Waste, 1988.

— "Drinking Water: Is It Safe?," E. J. Kahn III, *Boston Magazine*, May 1987.

— "Evaluation of Activated Carbon Filters," *Practical Homeowner*, Rodale Press, Emmaus, Pa., January 1987.

— *A Guide to the Clean Water Act Amendments*. Washington, D.C.: EPA, 1978.

— "Heavy Metal on Tap," Michael Kantor, *Sierra*, November/December 1987.

— *Lead and Your Drinking Water*. Washington, D.C.: EPA, Office of Water report #EPA-87-006, 1987.

— "New Age of Aqueous" (evaluation of bottled water), William C. Banks, *Money*, September 1986.

— *Troubled Water*, Jonathan King. Emmaus, Pa.: Rodale Press, 1985 (excellent book, includes material on filter testing).

— *Troubled Waters on Tap*. Duff Conacher. Washington, D.C.: Center for Study of Responsive Law, 1988.

— *Water Conditioning and Purification Magazine*, 4651 North First Avenue, Suite 101, Tucson, AZ 85733.

— "Water Filters," *Consumer Reports*, February 1983, March, July, and October 1986.

— *Water Fit to Drink*, Carol Keough. Emmaus, Pa.: Rodale Press, 1980.

— "The Water Issue," *ENVIRON*, No. 6, Wary Canary Press, Fort Collins, CO, 1988.

— *Water Pollution*, Julian McCaull and Janice Crossland. New York: Harcourt Brace, 1974.

— *Water Technology Magazine*, 13 Century Hill Drive, Latham, NY 12110-1281.

— "Water, Water Everywhere," (evaluation of bottled and tap water), *Consumer Reports*, January 1987.

— "You and Your Drinking Water," *EPA Journal*, December 1986.

ENDNOTES

1. Joanna Poncavage, "Sold on Organic," *Organic Gardening*, June 1989, p. 43.

2. Michael Rozyne, "Organic Foods: How Can You Be Sure?," *Whole Life Times*, August 1983.

3. Poncavage, "Sold on Organic," p. 46.

4. Debra Lynn Dadd, *Nontoxic and Natural* (Los Angeles: Jeremy P. Tarcher, 1984), p. 107.

5. Based on information from *Chemical Cuisine* (Washington, D.C.: Center for Science in the Public Interest, n.d.) and *Food Adulteration* (London: Unwin, London Food Commission, 1988), pp. 52-60.

6. Dadd, *Nontoxic and Natural*, p.110.

7. Stephen U. Lester and Brian Lipsett, *Drinking Water, An Endangered Resource* (Arlington, Va.: Citizen's Clearinghouse for Hazardous Waste, 1988), pp. 8-9.

8. Lisa Y. Lefferts and Stephen B. Schmidt, "Water: Safe to Swallow," *Nutrition Action*, November 1988, p. 7.

9. *Consumer Reports*, January 1987.

10. *New Scientist*, November 19, 1988, cited in "Water: Unsafe In Any Form?" *Utne Reader*, September/October 1989.

11. An excellent overview of different systems is given in *Drinking Water Filters: What You Need to Know* (Arlington, Va.: Citizen's Clearinghouse for Hazardous Waste, 1988).

12. Study on skin and waterborne toxics done by Massachusetts Department of Environmental Quality Engineering in 1984, cited in *Environ* magazine, no. 6, 1988.

13. *Home Safe Home* (Belmar, N.J.: Clean Water Fund, New Jersey Environmental Federation, 1989).

14. Based on information from *A Survey of Household Hazardous Wastes and Regulated Programs*, EPA/530-SW-86-038 (Washington, D.C.: EPA, 1986); *Household Hazardous Waste Safety* (Philadelphia: Clean Air Council, n.d.); and *Hazardous Wastes from Homes*, (Santa Monica, Calif.: Enterprise for Education, n.d.).

15. Estimate of the German Ministry of the Environment, cited in "Promising Initiatives," *World Watch* magazine, May/June 1989, p. 6.

16. Ibid..

AFTERWORD

Positive Ecology
Moving from Pollution to Solution

"Producing pollution is negative ecology.
Preventing it is positive ecology."
– Jacques Cousteau

In this book we have shown how different types of pollution can be – and are being – cleaned up and prevented. Although modest progress has been recorded in some areas, much more remains to be done. Crucial questions we must answer are: What will be the effects on ourselves and future generations of the pollution to which we are exposed on a daily basis? How can we prevent further ecological disasters such as Chernobyl, Love Canal, and Exxon *Valdez*? Will we take decisive measures nationally and globally before we arrive at what some people foresee as the "end of nature"?

In the view of Ernest Callenbach, author of the prophetic novel *Ecotopia*, it will take a catastrophe of epic proportions to move humankind to an ecologically healthy society: "One of these days a nuke is going to blow in this country, as surely as the sun goes up and comes down. It . . . will put a whole new complexion on environmental politics."[1] He may be right, but we don't have to sit around waiting for another Chernobyl to find out.

As suggested throughout this book, cleaning up the environmental mess requires changing our lifestyles and the way we run our society. The choice, then, is to be Chernobylized into change, or to take action now before a point of ecological no return is reached.

Although some, perhaps many, of the earth's ecosystems have been irreparably damaged by our ignorance, stupidity, and greed, there is still time for learning and healing. There are signs of hope, if not grounds for optimism. Although we don't know all the answers to the problems of pollution, we have a good idea of the causes and thus of how to solve them. Some causes, we have seen, are common to several types of pollution. Petroleum-based products, for example, generate air pollution, acid rain, global warming, hazardous pesticides, and toxic waste. And some solutions are so obvious that one wonders why they have not already been implemented. As Peter A. A. Berle, president of the National Audubon Society, points out, *a mere 1.7-mpg improvement in fuel efficiency standards for cars would save more oil than drilling in the Arctic refuge could ever produce.*

> *Callenbach may be right, but we don't have to sit around waiting for another Chernobyl to find out.*

Conservation and more efficient use of our resources and energy could go far – perhaps as much as 50 percent of the way – toward cleaning up pollution. Switching from fossil fuel to renewable energy sources can achieve another 20 percent of the job, while exchanging our chemical-intensive agriculture for a more natural, organic type of farming could achieve 15 percent more. Reducing the use of plastics is a significant way of saving oil and waste at the same time, saving perhaps a further 5 percent. The remaining 10 percent of the cleanup could come from new energy and antipollution technologies presently under development.

If we know the basic causes and the directions to be taken, why aren't we doing more to solve the problems? Why isn't the saving of our environment – in which we *all* have a vital personal stake – given a higher priority than, say, building a fleet of 132 Stealth bombers at $79 billion?[2] The answer lies in the nature of our political process and what we perceive to be our national interests.

Since the end of World War II the United States and the Soviet Union have engaged each other in a cold war almost as costly in terms of gross national product as the hot one against Nazi Germany and Japan, in which we and the U.S.S.R. were allies. Although the justification for such an huge nonproductive investment is no longer valid, the idea of winding down a 45-year military confrontation makes many of our political, industrial, and labor leaders uneasy. Whenever the administration considers even minor cuts in the $300 billion defense budget, it is met with an outcry of protest from legislators representing states and districts with lucrative military contracts. "You are putting Grumman out of business!" objected Representative George Hochbrueckner of Long

Trade-Offs between Military and Environmental Priorities[1]

Military Priority	Cost	Social/Environmental Priority
Trident II submarine	$100 billion	One-third of estimated clean-up cost for U.S. toxic waste dumps over 50 years
F-16 jet fighter programs Stealth bomber program	$79 billion	80 percent of estimated costs to meet U.S. clean-water goals by 2000.
MK-50 advanced light weight torpedo	$6 billion	Annual cost to cut U.S. sulfur-dioxide emissions by 8-12 million tons a year to combat acid rain, over five years.

Island when the secretary of defense proposed stopping production of the Navy F-14D fighter plane.[4] A few years ago I visited the same company when it was testing, under contract from the Department of Energy, a promising new wind-turbine system.[5] Unfortunately, Grumman (along with many other companies) was forced to discontinue its renewable-energy program when the Reagan administration switched its funding into nuclear power and increased military budgets. In the kinder, gentler America promised by the "environmental president" Bush, the workers at Grumman could turn their skills back to making wind turbines and solar thermal collectors, instead of unproductive weapons for a war that need never be fought.

The war we must wage is against a way of life, practiced mainly by the industrial countries, that depends obscenely on our consuming so much of the world's fossil-fuel and food resources and thereby producing so much of its waste. In this war all the nations of the world are essentially on the same side. The enemy, as Walt Kelly's Pogo said, is us. We are the ones who create the pollution, we are the ones who must clean it up. Winning this war calls for a concerted effort as great as we expended on winning World War II. To mobilize for it, we must radically change our priorities to include proper health care, affordable housing, sustainable food production and distribution, and to provide the education our children need to make the planet a decent one to live on. These are priorities not just for the affluent countries of the world but for human society as a whole. *Those of us who are more aware of the need for change must take first responsibility in bringing it about, starting with ourselves.* Pending inspired leadership from above we must begin the pressure from the grass roots below. The soil is fertile. The time is ripe.

Here, in summary, are the basic steps we must take:

What We Can Do to Clean Up the Environment

1. **Environmental cleanup begins with ourselves**, with an awareness that how we live affects both our immediate surroundings of home, work, and neighborhood and the broader contexts of city, state, nation, bioregion, and ecosphere.

2. We must increasingly **see the connections** between our daily acts and the ecology of the earth. (Eating hamburgers *does* contribute to rain-forest destruction thousands of miles away.)

3. **Break through the plastic membrane** that separates us from nature and from one another. Look at the stars and trees. Listen to the songs of birds, before they all disappear. Grow trees and, however modestly, some of your own food.

4. **Understand that the whole earth is part of our body**, to be respected as we respect ourselves, that nature exists for all species indiscriminately,[6] that its resources are limited and must not be wasted, and that our priority (and that of government) must be to save the environment.

5. With this understanding you will **gain the ecological awareness to deal with pollution** in all its forms and discover how to prevent it before it happens

6. **Develop a lifestyle that is less intrusive on the environment**. As you reduce your use of energy and things, you will be reducing waste and pollution. A lifestyle that is more in tune with natural cycles is physically, mentally, and spiritually healthier. It will make you feel better and more able to practice positive ecology.

7. **Move closer to your work**, or, if you can, work at home (with the "electronic workplace," more and more people are doing this).

8. **Reuse**. Recycle. Refuse to buy products that are environmentally harmful.

9. **Keep your eye on the big picture** (environmental cleanup) but remember it's made up of small brush strokes. Picking up a single discarded soda can, reusing a manila envelope, and not buying groceries in excessive packages may not sound very important. However, when you multiply these small actions by millions of other people doing the same thing, they add up significantly.

10. From your base of individual action, **work outward in ever widening circles**. Join a local action group that is working on an issue important to you and support at least one national organization concerned with environmental conservation and cleanup.

11. **Get involved politically** and not just at election times. Work to elect and support ecologically minded legislators. Write them letters; they do make a difference! Get them to honor their election promises.

12. **Use all the help you can get** to take on the big polluters and the big problems.

13. You'll come across individuals who agree that pollution is terrible but who excuse their lack of action with "You can't beat City Hall," or "It's too late now." Remind them that, instead of making excuses, many people, as we noted in the introduction of this book, just went ahead and changed the system. Not everyone wants to be a leader, but you can at least support those who are taking the initiative locally and nationally.

14. **Appreciate the contributions of the movers and shakers** and the work of many ordinary citizens described throughout this book. Be inspired to follow their examples. *After all, it's in a good cause – your own and that of the world you live in.*

RESOURCES

Some of the following books have already been listed in other Resources sections of the book. They are given again along with other titles because I find them particularly inspirational and because they offer valuable insight and meaning to the broader themes outlined in this Afterword.

— *The Ages of Gaia: A Biography of Our Living Earth*, James Lovelock. New York: W.W. Norton, 1988.
— *Deep Ecology*, Bill Devall and George Sessions. Salt Lake City: Gibbs Smith, 1985.
— *Design with Nature*, Ian L. McHarg. New York: Doubleday, 1971.
— *Ecology for Beginners*, Stephen Croall and William Rankin. New York: Pantheon, 1981.
— *Ecology and Our Endangered Life-Support Systems*, Eugene P. Odum. Sunderland, Mass.: Sinauer, 1989.
— *Gaia: The Human Journey from Chaos to Cosmos*, Elisabet Sahtouris. New York: Pocket Books, 1989.
— *Gaia: A Way of Knowing*, edited by William Irwin Thompson. Great Barrington, Mass.: Lindisfarne, 1987. Includes essays by Henri Atlan, Gregory Bateson, Hazel Henderson, James Lovelock, Lynn Margulis, Humberto Maturana, William Irwin Thompson, John Todd, and Francisco Varela.
— *The Gift of Good Land*, Wendell Berry. San Francisco: North Point, 1981.
— *How Nature Works: Regenerating Kinship with Planet Earth*, Michael J. Cohen. Walpole, N.H.: Stillpoint, 1988.
— *Living in the Environment: An Introduction to Environmental Science*, G. Tyler Miller, Jr. Belmont, Calif.: Wadsworth, 1988. The best textbook on the subject.
— *Meeting the Expectations of the Land: Essays in Sustainable Agriculture and Stewardship*, edited by Wes Jackson, Wendell Berry and Bruce Colman. San Francisco: North Point, 1984.
— *A Sand County Almanac*, Aldo Leopold. New York: Oxford, 1987.
— *Toward an Ecological Society*, Murray Bookchin. Montreal: Black Rose, 1981.
— *The Unsettling of America: Culture and Agriculture*, Wendell Berry. New York: Avon, 1977.
— *Walden and Other Writings*, Henry David Thoreau, edited by Joseph Wood Krutch. New York: Bantam, 1971.

ENDNOTES

1. *Time*, October 31, 1988.
2. See John R. Kasisch (Republican of Ohio, Member of the House Armed Services Committee), "$600 Milion per Stealth Bomber," *New York Times*, July 18, 1989.
3. *World Watch*, September – October 1989, p. 10.
4. Anthony Lewis, "Cold War Comfort," *New York Times*, April 27, 1989.
5. Jon Naar, *The New Wind Power* (New York: Penguin, 1982), pp. 180-183.
6. The rights of animals and inanimate objects (soil,water, plants, and trees) are eloquently expressed in two important books: Aldo Leopold, *A Sand County Almanac* (New York: Oxford, 1981), especially pp. 237-239; and Christopher D. Stone, *Earth and Other Ethics* (New York: Harper & Row, 1988).

ACKNOWLEDGMENTS

Writing a 150,000-word book can be a solitary occupation. However, my lonely world was enlivened by a steady stream of helpers – researchers, consultants, experts, contributors, critics, and friends.

First among the more than 100 people who made this book possible is my co-worker and son, Alex Naar, whose encouragement, assistance, and integrity kept me on the right track from initial concept to finished form. He devoted long hours to locating and evaluating source material, particularly on renewable energy, acid rain, and environmental law, wrote many of the section headings, photographed the wind farm in Altamont Pass and the Three Mile Island nuclear plant, and came up with the idea for our beautifully executed cover, among many other contributions.

I want to thank my agent, Sarah Jane Freymann, who found me the best of publishers and editors and played a key role in making *Design for a Livable Planet* as positive as it is. To my editor, John Michel, I give highest credit for his enthusiasm, encouragement, and unerringly sure decision making at every critical point of the book's progress.

An important influence at a very early stage was my friend Bill McDonough, whose own work is described in chapter 4 and who introduced me to Fred Krupp, executive director of the Environmental Defense Fund. Fred helped me focus more clearly on making the book a practical guide to cleaning up the environment, took time out of an incredibly busy schedule to write the Foreword, and generously made the considerable resources of EDF available to me whenever I needed them. He put me in touch with EDF scientist Dr. Rodney Fujita whose expertise made chapter 7 (Global Warming) more accurate and more understandable. Another key Krupp connection was Michael Herz, assistant professor of law at Cardozo School of Law and former lead attorney for EDF. At incredibly short notice he gave me nothing less than a crash course in environmental law which forms the basis of chapter 10. My special gratitude also to EDF's Diana Widener who provided me with a never-ending flow of information and contacts I could not otherwise have obtained.

Another significant contributor was Charles Komanoff, the internationally known energy economist and president of *Transportation Alternatives*. With scalpel-like precision he put chapters 8 and 9 into more objective and credible perspective; he also contributed the report "Renewable Pedal Power" for chapter 9. The chapter on acid rain and water pollution benefitted immeasurably from the critiques of Dr. Paul Godfrey and his colleagues Marie-Françoise Walk and Ed Kaynor, of the University of Massachusetts Water Resources Center at Amherst. Special thanks also to my good friend and colleague Dr. Joseph Goldman, director of the International Center for the Solution of Environmental Problems in Houston who advised me on many aspects of climate change, agriculture, and ecology. Valuable help on chapter 8 was also given by the medical writer Linda Ketchum, coauthor of *Living with Radiation*.

I am indebted to numerous friends in the environmental movement, including: Dick Russell who gave me permission to use parts of his devastating report on toxic waste in Arkansas (see chapter 2) and his moving account of the work of Earth First! in chapter 11; Tim Connor, research director of the Hanford Education League, who wrote the special report *Silent Holocaust* for chapter 8; Lois Marie Gibbs, founder of the Citizen's Clearinghouse for Hazardous Waste and an inspiring leader of the environmental movement; Tim Knipe and Karen Brazeau of the Cousteau Society; Dave Foreman of Earth First!; Nancy Jack Todd, editor of *Annals of Earth*; John Todd, Ocean Arks International; Drs. Barry Commoner and James Quigley at the Center for the Biology of Natural Systems; Robert Rodale for much of my information on organic farming; David Levine, Learning Alliance, New York, for his contribution to chapter 11; Dr. Michael J. Cohen, founder of the Audubon Expedition Institute, for his understanding of how Nature really works; Jeremy Rifkin; Hunter and Amory Lovins and the entire staff of the Rocky Mountain Institute for a steady flow of important information and insights; Jay Halfon, Steve Romalewski, and Arthur Kell, all from NYPIRG, for their special help on chapter 11; Gene Karpinski, executive director, USPIRG; Lee Wasserman, executive director of the Environmental Planning Lobby, Albany, N.Y.; Kenneth Boley and Nancy Rader of Public Citizen's Critical Mass Energy Project; Irmgard Hunt, the Nature Conservancy; Tina Hobson, Renew America; Deborah Gangloff, director of communications, American Forestry Association; Diane D'Arrigo, Nuclear Information and Resource Service; Neil Seldman, Institute for Local Self-Reliance; H. David Davis, consultant to the World Bank, who provided me with a steady flow of material on that agency's work; Sara Nichols, Esq., staff attorney, Clean Air Council, Philadelphia; Abigail Allen, Environmental Research Foundation; Dr. Paul Connett, Work on Waste, David Collins, Council on Economic Priorities; Michael Pilarski, editor of Friends of the Trees *International Report*, Irmgard Hunt, formerly with Inform now with Nature Conservancy, Susan Machum, Ecology Action Centre, Halifax, Nova Scotia.

There are also important contributions to the book from Greenpeace, the Natural Resources Defense Council (particularly Kathy Dold and Jeffry Oliver), Concern Inc., the Audubon Society (including the excellent *Audubon Activist*), the Sierra Club, and Earth Island Institute as well as from a network of concerned citizens – Mari Mennel Bell, Erich Bollhorst (my indefatigable "in-house" researcher), Oliver Williams, Mirjana Hamburg, Janelle Winston, Terry Blount, David Feldman, Randy Acker, Peter Bronner, Susan Stein, Hans Webber the incomparable birdwatcher, and my organic gardening neighbor and consultant Lee Reich.

From government and industry I received a great deal of assistance. At the EPA I am most grateful to Dr. Paul Giardina, radiation officer, Dennis P. Carey, librarian, and Margaret Randol, deputy director, all at Region 2 in New York where I spent many productive hours, and to Dr. Jerry Moore, David Kling, Ruth Barker, and Melba Meador among many others at EPA's headquarters in Washington, D.C. My special thanks go also to: Terry Clausen and Ken Zweibel, Solar Energy Research Institute, Golden, Colo., Scott Sklar, executive director, the Solar Energy Industries Association, Carlo LaPorta who organized the important Forum on Global Warming and Renewable Energy in Washington, D.C. in June 1989, Tom Gray, then executive director of the American Wind Energy Association, Scott Lewis, chairperson, Northeast Solar Energy Association, James Amick, Mobil Solar Energy Corporation, Mike Bergey, Bergey Windpower, William E. Rogers, chairman, Power Kinetics, Inc., Stanford R. Ovshinsky, president, Energy Conversion Devices, Bob Hamburg, Omega-Alpha Recycling Systems, Orma, W.Va., AnnaLisa Erickson, Luz International, Jerry Goldstein, publisher *BioCycle* magazine, Ros Davidson, editor *Windpower Monthly*, Pamela Alper, director, sculpture survey, Art Commission of the city of New York, Alan Van Arsdale, Massachusetts Department of Environmental Quality, Michael Pertschuk, the Advocacy Institute, David McClean, California Energy Company, Larry O'Connell, Mary Ann Garneau, and Lori Terson, all of the Electric Power Research Institute, and my good friend Thomas Sahagian, director of weatherization for the city of New York for being there whenever I needed him.

My warmest appreciation to Beverly Russell, editorial director of *Interiors* and *Architecture* magazines, for her unflagging encouragement and constructive criticisms, and to the Very Reverend James Parks Morton, dean of the Cathedral of St. John the Divine for his love and inspiration.

And to Joe Santoro I want to acknowledge his concern and loving care for the cover-to-cover design of *Design for a Livable Planet*, transforming what could have been an indigestible mass of words, diagrams, and pictures into the visually exciting guidebook for environmental action in the 1990s.

Page numbers in italics are references to the Resources section at the end of each chapter.

American Wind Energy Association, *222*
Americium-241, 176
Amicus Journal, 31
Ammonia, 87
disposal of, 304
Ammonia-based cleaners, disposal of, 304
Ammonium chloride, 87
Animals, laws for the protection of, 238-39
Antarctica, hole in ozone layer above, 139
Antarctica Project, 73, *254*
Antifreeze, disposal of, 304
Antinuclear groups, 167-70
Ants, 302
Apples, Alar-treated, 259-61
Appliances, 27, 28
energy-efficient, 107, 217
National Appliance Energy Conservation
    Act, 240-41
Applied Energy Services Thames, 127
Appropriate Technology Transfer to Rural
    Areas, *222*
Arco Solar, 203, *223*
Army Corps of Engineers, U.S., 234
Art and Craft Materials Labeling Act, 306
Art materials, 299
Asbestos, 84-86
hotline, *29*, 85
Asbestos School Hazard Abatement Act
    (ASHAA) hotline, 86
Ash from incinerators, 13
Aspartame, 291
Asthma and Allergy Foundation of America, *94*
Atomic Energy Act, 239
AT&T, 143
Auro Products, 308
Automatic dishwashing detergents, 299
Automobiles. *See also* Gasoline
acid rain and, 105
air conditioners for, 140, 141, 143, 147
alternative fuels for, 81, 241
Clean Air Act and, 233
economizing on gas, 108-9
fuel economy, 194-95
greenhouse effect and, 146
lead in exhaust fumes, 87
pollution inside, 89-90
Automotive Dismantlers and Recyclers
    Association, 31
Automotive fluids, disposal of, 304
Auto waxes and polishes, disposal of, 304
Avoidables, in garbage, 15-16

B

Bacteria, in drinking water, 69, 294
Bags. *See also* Packaging
plastic, 22
reusing, 26-27
Baking soda, 303
Barbecue lighter fluid, disposal of, 304
Bark, Jed, 170
Barnwell (NC) landfill, 162

Bathrooms
air pollution in, 87
energy conservation tips, 220
Batstone, Roger J., *29*, 42-43
Batteries
disposal of, 304
for electric automobiles, 195
Baubiologie Hardware, 299, 308
Baucus, Max, *148*
Bazor, James C., 205
Beatty (NV) landfill, 162
Beef, from tropical rain forests, 130
Beepers, 181
Beeswax, 303
Beetles, 302
Ben and Jerry's, 127
Bence, Bryan, 17
Benzoates, 291
Benzyl chloride, 38
Bergey Windpower, *224*
Berkeley (CA), 17
Berle, Peter A. A., 314
Best Available Control Technology (BACT)
    requirement, 252
Beta rays, defined, 154
Bethlehem Steel, 249
Beverage containers, plastic, 21, 23
reusing, 27-28
Bhopal (India) disaster, *29*
BHT (butylated hydroxytoluene), 291
Bicycles, 220-21
Binary geothermal plants, 207
BioAct EC-7, 143
Biofuels, 209-10
Biogas, 209
Biomass, 208-10
Bioregion, defined, 5
Bioregionalism, 281-82
Biosphere, defined, 5
Bleach, 299
Blue Angel program (West Germany), 305
Body Shop, The, 308
Borax, 303
Bottled water, 295
Bottle laws, 19-20
Bottom ash, defined, 11
Brazil, 54
Amazon rain forest, 124-27
Brazil nuts, 127
radioactivity of, 158
Brooklyn Navy Yard, 12
Brown, Jerry, 199
Brown, Jr., George E., 166
"Bubble concept," 105
Bugvac, 54
Building Owners and Managers Association,
    94
Burning. *See* Incineration
Bush, George (Bush administration), 48
acid rain and, 104-5
BVO (brominated vegetable oil), 291
Byrd, Robert, *110*

C

Cactus Alliance, 169
Cadmium, 13
CAFE standards, 241
California Public Utilities Commission, 193
recycling agency hotline, 30
Safe Drinking Water and Toxics
    Enforcement Act, 243-44
wind energy, 199
California Certified Organic Farmers, 56
California Energy Commission (CEC), 199,
    222, 223
Callenbach, Ernest, 314
Calvert Social Investment Fund, 307
Canada, 306
acid rain and, 99-102
recycling in, 18-19
Canadian Coalition on Acid Rain, 110
Canadian Wind Energy Association, 222
Cancer
electromagnetic fields and, 177-79
skin
    fluorescent lighting and, 180
    ultraviolet (UV) radiation and, 140
Captan, 51
Carbon dioxide (CO_2)
deforestation and, 115, 127
geothermal energy and, 207
global warming and, 136, 139, 144, 145
reducing emissions of, 139
trees and, 128
Carbon-14, 120
Carbon monoxide (CO), 79, 81
Carcinogenic, defined, 154
Carcinogens, California's Proposition 65
and, 244
CARE, 121, 127
Carpet and upholstery cleaners, 299-300
Carpets and rugs, 92, 299
Carson, Rachel, 52, 97, 251
Carter, Jimmy (Carter administration), 198
Cashew trees, 123
Catalyst, 131
Cataracts, ultraviolet (UV) radiation and, 140
Ceiling fans, 107
Center for Environmental Education, 73, 254
Center for Plastics Recycling Research, 30
Center for Science in the Public Interest, 56,
    310
Center for the Study of Responsive Law, 70,
    254, 310
Center for the Biology of Natural Systems, 30
Ceramic glazes, uranium oxides in, 176
CERCLA (Comprehensive Environmental
    Response, Compensation, and Liability
    Act), 38, 45-49, 235-36
hotline, 56
Cesium-137, 158
Cesspool cleaners, disposal of, 304
CFC-113, 143
Chafee, John H., 148

Chameides, William, 81
Chemical Emergency Preparedness Hotline, 29
Chemicals, toxic. See Toxic chemicals
Chequamegon National Forest, 118
Chernobyl disaster, 153, 155
Cherokee National Forest, 116
Chesapeake Bay Foundation, 249
Chesapeake Bay Foundation v. Bethlehem
    Steel Corporation, 249
Children, 28
Children of the Green Earth, 121
China, 53-54, 103
Chipko, 121-22, 131
Chlorinated solvents, 44-45, 69
Chlorine, 38, 44, 87
in drinking water, 294
in swimming pools, 297
Chlorine bleach, disposal of, 304
Chlorofluorocarbons (CFCs), 21
alternatives to, 141-44
global warming and, 140
ozone layer depletion and, 139-40
reducing use of, 141-42, 147
Chromotropic acid test, 87
Chronar, 202-3, 223
Cicoria, Anthony, 276
Cigarette smoking, 88
as indoor air pollution, 87
radioactive lead and polonium and, 176
Citizens Acid Rain Monitoring Network, 110
Citizen's Clearinghouse for Hazardous Wastes
    (CCHW), 30, 50, 56, 265, 283
Citizens for a Better Environment, 283
Citizens for Ocean Law, 73, 254
Citizens' suits, 247, 248
under Superfund, 49
Citrus Red No. 2, 291
Civil disobedience, 278, 280
Clamshell Alliance, 169, 182
Clean Air Act (CAA), 232-33, 242, 252
acid rain and, 105
Cleaners. See also Detergents
all-purpose, 298-99
carpet and upholstery, 299-300
disposal of, 304, 305
drain, 300
glass, 300
oven, 301
toilet, 304
Clean Water Act (CWA), 64, 65, 233-34,
    242, 249, 252
Clean Water Action Project, 73, 283
Clean Water Fund of North Carolina, 74
Clearcutting, 117
Clearwater (sloop), 66-67
Climate Institute, 148
Clinton (NJ), radon in, 173
Clothing, 300
Coal, 190
gasification of, 205
Coalition for Peace and Justice, 169
Coalition for Recyclable Waste, 21, 30

radon problem and, 92, 172, 173
Radon Reduction in New Construction (booklet), 92
record of, 46-48
regional offices, *29-30*
Superfund and, 235-36
Toxic Substances Control Act (TSCA) and, 237
Vertac chemical (Jacksonville, AR) and, 40, 41
writing to, *29*
Environmental Research Foundation, 31, 56, *283*
Environmental Task Force, 169
Environmental Testing and Technology, 308-9
Ethanol, 81, 209, 241
European Community (EC), reduction of CFCs and halons and, 141
Exxon Valdez (tanker), 63, 190

F

AFCO Inc., *223*
Fallout, defined, 154
Fans, 217
ceiling, 107
Farm Conservation and Water Protection Act, 289
Fast-food chains, 21-22
FC134a (sterilant), 143
Fecal coliform bacteria, 71
Federal Energy Regulatory Commission, *222*, 240
Federal government. *See also specific agencies and departments*
cooperation between states and, 269
Federal Insecticide, Fungicide, and Rodenticide Act of 1972 (FIFRA), 50, 237-38
Federal Power Commission (FPC), 249-50
Federal Register, 246
Feedback, defined, 6
Feldman, Jay, 50
Fertilizers, 210, 211
Filters, drinking-water, 295-96
Fingernail polish remover, disposal of, 305
Fire extinguishers, 144, 147
Fire extinguisher simulators, 144
Fireplaces, 92
Firewood, 114
Fish, acid rain and, 99, 100
Fission, defined, 154
Fixation of toxic chemicals, 44
Fleas, 302
Flies, 302
Floor and furniture waxes/polishes, 300
disposal of, 305
Florida Solar Energy Society, *223*
Fluorescent lighting, energy conservation, 218
Fly ash, defined, 11
Foams
CFC-containing, 140, 142

packaging, 140, 142, 147
polystyrene, 23, 147
polyurethane padding, 299
styrofoam, 21, 22, 27, 28, 142
urea-formaldehyde insulation, 86
Food. *See also* Agriculture
advertising claims, 290
chemical additives in, 290-92
irradiation of, 174
organic, 54-55, 175, 219, 288-92
pesticides in, 53-55
radioactivity of, 158, 181
Food and Agricultural Organization (FAO), *130*
Food and Drug Administration (FDA), 56, 174, 175, *310*
Food and Water, *182*
Food chain, defined, 6
"Food-chain gang," 260
Food Irradiation Response Newsletter, *183*
Food web, defined, 6
Ford Motor Co., 105
Foreman, Dave, 281
Forests. *See also* Deforestation; Trees
acid rain and, 99
clearcutting, 117
continuous-tract management of, 118
"debt for nature" swaps, 126
myths and realities about, 118
selective cutting of, 117
slash-burning, 117-18
Forest Services, U.S. (USFS), 115-18
Formaldehyde, 38, 86-87
Fossil fuels. *See also* Oil (petroleum)
CO_2 emissions from, 139
defined, 6
disposal of, 305
Fowler, Wyche, 289
France, nuclear energy in, 211
Frase, Patty, 40
Freedom of Information Act (FOIA), 246-47
Free radicals, 156
Freezers, 140, 142-43
energy conservation tips, 219
Freon (R-12), 142-43, 147
Friends of the Earth (FOE), *131*, 266, *283*
Friends of the Earth International, 266
Friends of the Trees, *131*
Fuel
defined, 6
fossil. *See* Fossil fuels
Fuller's earth, 303
Furniture polish, 300
Fusion, 214

G

AC (granular activated carbon filtration), 70
Gaia, defined, 6
Galileo (space probe), 166
Gamma rays, defined, 154
Garbage, 9-35

Wald, George, 158
WARD (Warwick Against Radioactive Dump), 170
Washer, clothes, 219-20
Washington, recycling agency hotline, 30
Waste Management, 23
Waste Management Inc. (WMI), 17
Waste stream, defined, 12
Water. *See also* Water pollution
conservation of, 218-19
drinking, 68-71
    acid rain and, 98, 100
    bottled, 295
    evaluating safety of, 292-94
    knowing your rights, 72
    purifiers and filters for, 295-97
    resources, *73-74*
    Safe Drinking Water Act (SDWA) and, 234-35
    what you can do about unsafe, 294-98
Water Information Network, *74*
Water pollution, 61-75. *See also* Water, drinking
Clean Water Act (CWA) and, 233-34
coast and river cleanups, 65-67
oil spills, 62-64
resources, *73-74*
Water power, 196-98
Water purifiers, 295
Water Quality Association, *74*
Water Resources Research Center, *110*
WaterTest Corporation, *74*
Water-testing laboratories and consultants, *74*
Watson, Paul, 279
Watt, James, 237
Waxman, Henry A., 78, *110*
Webster Industries, 22
Weevils, 302
Wellesley (MA), recycling center in, 16
Wellman, 23
West Germany, 21
acid rain in, 99, 103
West Linn, Oregon, 18
Wilderness Society, 117, 123, *132, 284*
Wildlife and habitat protection laws, 238-39
Wiles, Richard, 52
Wind energy, 198-200
manufacturers, 224
Windows, 217
cutting heat loss, 107
Wirka, Jeanne, 22
Wirth, Timothy, 139, *148*
Wirth, Timothy E., *110*
Wisconsin, 24
Wood, as fuel, 208
Woods Hole Research Center, *149*
Wood stoves, 89, 92, 208
Woodwell, George, 145
Working Assets Money Fund, 308
Working Group on Community Right-to-Know, 57

Work on Waste, 31
World Association for Solid Waste, 32
World Bank, 145
Amazon rain forest and, 125-26
World Meterological Organization (WMO), *148*
World Neighbors, 124, *132*
World Resources Institute, 267
Worldwatch Institute, 14, *223*, 267
World Wildlife Fund, *132*

X-rays, 174
from color TV sets, 176-77
defined, 154

Yale Materials Handling Corporation, 42, 43
Yucca Mountain (NV), 162
Yusho incident, 45

Production Notes

In keeping with the timely ideas expressed in *Design for a Livable Planet*, a wide array of tools and work methods were incorporated in writing, designing and producing this book. The attempt was to put into practice some of Jon Naar's recommendations as *fuel* for a new way of working.

Through the "electronic office" namely, fax machines, modems and desktop publishing, much time was conserved and material waste kept to a minimum. During the process of passing information between author, publisher, designer and services, mailing envelopes were recycled, cardboard tubes which contained each shipment of typesetting were returned to the typesetter for reuse, and illustration boards, normally used for mounting final camera-ready artwork, were not required for printing.

The following electronic and traditional tools aided in the realization of the marvelous product at hand:

Writing – Hardware/IBM AT and an Epson Dot Matrix printer. Software/WordPerfect 5.0.

Designing – Hardware/Macintosh IIx & IIcx, Apple CD-ROM, Apple Scanner, and a LaserWriter NT printer. Software/Microsoft Word 4.0, Quark Xpress 2.12, Adobe Illustrator 88, Adobe Streamline, Adobe Type Manager, Letraset ImageStudio 1.6, and Olduvai Read-It OCR.

Typesetting – Hardware/Linotronic L300, RIP 3, and Maxcess Syquest 44mb Removable Drive. Type/Univers Condensed Bold, Janson Text and Zapf Dingbats all from the Adobe Type Library.

Printing – Traditional page-proofs and offset printing and, as expected, *this book was printed on recycled paper!*